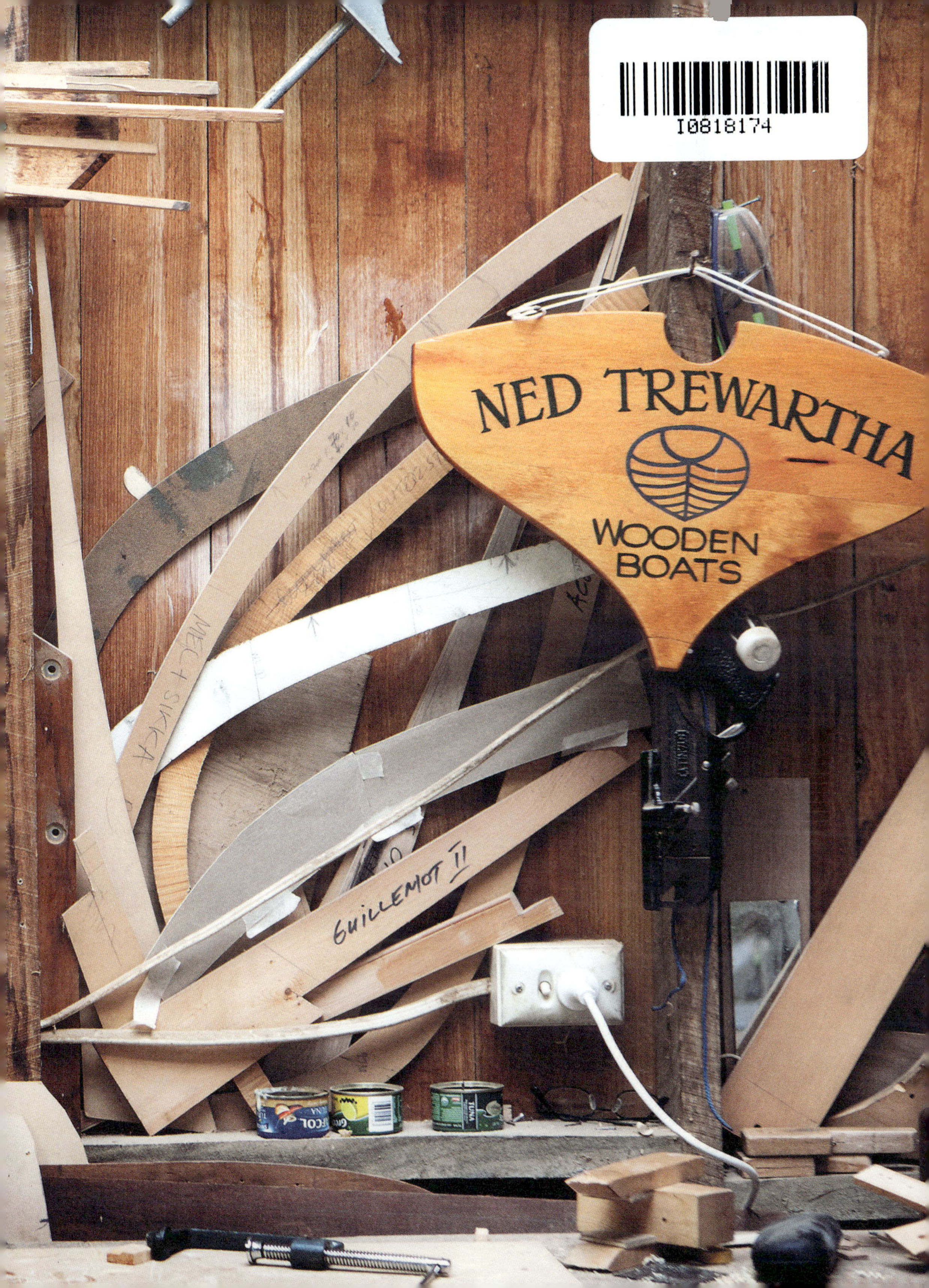
NED TREWARTHA
WOODEN
BOATS
GUILLEMOT II

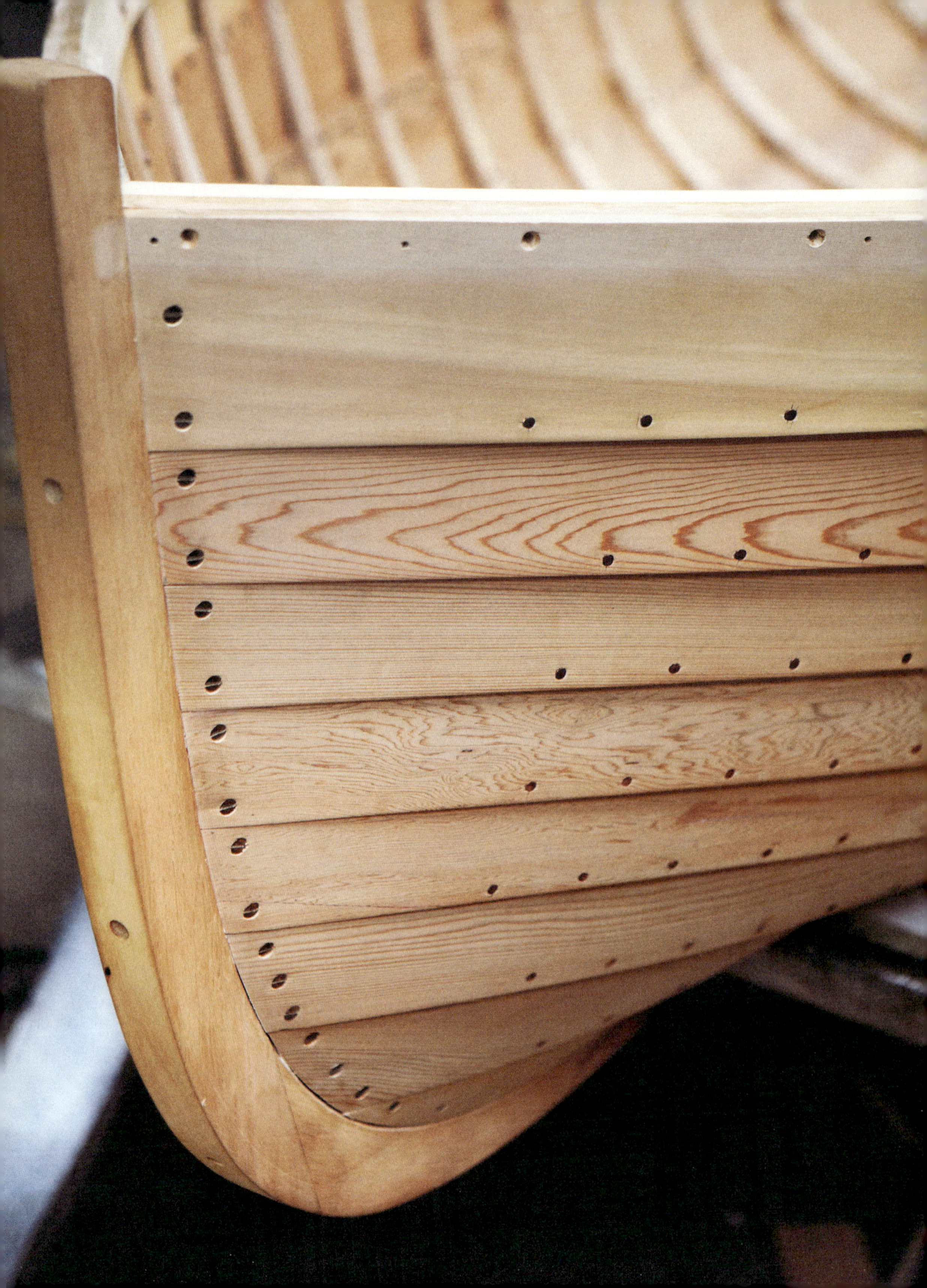

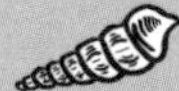

SIMON GRIFFITHS is a leading photographer of food, interiors and gardens. His photography appears frequently in the major lifestyle magazines, and in books such as *Stephanie Alexander's Kitchen Garden Companion* and *Kylie Kwong: My China*. In the field of gardening and landscape design he has collaborated with Rick Eckersley and Lisa Stafford on their book *Outside*, with Jenna Reed Burns on *Australian Gardens for a Changing Climate*, and with noted rosarian Susan Irvine on *The Garden at Forest Hall*. He has also worked closely with leading Australian garden designer Paul Bangay on all his books, most recently *The Garden at Stonefields*. This is his third solo book following *Shack* and *Shed*.

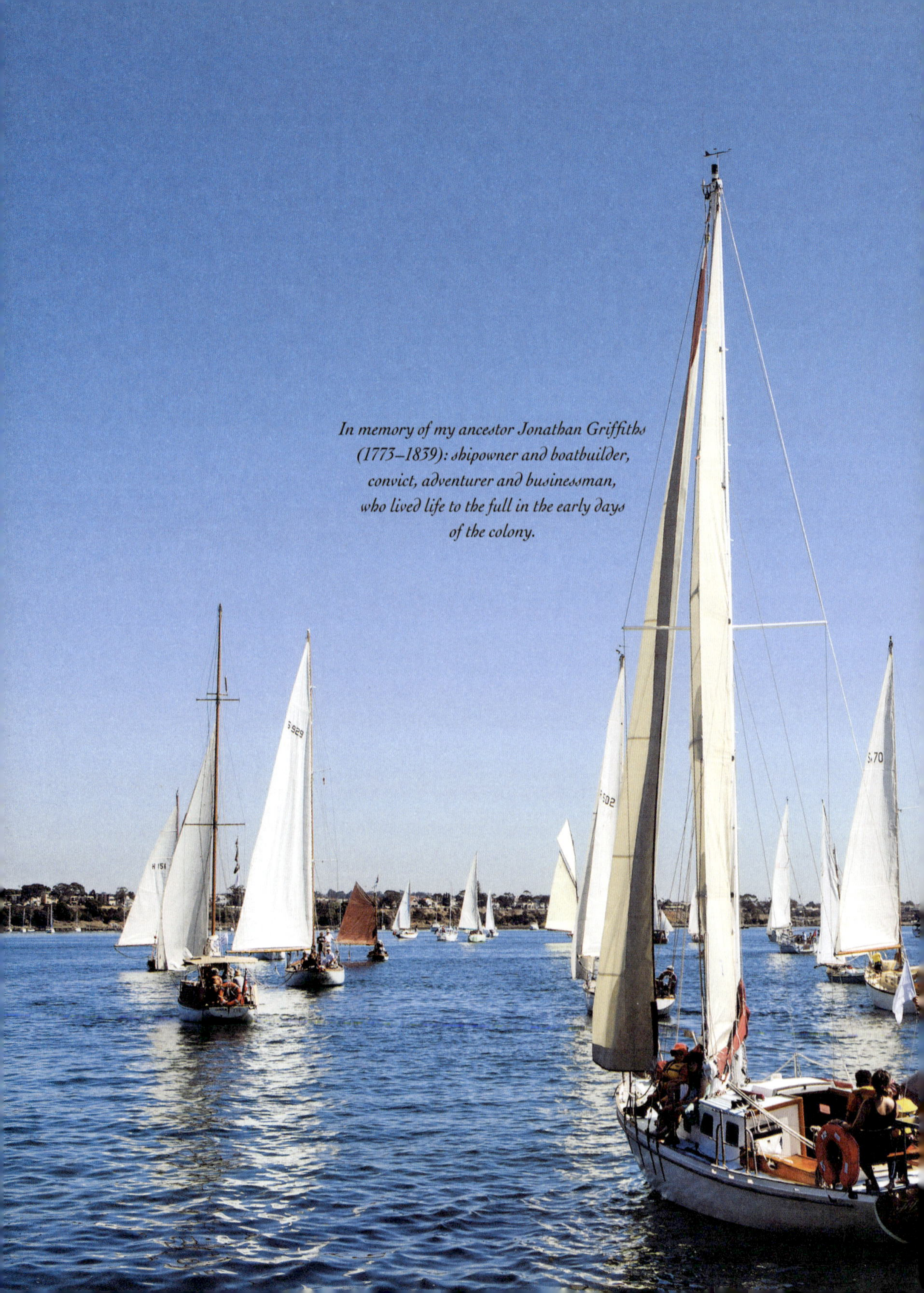

In memory of my ancestor Jonathan Griffiths (1773–1839): shipowner and boatbuilder, convict, adventurer and businessman, who lived life to the full in the early days of the colony.

BOAT

SIMON GRIFFITHS

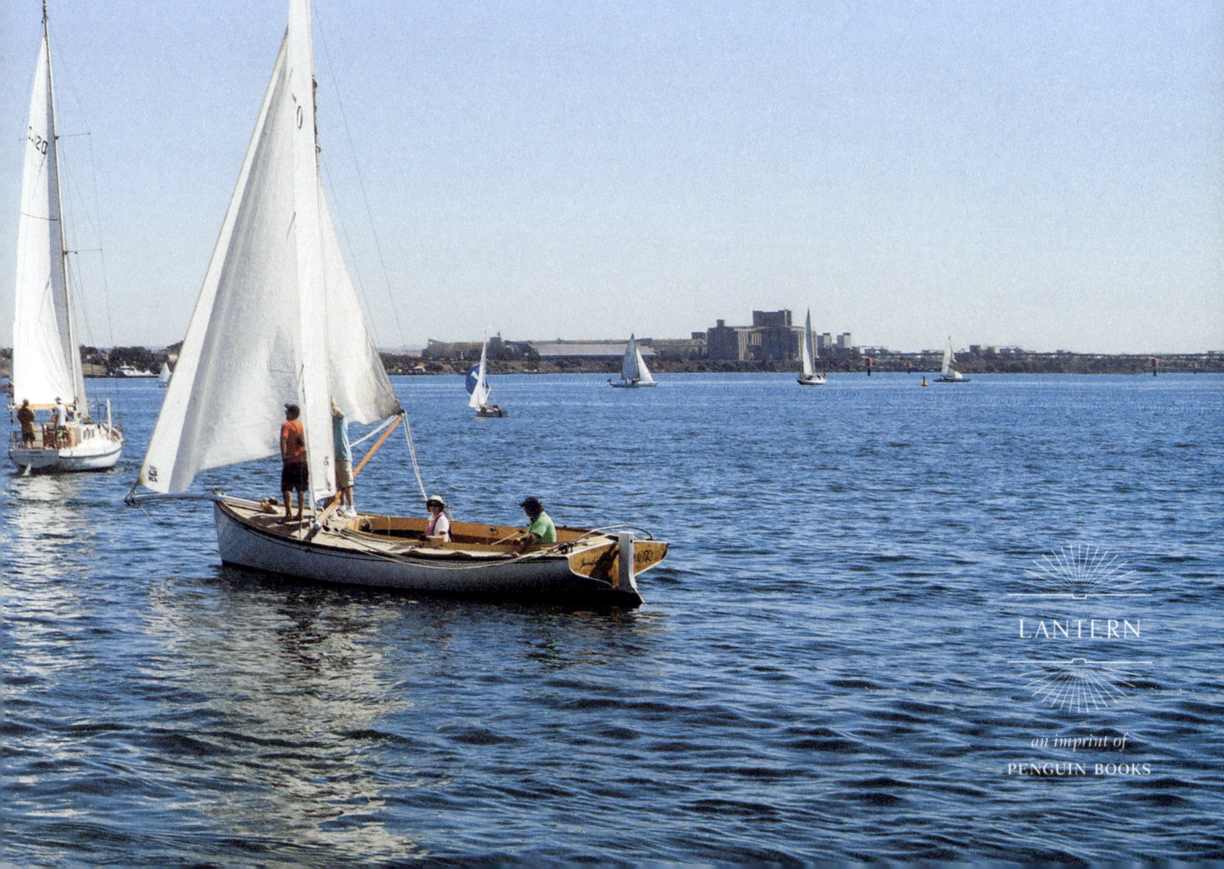

LANTERN
an imprint of
PENGUIN BOOKS

BOAT

A WATERCRAFT OF ANY SIZE DESIGNED TO FLOAT, GLIDE, WORK OR TRAVEL ON WATER

Boats come in all shapes and sizes. Whether it's a million-dollar yacht, an ancient wooden rowboat, a speedboat or a model boat you have built from scratch, there is a boat for every need and every budget. It could be a small, oar-powered fisherman's dinghy or a steam-powered launch chugging down a river; a glamorous yacht under full sail, or a diesel-powered working boat; a fishing boat or a police patrol boat driven by powerful twin diesel engines.

Australians are renowned for their love of the water, and beaches and boats have always been important on this large island continent. The first white settlers came to Australia by boat, and the original inhabitants used boats; indeed it is thought they came to Australia over 40 000 years ago by sea.

After white settlers and convicts arrived here, boats were the main form of transport: passenger boats, trading boats and freight, moving back and forth between Australia and England. My ancestor Jonathan Griffiths (1773–1839), who arrived in Australia by boat on The Second Fleet, was taught boatbuilding while doing seven years' hard labour on Norfolk Island, and became one of the colony's earliest boatbuilders. By 1804 Jonathan had built *Speedy*, *Elizabeth and Mary*, *Nancy* and *Rosetta*, among others. His second son, John Griffiths (1801–1881), also became a shipowner and boatbuilder. John built *Glory*, *Resolution*, *Henry*, *William* and *The Brothers*, as well as the barque *Sydney Griffiths*, which carried the first cargo of wool directly to London from Port Fairy. William Dutton (see the Portland whale boat named after him on pages 21–23) worked as a whaler and sealer for John Griffiths.

Boatbuilding yards can be just as fascinating as the boats themselves. The age-old craft of boatbuilding evokes the scent of beautiful woods being steamed to bend the timber; the copper and bronze nails being hammered into place; rows of tools hanging neatly on walls; sanding, shaping, sealing, oiling and painting. There is an alchemy that takes place in a boatbuilder's yard; a boat is much more than the sum of its parts.

Boat festivals are a great way to see lots of different boats and meet boat owners. If you're searching for a boat, it's a great way to start – you can have a good look around before deciding what's right for you. Even if you just like looking at boats, Australia has some fantastic boat festivals that are well worth a visit.

This book is a collection of boats large and small and every size in between: working boats and pleasure craft, models, steam-, diesel- and sail-powered ones as well as oar-driven vessels, both new and old. They all speak of humanity's fascination with the water and of our love for adventure, travel and freedom.

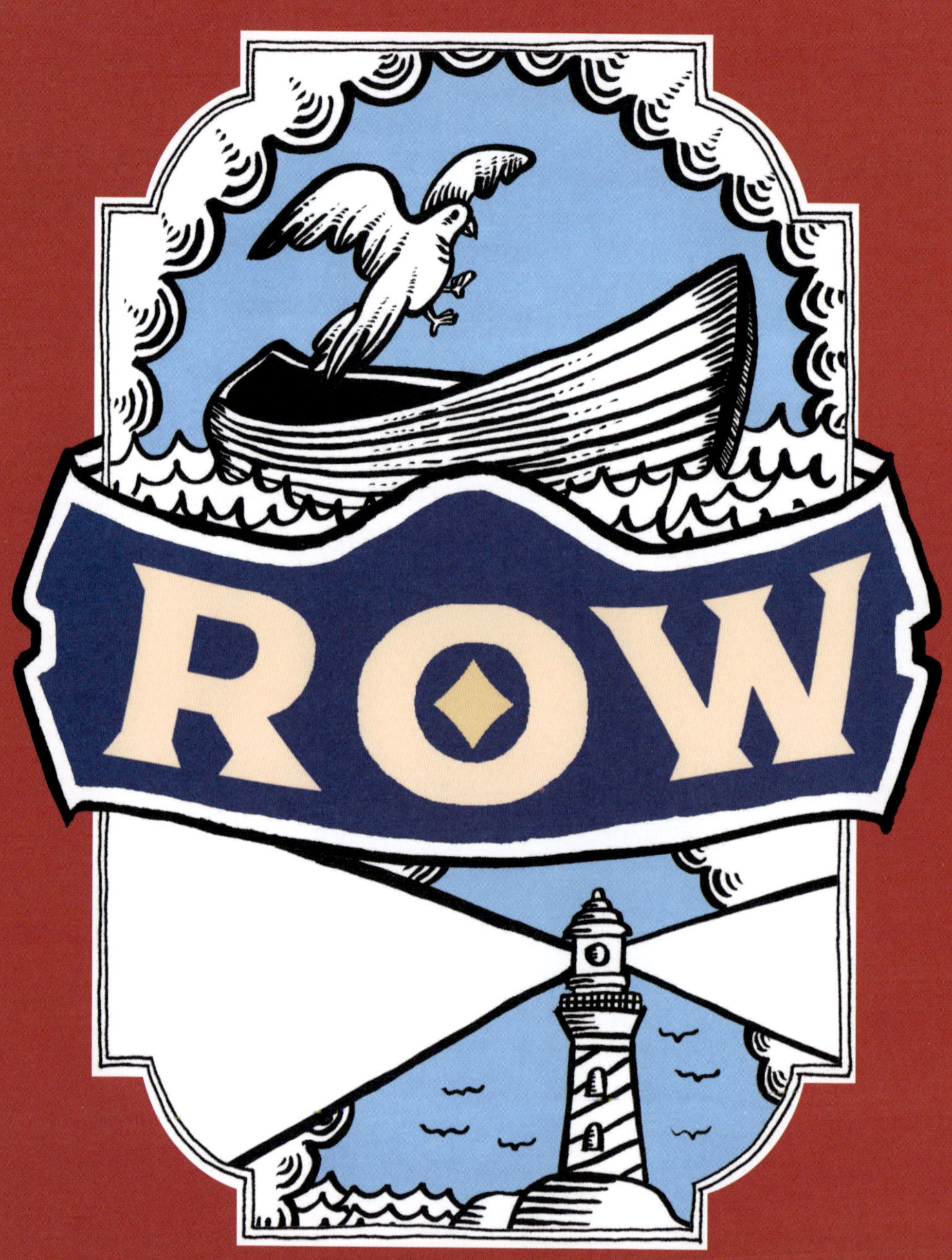
ROW

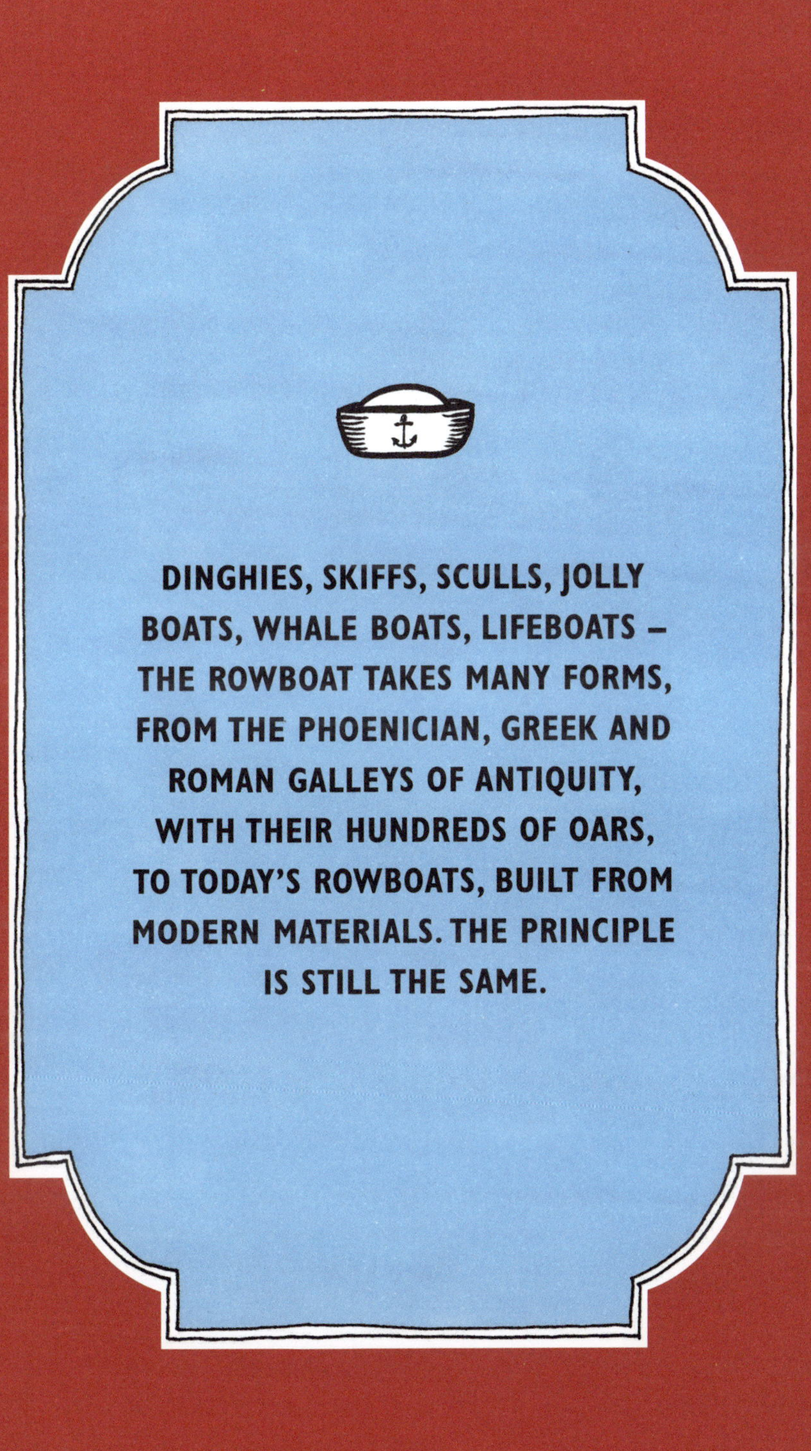

DINGHIES, SKIFFS, SCULLS, JOLLY BOATS, WHALE BOATS, LIFEBOATS – THE ROWBOAT TAKES MANY FORMS, FROM THE PHOENICIAN, GREEK AND ROMAN GALLEYS OF ANTIQUITY, WITH THEIR HUNDREDS OF OARS, TO TODAY'S ROWBOATS, BUILT FROM MODERN MATERIALS. THE PRINCIPLE IS STILL THE SAME.

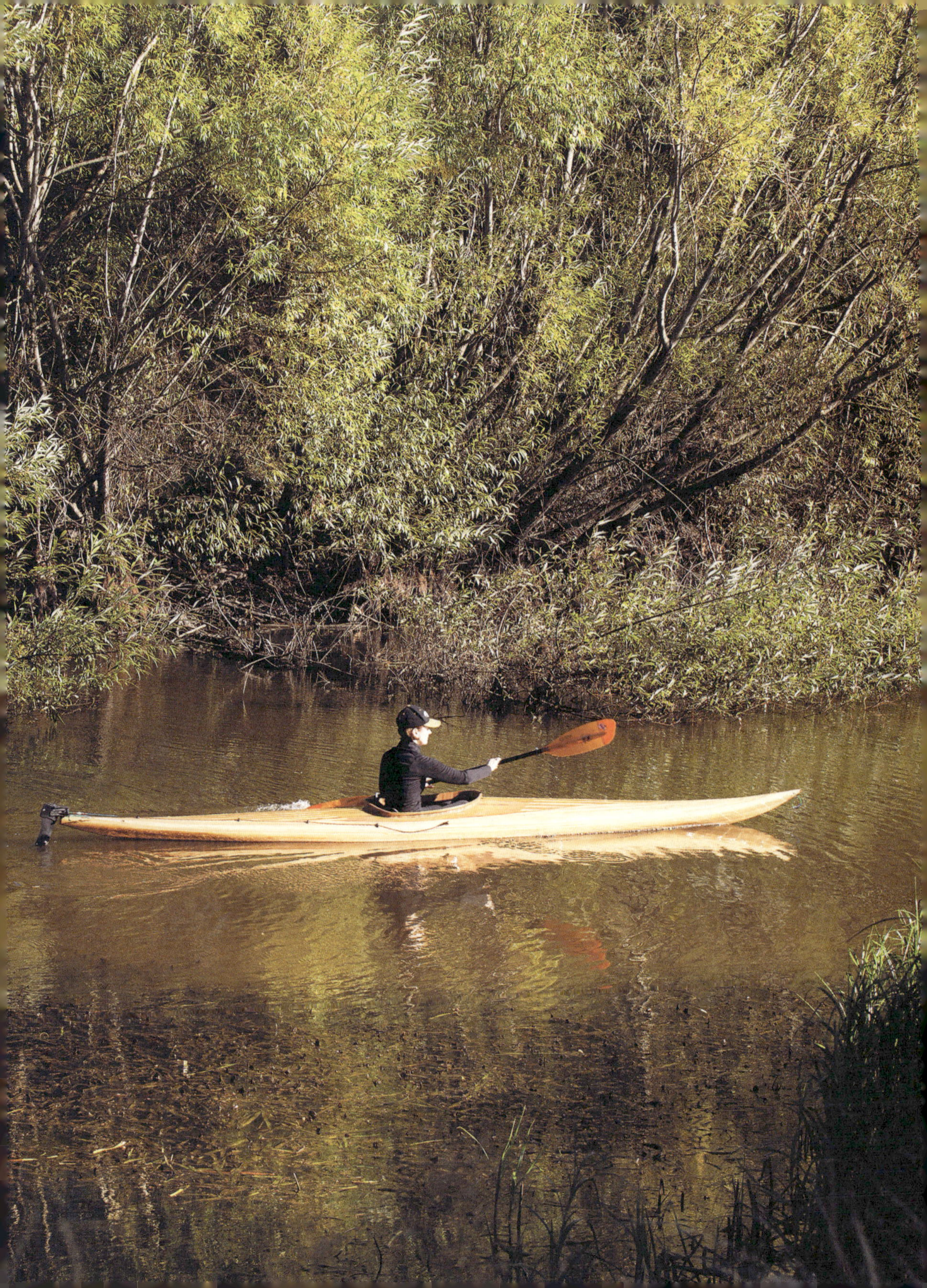

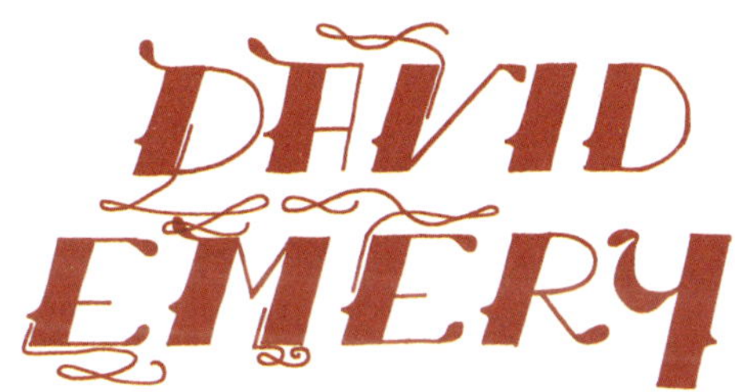

David Emery is a celebrated furniture-maker who works in the Central Victorian town of Kyneton. His furniture can be found in Parliament House in Canberra and design stores, and he has even outfitted a cathedral. David also loves making strip-built kayaks, using the designs of internationally renowned small-boat designer Nick Schade of Guillemot Kayaks in Connecticut.

To strip-build a kayak, first you make a spine from cross-sectional pieces of wood, then you cover it with thin strips of a lightweight wood glued together to form the body. The timber is then sanded and given a thin coat of clear fibreglass both inside and out, to seal it. The finished kayak is remarkably light and very strong. Having made quite a number of these, David now has the process down to a fine art, and can quickly taper and shape the strips into the required shapes.

Strip-built kayaks look good too. As designer Nick Schade says, 'What looks good to the water looks good to the eye.'

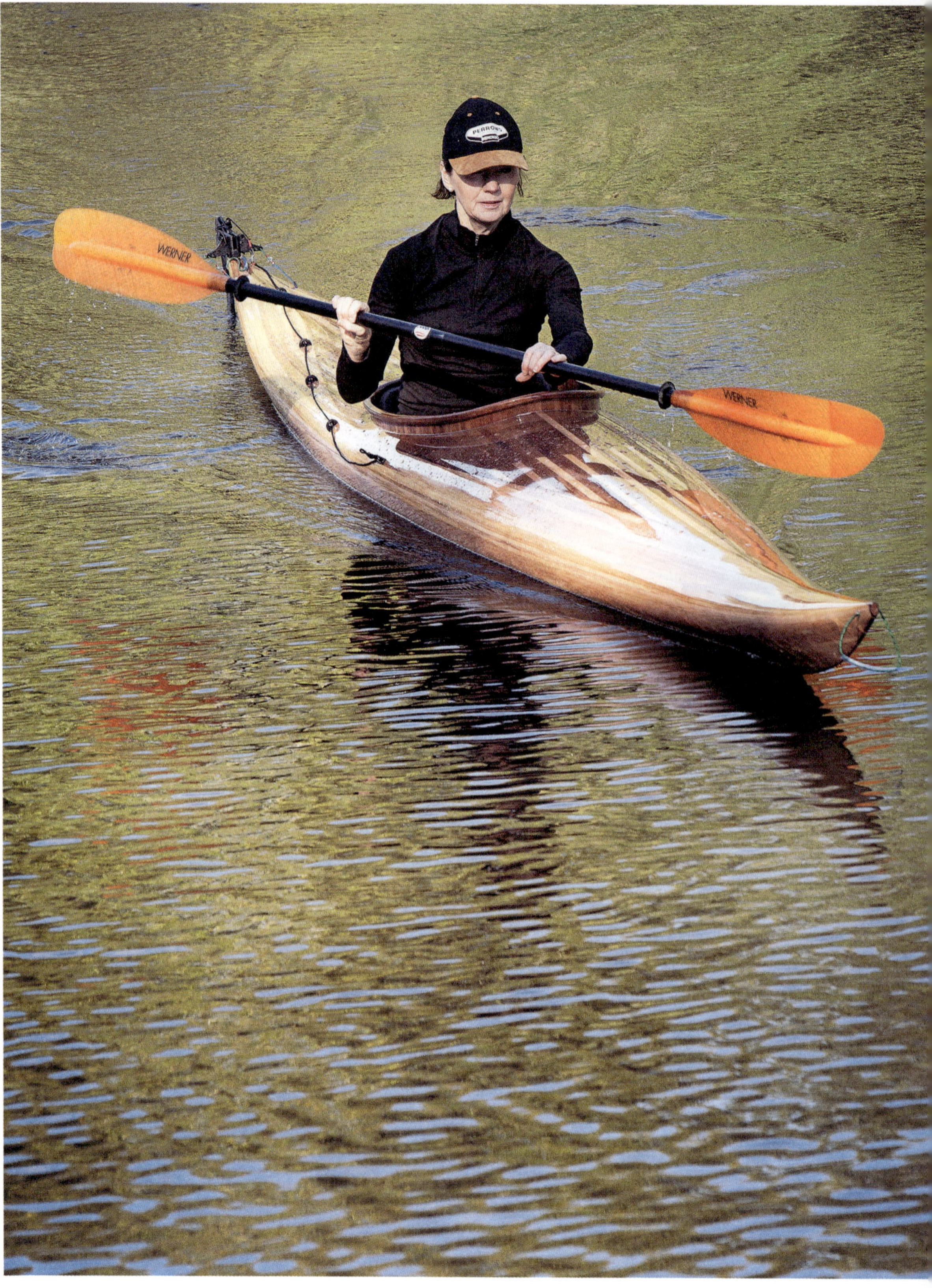
WERNER
WERNER

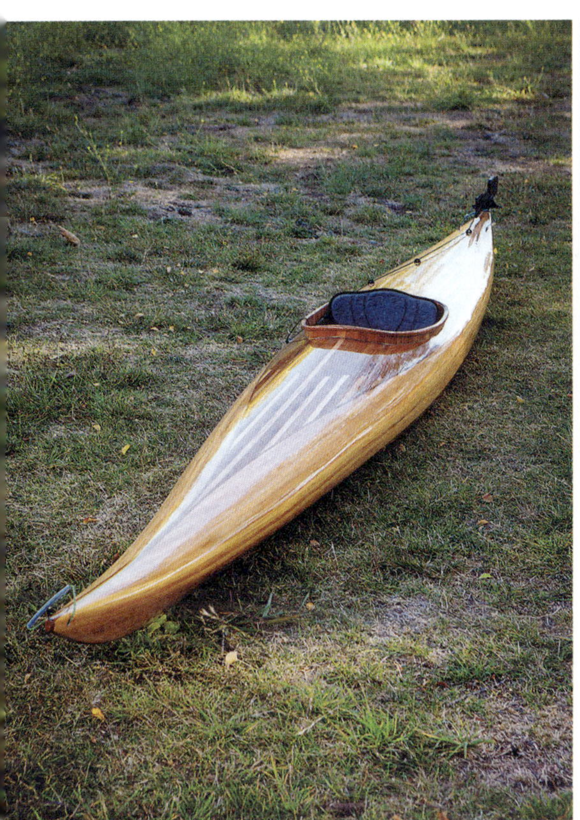

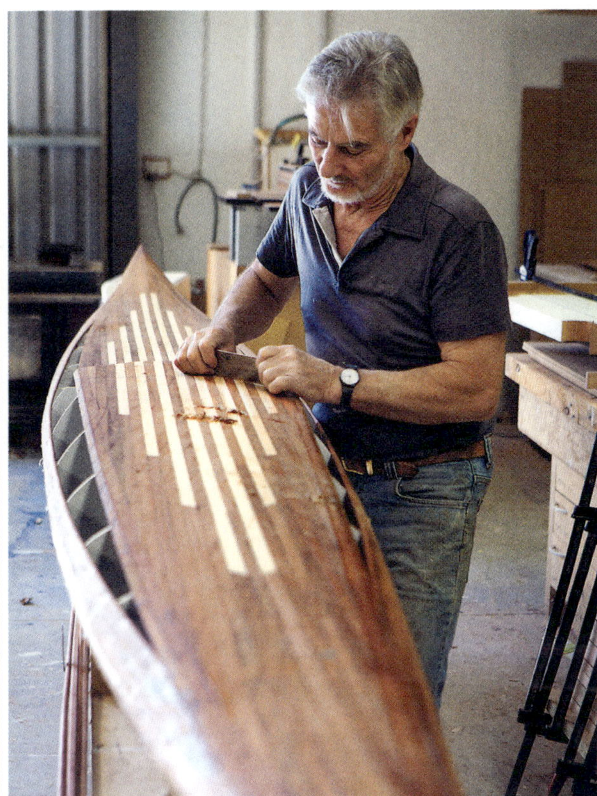

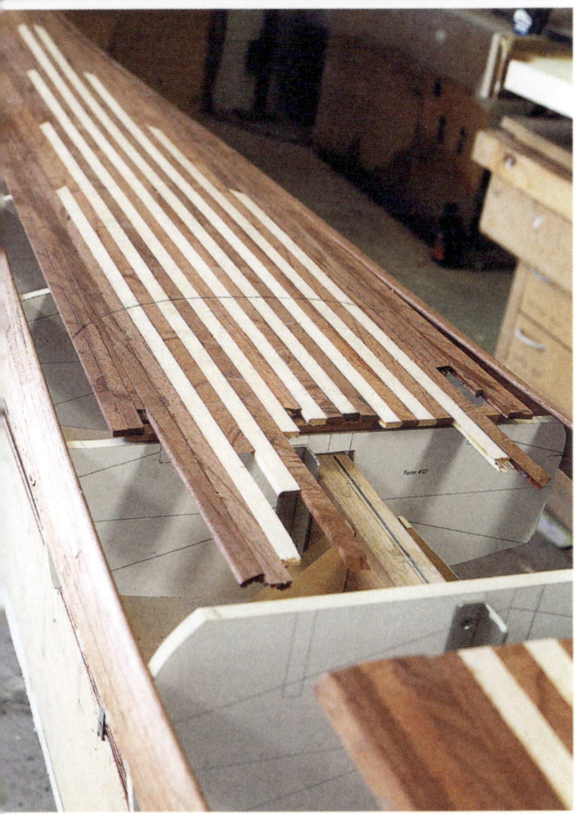

David made his wife, Jan, a beautiful kayak from two planks of Western Red cedar – one was the darkest piece he had ever seen, and the other the lightest. He then machined the timber into the strips he needed and, before too long, Jan's kayak emerged. Jan (pictured left) and David now go on kayaking adventures and holidays together.

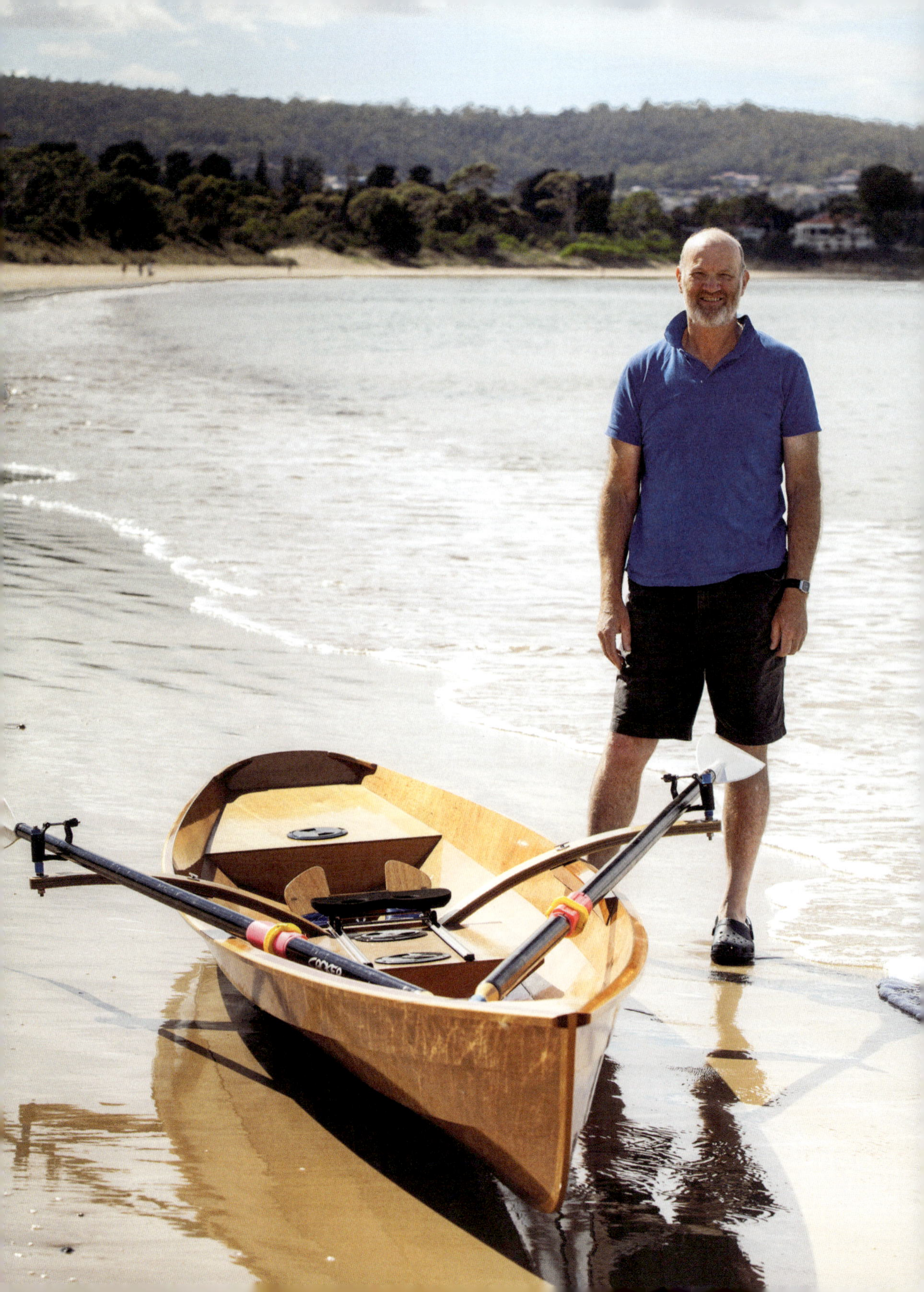

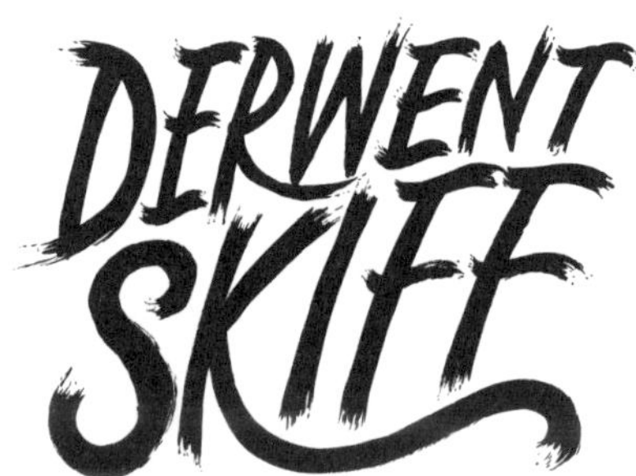

Designing boats seems to run in Allan Witt's family. Allan's first version of the Derwent Skiff was a boat he designed and built for his wife to help her get fit; and his father, Lou Witt, made a clinker-built version of the same design.

The final version of the Derwent Skiff was a mix of the two designs and won a design award at the 2007 Australian Wooden Boat Festival. It's a lightweight recreational rowing boat that is 18 feet long and designed to row with as much ease as a racing scull.

Allan designed the skiff so that you can either buy a kit and build it yourself; buy plans only, then cut the timber and build; or buy a fully made boat.

Allan gets a great response to the Derwent Skiff – while we were shooting the pictures for this book, three people came up and asked for his business card. There's something about wooden boats that seems to attract people. His Derwent Skiff slices through the water at a great rate, and I can see why it almost has a cult following. Next for Allan is a new, super-lightweight version.

Alan Witt with one of his Derwent Skiffs at Bellerive Beach, just outside Hobart. They are specially designed and built to suit the conditions on the Derwent.

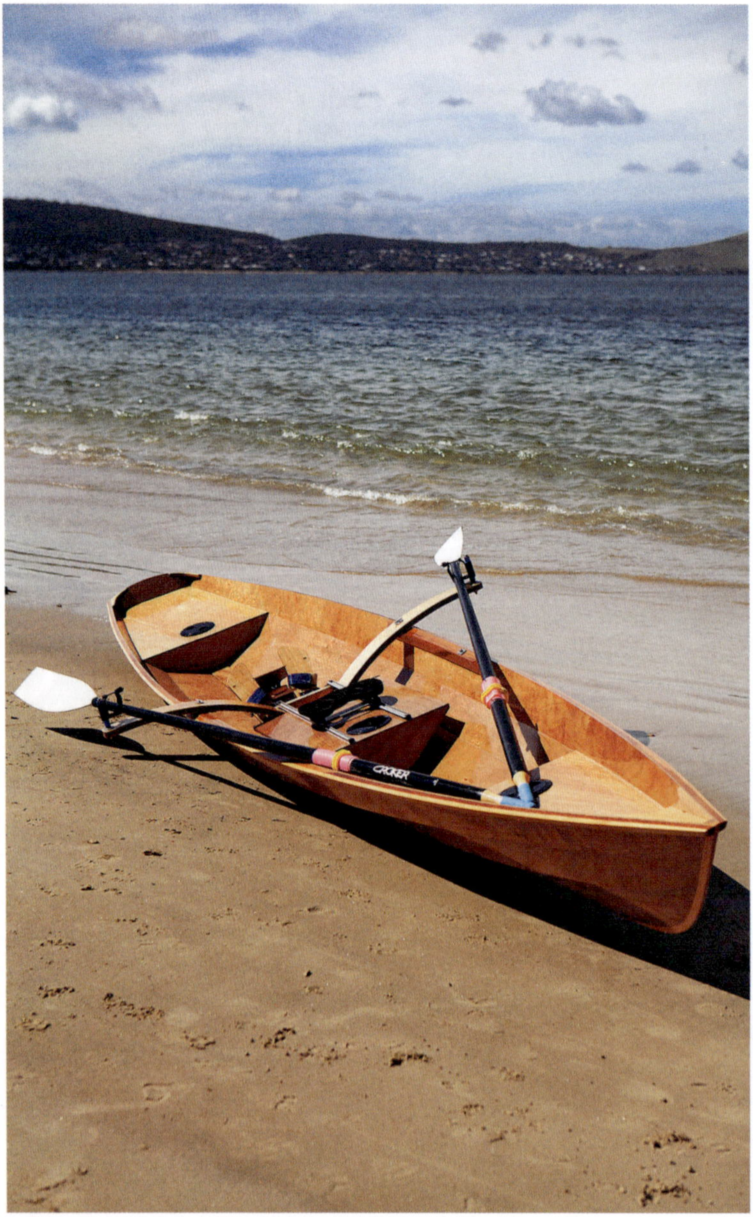

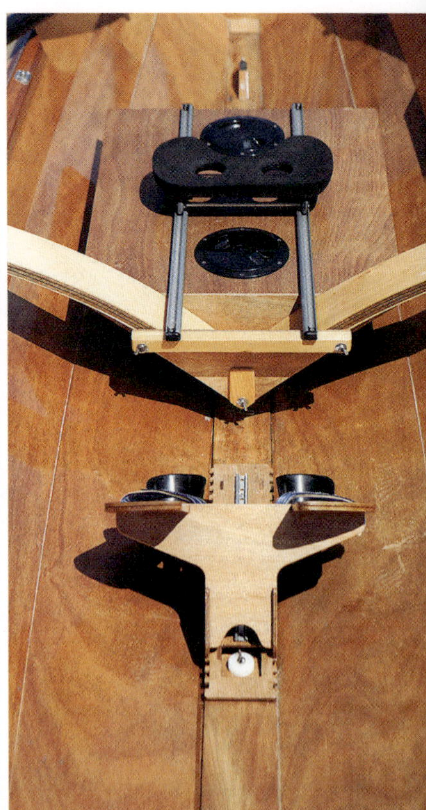

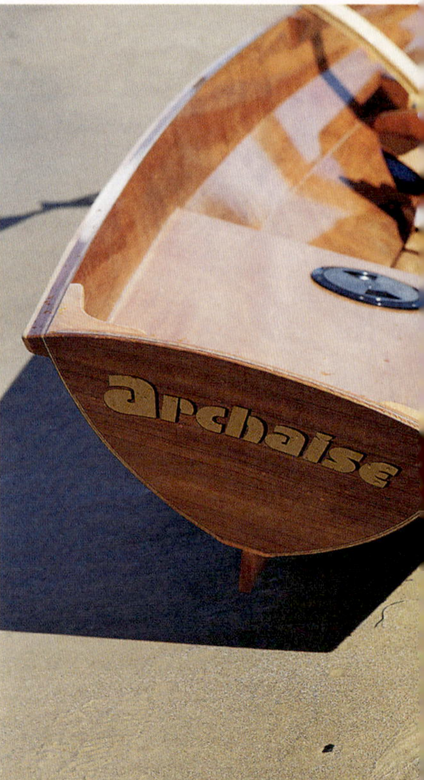

The sliding rowing seat on the Derwent Skiff enables you to use your whole body to row.

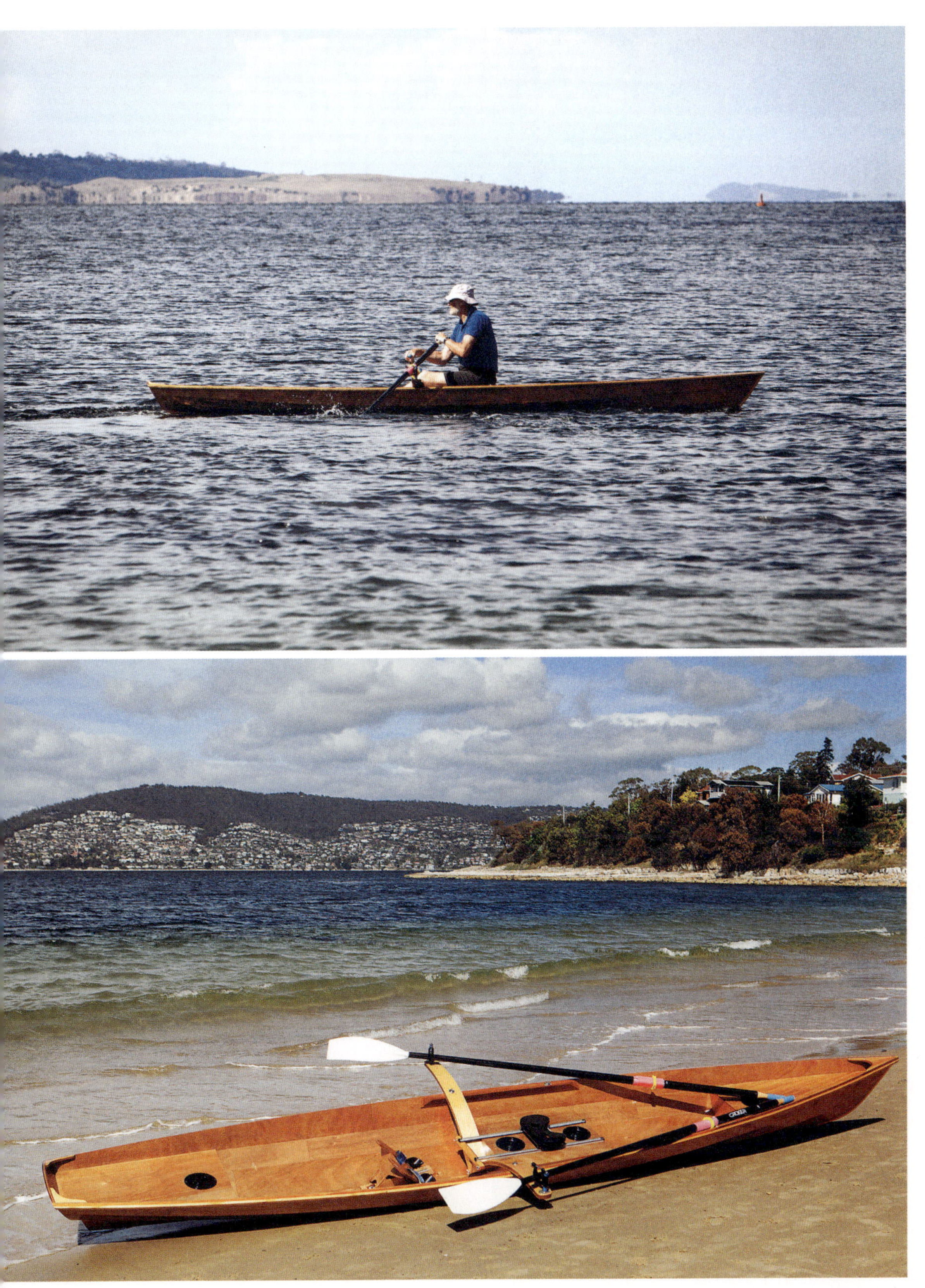

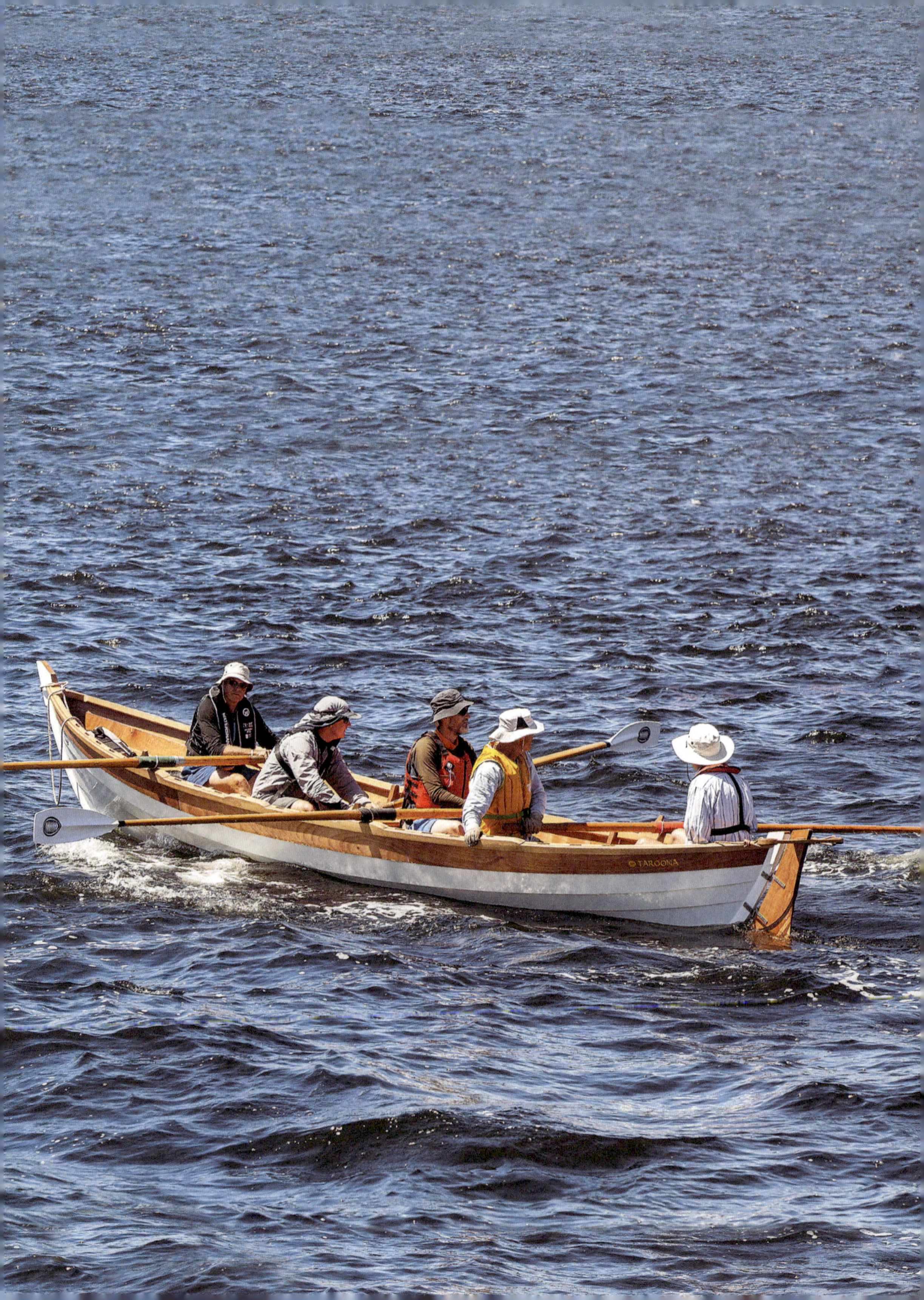
TAROONA

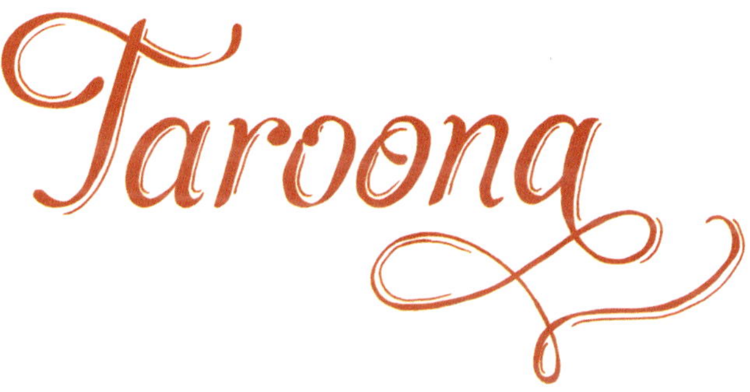

This St Ayles Skiff was built by the Taroona Community Association as a community development project funded by the Kingborough Council to encourage rowing along the beautiful coastline south of Hobart, Tasmania.

The first St Ayles Skiff was commissioned in 2009 by the Scottish Fisheries Museum in Fife and was designed by Iain Oughtred, an expert in historic boats. His brief was to design a fast, attractive and safe skiff that was easy and relatively cheap to build and could be rowed by the people who built it. He designed a 22-foot clinker plywood rowing skiff for four rowers and a cox. The boat comes as a kit, with pre-milled plywood planks and components, and requires about 500 hours' labour.

The St Ayles Skiff has been a successful community project in over 100 coastal communities in the United Kingdom, Canada, Australia and New Zealand.

With four rowers on board, *Taroona* can move through the water in a very sprightly way.

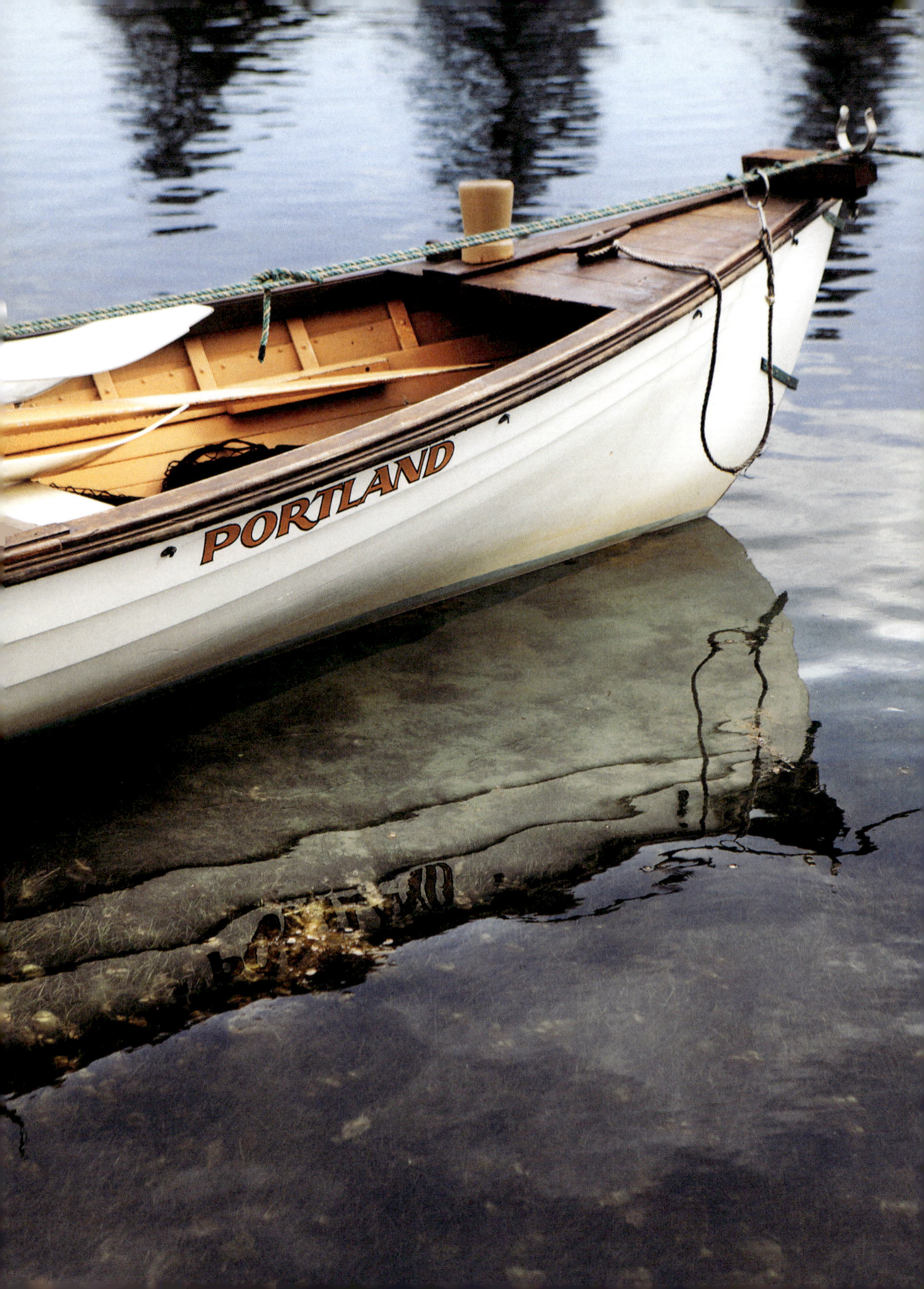
PORTLAND

WILLIAM DUTTON

Built by the community group Promoting Portland Maritime Heritage Inc, *William Dutton* was launched in October 2010 to promote Portland's maritime heritage and to raise money for the area's maritime museum. She is a whale boat, named after the area's most famous whaler, William Dutton, who started whaling in this south-western Victorian town in the early nineteenth century.

William Dutton is built to a traditional whale boat design from Oregon timber planks on a spotted gum keel and ribs, with copper fastenings. She has five oars and one sweep and is 29 feet 6 inches long. Her beam is 7 feet 2 inches and her draught is nearly 9 inches.

William Dutton is used to practise for the Australian Whale Boat Racing Championships and other whale boat competitions. The crews are male, female and mixed, and the boat is also used by the local Rotary Club. The crews train three nights a week, so the boat gets plenty of use. She has united a lot of people in the Portland community, leading to many new friendships.

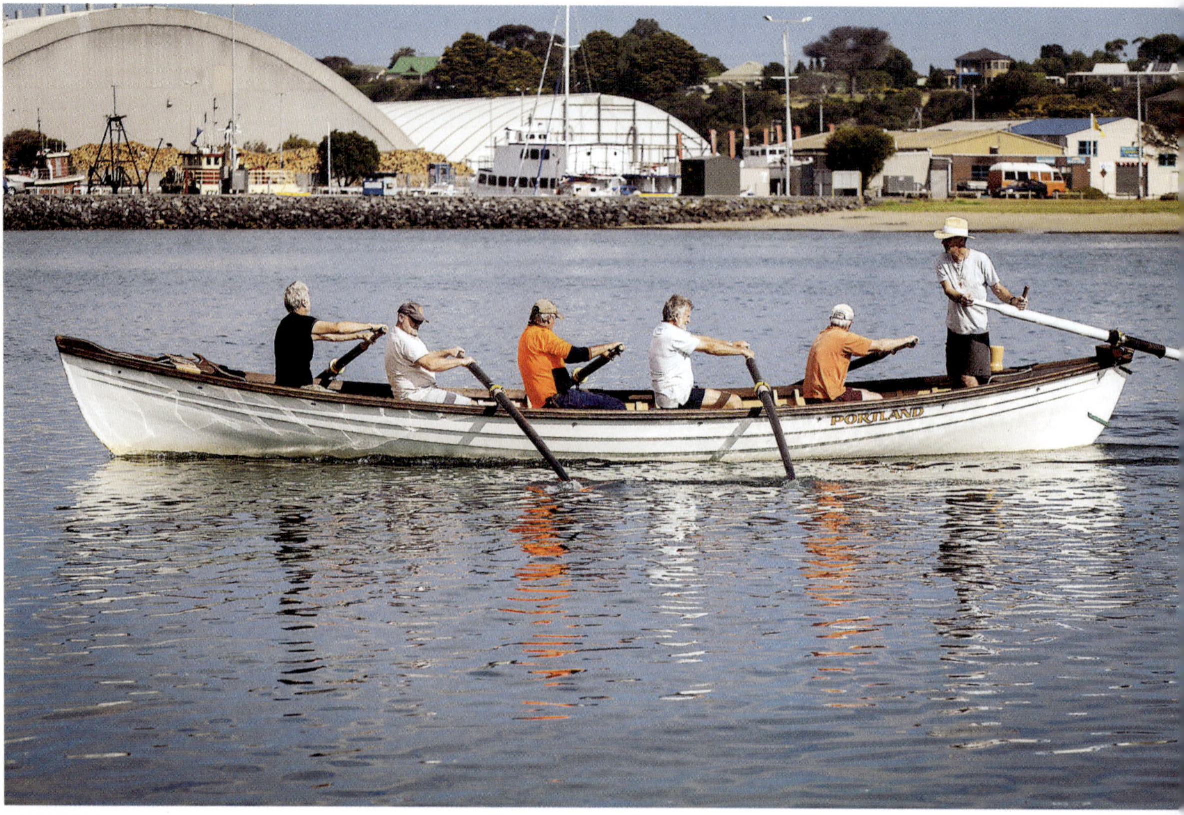

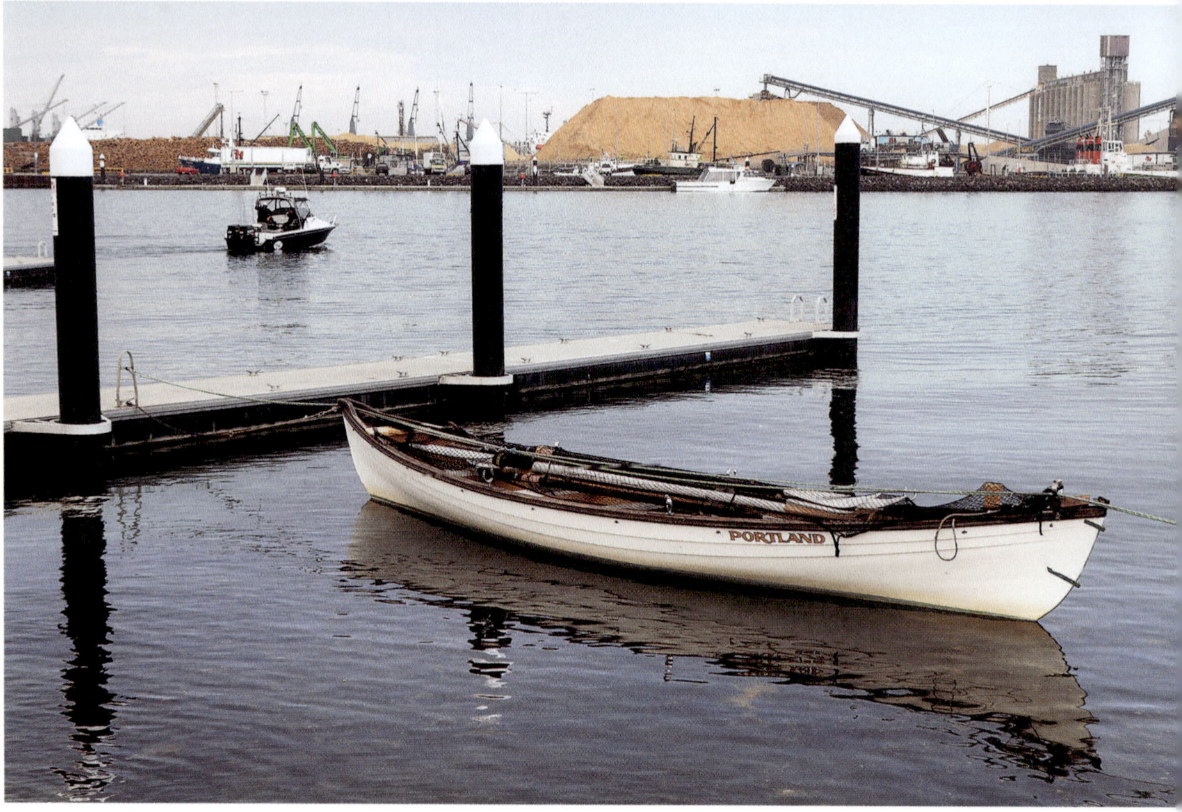

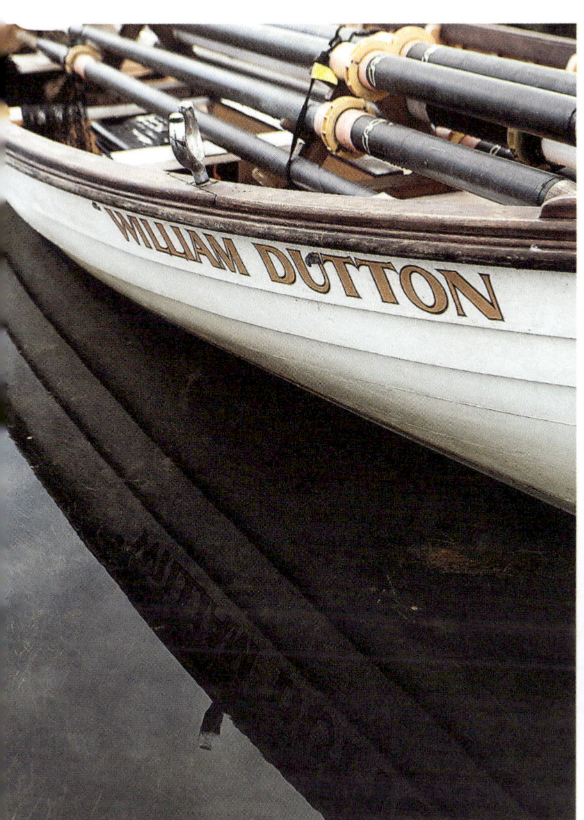

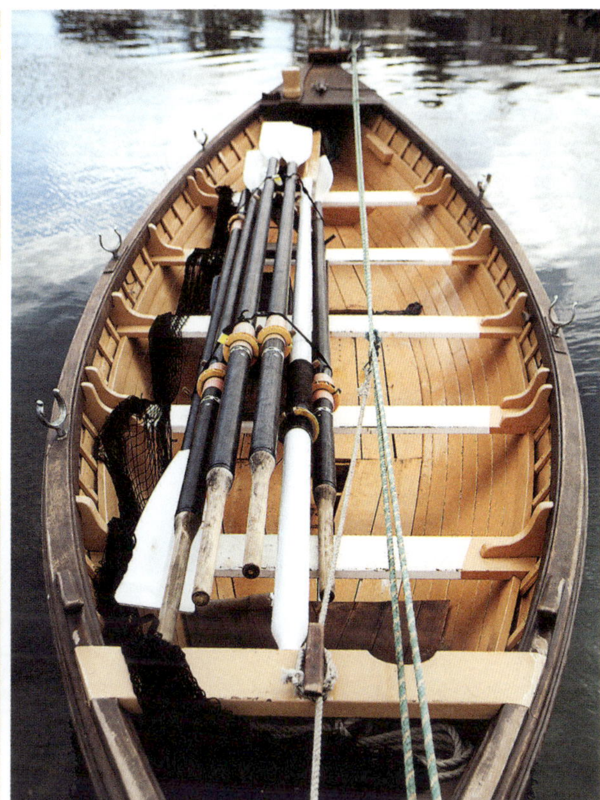

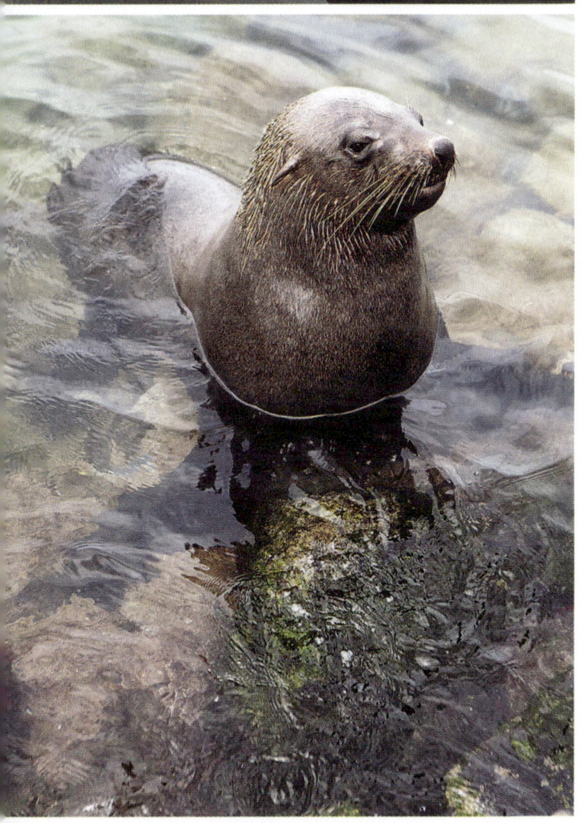

Back in the nineteenth century, boats like *William Dutton* were mainly used for whaling and sealing. Today, it's nice to see seals swimming around in the shallows where she is moored.

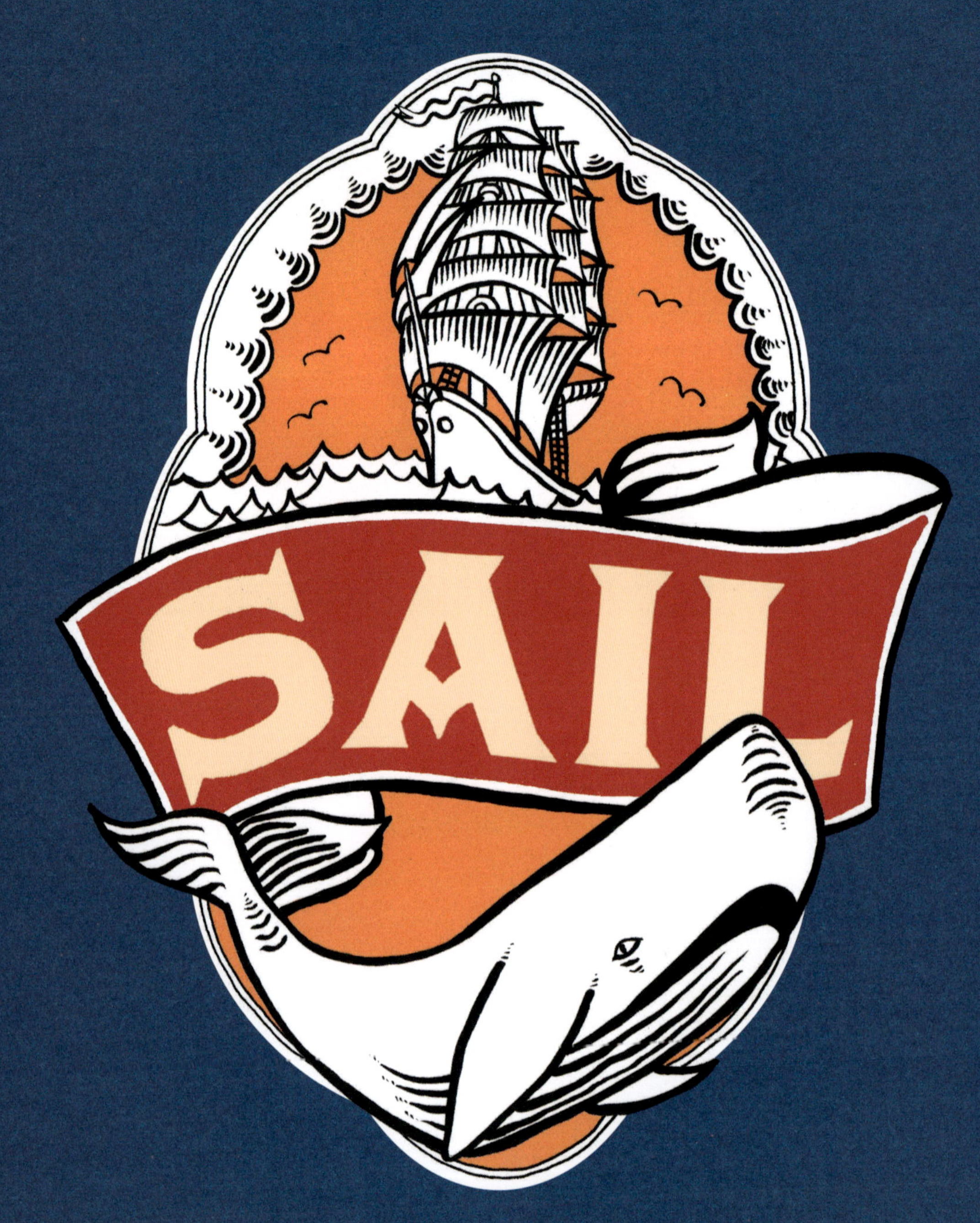
SAIL

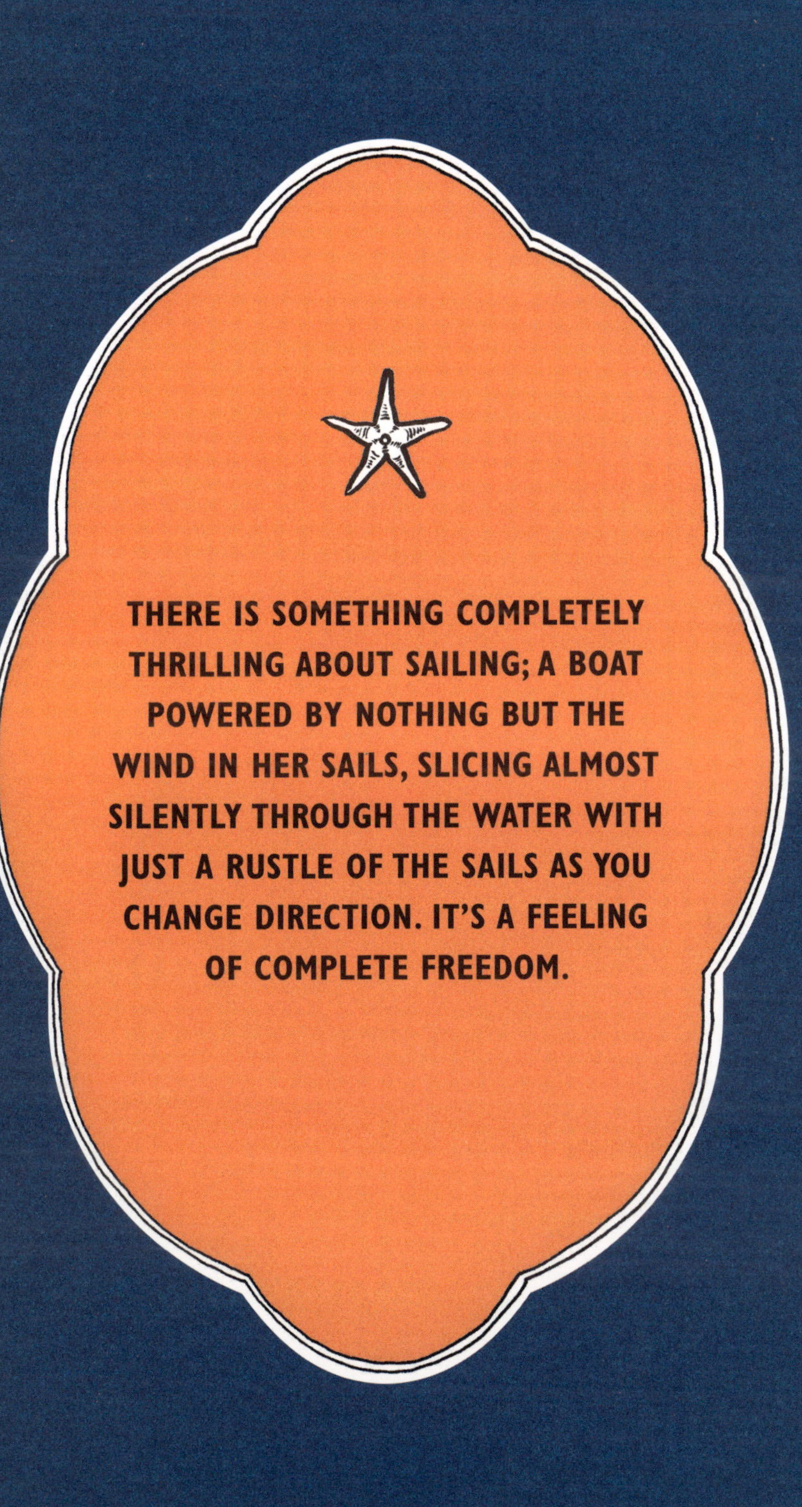

THERE IS SOMETHING COMPLETELY THRILLING ABOUT SAILING; A BOAT POWERED BY NOTHING BUT THE WIND IN HER SAILS, SLICING ALMOST SILENTLY THROUGH THE WATER WITH JUST A RUSTLE OF THE SAILS AS YOU CHANGE DIRECTION. IT'S A FEELING OF COMPLETE FREEDOM.

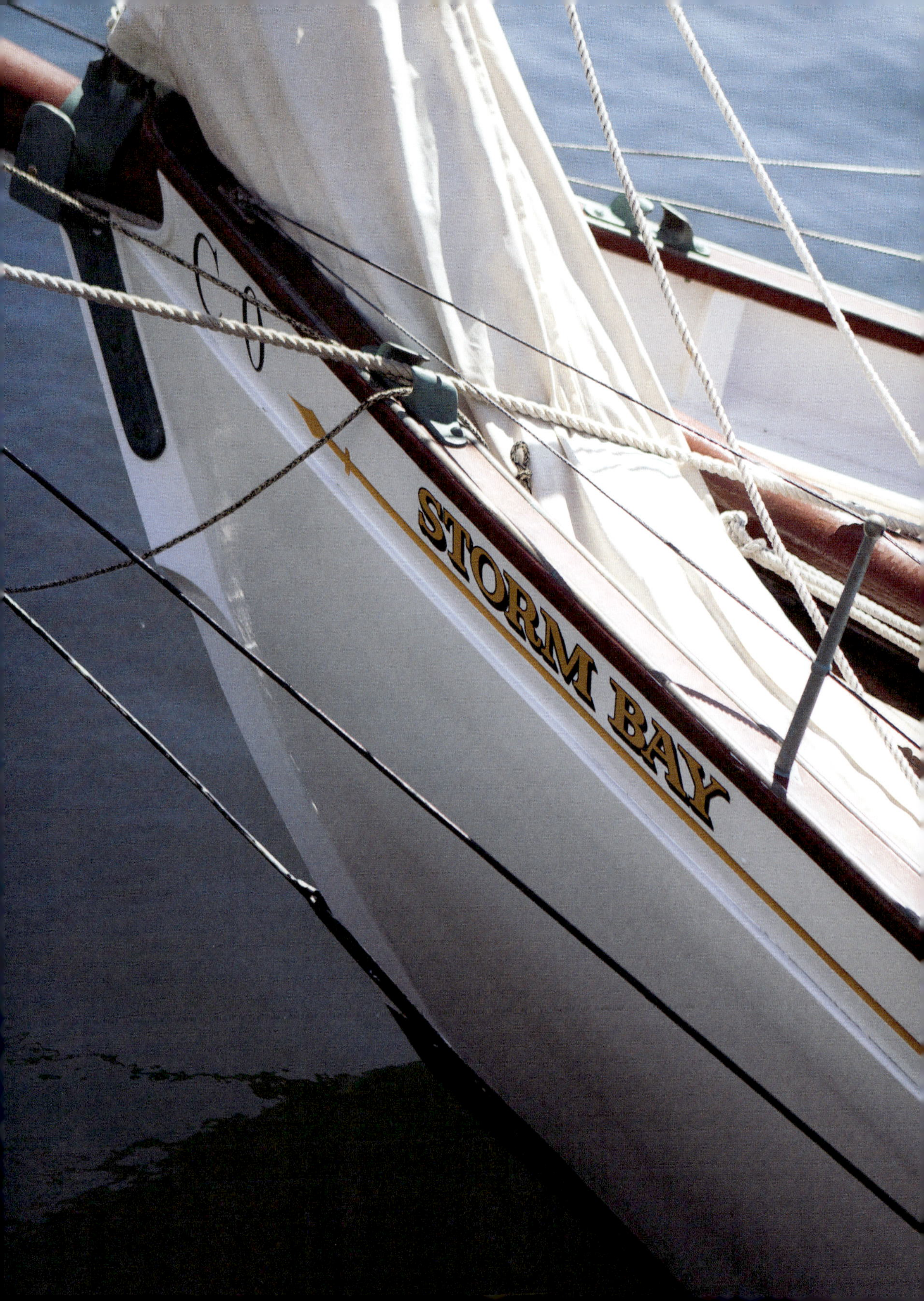
STORM BAY

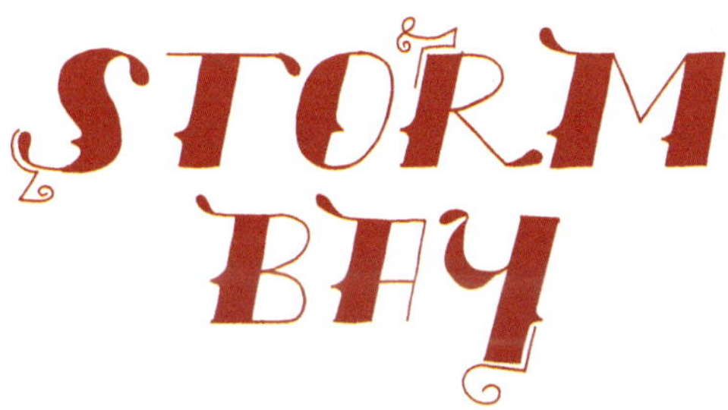

The *Storm Bay* tale is another of those love stories between owners and their boats. Tim Phillips of the Wooden Boatshop in historic Sorrento, Victoria, fell in love with sad, unloved *Storm Bay,* whose owners had neglected her badly, and bought her in 1996, then spent ten years restoring her to her original condition as a sailing boat. Tim and his team are passionate about the restoration and preservation of Australia's wooden boat heritage, so it's hard to imagine a better owner for *Storm Bay*.

She was built in Hobart in 1925 by Percy Coverdale, a legendary shipwright, as a barracouta and crayfishing boat. She is probably the most beautiful fishing boat you will ever see, with her elegant lines, gaff-rigged with a top sail. Designed by Alf Blore, she has blue gum frames and her hull and decks are planked with Huon pine.

Under full sail she is nothing short of magnificent. She is 54 feet tall, her beam is 13 feet 2 inches, and her draught board is 6 feet 6 inches up and 10 feet 6 inches down.

Prior to her restoration, *Storm Bay* was a fishing boat operating out of St Helen's, Tasmania.

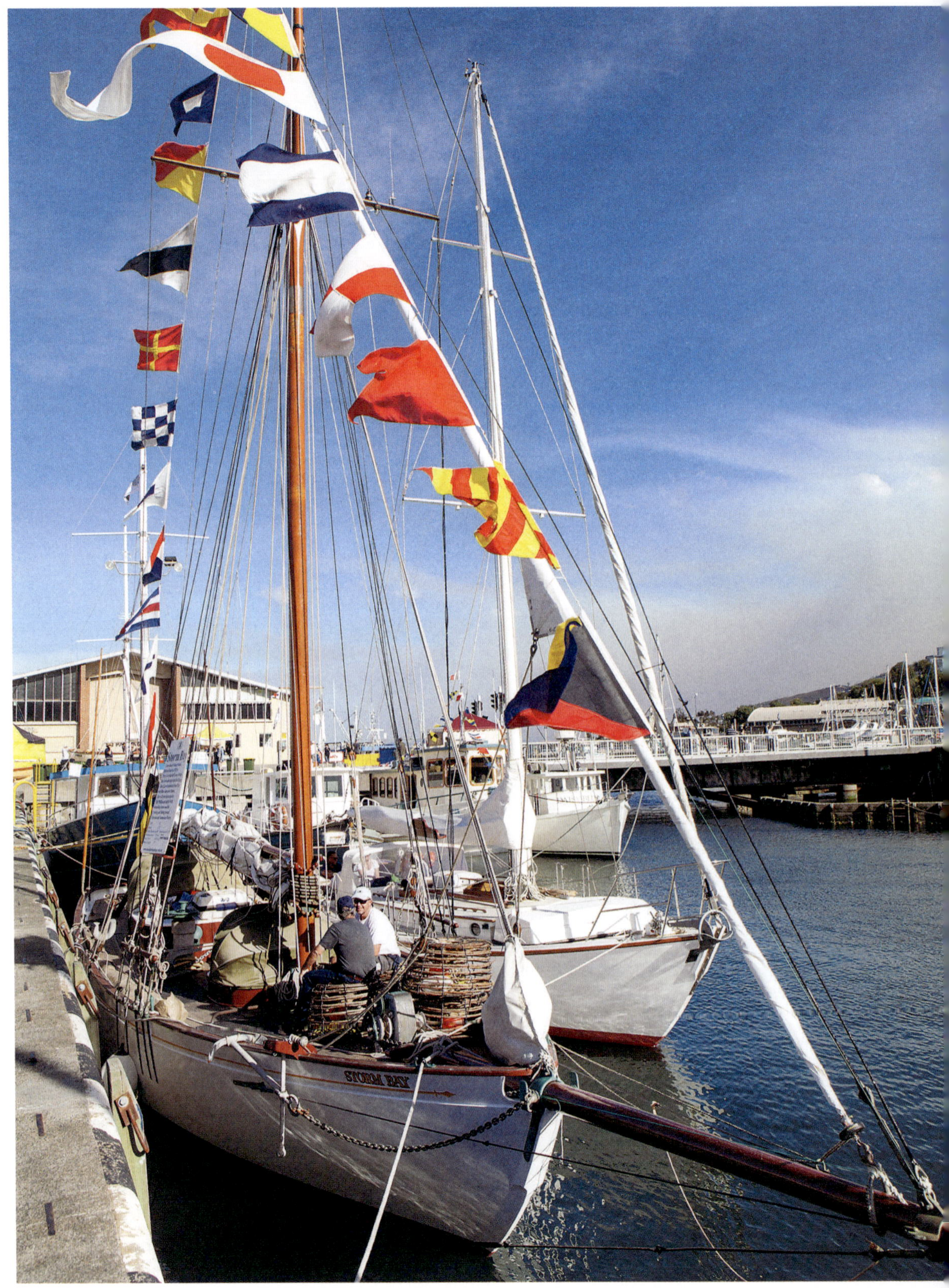
STORM BAY

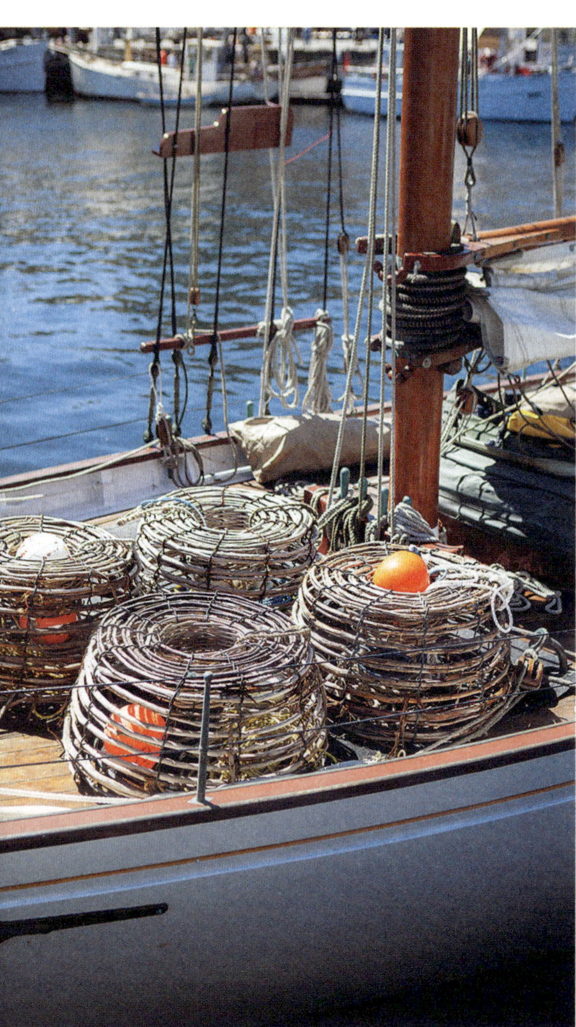

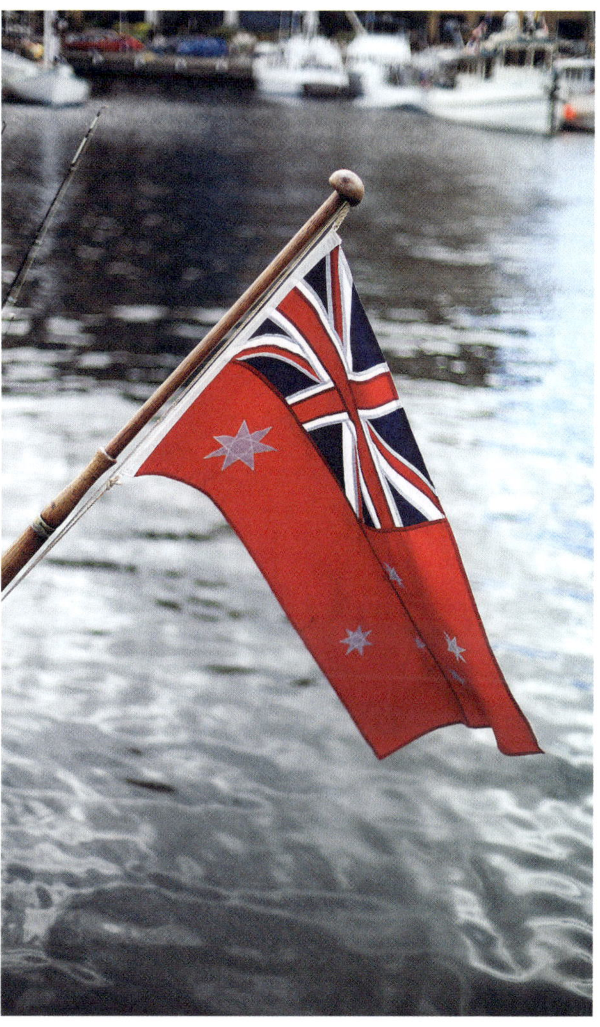

Storm Bay is a working fishing smack (boat), hence the cray pots on her deck.

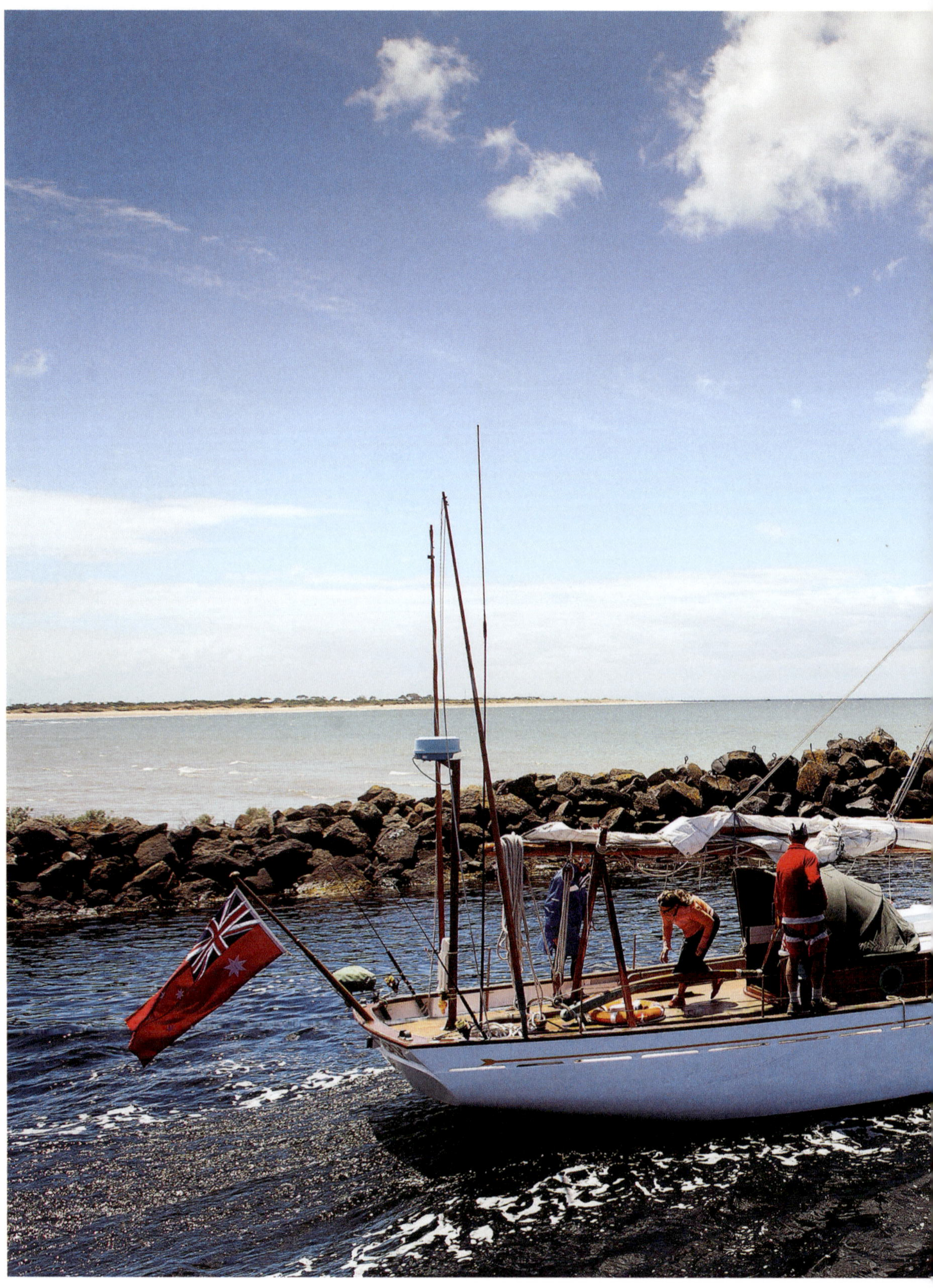

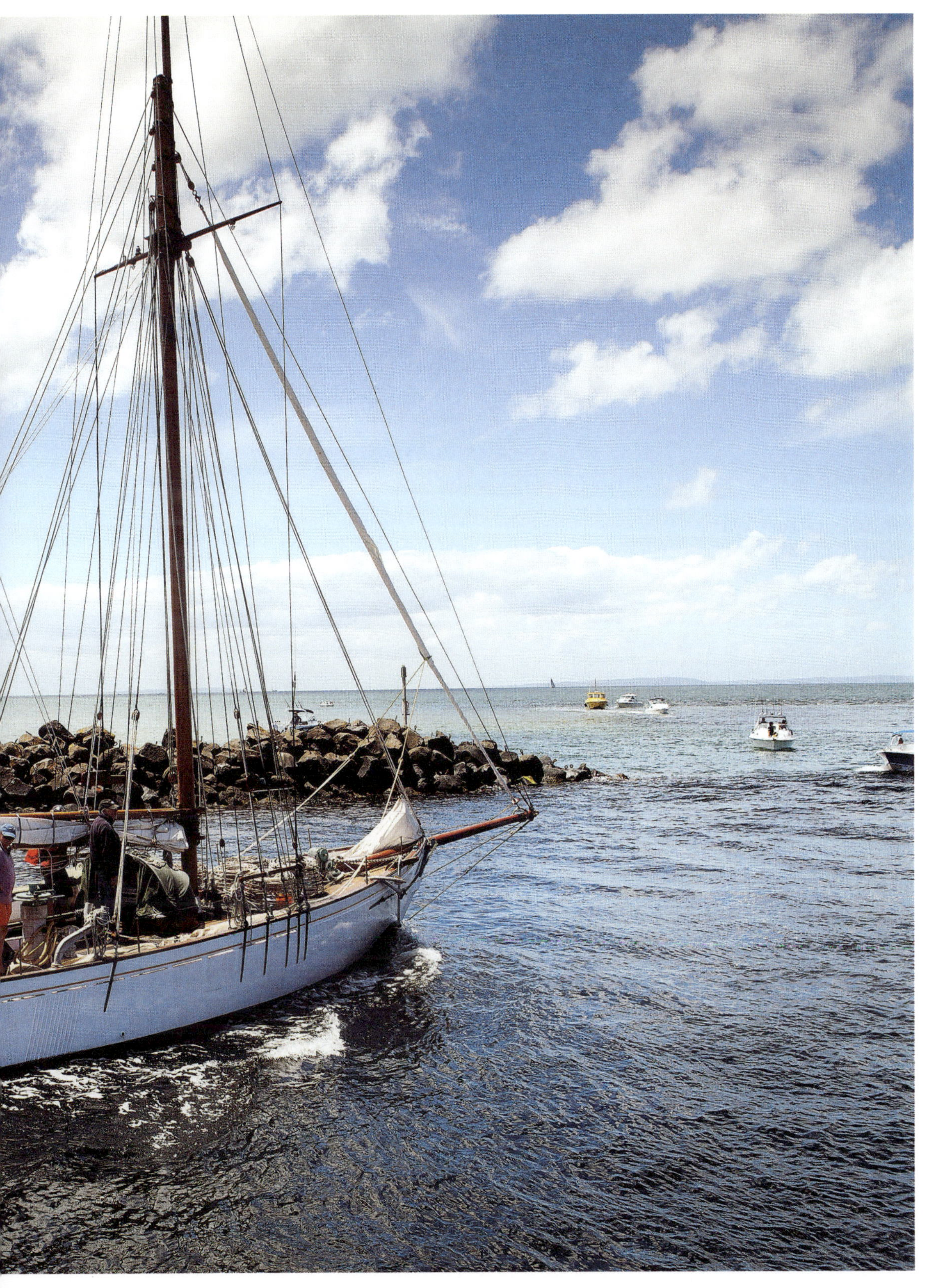

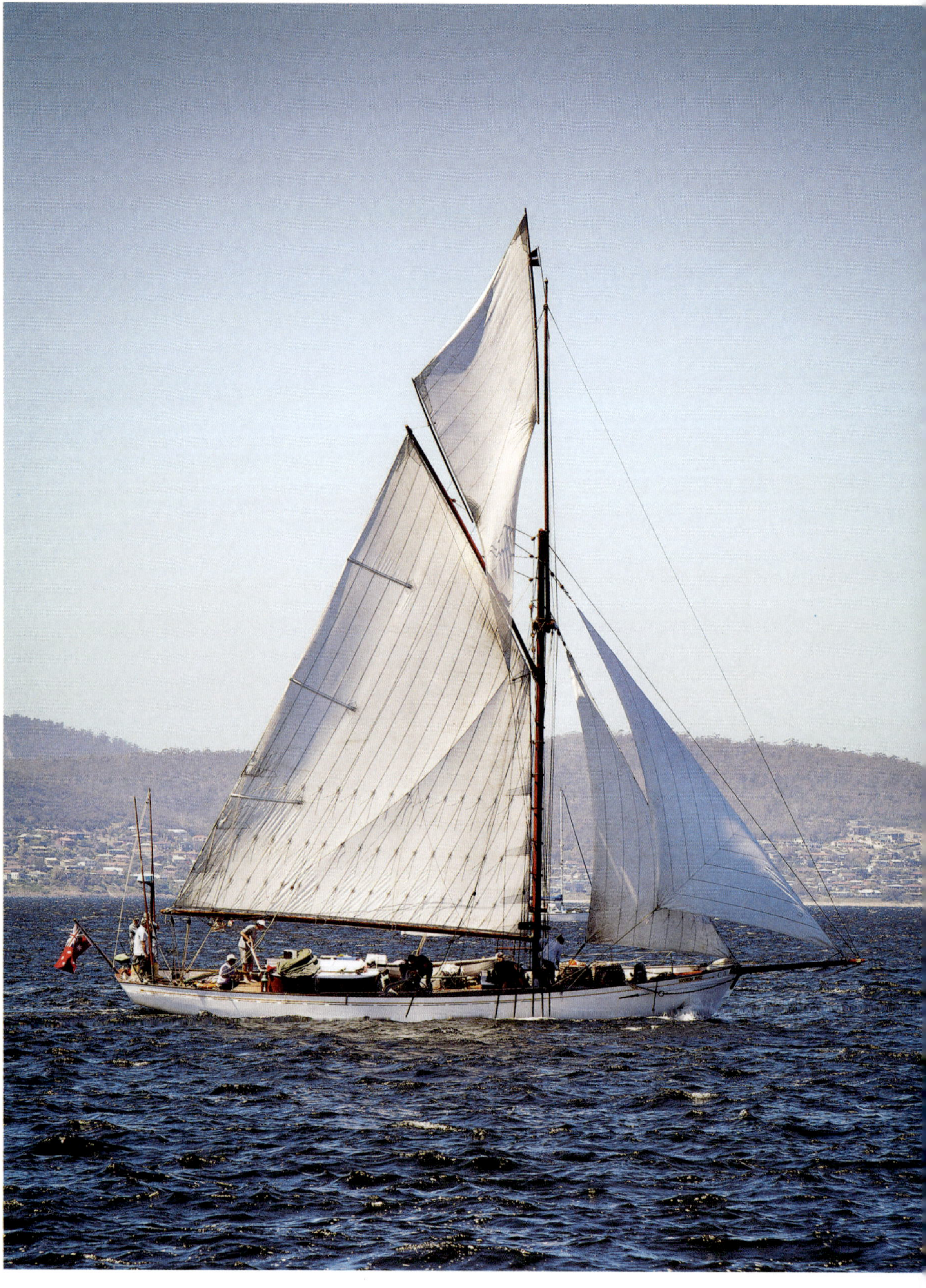

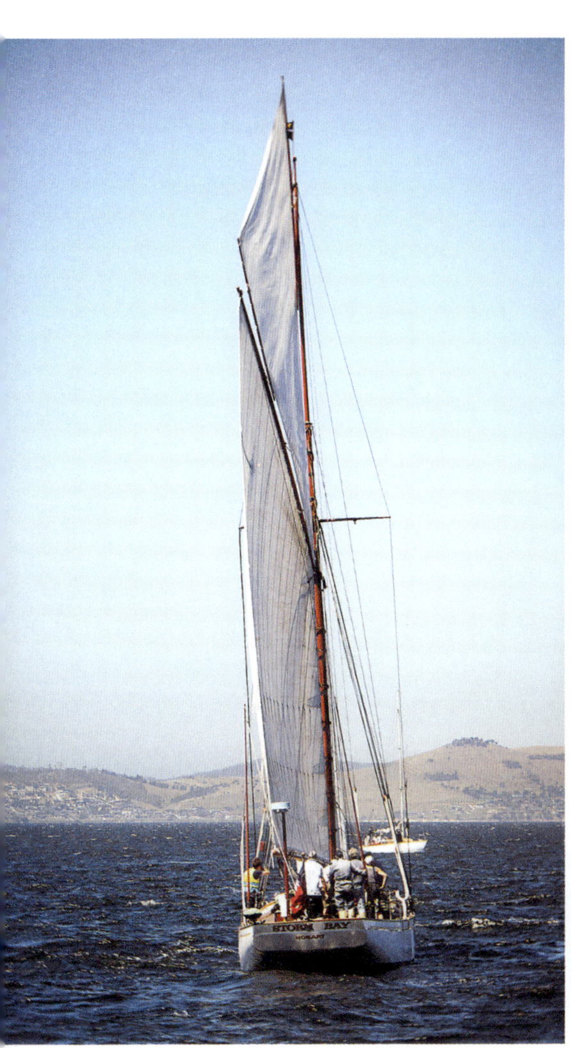

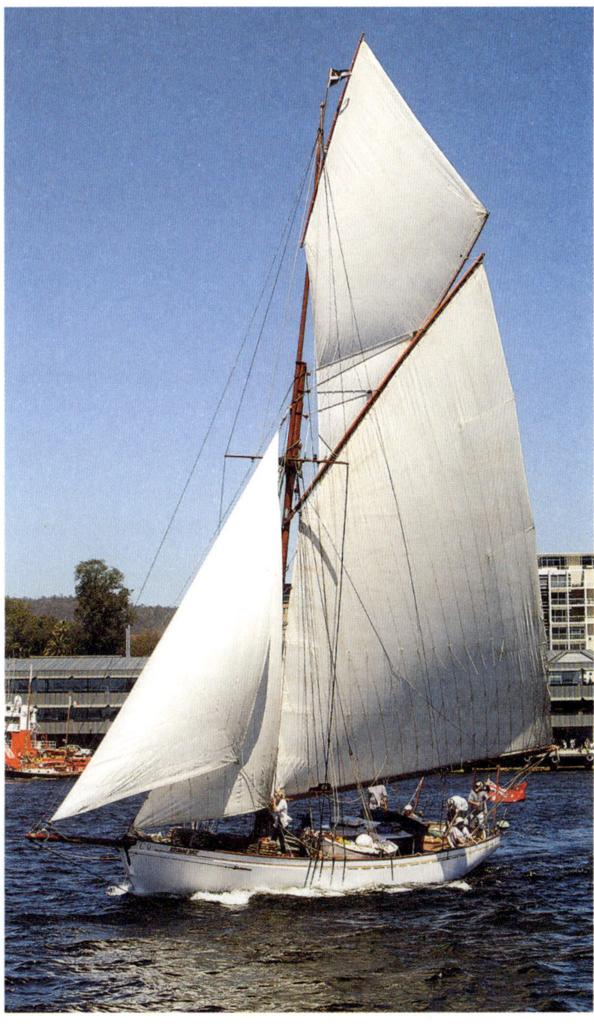

The Mercury newspaper announced at *Storm Bay*'s launch: '*Storm Bay* is a very handsome addition to the Tasmanian fishing fleet. Looking at the smack as she stands at present, she resembles a cruising yacht rather than a fishing vessel – her lines are graceful and she should prove to be speedy under sail.'

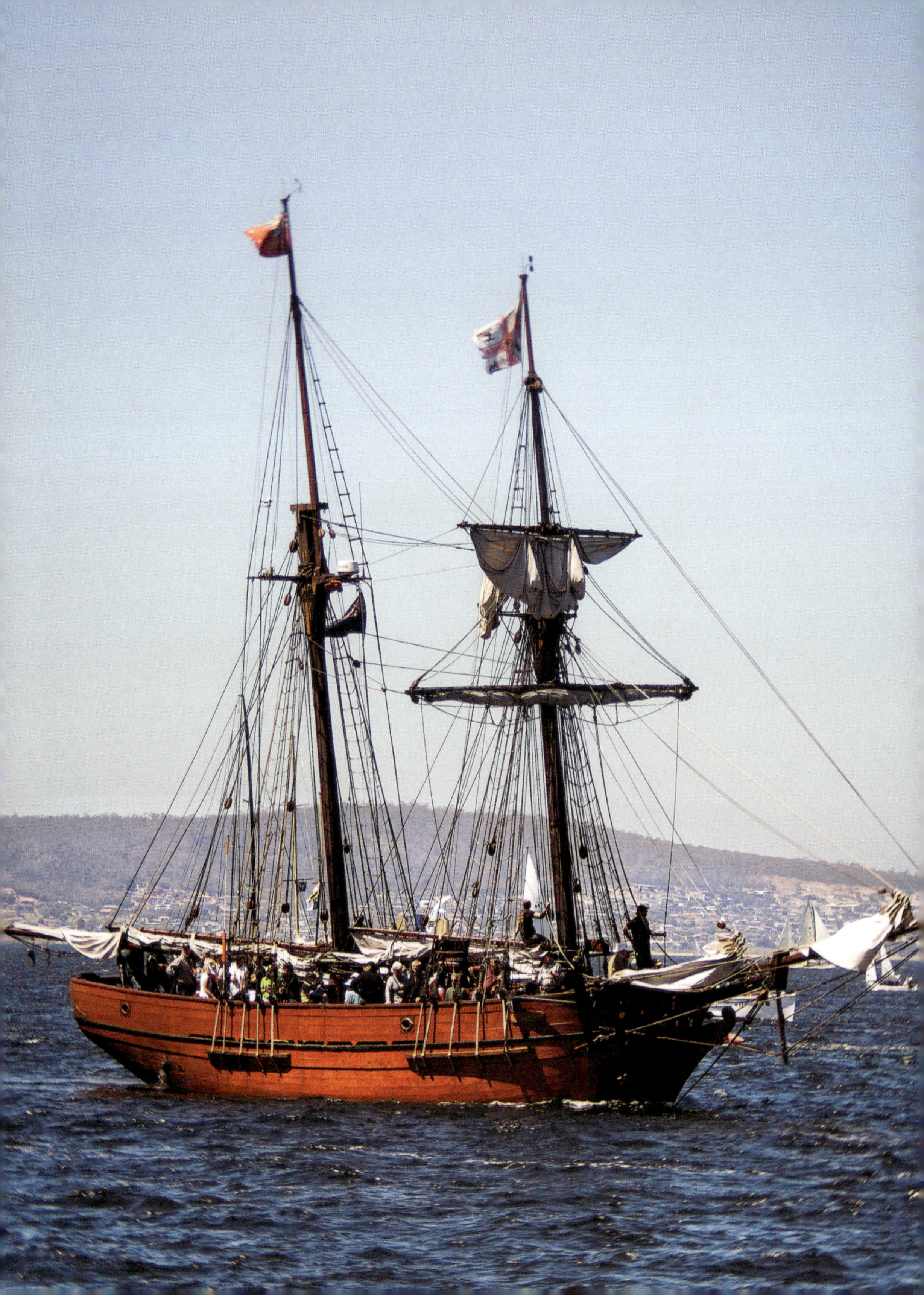

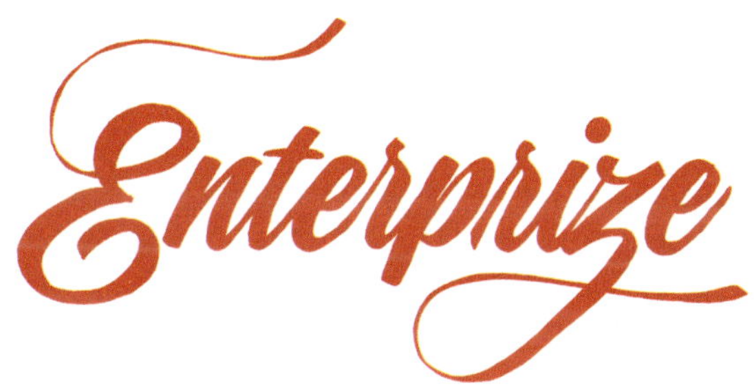

Stepping onto *Enterprize* is like stepping back in time.

She launched in 1997, and was the first square-rigged ship built in Melbourne in over 120 years. She is a replica of the original *Enterprize* schooner, built in Hobart in 1830 and purchased by John Pascoe Fawkner in 1835 to search for a new settlement. She eventually sailed into Port Phillip Bay and north to the Yarra River – the settlement of Melbourne had begun.

Enterprize is operated today by the Enterprize Ship Trust, a not-for-profit organisation dedicated to preserving and promoting tall ships. She is crewed and maintained by volunteers from all walks of life.

Her deck length is 16.1 metres, overall length 27 metres, beam 5.4 metres, draught 3 metres, height from mast to deck 17.7 metres, displacement 72 tons and sail area 185 square metres.

Happily, *Enterprize* is now open to the public, so it's easy to book a ticket and experience the thrill of nineteenth-century sailing for yourself.

FOLLOWING PAGES
It is a feeling like no other to be aboard *Enterprize* under full sail, hearing the wind in her sails.

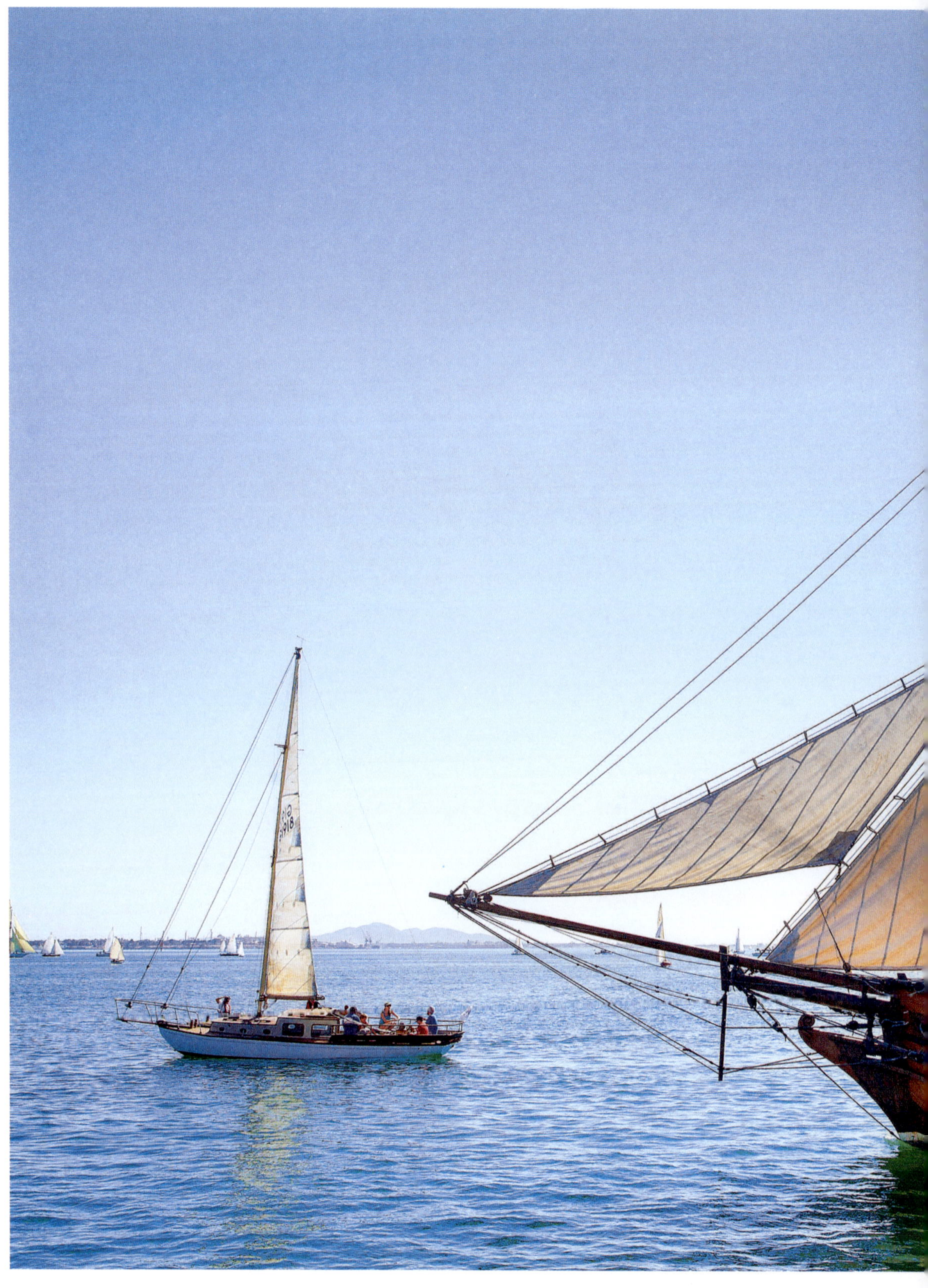

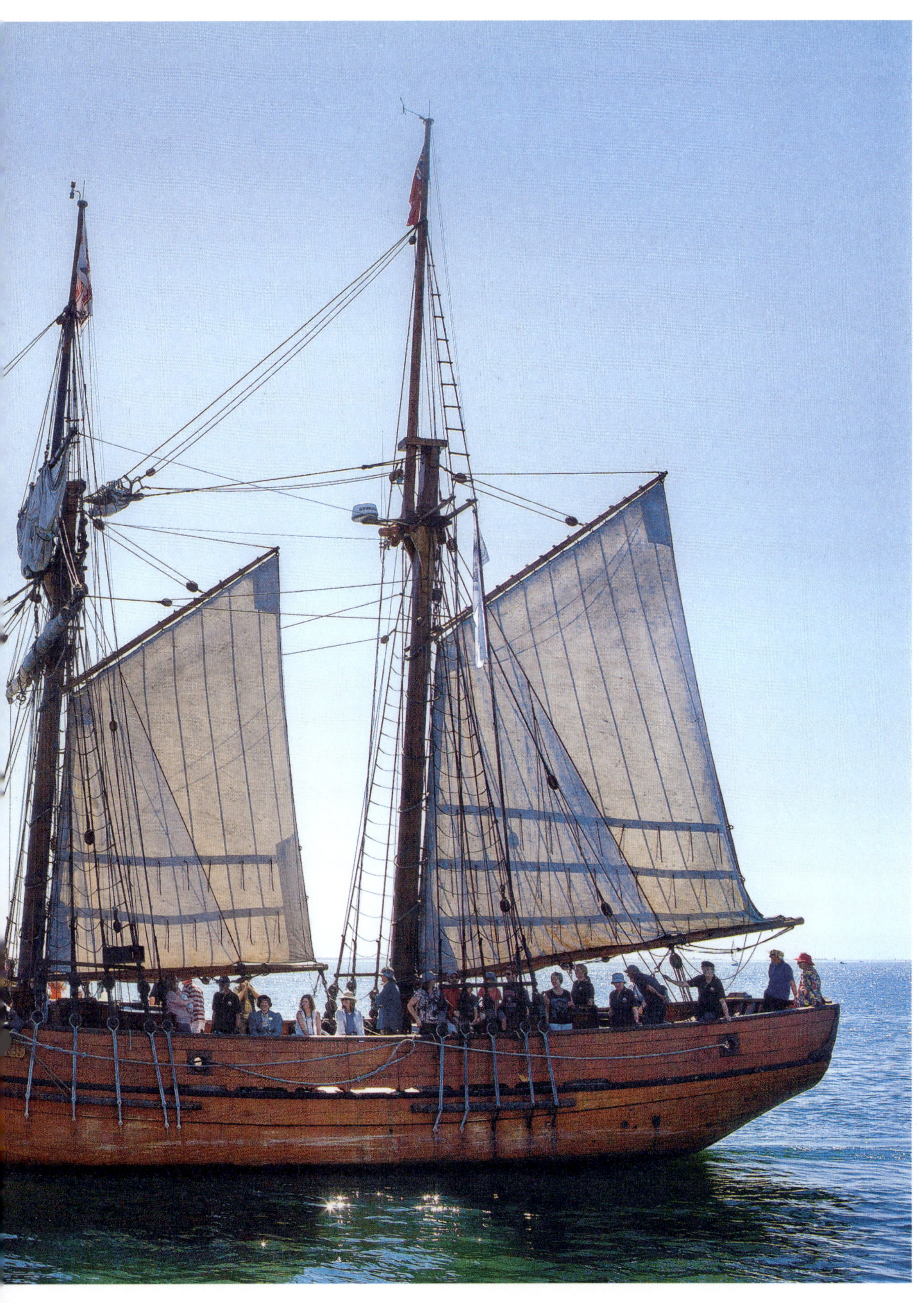

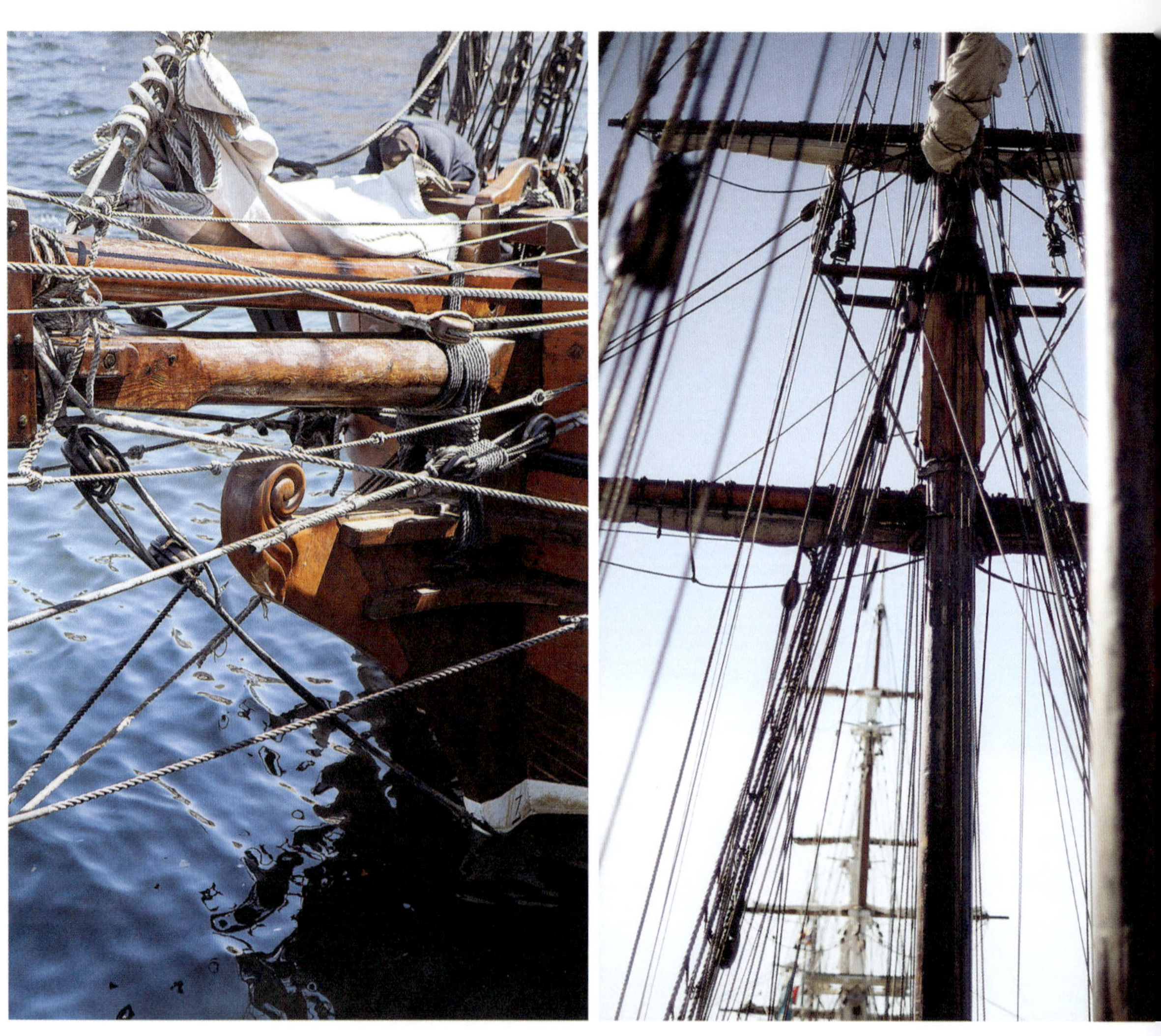

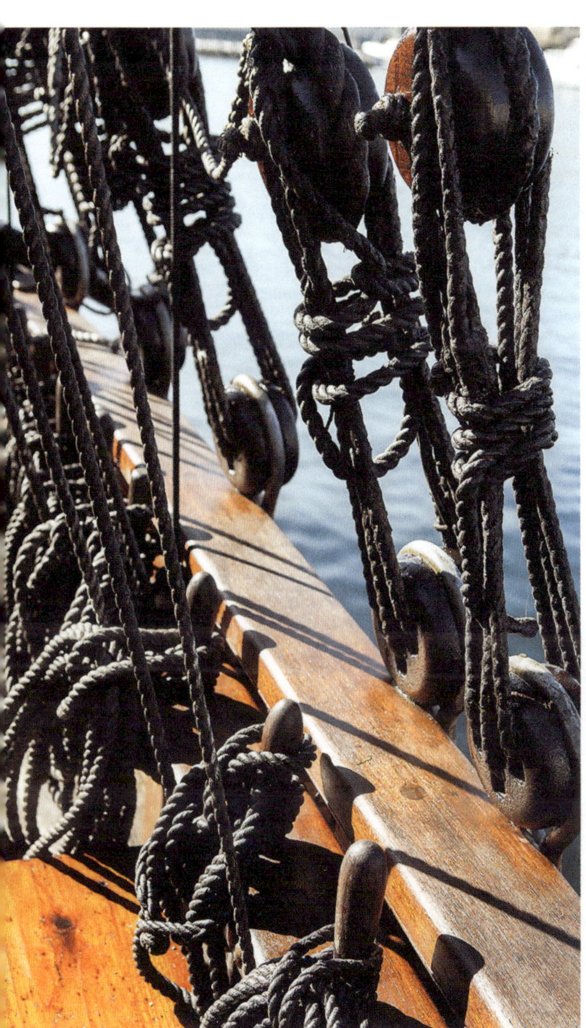

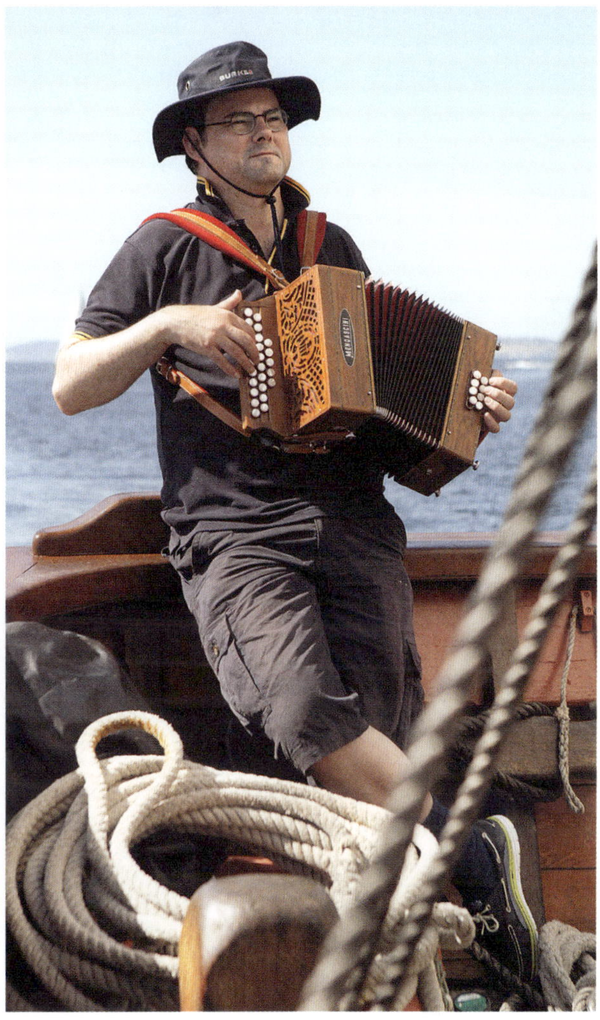

Enterprize's keel was laid in 1991: a single piece of ironbark. The rest of the timber was recycled: 100-year-old wharf timbers, the staves of old brewing vats, floor joists from an old wool store in Western Australia, and cypress pine from the Royal Melbourne Golf Course. Her masts are Californian redwood.

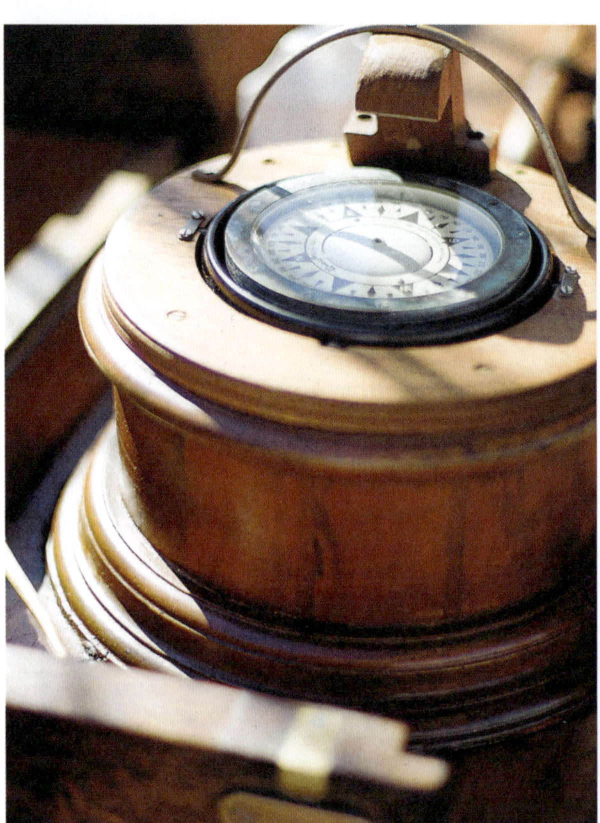

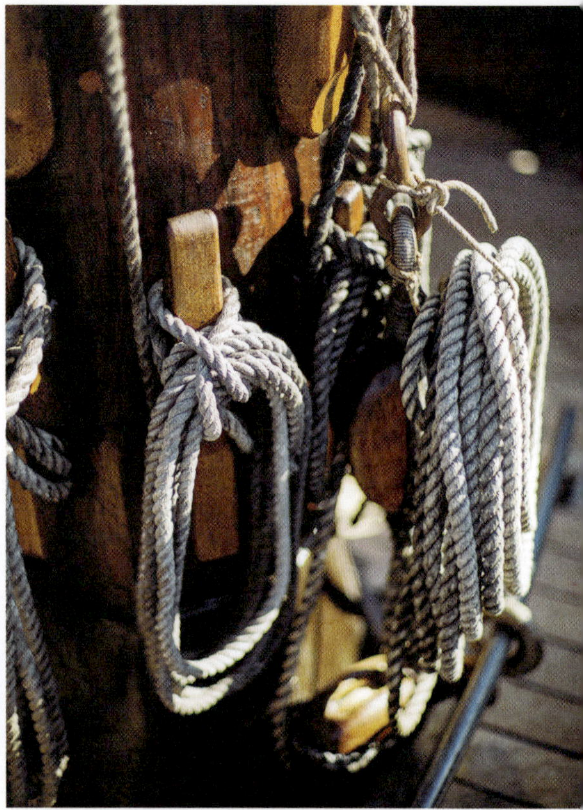

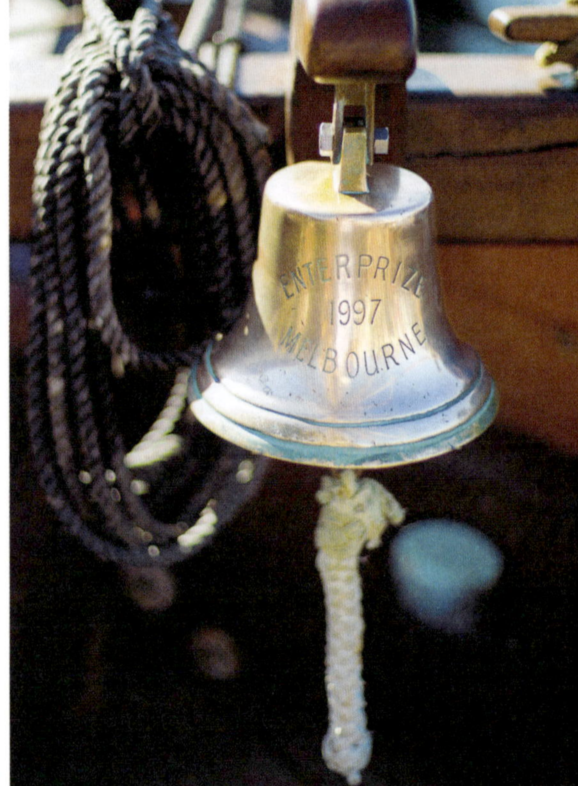

Enterprize is as close to the original as possible. Sails are hand-sewn from flax cloth imported from Scotland, while the rigging is hemp fibre rope from Holland, protected by coatings of Stockholm tar.

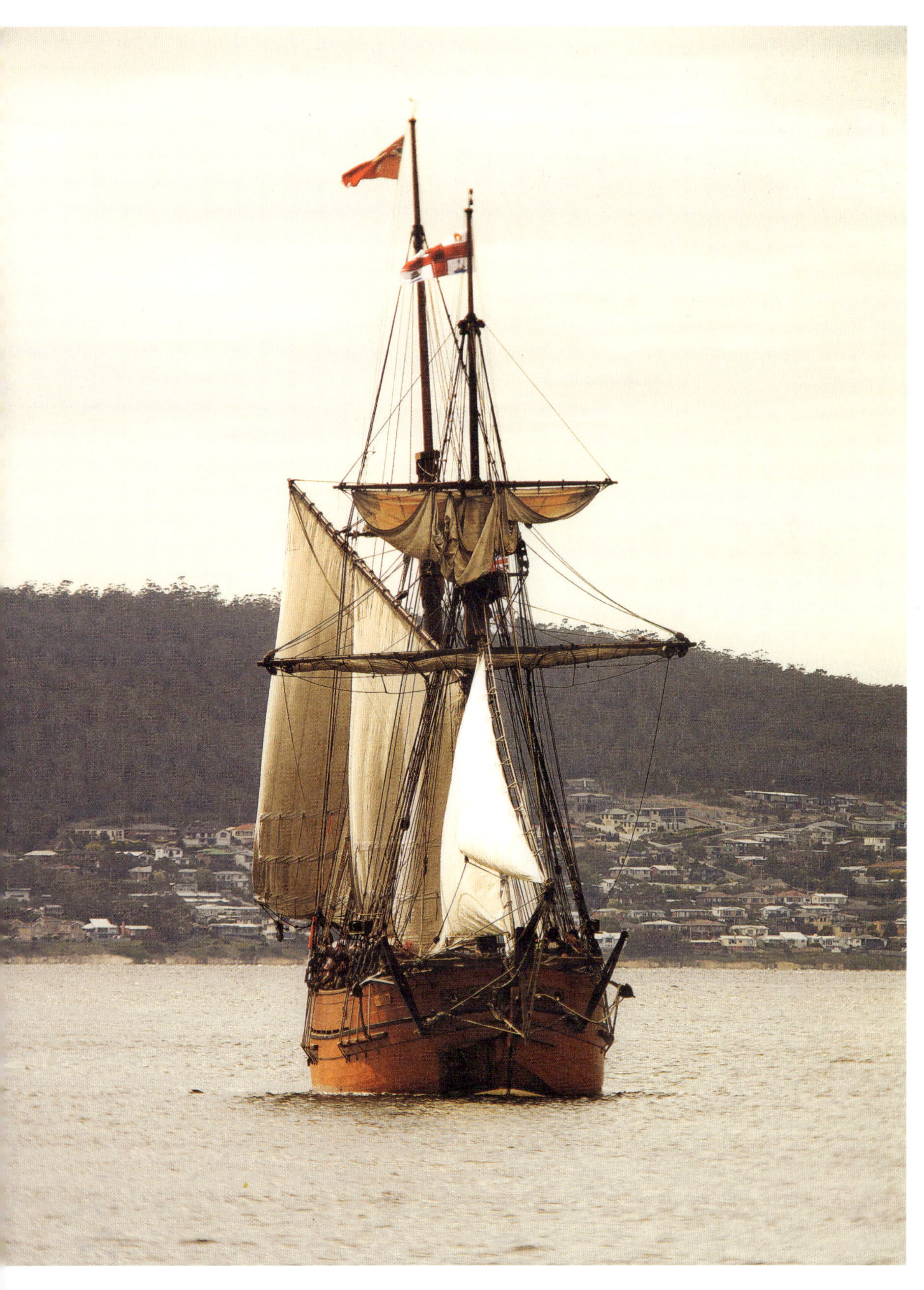

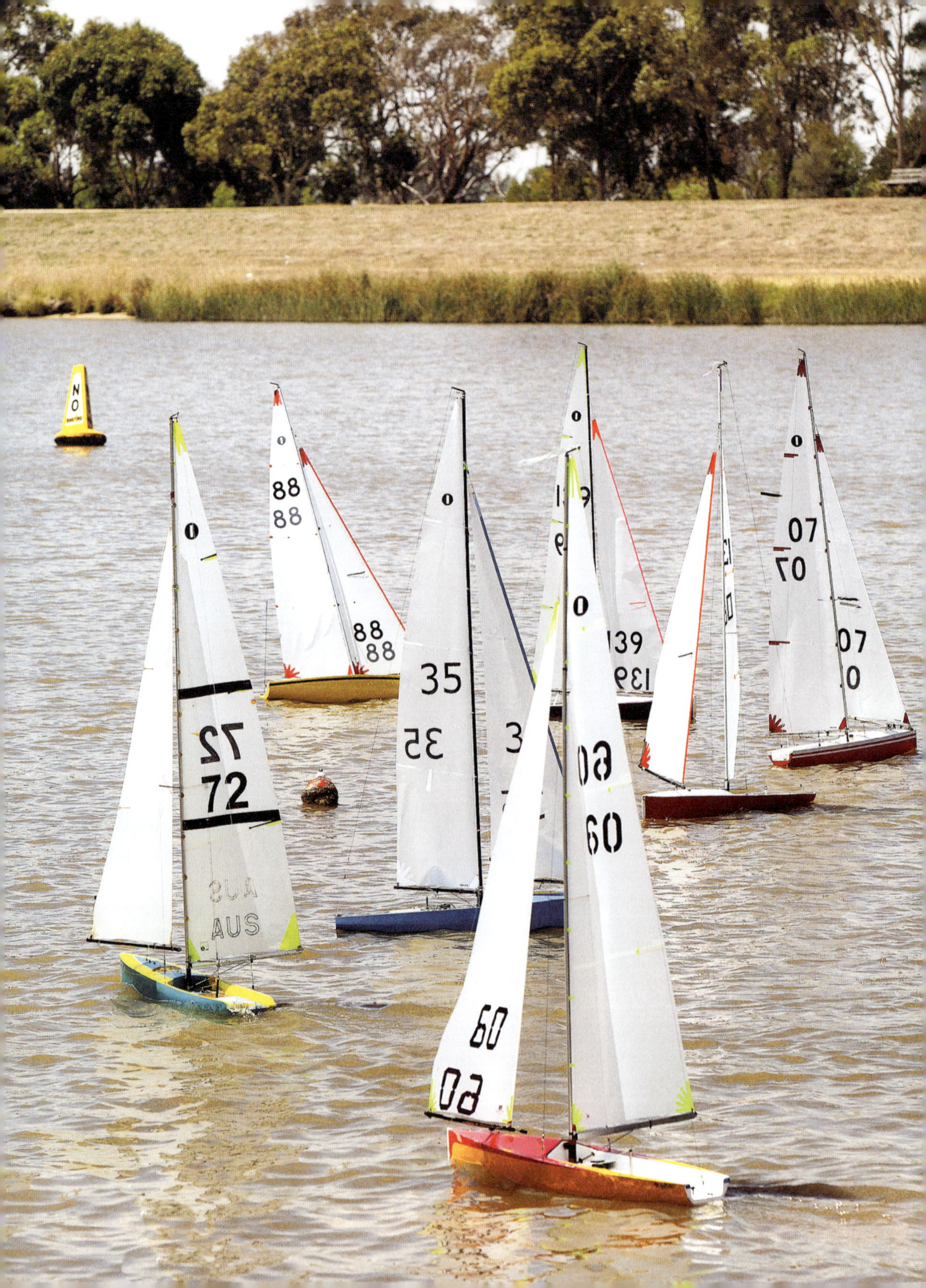
88
35
72
AUS
60
07
139

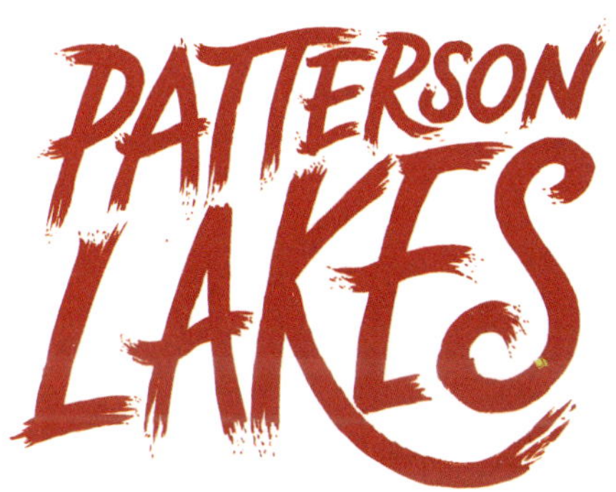

It's a warm, sunny summer afternoon and Melbourne's Patterson Lakes Radio Model Yacht Club, formed in 1981, is meeting. It's Tuesday, a race day, and the club members are setting up their model yachts. The yachts are mostly International One Metre (IOM) class – meaning the hull is 1 metre long. They do also sail other classes at the club: Micro Magics, whose hulls are 525 millimetres long, Lasers, whose hulls are 1.05 metre long and Marbleheads, whose hulls are 1.29 metres long.

The model yachts are scaled-down versions of the big ones. The radio controls only steer the yachts; the wind is their sole propulsion. There is quite an art to adjusting the sails to get the optimal speed.

There must be at least twenty-five members with boats racing today. There are ten races of eight minutes each. It's a fun afternoon, with the members laughing and ribbing each other, and there are quite a few thrills and spills. The models are fairly high-tech and can cost anywhere from $1000 to $6000.

Club members range from a few retired sailors to people who have never sailed before and just love model boats. It's a great way to sail without having the upkeep and expense of a big boat. The guys all have big grins on their faces at the end of the day – it's a very pleasant way to spend an afternoon.

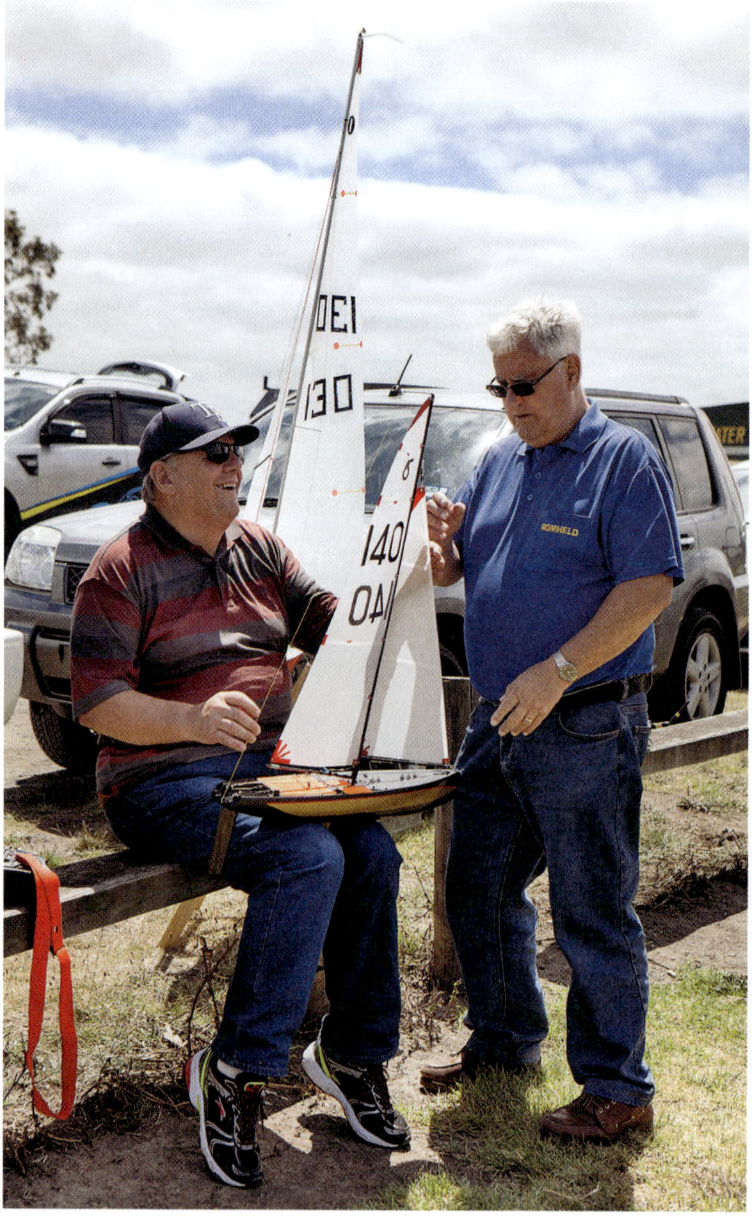

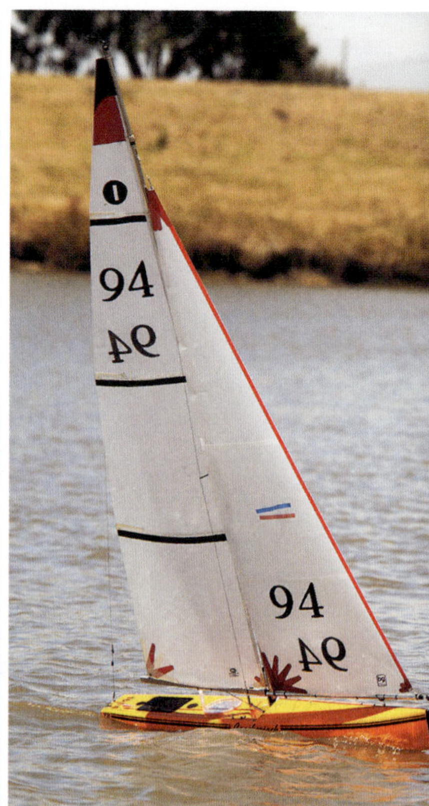

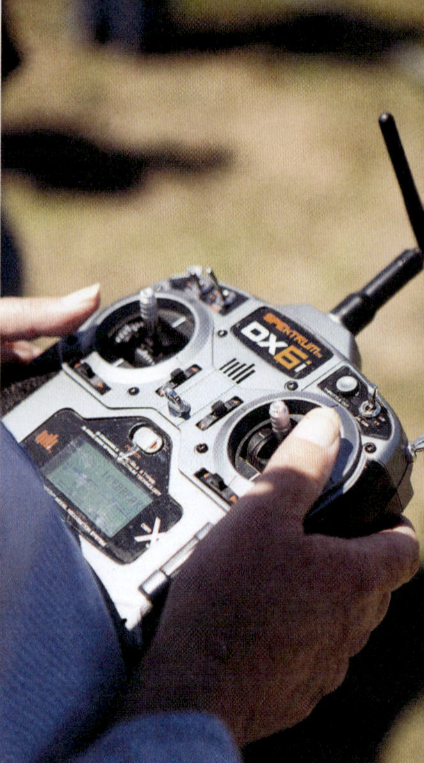

There's a lot of laughing and cheering amongst the club members; racing model boats is a very social activity.

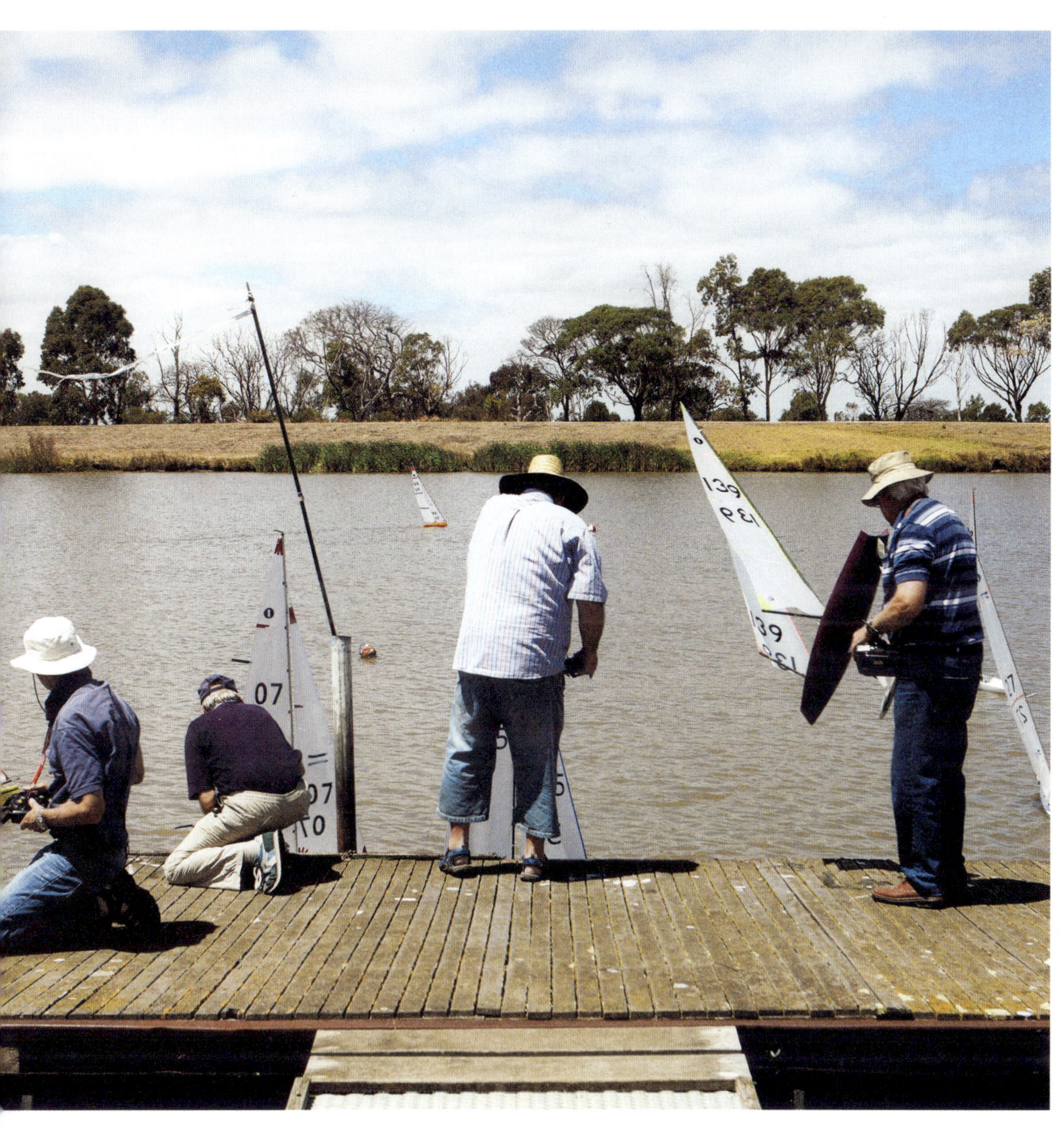

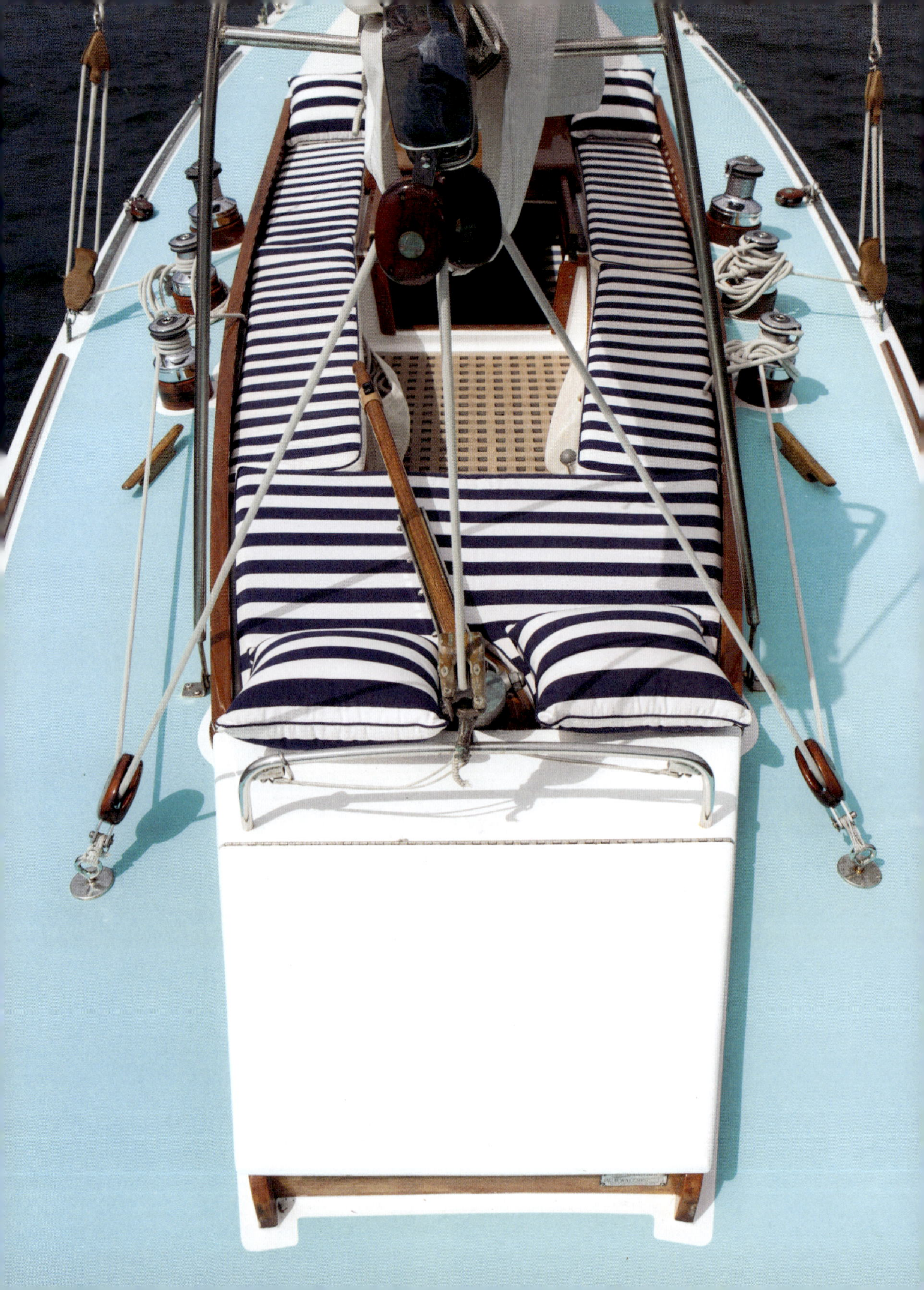

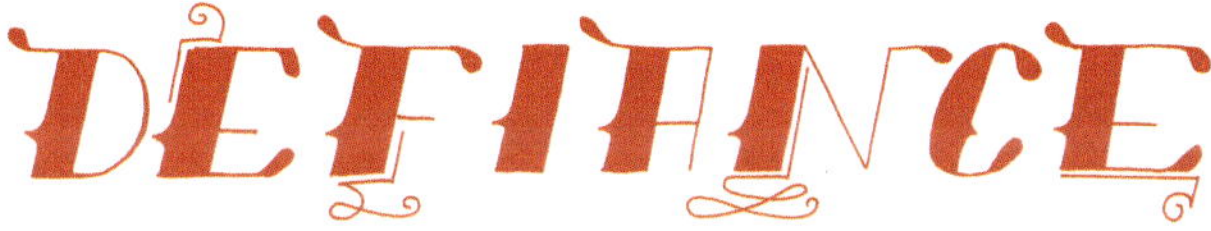

Beautiful, historic *Defiance* was the first 8-metre yacht to be completely designed and built in Australia. Shipwright Ernest Digby and his three sons built her in 1935 in their backyard in Williamstown, Victoria. Ernest was quite unusual in that he was a designer, owner, builder and racer of boats. He was also commodore of the Hobsons Bay Yacht Club for a time.

Defiance is famous for having participated in five Sydney to Hobart Yacht Races, and has had a colourful racing life, winning races in Victoria and New South Wales. Nicole has plans to take her to Europe to compete in the International 8-metre World Cup in Brittany.

Her current owner, Nicole Shrimpton, has restored her to beautiful condition, painting her a '1930s green'. She says, 'It was love at first sight when I saw *Defiance*. Boats bring out the best in you, and *Defiance* has brought out the best in me.'

Nicole has sought out the most talented people to work on her, and all the love, time and money she has invested make *Defiance* one of the most stylish yachts on Sydney Harbour.

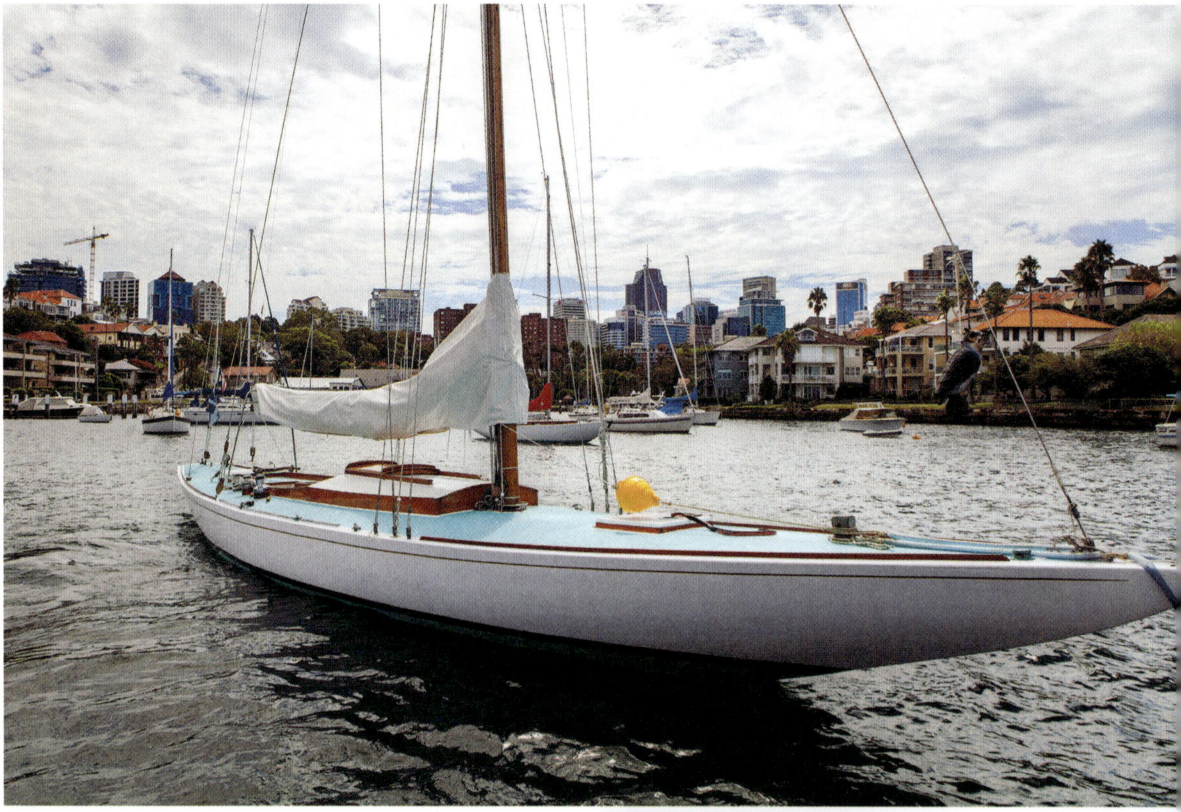

All the planking for the hull came from a single log of Huon pine. *Defiance* also has a hardwood stem, Celery Top wood top and King Billy pine in her construction.

As her owner Nicole puts it, 'I don't want to over-restore her, but it is important that she is looked after properly.'

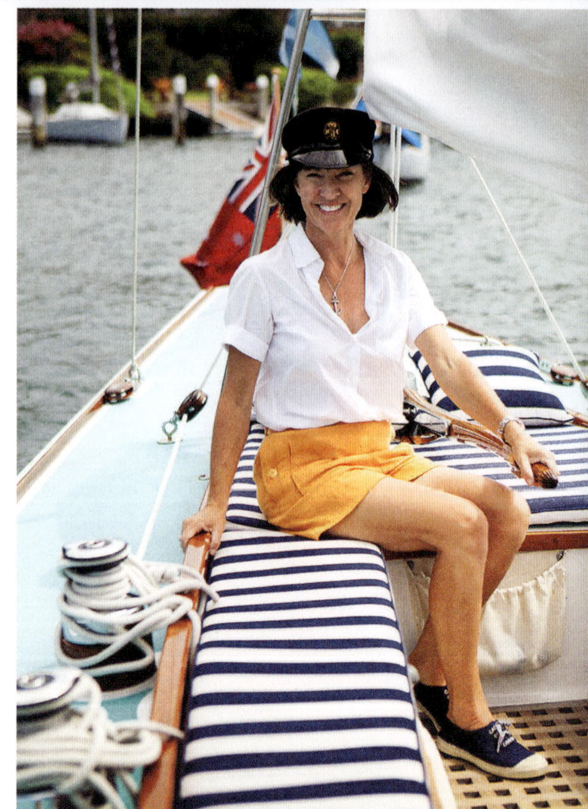

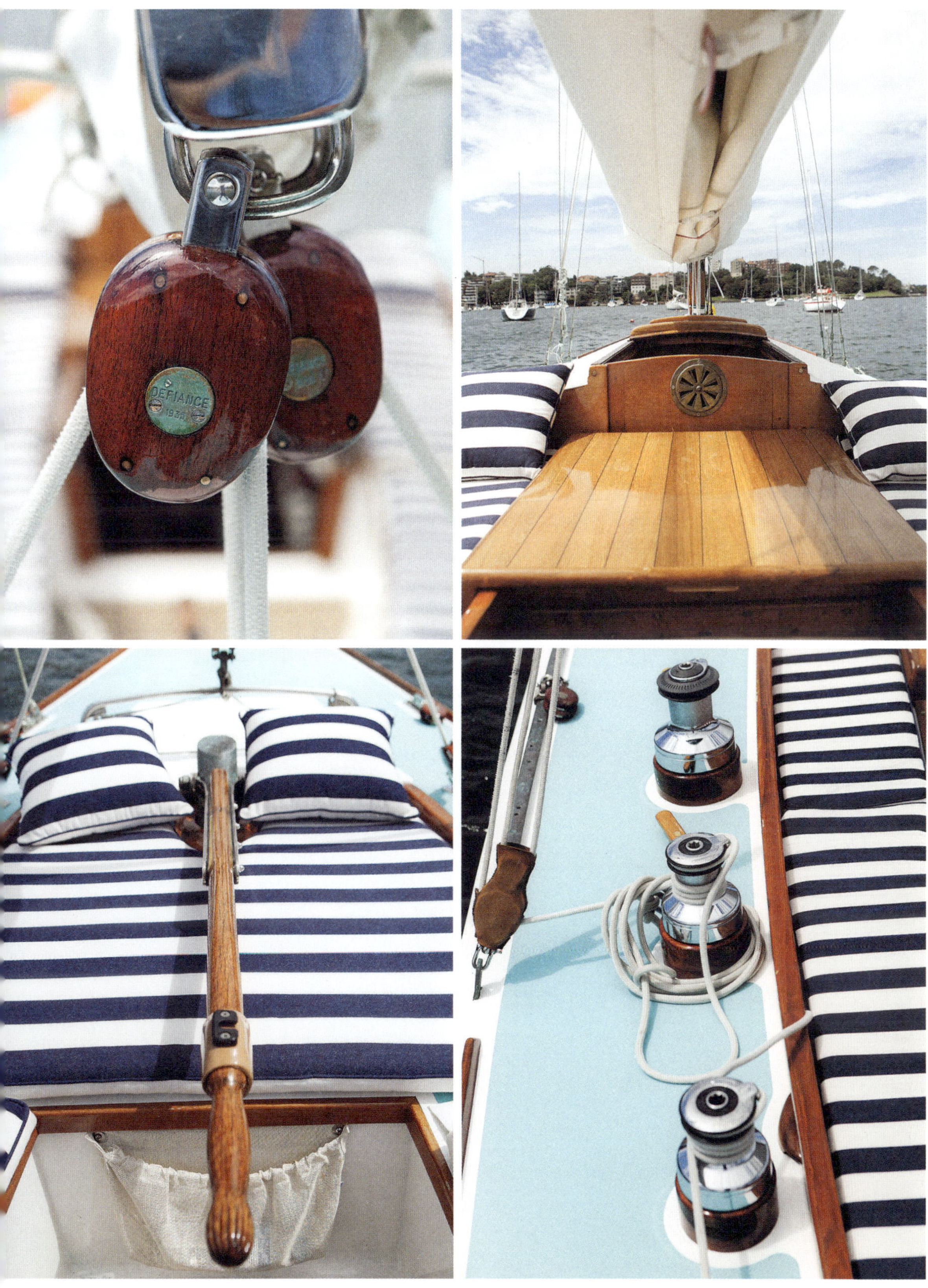
DEFIANCE

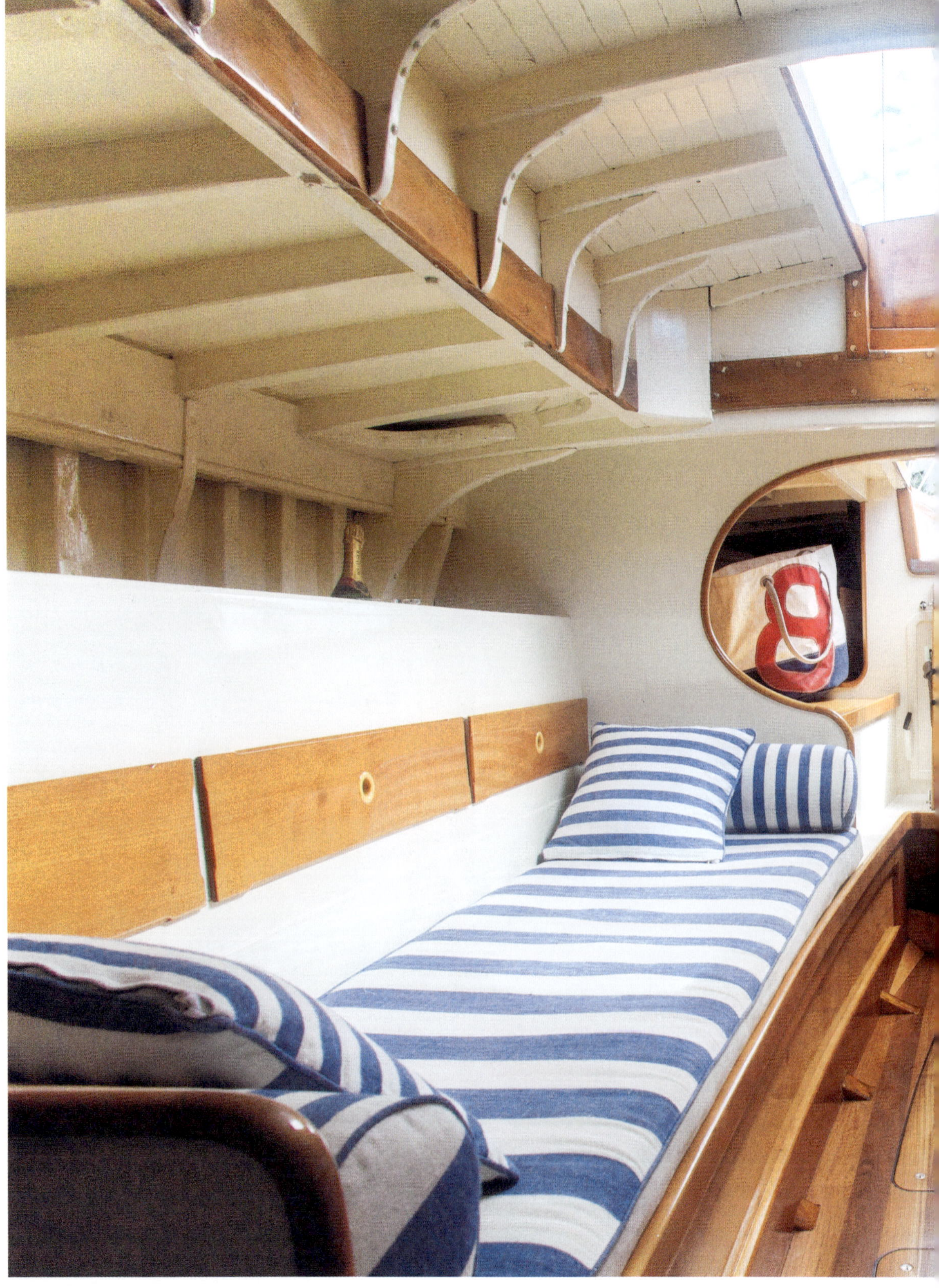
8

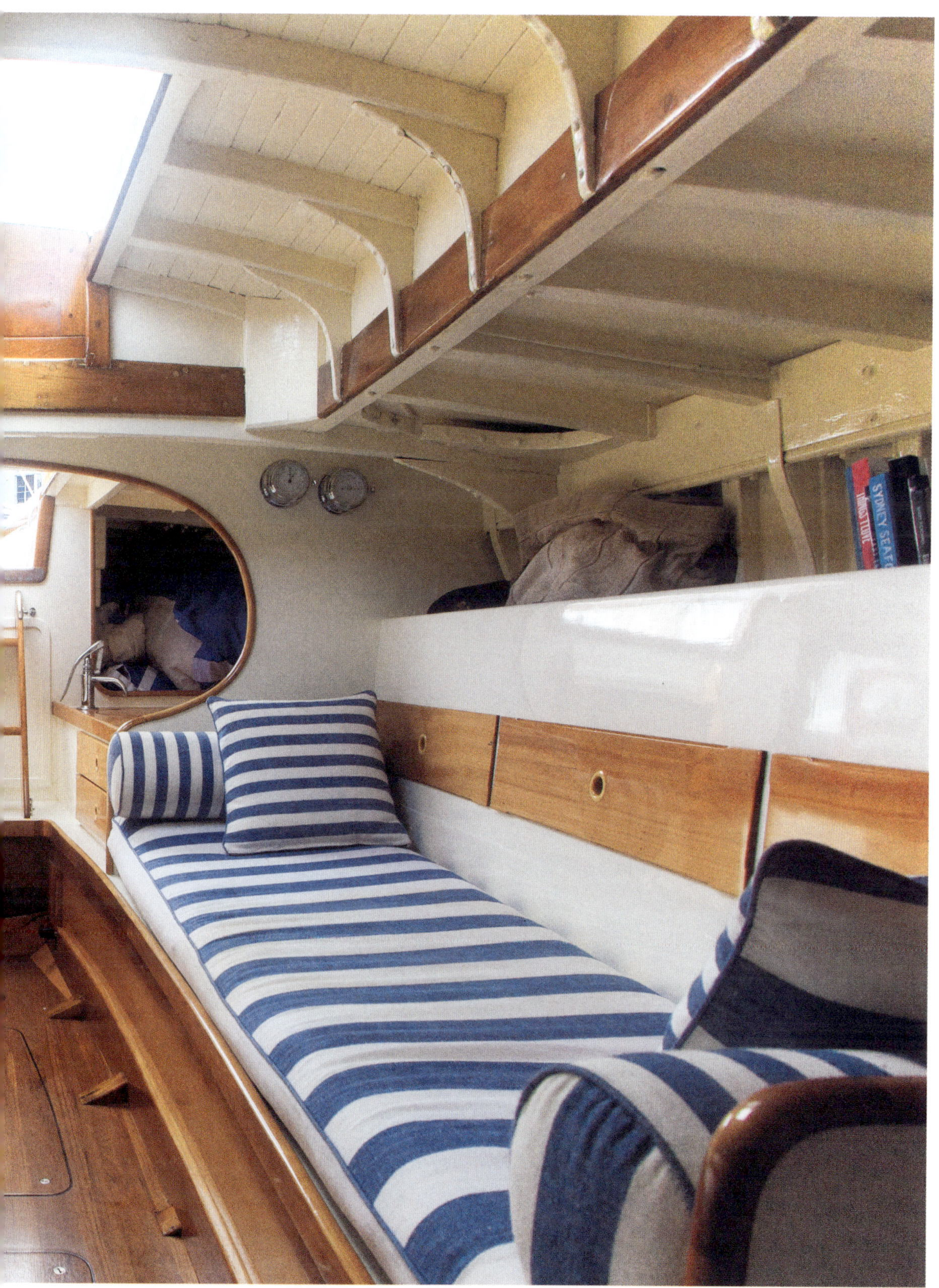

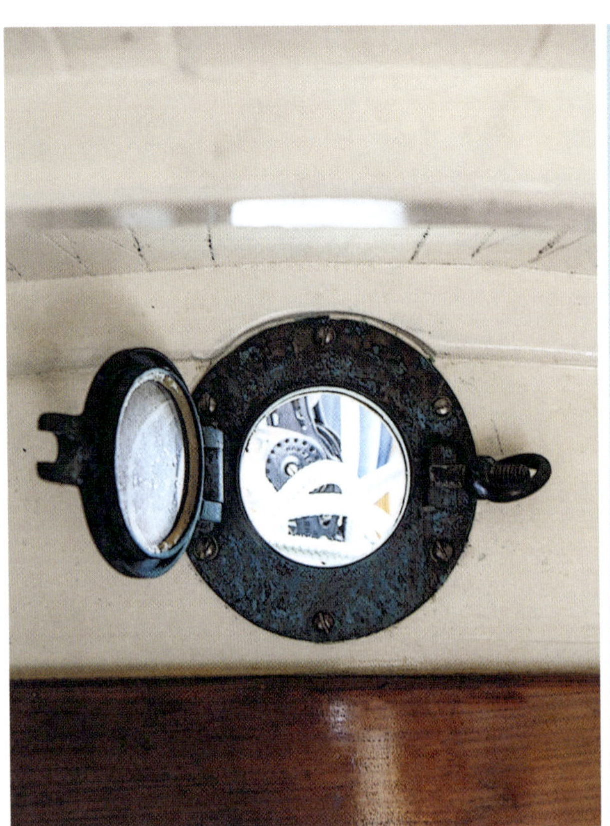

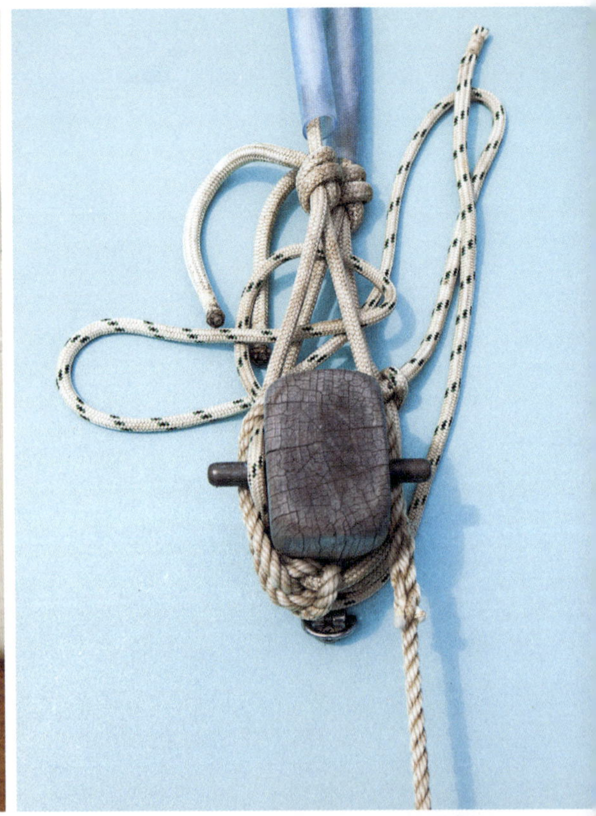

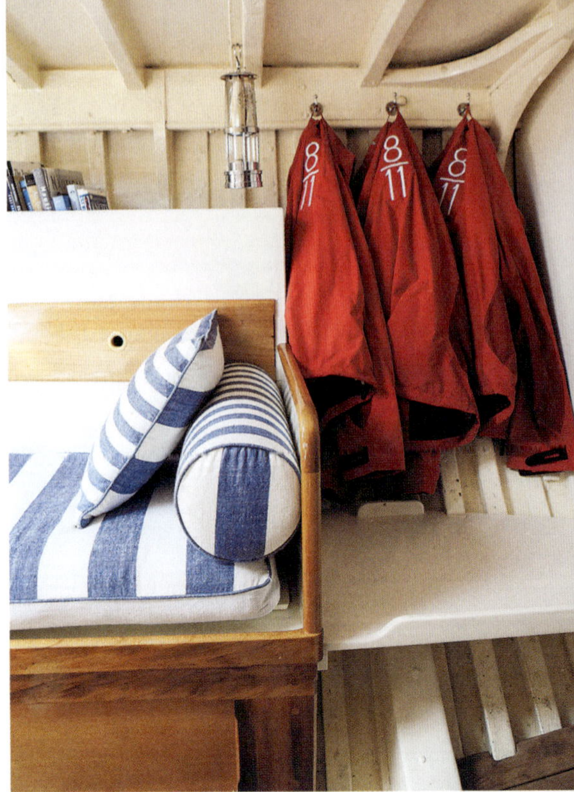

ABOVE, LEFT One of *Defiance's* bronze portholes.

RIGHT Wet weather gear is neatly stowed below decks.

OPPOSITE *Defiance* is known for her elegant lines in the water.

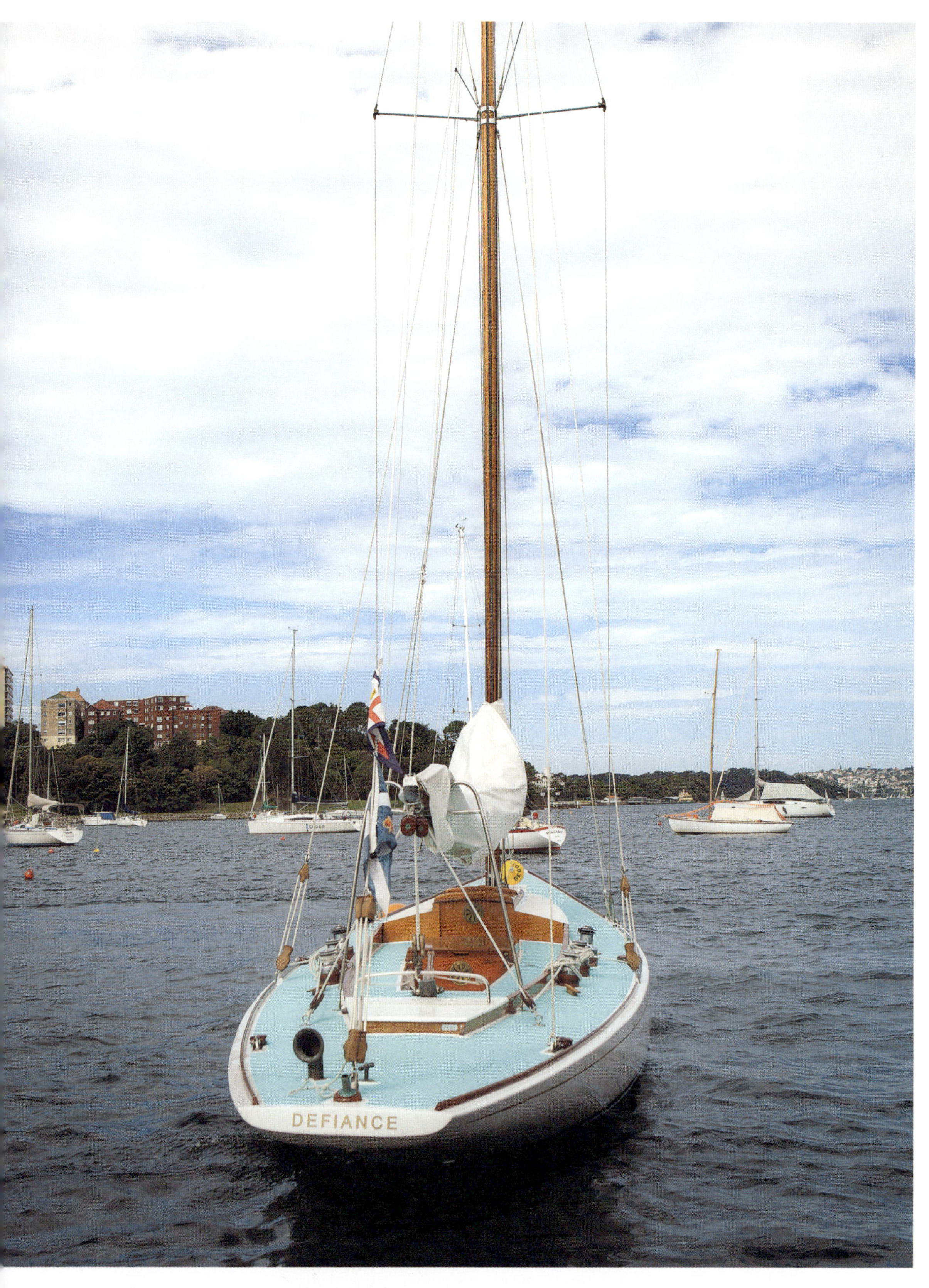
DEFIANCE

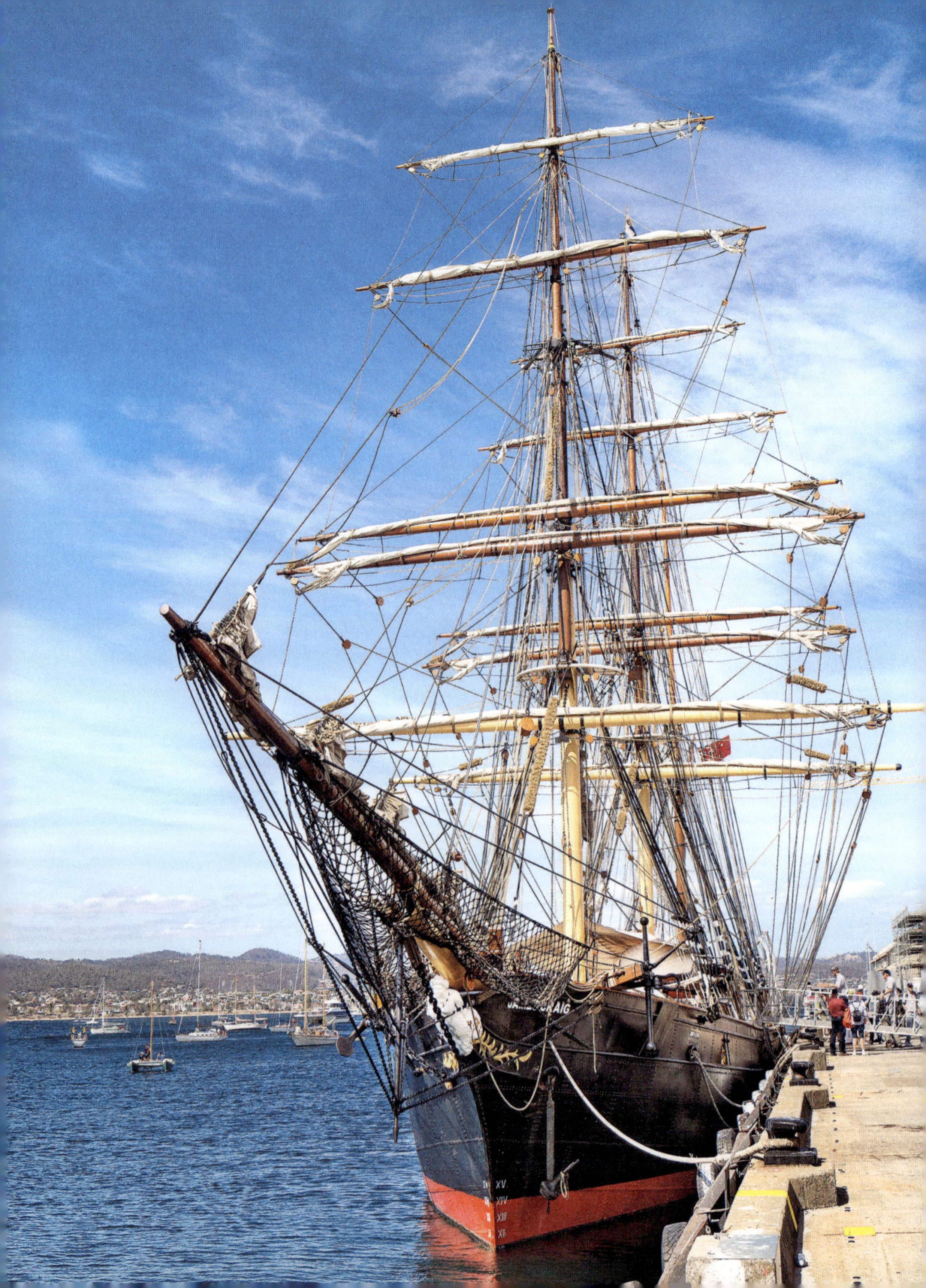

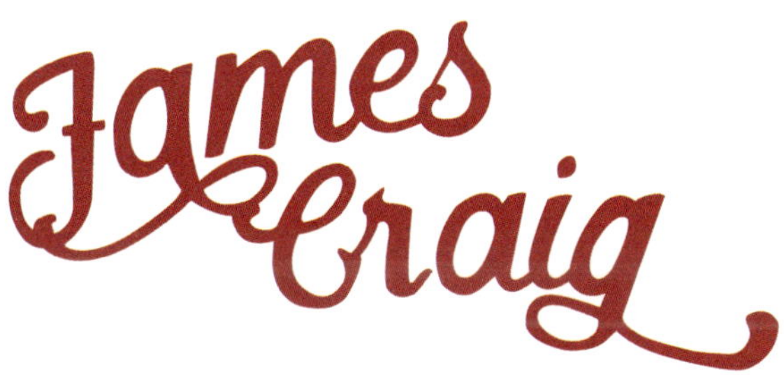

James Craig, part of the Sydney Heritage Fleet, is one of only four nineteenth-century barques in the world that still regularly go to sea with passengers.

Built in 1874 in Sunderland, England, she was originally named *Clan Macleod* and carried cargo around the world. In 1900 she was acquired by Mr J.J. Craig, and in 1905 renamed *James Craig*. She sailed between New Zealand and Australia until 1911 when, unable to compete with steamships, she was eventually abandoned. In 1932 she was sunk in Recherche Bay in Tasmania by some fishermen who blasted a 3-metre hole in her side.

In 1972 her luck changed and she was refloated by volunteers from the Port Jackson Marine Steam Museum, now the Sydney Heritage Fleet. She was towed to Hobart and then Sydney for repairs. The restoration took almost forty years and thousands of hours' work.

James Craig was relaunched in 1997 and restoration work was completed in 2001. Now given pride of place in the Sydney Heritage Fleet, she can enjoy semi-retirement at 141 years old.

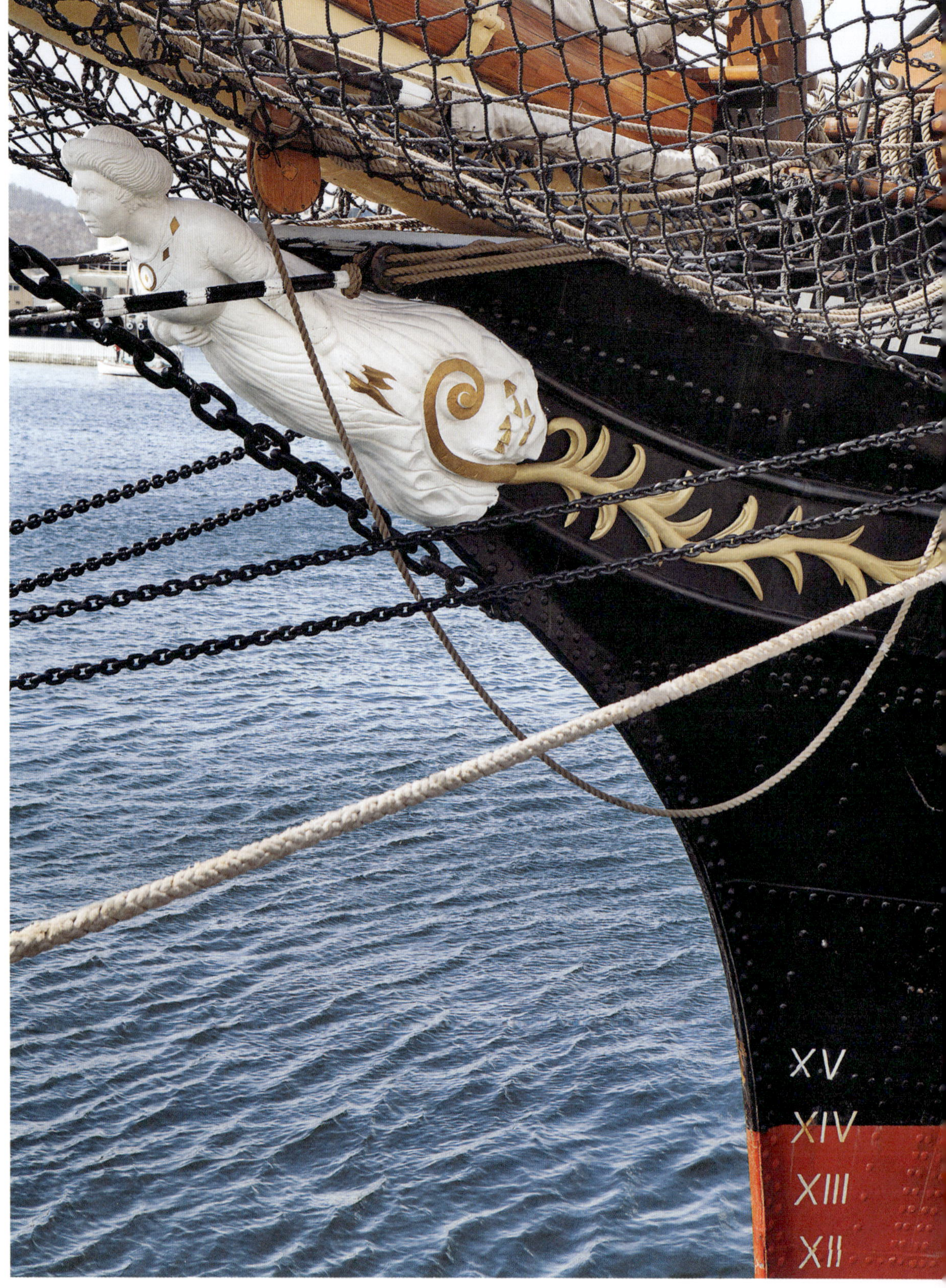
XV
XIV
XIII
XII

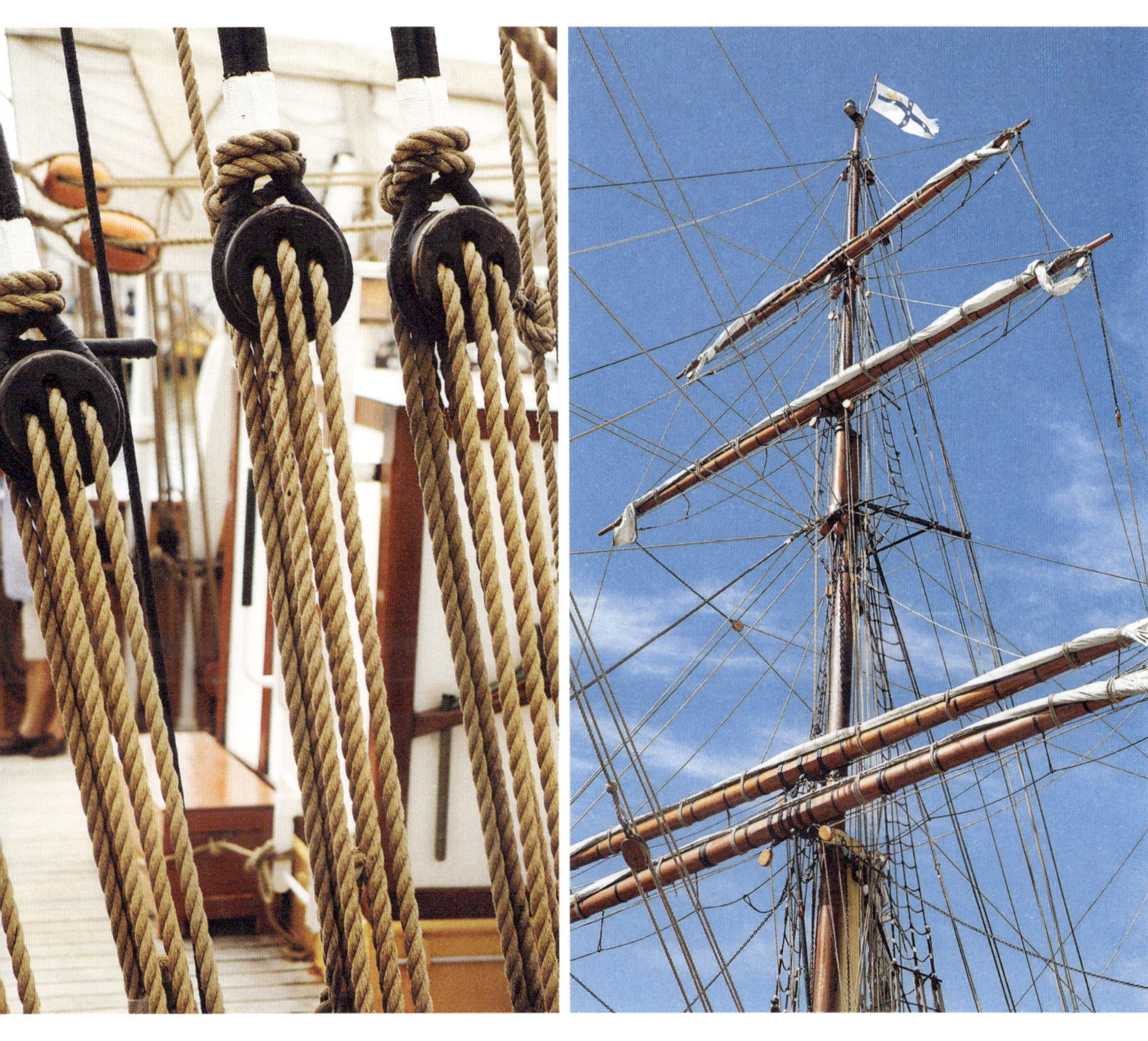

Details of the now fully restored and very smart *James Craig*. Her stint underwater is now nothing but a distant memory.

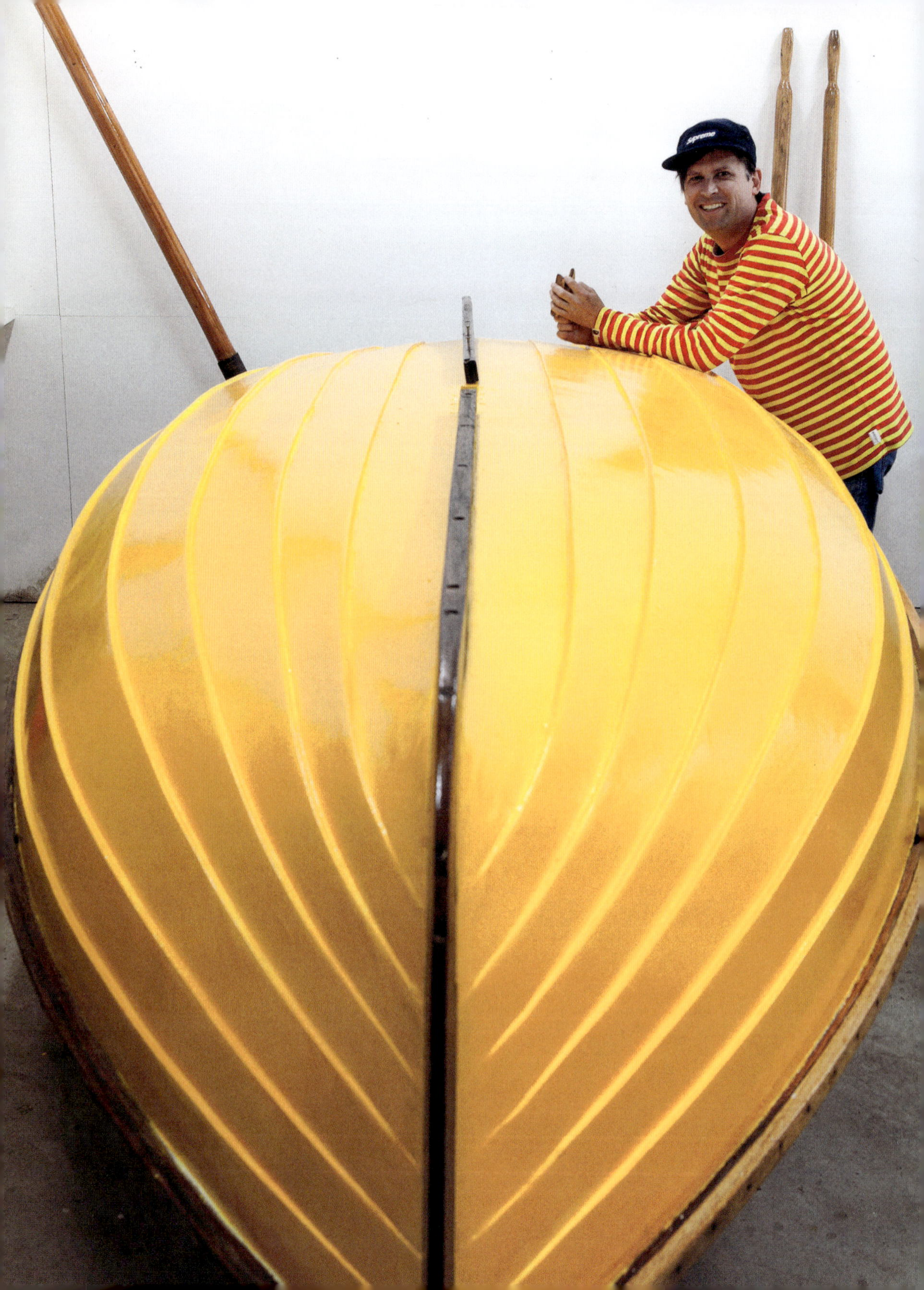
Supreme

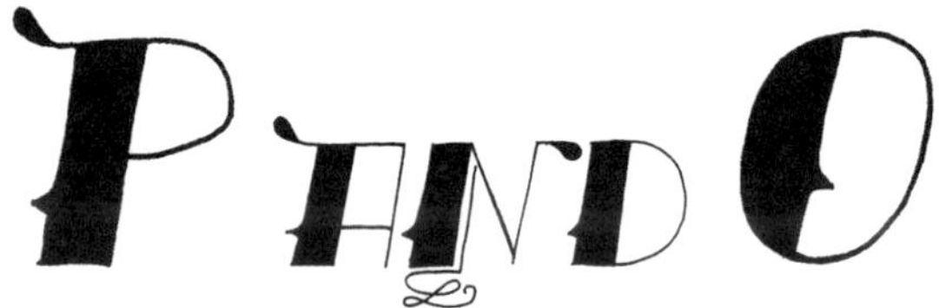

This is the boat Oliver Cole learnt to sail as a four-year-old with his father, Peter, in the bay off the Mornington Peninsula, south of Melbourne. Named *P and O*, for Peter and Oliver, she is a 12-foot marine plywood dinghy that Peter had converted to sail.

Oliver with newly painted *P and O*, a boat you are not likely to miss on the water.

Peter hand-planed the mast and made the spars, centreboard, rudder and blocks himself in the family living room. He also inlaid the centreboard with exotic timbers, making her a work of art.

After *P and O* sat unused in a woolshed for some time Oliver decided to restore her. After six months of sanding, painting and varnishing she's almost ready for adventures again. Her hull is painted an amazing marker yellow, the same colour used on marine buoys and hazard signs, so she will never get lost in a crowd. Her woodwork is beautifully varnished, and she still has her original tan sail. Oliver also updated her by replacing the hemp-rope rigging with something more modern.

So, *P and O* has had a new lease of life. She's hard to miss now, so if you see a bright-yellow boat whizzing past it's likely to be Oliver in *P and O*.

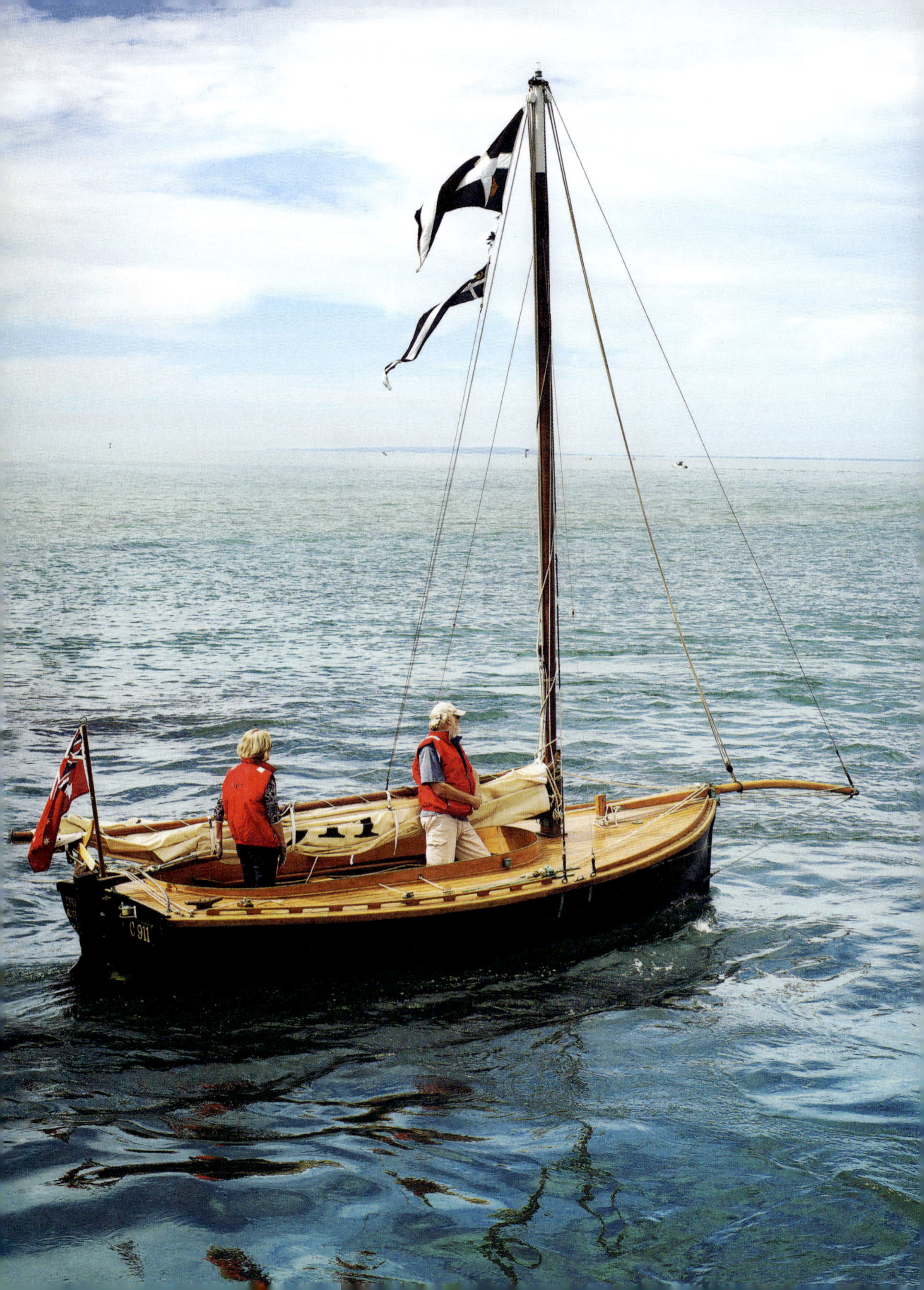
C 911

Lyndal Lea

'It was love at first sight,' says Carmen Bell of *Lyndal Lea*, her couta boat, and I can see why. She has the most beautiful lines and a striking, black-painted hull. When Carmen saw her moored at Queenscliff in Victoria with a scrap of plywood saying 'For Sale' with a telephone number scrawled on it, she couldn't believe her eyes.

Built in the late 1890s, probably by C. Blunt Boatbuilder in Geelong (see pages 88–97), she is a clinker-built boat, 18 feet long. 'I love the fact that these were working boats,' says Carmen.

Lyndal Lea was restored by Brett Almond, who found her in a paddock in nearby Portarlington. She was originally called *Blue Swan*, but Brett named her *Lyndal Lea* after his wife. Carmen has kept her as *Lyndal Lea*, as 'it's bad luck to change a boat's name and besides, I love the name.'

Lyndal Lea is now obviously well-loved. An elegant boat, now over 100 years old, she looks like she will be around for at least another 100 years.

THIS PAGE *Lyndal Lea* is quite striking with her black hull (unusual in the Australian heat) and black-and-white Couta Boat Club Pennant atop the mast.

FOLLOWING PAGES Her keel and stem are made from jarrah wood, the ribs are kauri and the planking is Huon pine. Her deck has been replaced with Celery Top pine.

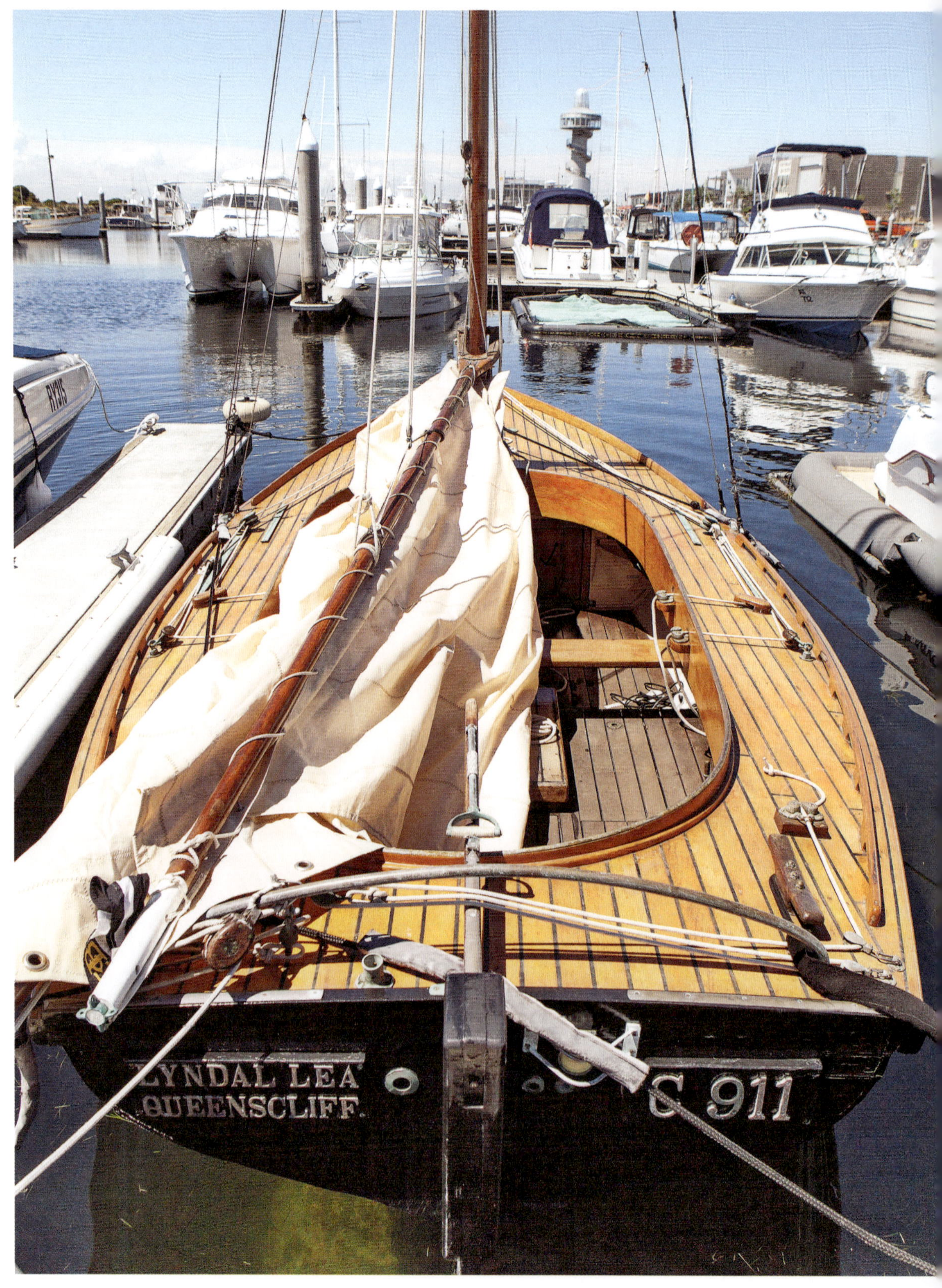
LYNDAL LEA
QUEENSCLIFF
C 911

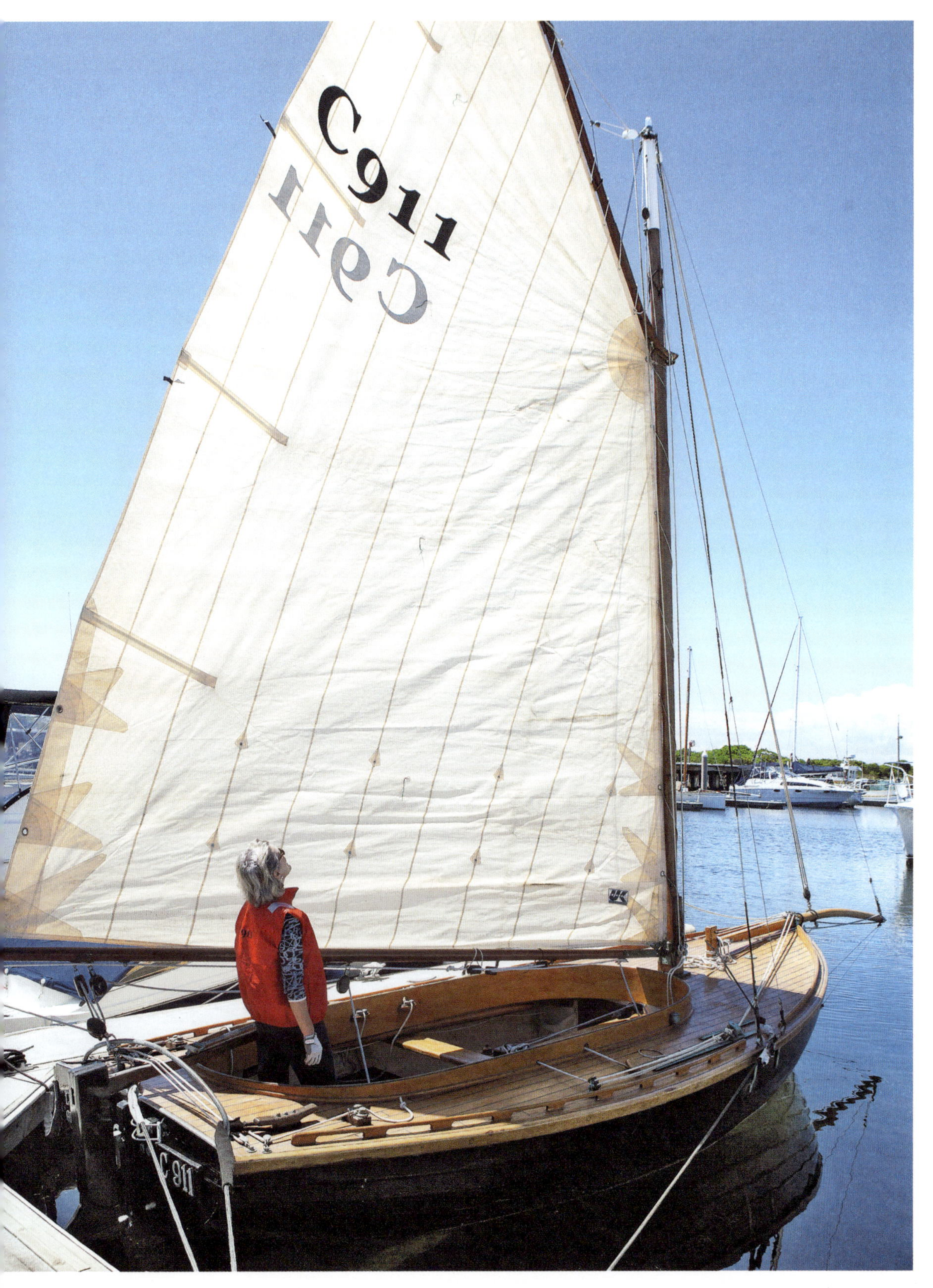
C911
C 911

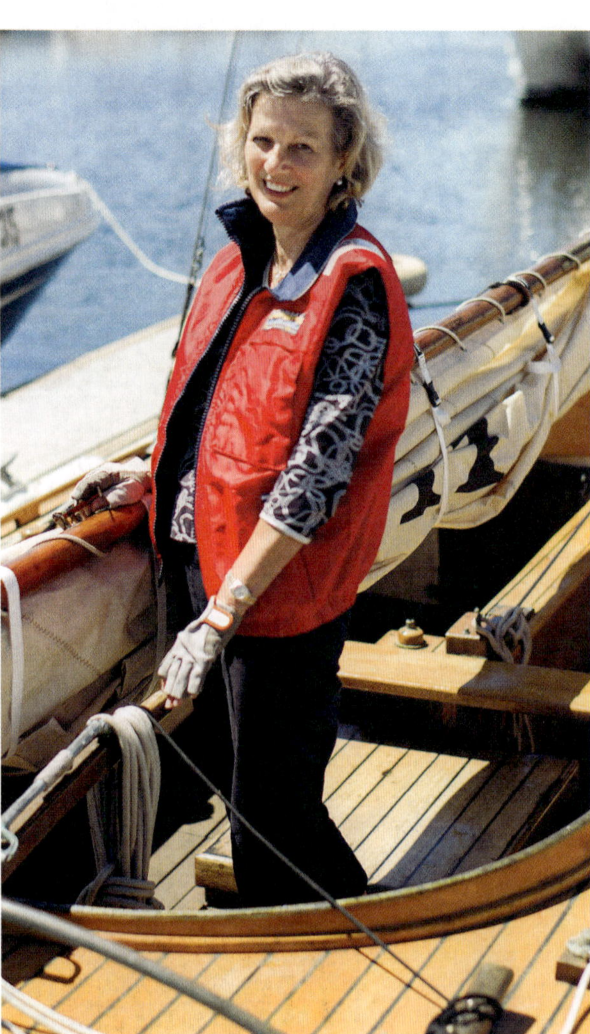

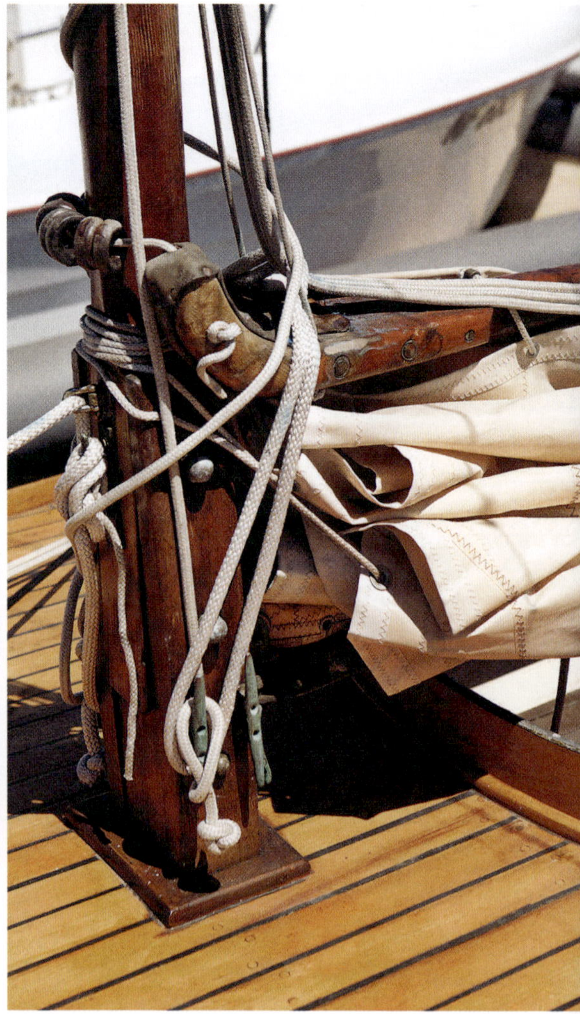

Carmen has gradually replaced many of *Lyndal Lea*'s fittings with brass and bronze. She has also replaced the old pulleys with wood-block pulleys found in antique shops over the years.

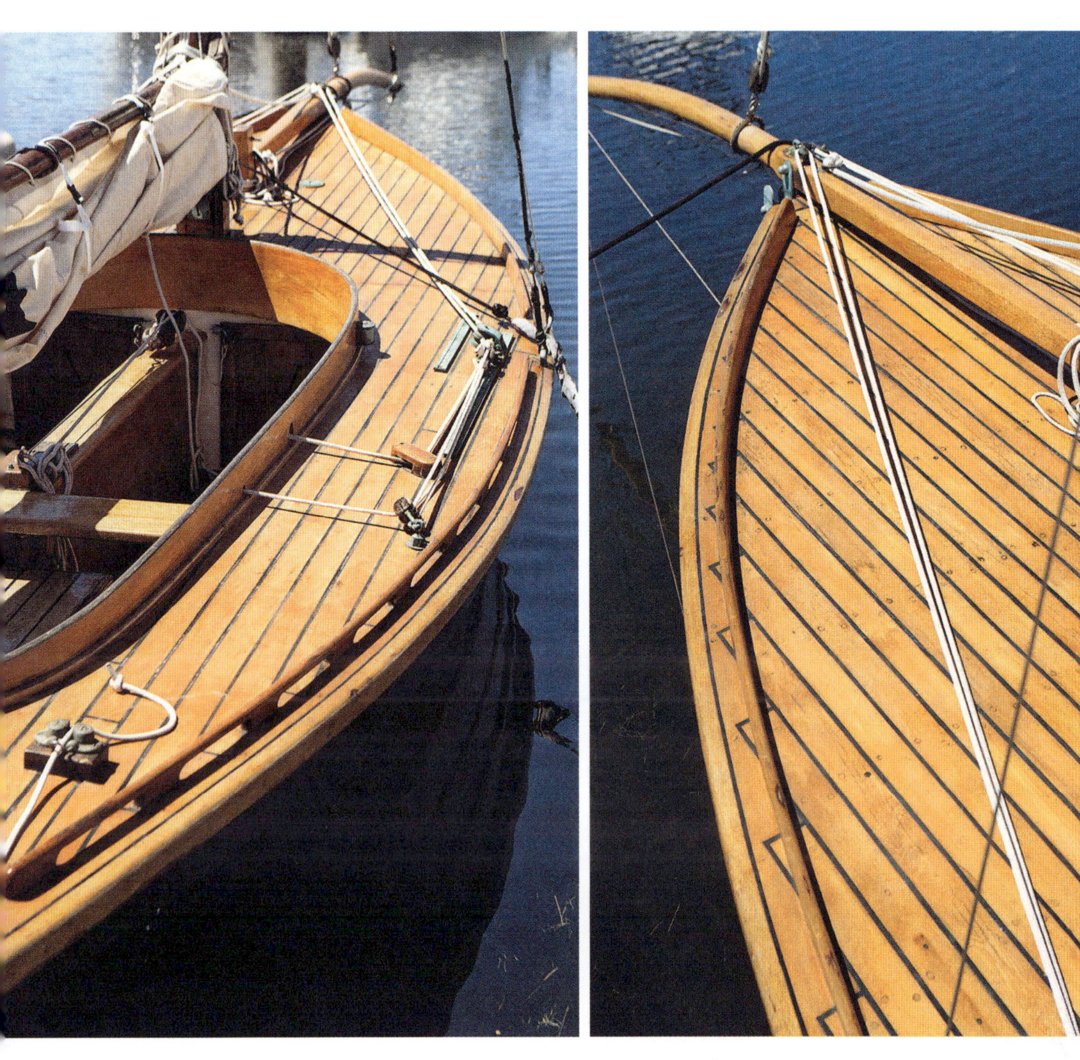

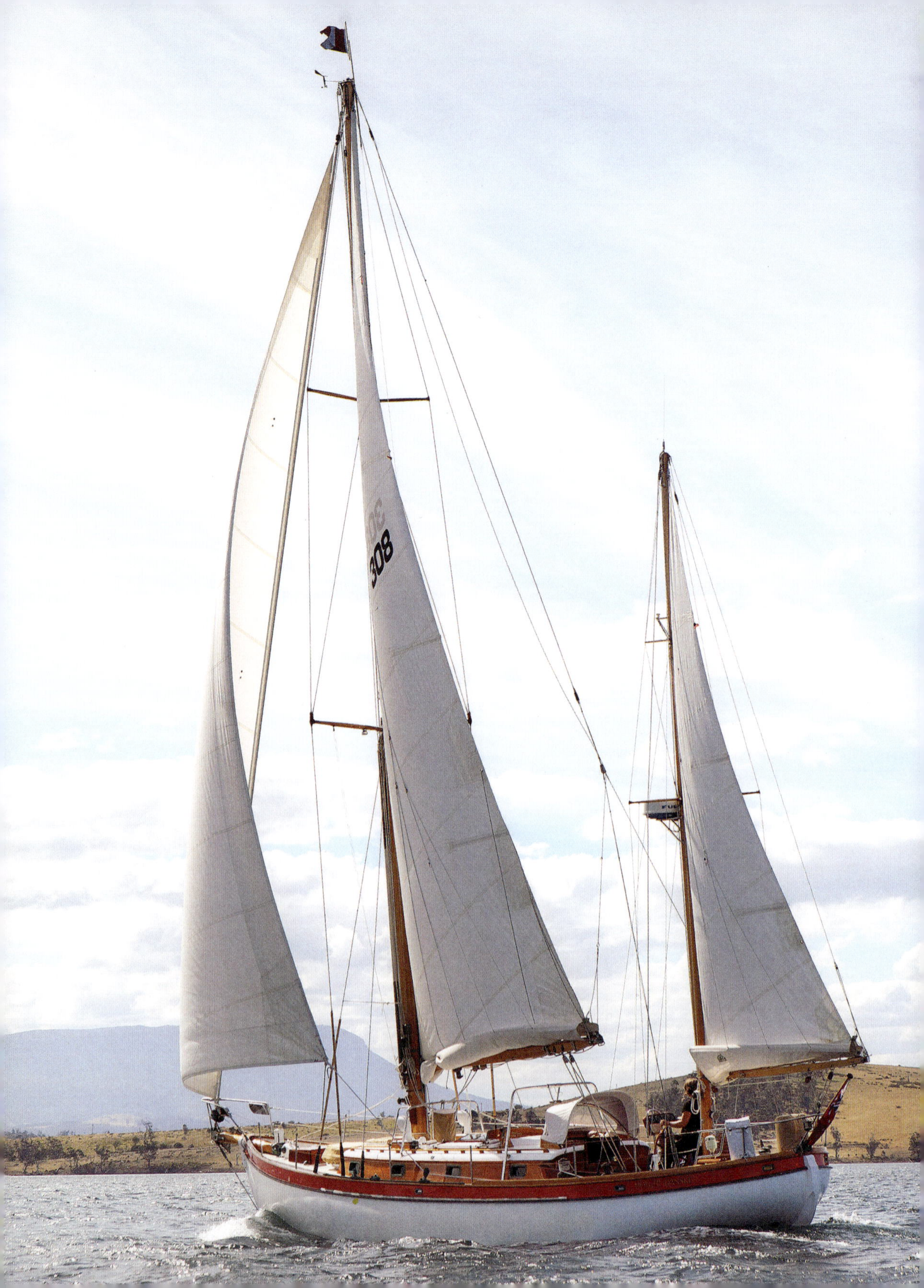
308

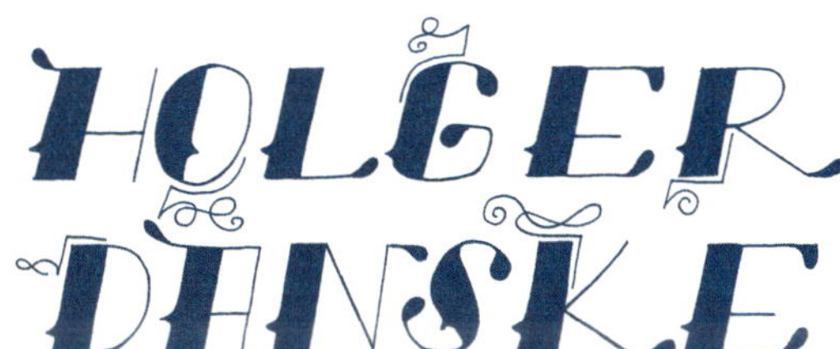

It's easy to see why people fall in love with their boats when they are as beautiful as *Holger Danske*, an offshore cruiser. Phillip Myer and Joy Phillips, her owners, adore her, keep her in immaculate condition and sail her often.

Holger Danske is a double-ender design, steered with a wheel rather than a tiller. She was built in Denmark in 1964 from Honduras mahogany at Aage Walsted's boat yard to the exacting standards of K. Aage Nielsen, one of the most famous yacht designers of the twentieth century. Every detail of his plans had to be followed exactly.

She is probably most famous for winning the 1980 Newport to Bermuda race by a large margin. She has had an adventurous life and has clocked up six transatlantic crossings. She now lives in Kettering in Tasmania.

Holger Danske was completely restored in 1997. Her overall length is 42 feet, six inches, her length at waterline 36 feet, her beam 13 feet 3 inches, her draught 6 feet and sail area 1083 square feet.

She is named after the iron- and steel-clad Danish folk hero who slumbers until his services are required to save Denmark.

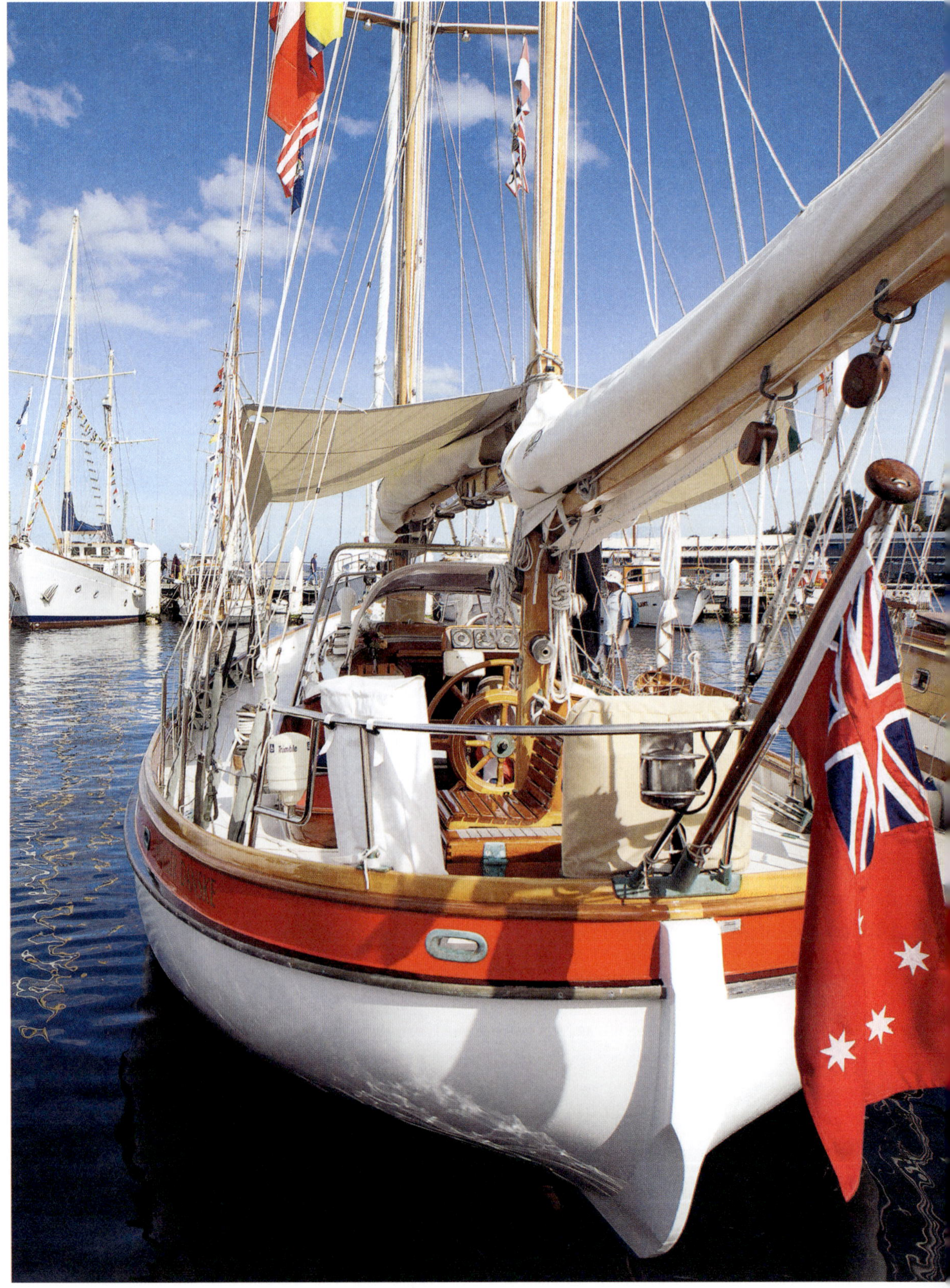

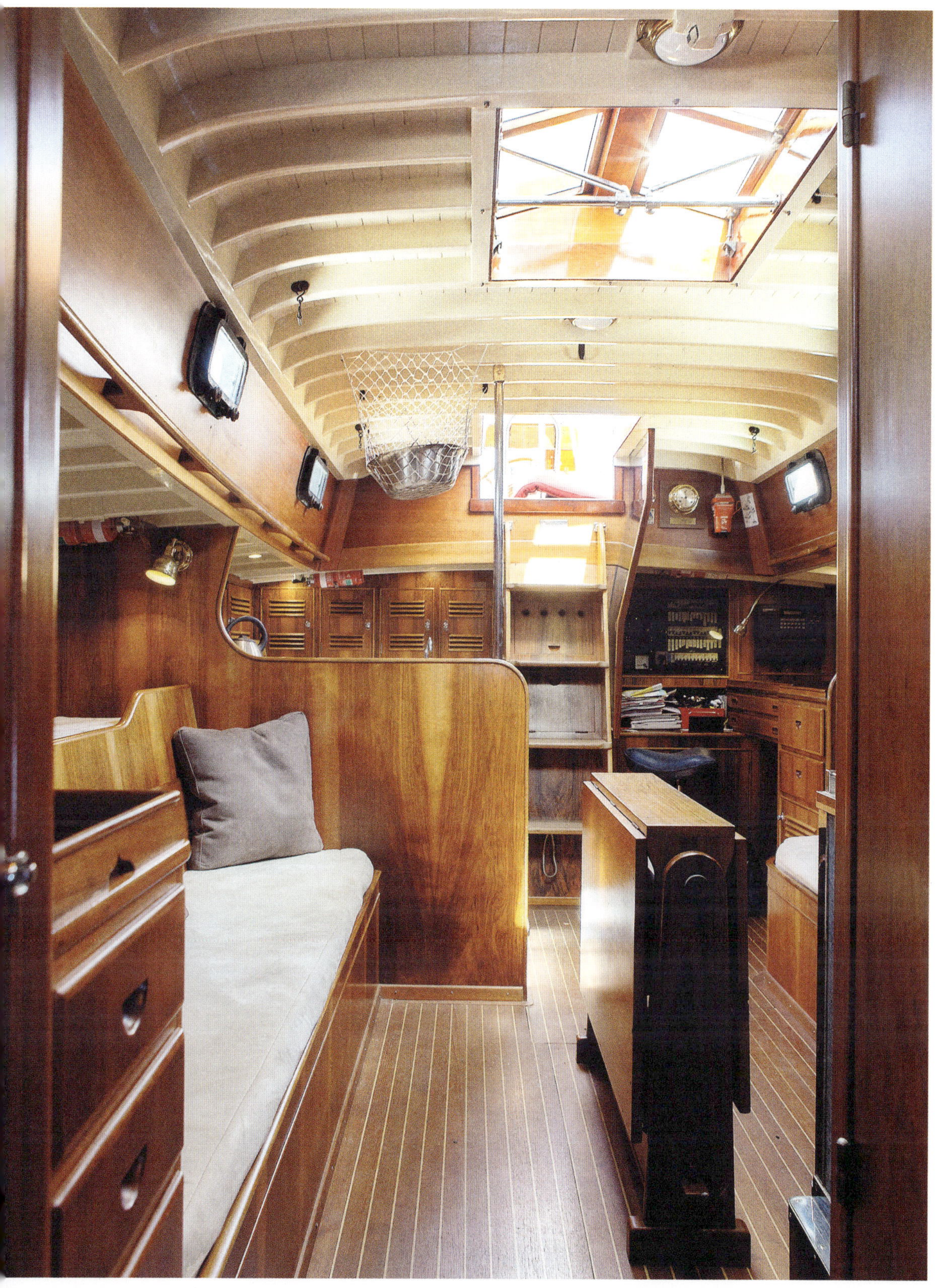

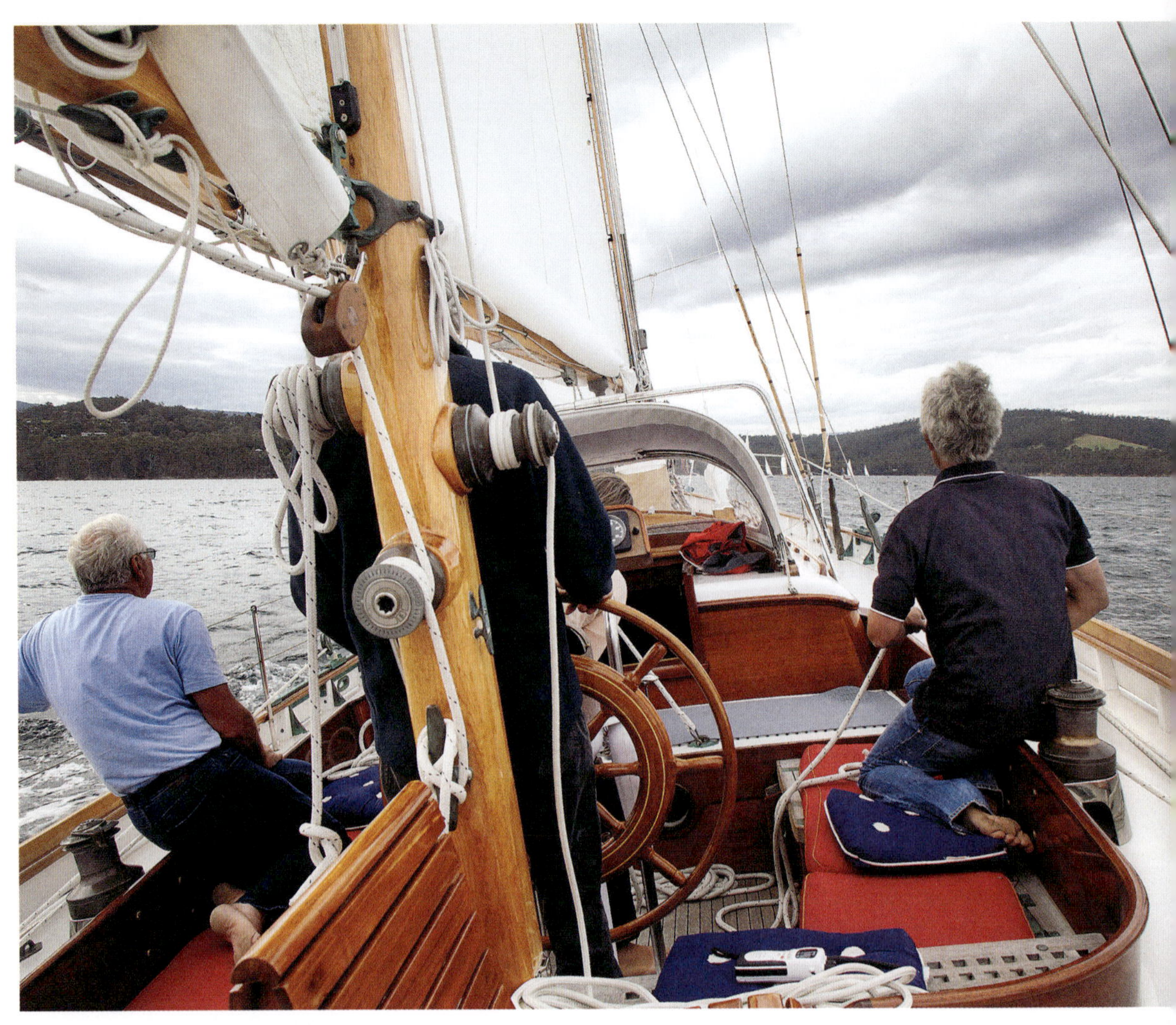

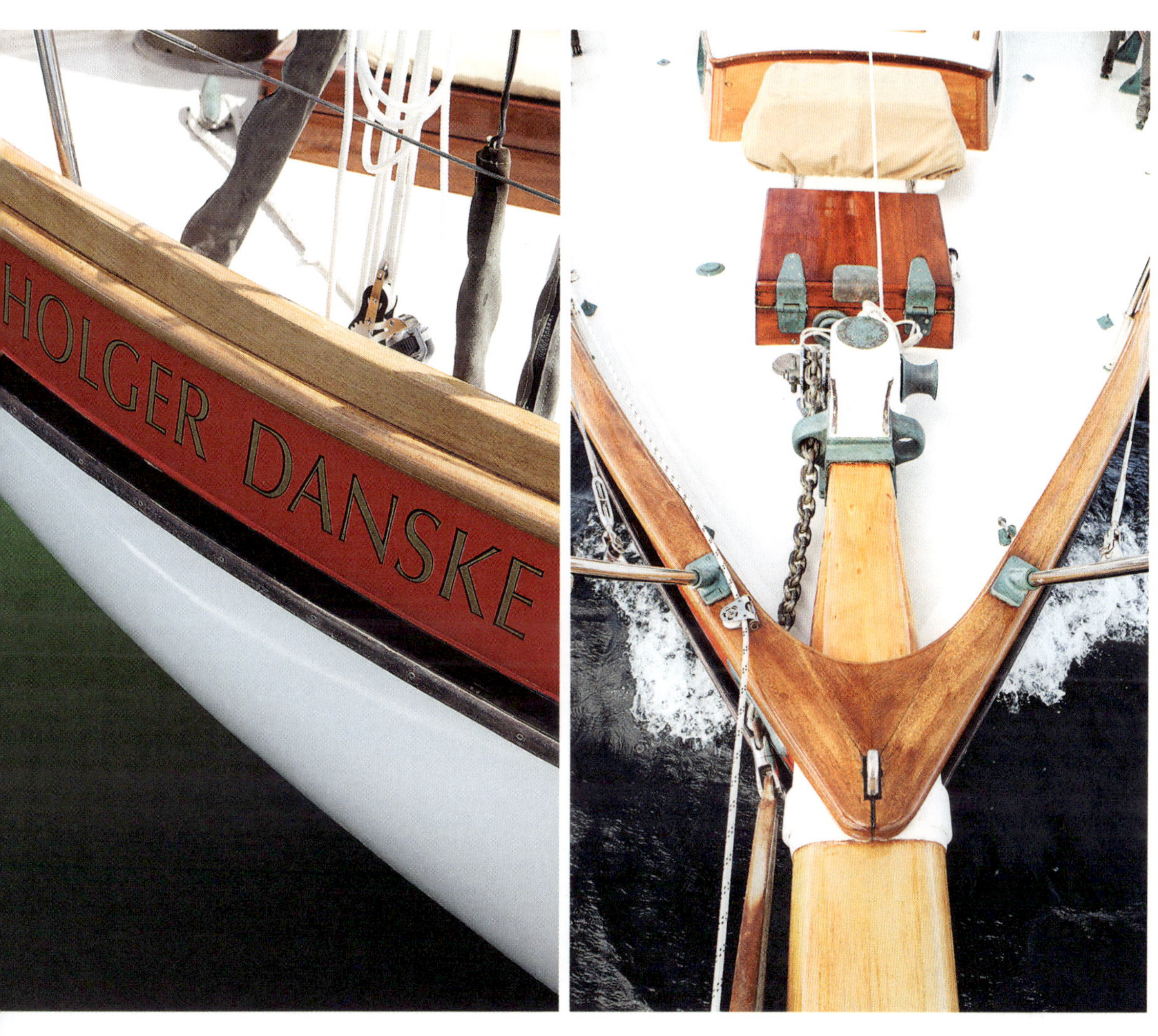

Holger Danske out on an evening sail from Kettering. She travels at a great pace, her elegant lines slicing through the water.

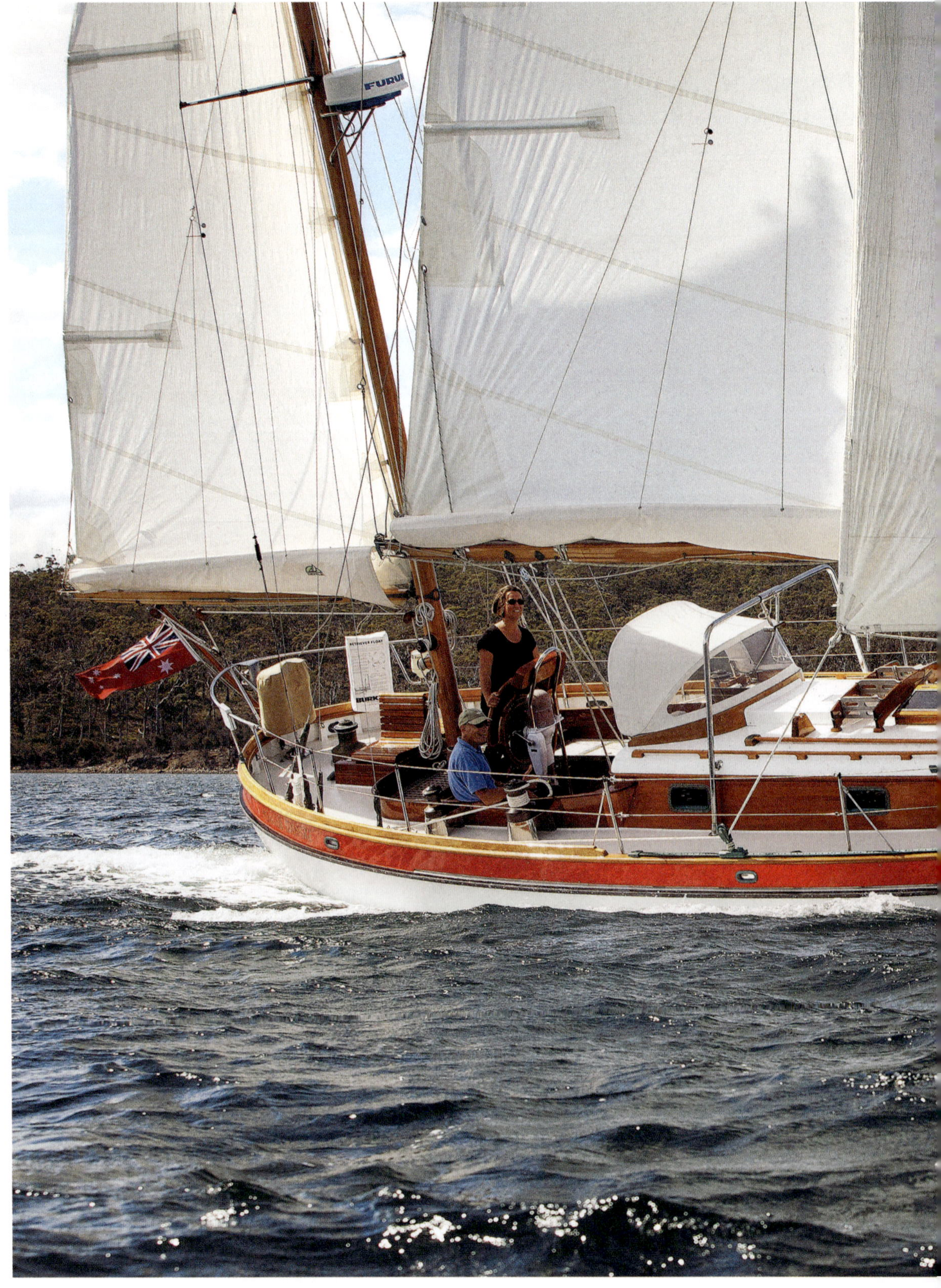
RETRIEVER FLOAT

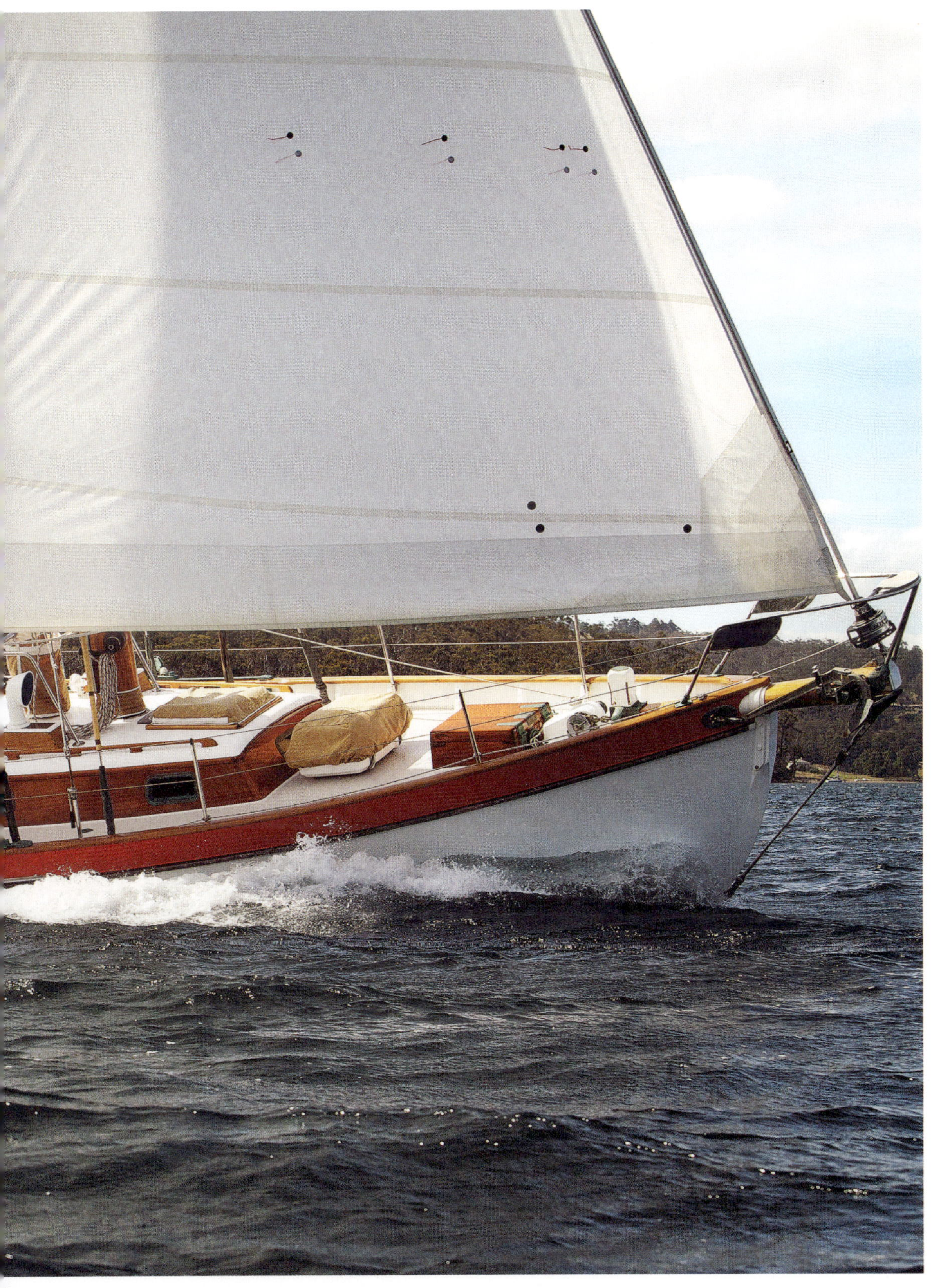

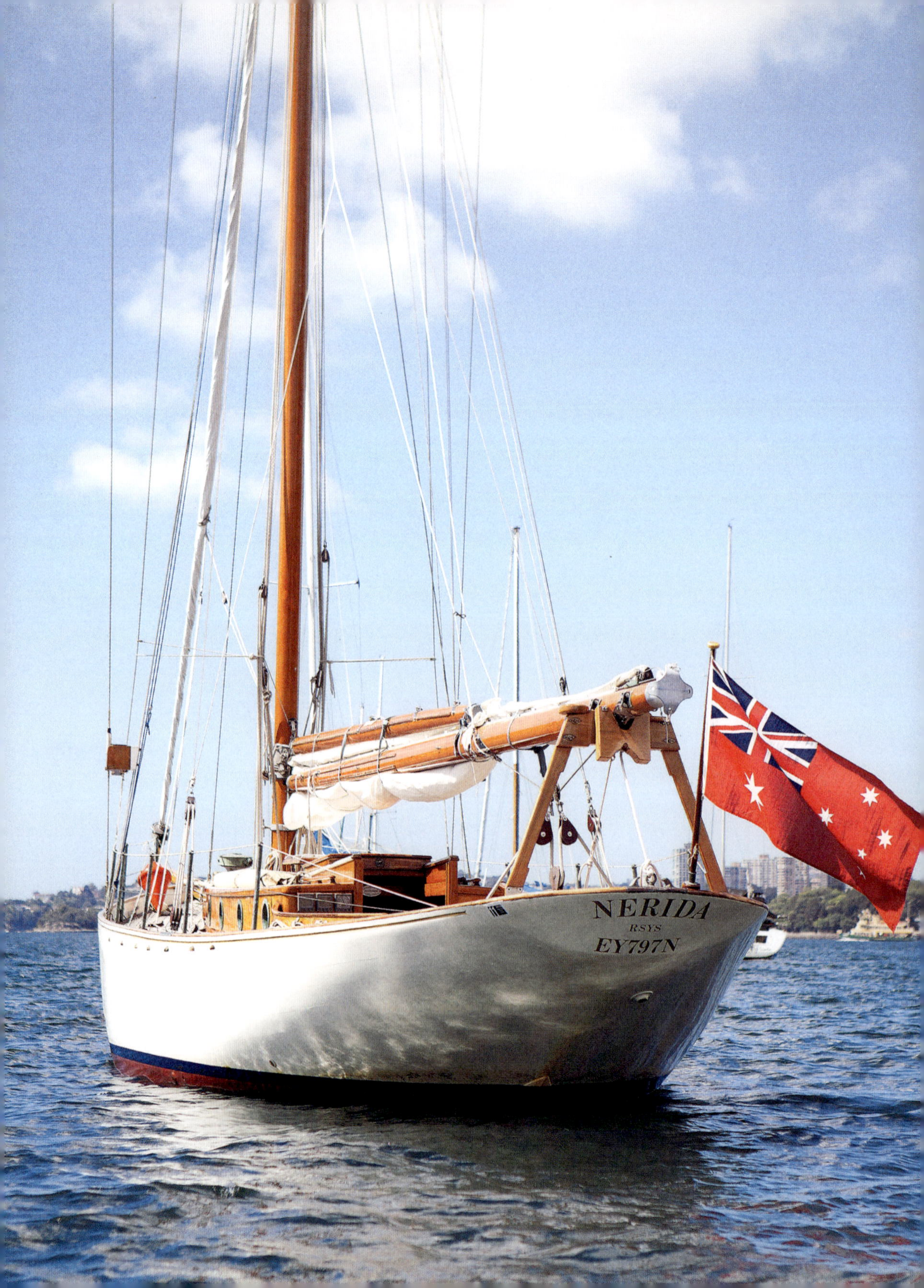
NERIDA
RSYS
EY797N

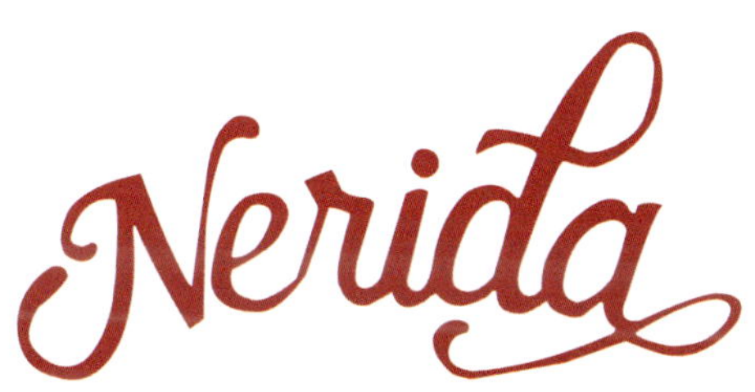

Nerida is, without a doubt, one of the most beautiful and celebrated yachts on Sydney Harbour. She was built for Tom Hardy, father of her current owner, Sir James Hardy, to a design by Messrs A. Mylne and Co. in Glasgow. She launched in 1933.

Tom Hardy was tragically killed in an air crash in 1938 and *Nerida* left the family for a period of time. She was refitted into a yawl and her tiller was replaced by a wheel. She won the 1950 Sydney to Hobart Yacht Race with this configuration.

Thomas Hardy & Sons purchased her in 1971 and Sir James had her restored to her original configuration, with tiller. In 2007, during a severe storm, a yacht moored near *Nerida* broke loose and hit her, leaving a gaping hole. In a second storm one week later, she slowly sank. Sir James was devastated.

The *Nerida* was raised and once again restored to her former glory. The only change to her original design was the addition of electric winch-halyards for the main sail, making her easier to operate. Sir James' son David Hardy continues the family tradition by sailing *Nerida*.

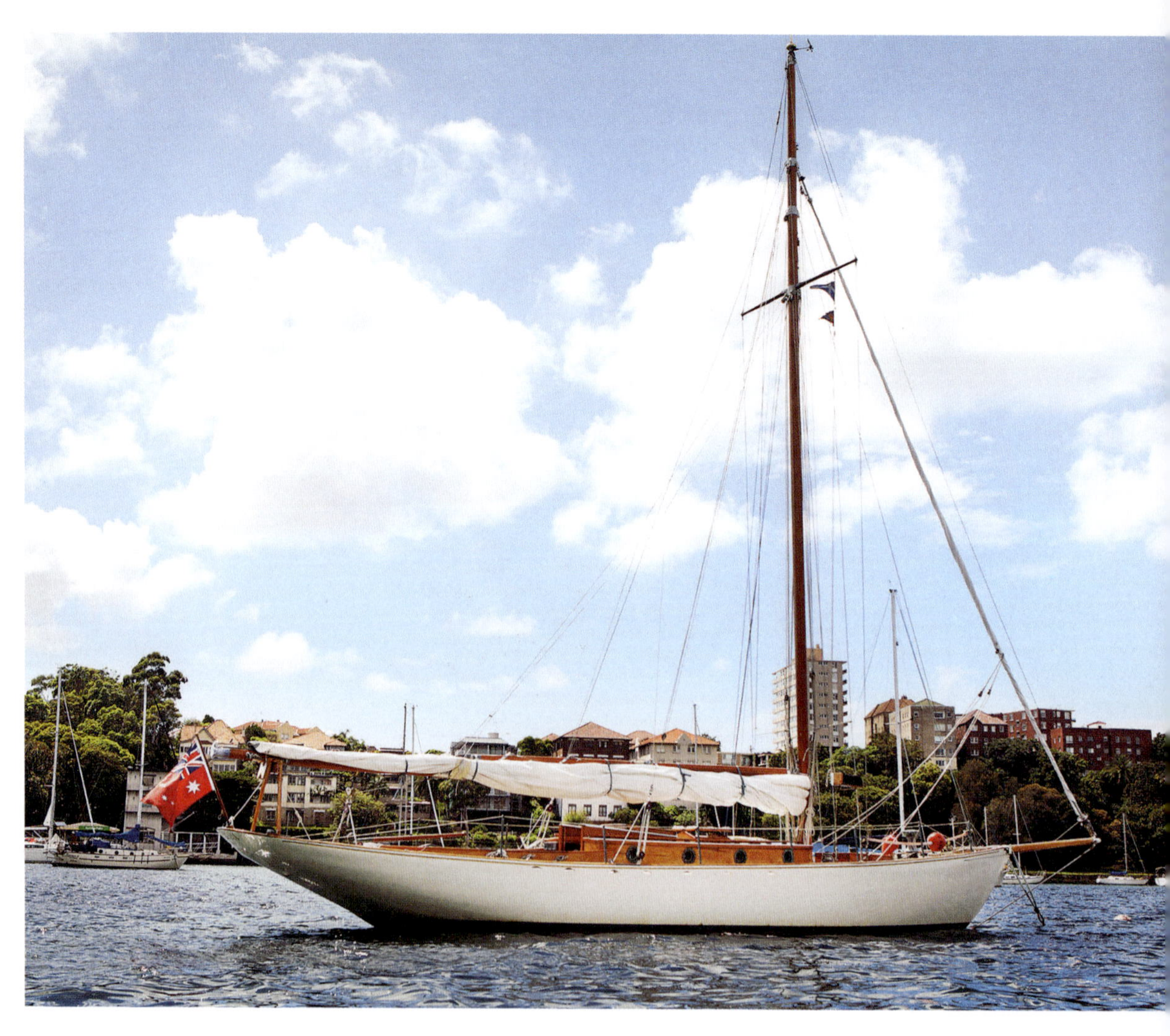

Nerida at her mooring, outside the Royal Sydney Yacht Squadron.

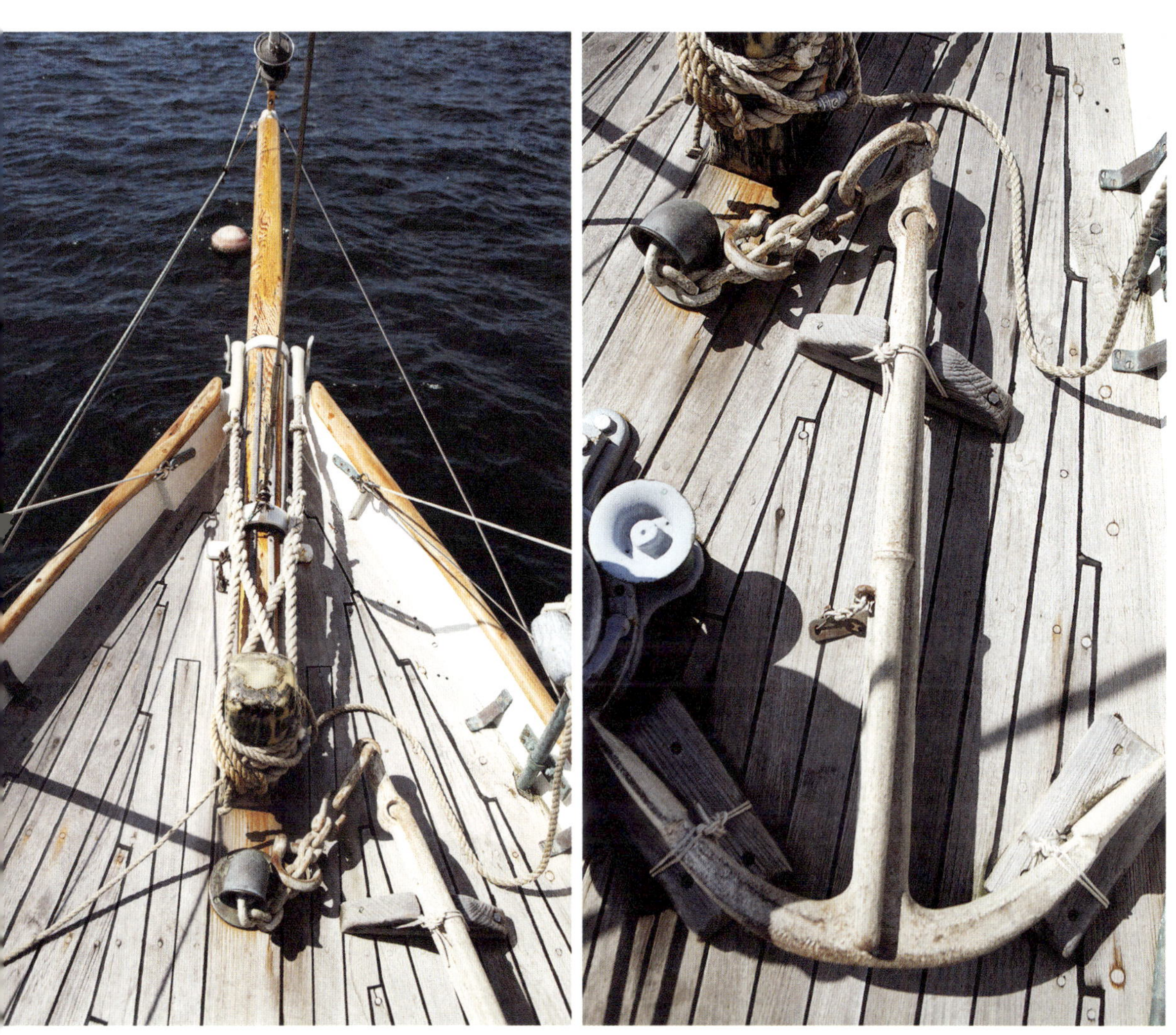

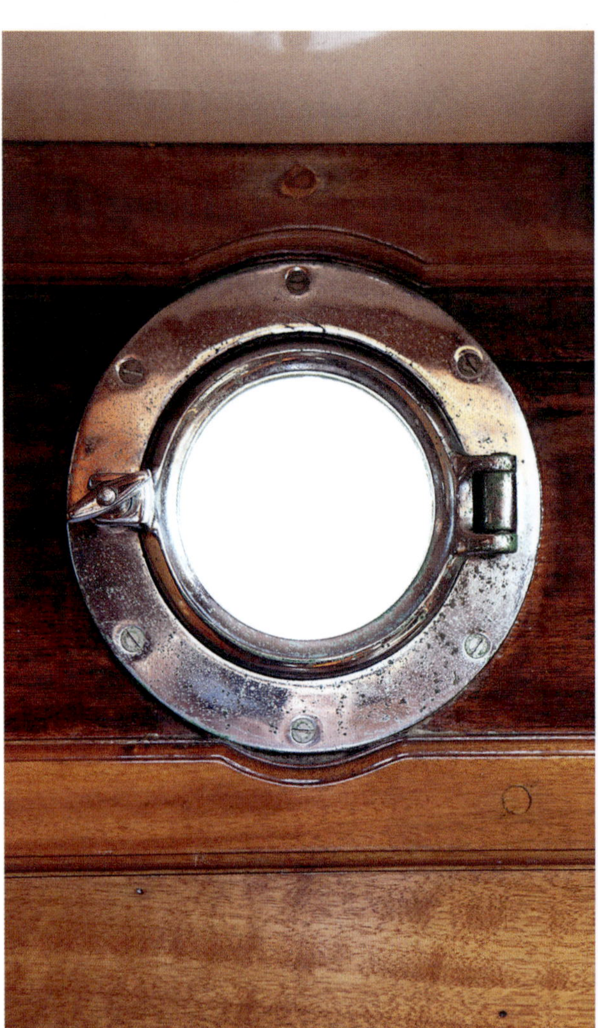

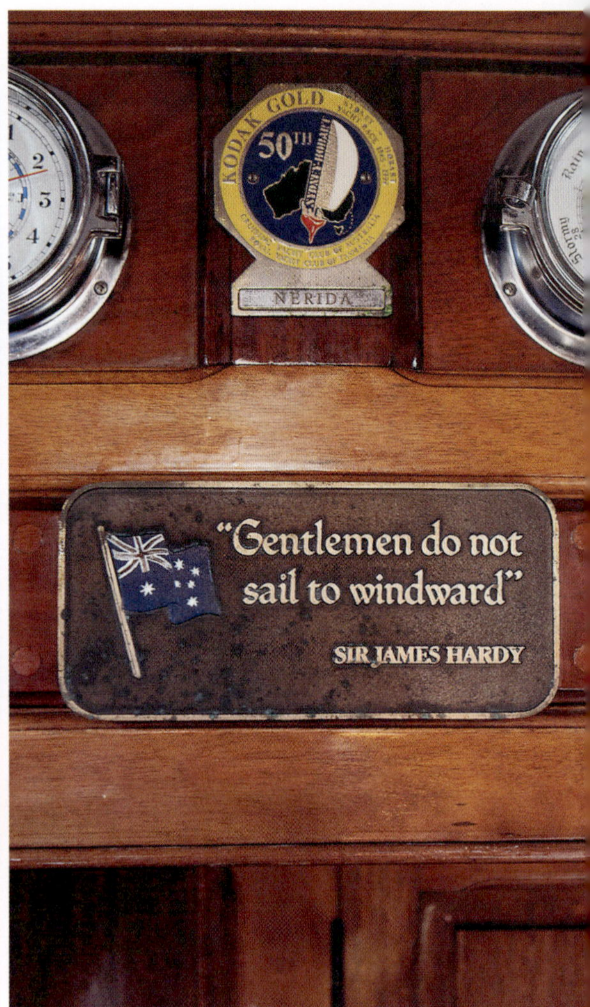

TOP RIGHT A piece of boating wisdom from Sir James Hardy.

OPPOSITE *Nerida*'s picture-perfect interior is all original.

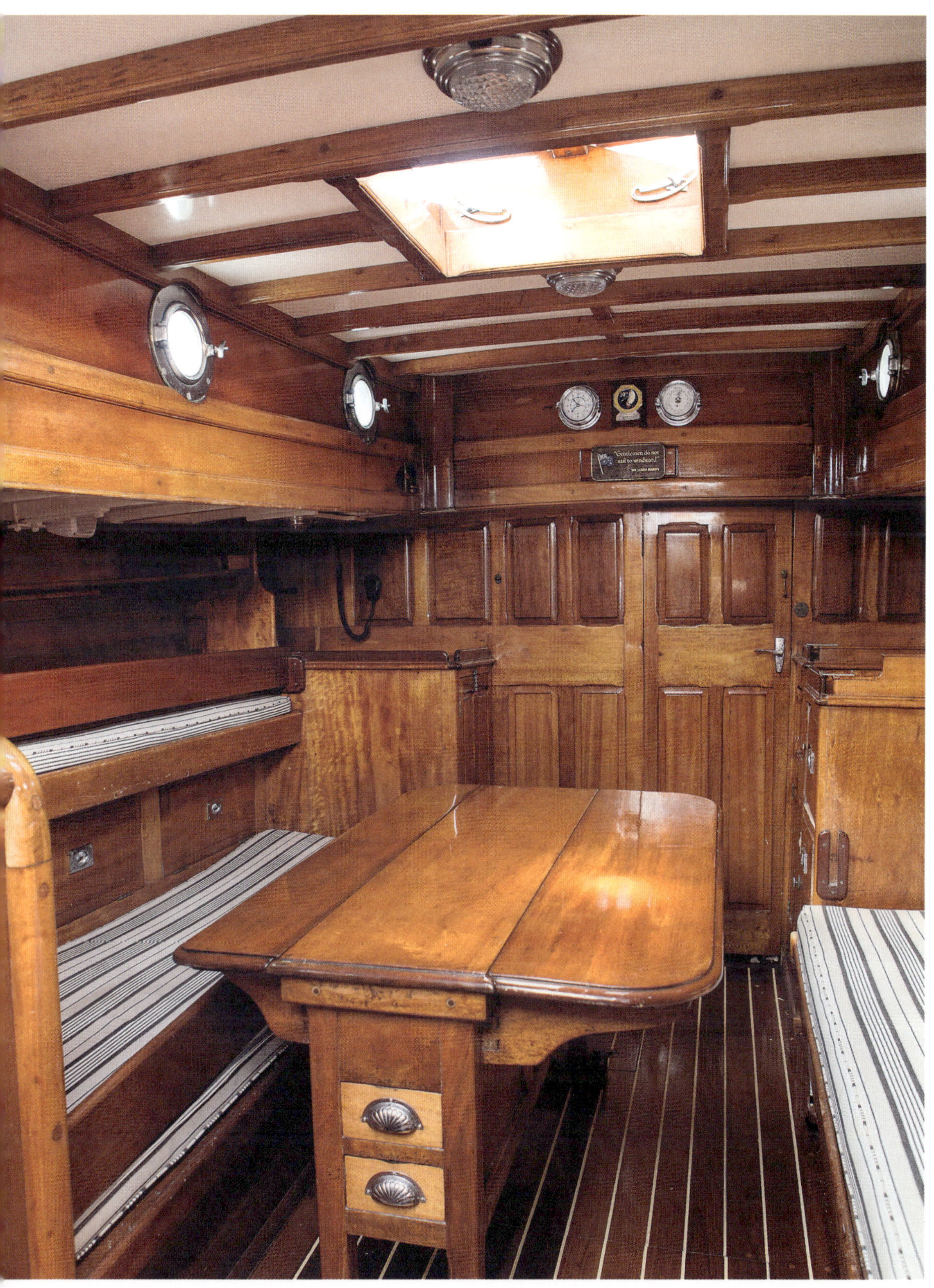
"Gentlemen do not
sail to windward"

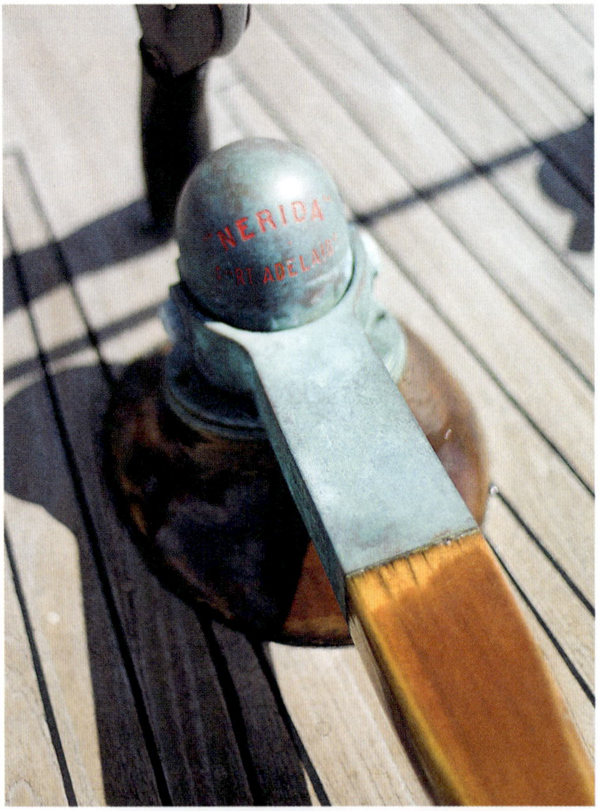

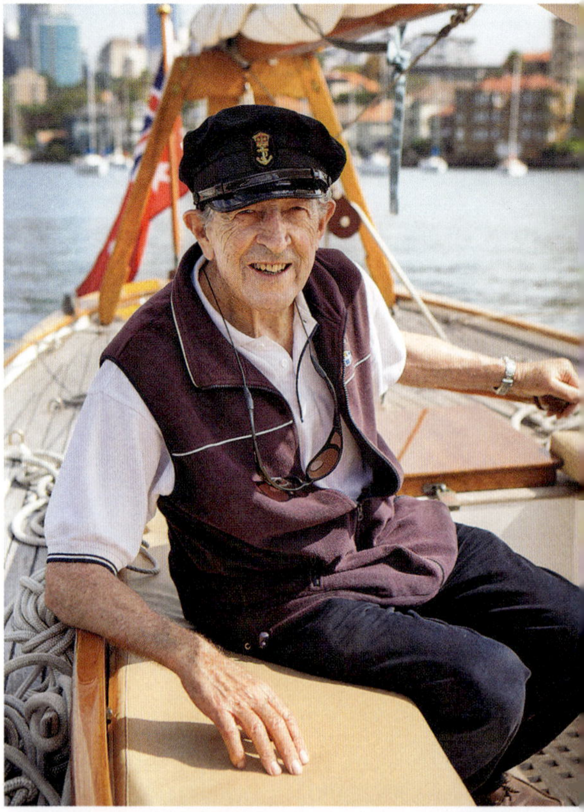

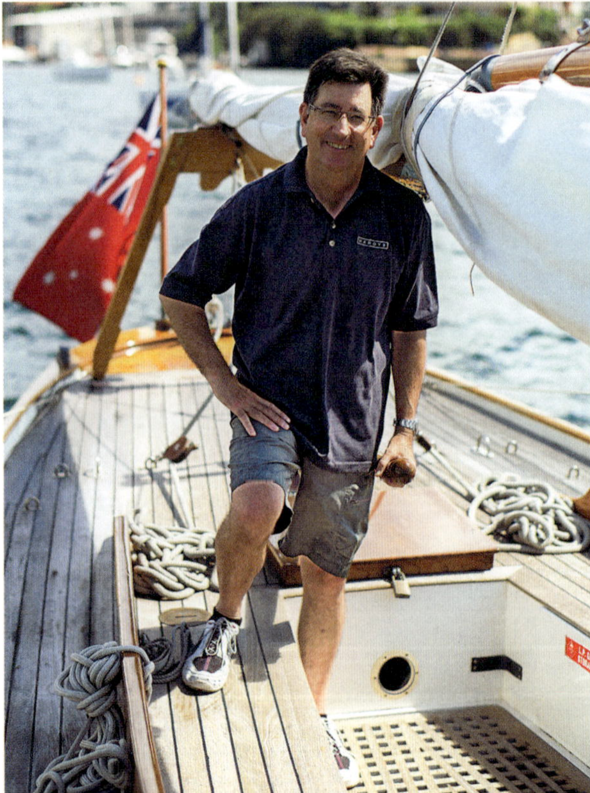

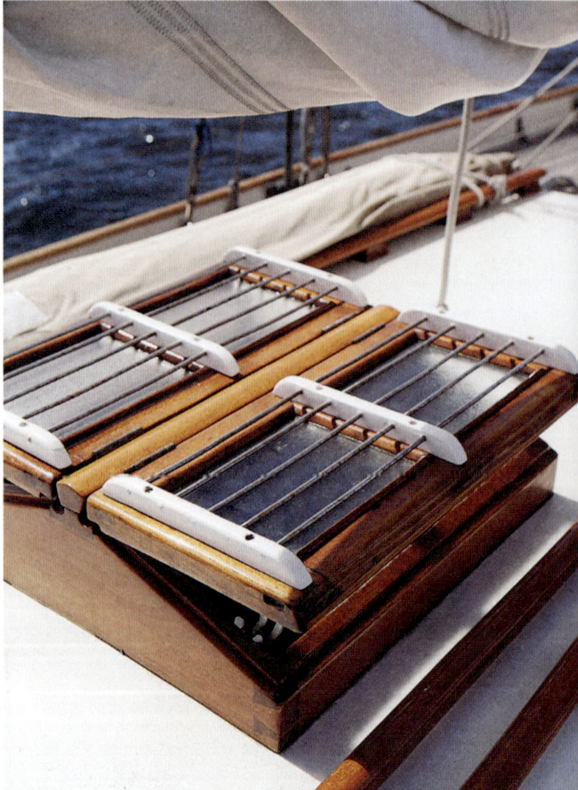

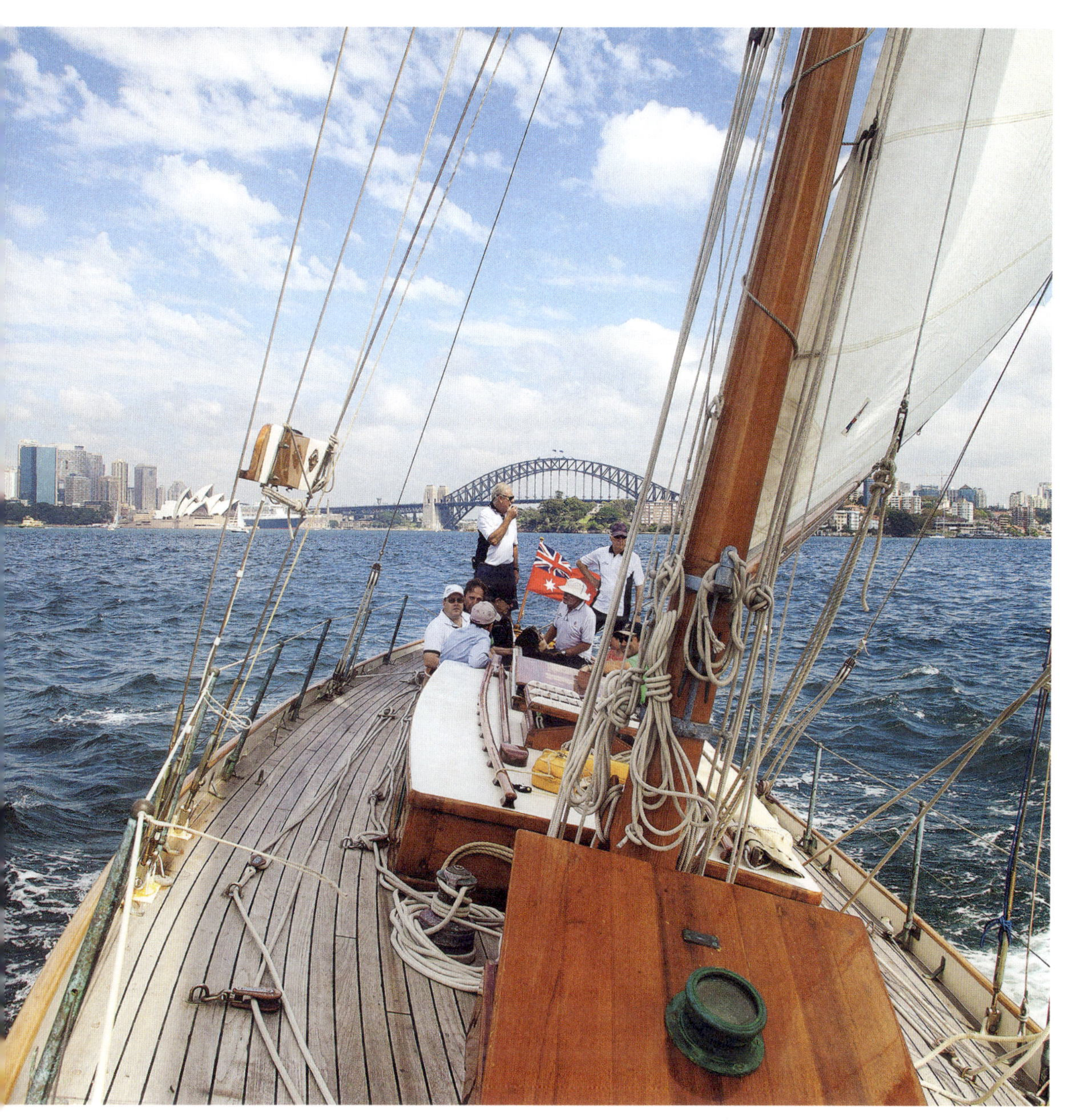

OPPOSITE Sir James Hardy (top right) and his son David Hardy (bottom left): second and third generations aboard *Nerida*.

Nerida is 45 feet long, with a 7-foot bowsprit. Her length at the waterline is 33 feet, her beam 11 feet and her draught 6 feet 3 inches. She cuts quite a dash on Sydney Harbour.

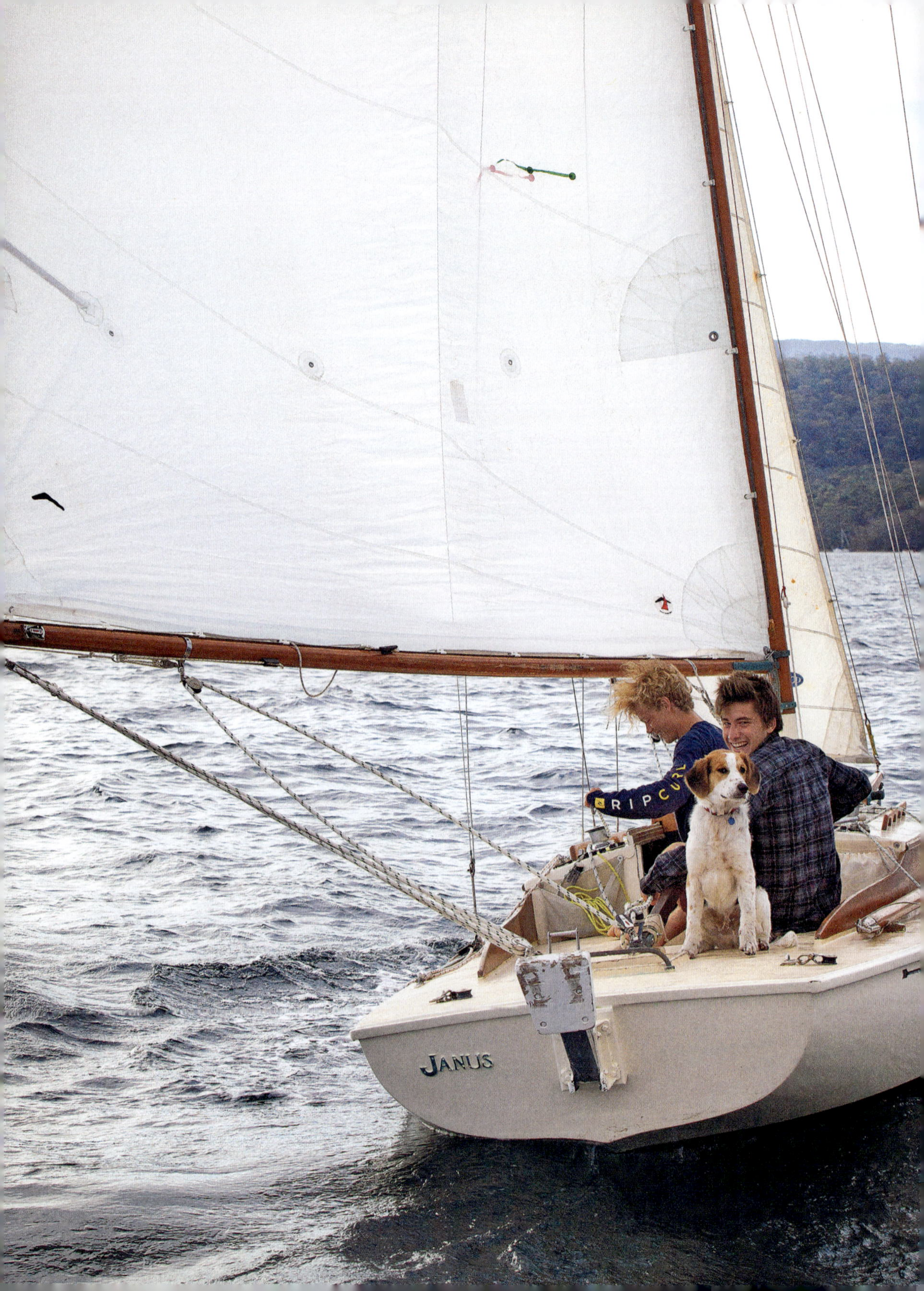
RIPCURL
JANUS

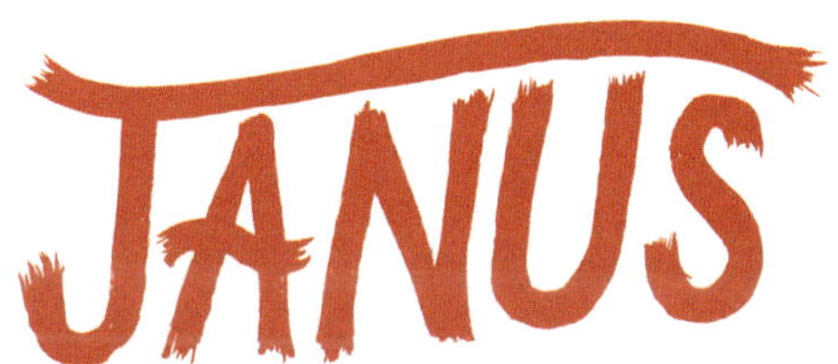

Ollie, Max and Scuppers heading out for the weekly race at Kettering Yacht Club.

Ollie McKay's boat *Janus*, a Derwent class sloop, was built in 1946. He has been sailing the family-owned boat for seven years. She is 24 feet 6 inches long, 6 feet 10 inches wide and her draw is 4 feet and 1 inch. She has a Celery Top hull and is named after an ancient Roman god associated with beginnings and transitions.

Ollie's newest crew member is his dog, Scuppers, who loves sailing. Ollie, his friend Max McLagan and Scuppers can be found most weeks racing in the Kettering Yacht Club races. At nineteen Ollie is already a seasoned sailor.

The D class or Derwent class yacht is part of Tasmania's maritime history. The design dates back to the 1920s, when Derwent Sailing Squadron had a design competition; they wanted a craft that could withstand the strong winds of the Derwent River.

D class yachts usually had names relating to myths, fantasy or fairytales, and the early ones were built from Huon pine. They are perfect cruisers/racers for Tasmanian conditions.

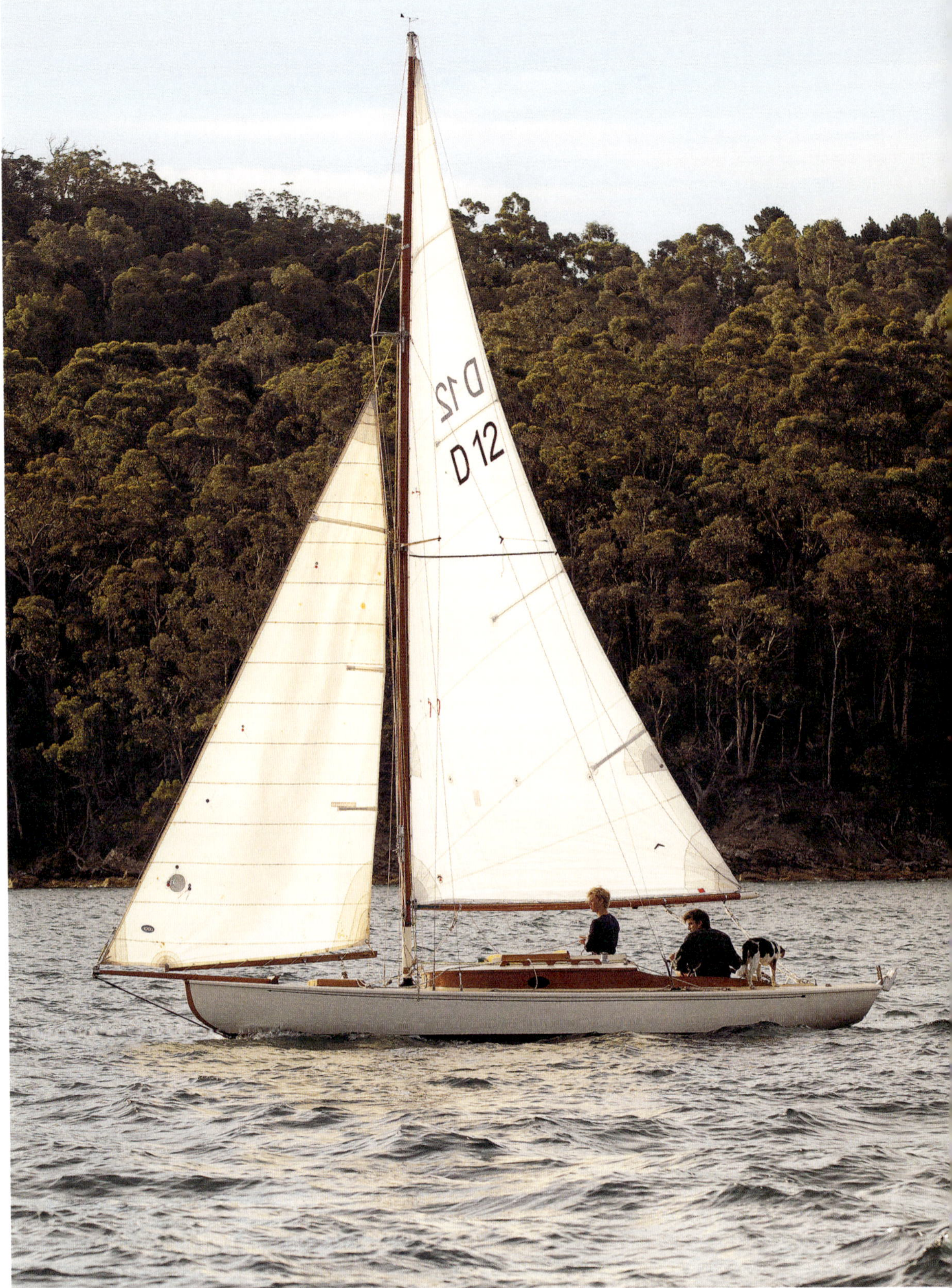
D 12

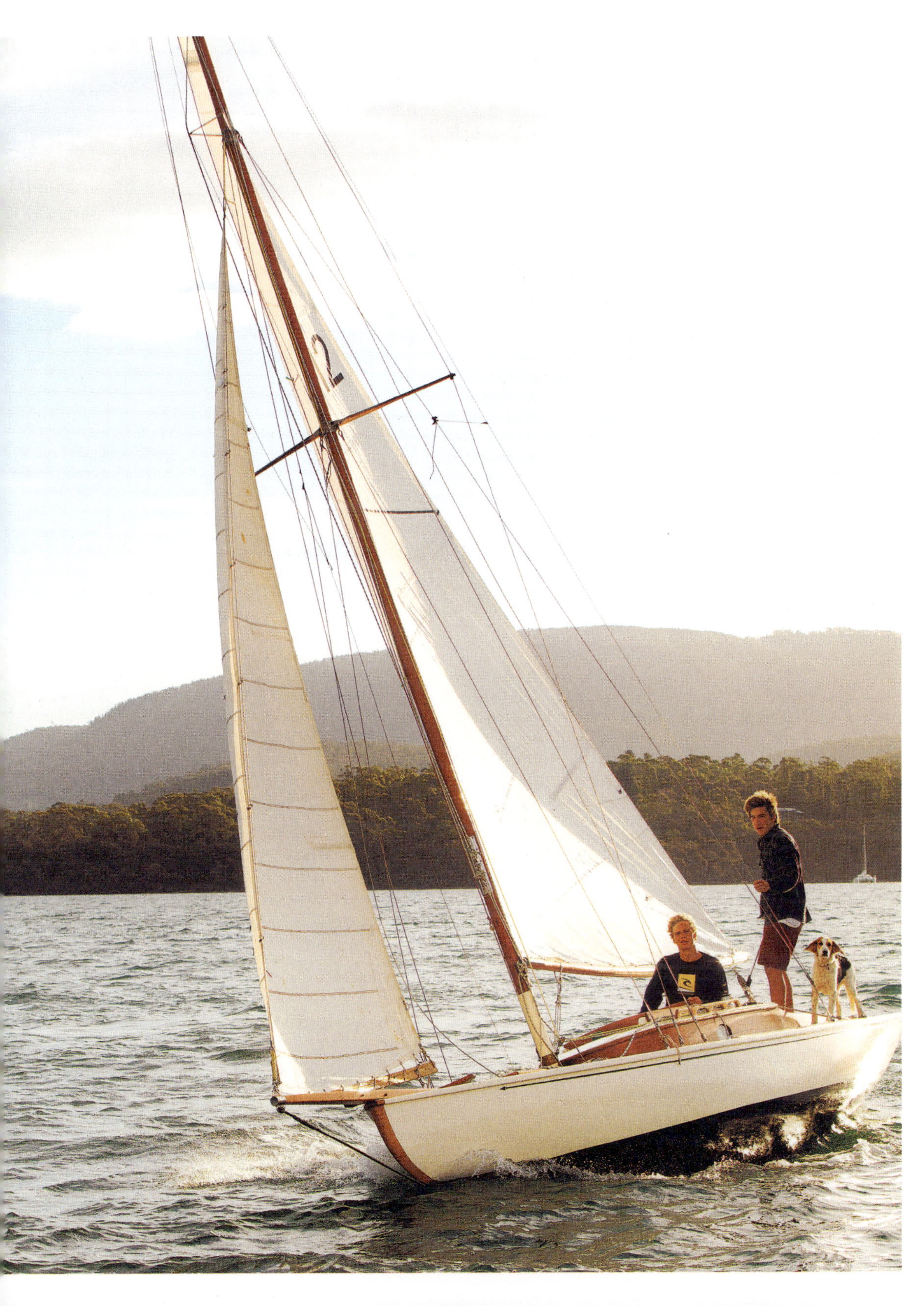
2

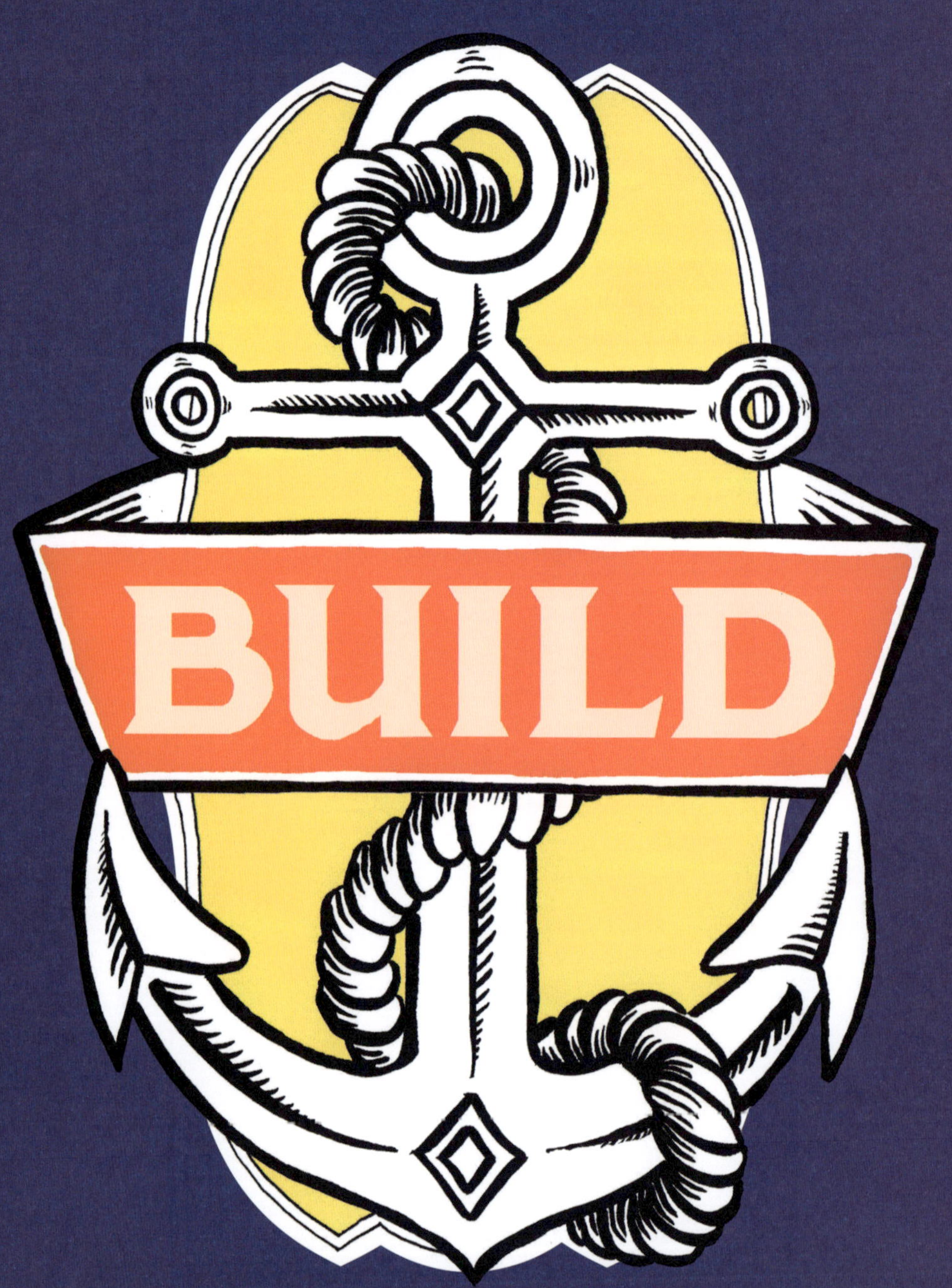
BUILD

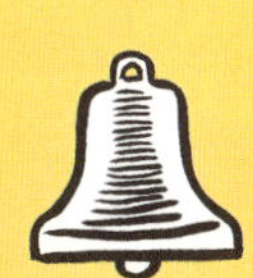

THE SMELL OF BEAUTIFUL TIMBER, GLUE AND VARNISH FILLS THE AIR. FROM THE EARLIEST TIMES, MAN HAS USED HIS SKILLS TO SHAPE TIMBER INTO BOATS, AND THE TRADITION CONTINUES TODAY IN A FEW BOAT YARDS AND SHEDS AROUND AUSTRALIA. IT MIGHT BE ANYTHING FROM A 50-FOOT HULL TO AN EXQUISITELY DETAILED SCALE MODEL.

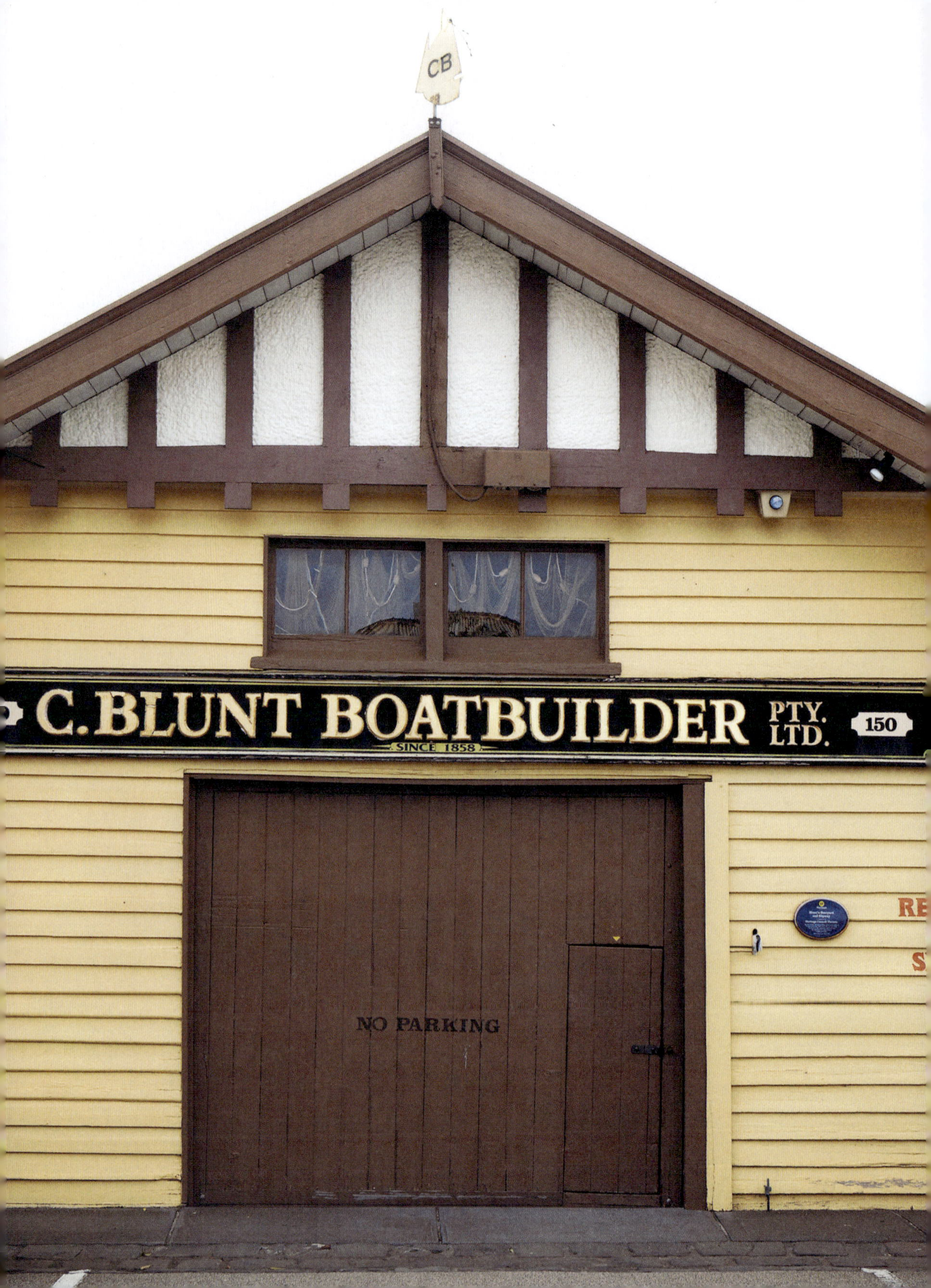
CB
C. BLUNT BOATBUILDER PTY. LTD.
SINCE 1858
150
NO PARKING

C. BLUNT BOAT BUILDER

Greg Blunt is a fifth-generation boatbuilder – a pretty rare thing in Australia. For over 150 years the Blunts have been building wooden boats and launching them into the waters of Port Phillip, Victoria.

Clement Blunt and his wife, who arrived in Australia from England in the early 1850s, had a rough start, losing their first home and all their possessions in a bushfire. Undeterred, they opened a boatbuilding business in Geelong in 1858. In 1887 Clement's eldest son, also called Clement, set up his own business on the Williamstown foreshore and was soon quite a success. The business thrived, but in 1926 a fire gutted the Blunts' shed and they moved to their current site in Nelson Place.

Greg Blunt, who now runs the family business, is often repairing boats built by his forebears. The shed and boat yard have been listed by Heritage Victoria because of their historical and archaeological significance, as a rare operating example of the many boatbuilding businesses which operated on the Williamstown foreshore in the early nineteenth century. The Blunts are still working hard, and on any day you might visit, the boat yard is a hive of activity.

FOLLOWING PAGES
The shed is a treasure trove of early nautical memorabilia: framed pictures of famous Blunt boats line the walls, along with an incredible collection of old tools.

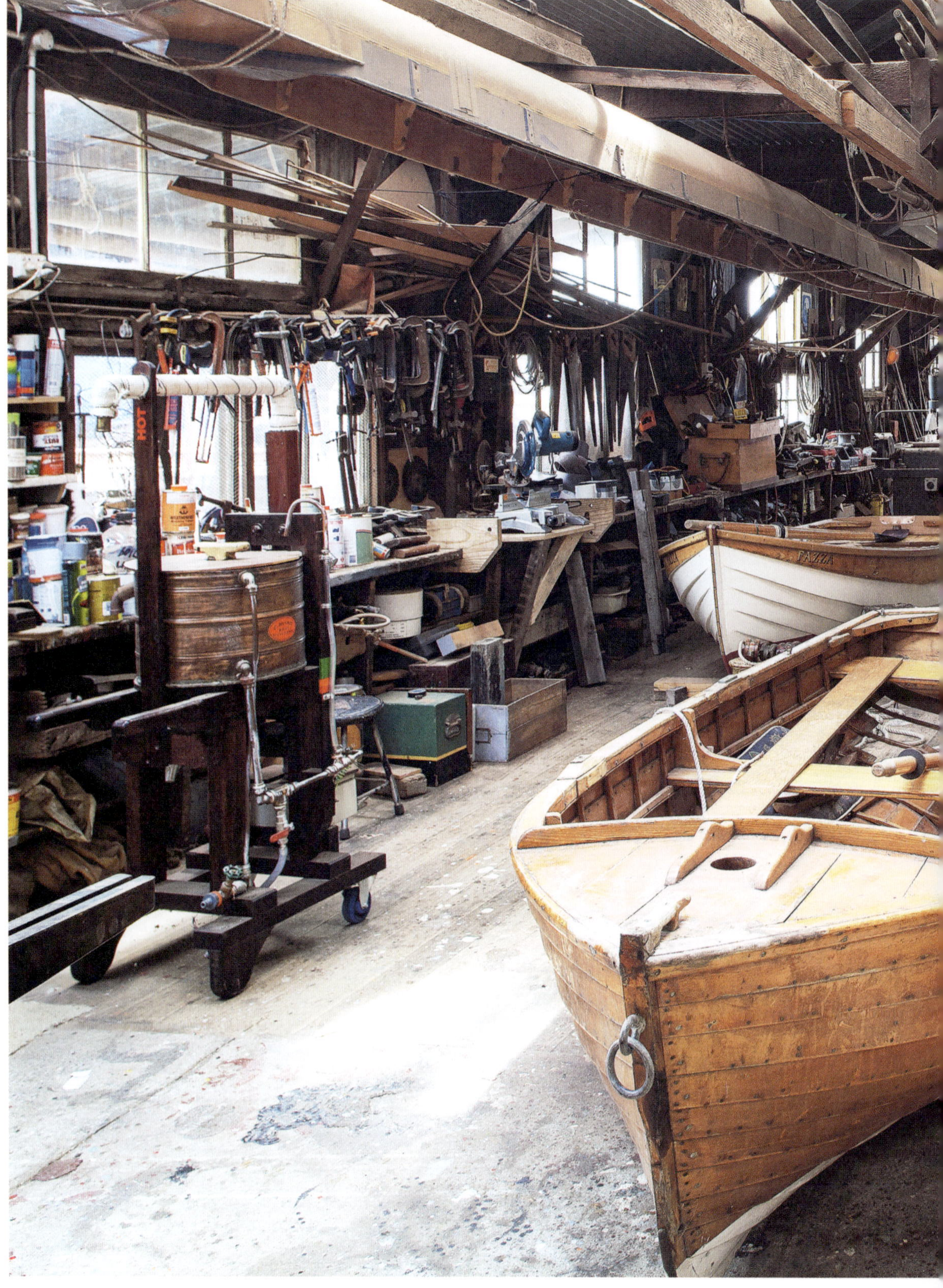
HOT
FAZZA

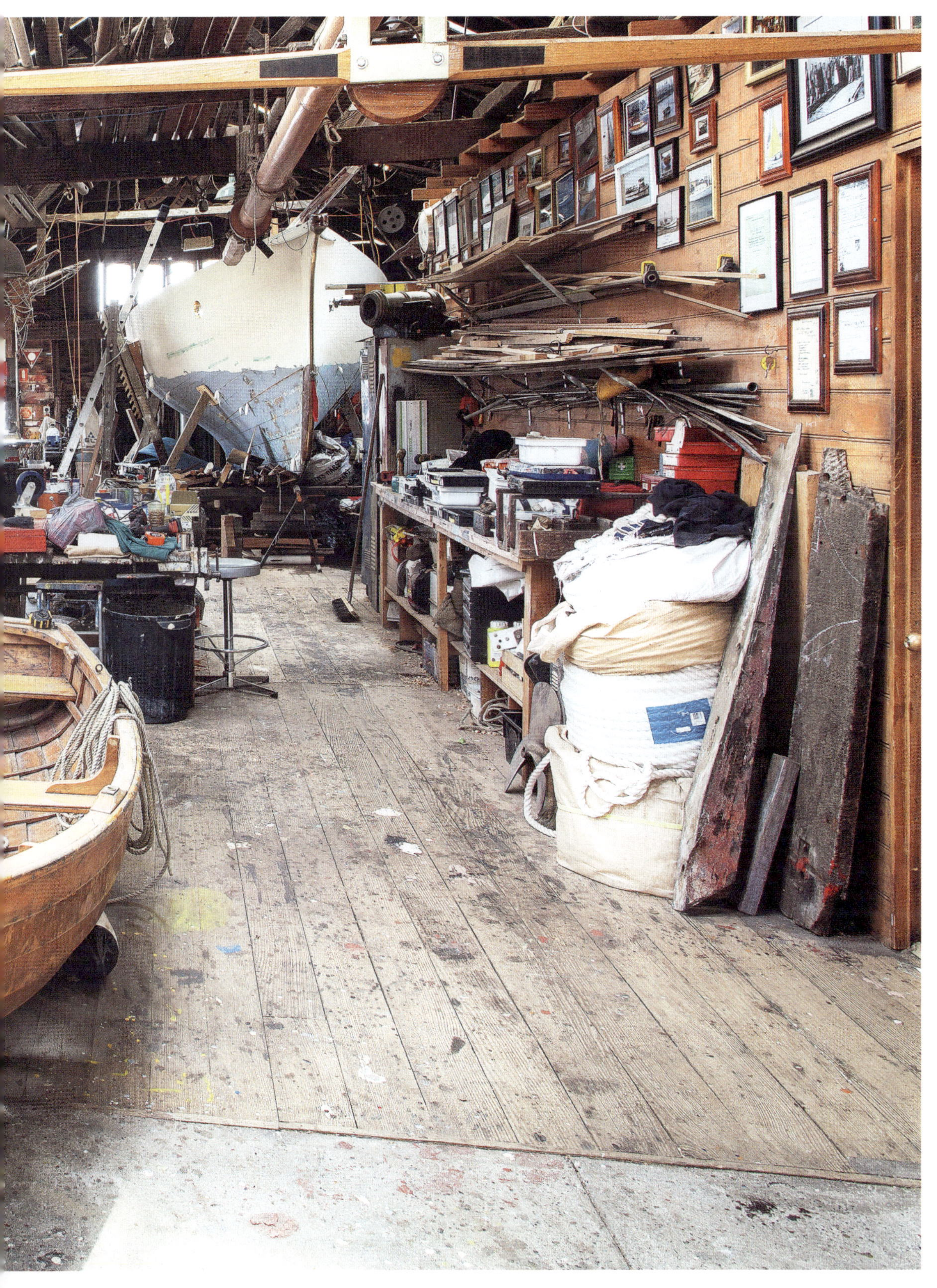

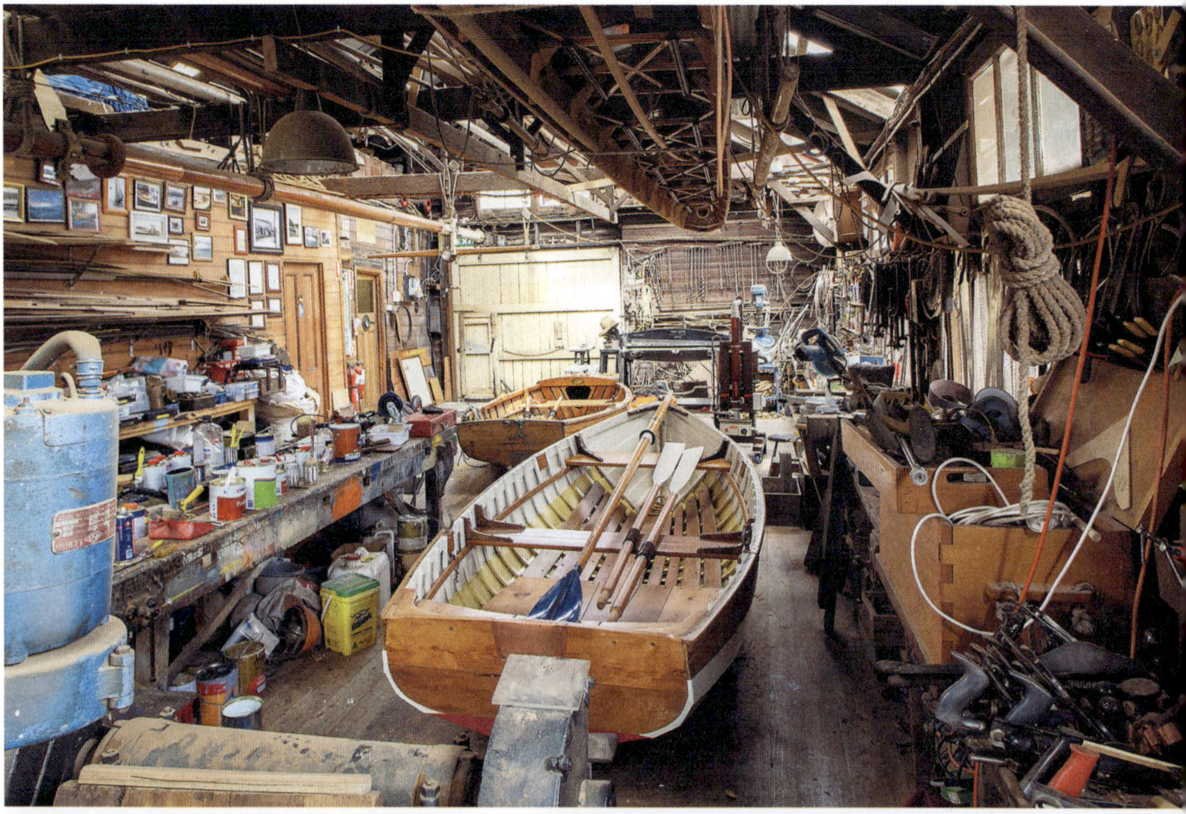

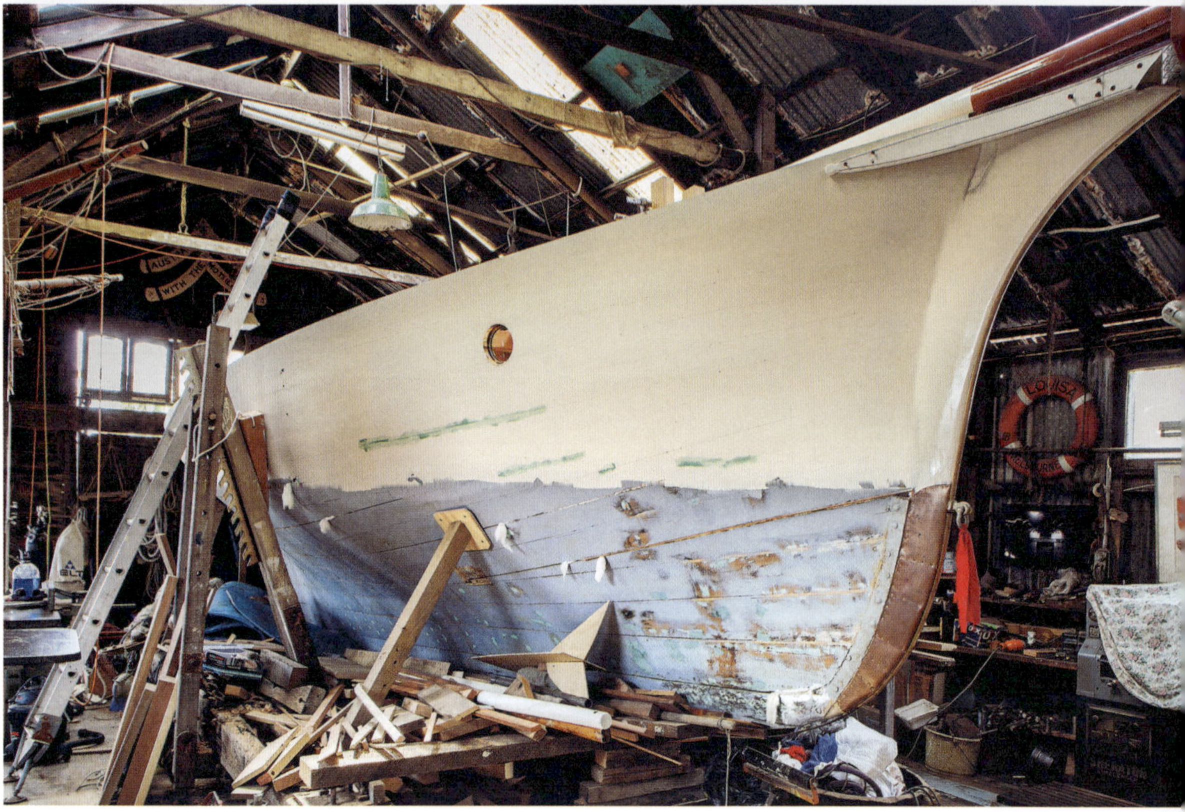

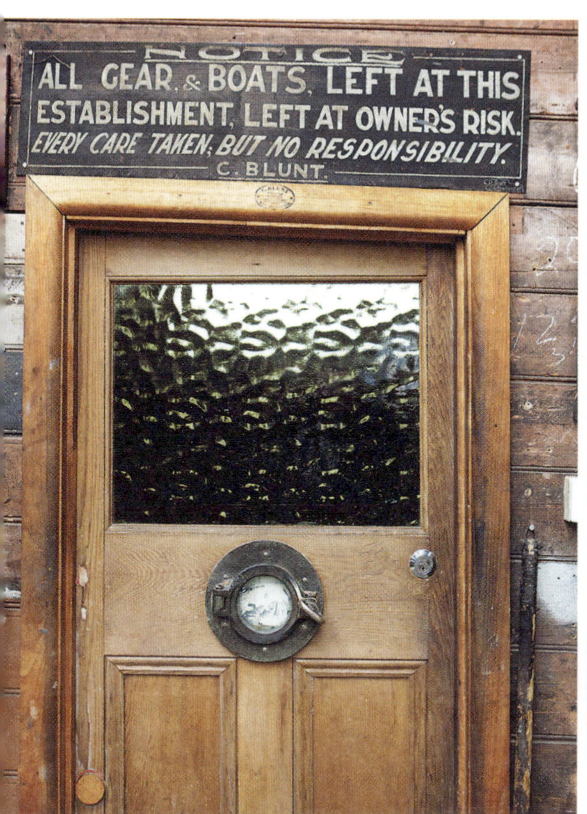

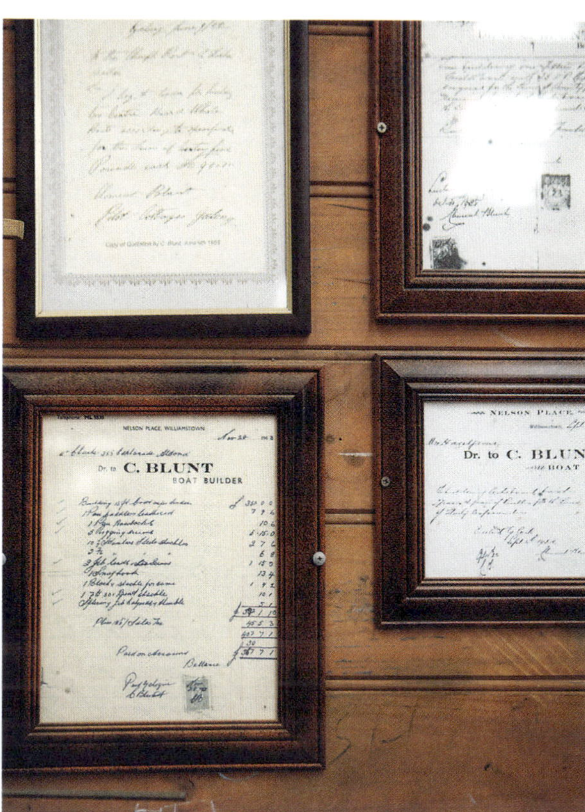

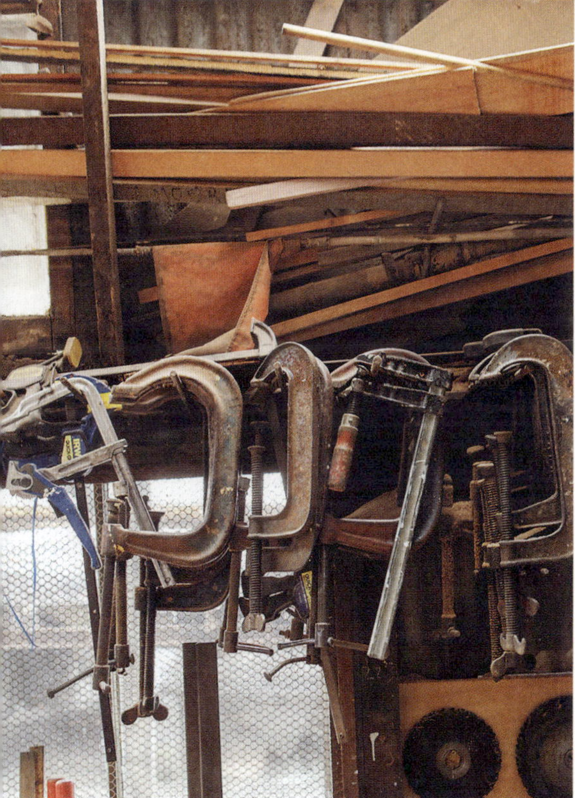

OPPOSITE, TOP The historic boatshed, as busy today as ever.

OPPOSITE, BOTTOM Greg is restoring this boat to sail himself once he retires.

ABOVE The door to Greg's office is surrounded by boating memorabilia and framed invoices for boats built by Blunts.

LEFT The shed is full of old boatbuilding tools.

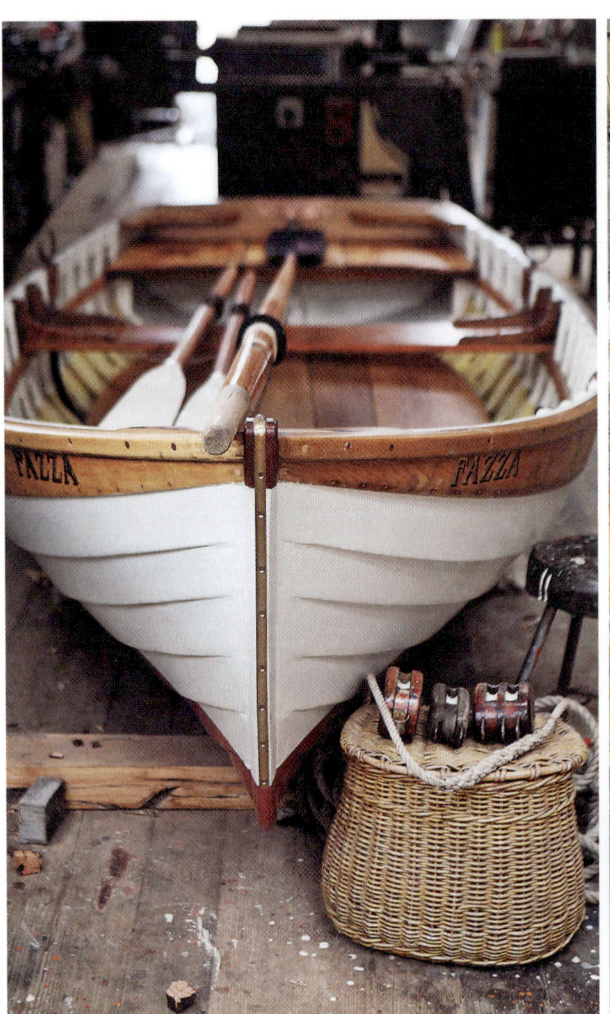
FAZZA
FAZZA

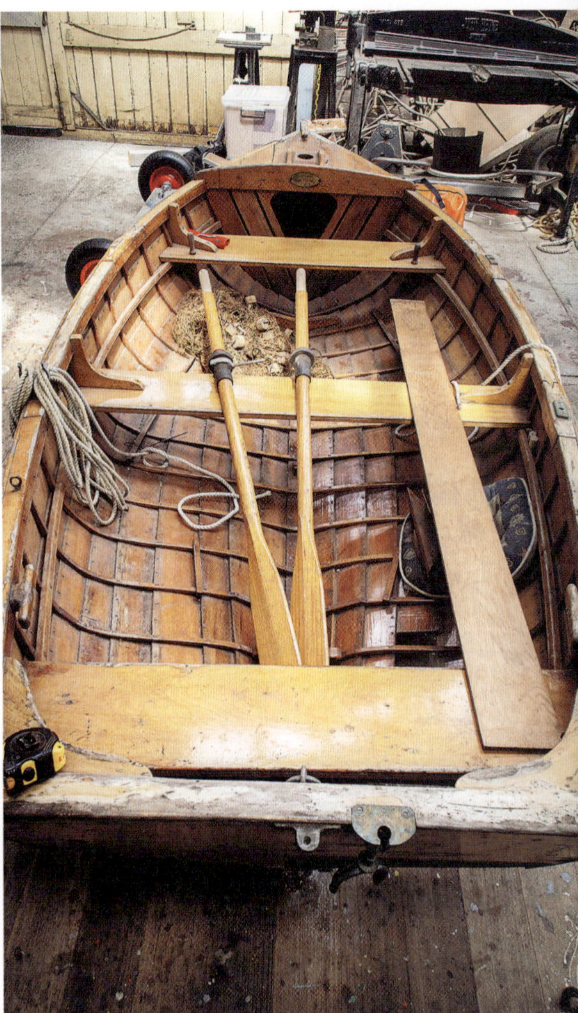

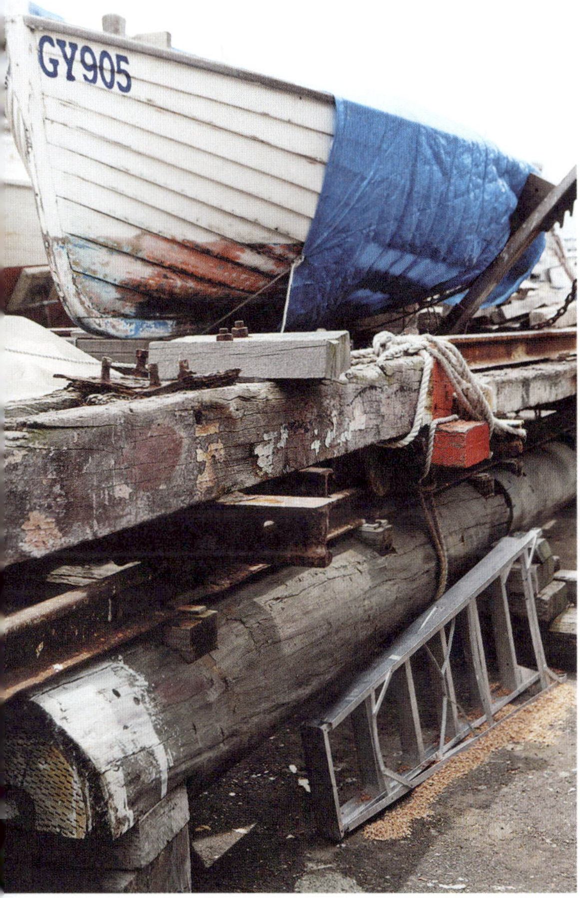

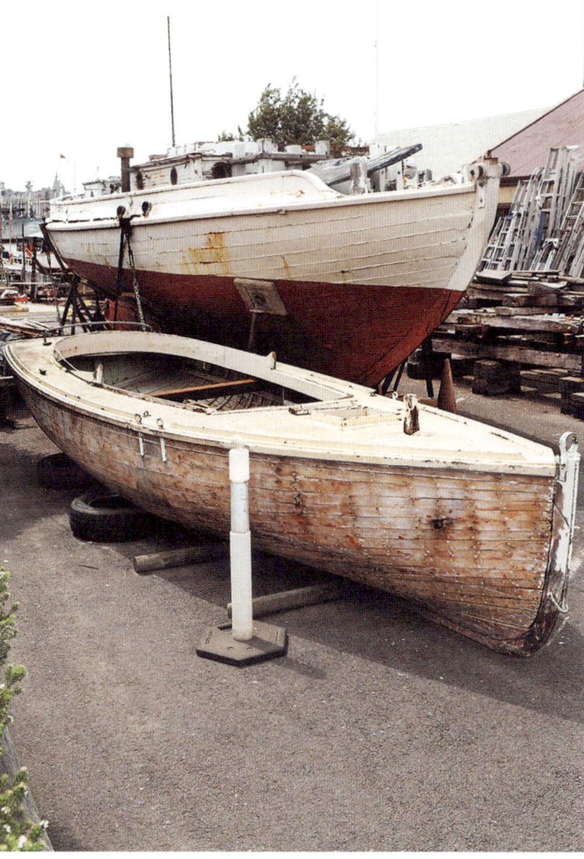

The boat yard is full of boats of every size and description, waiting to be restored. Many of them were built by Greg's father and his grandfather.

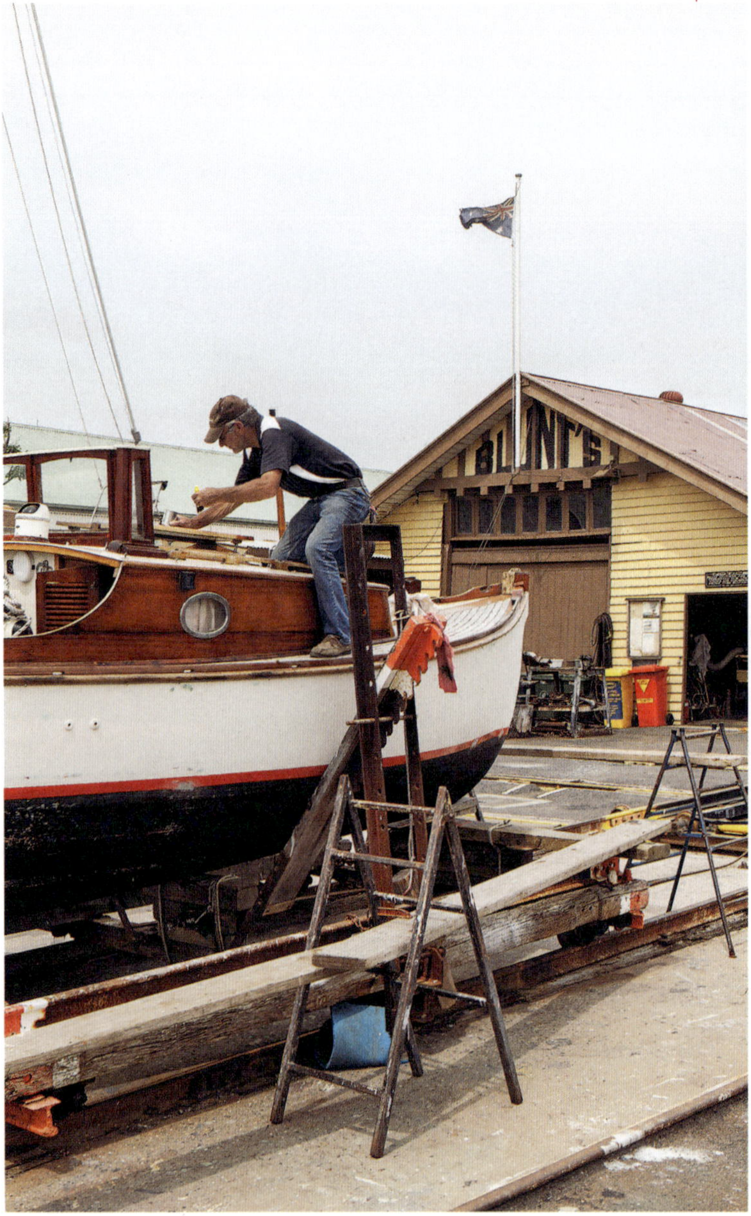

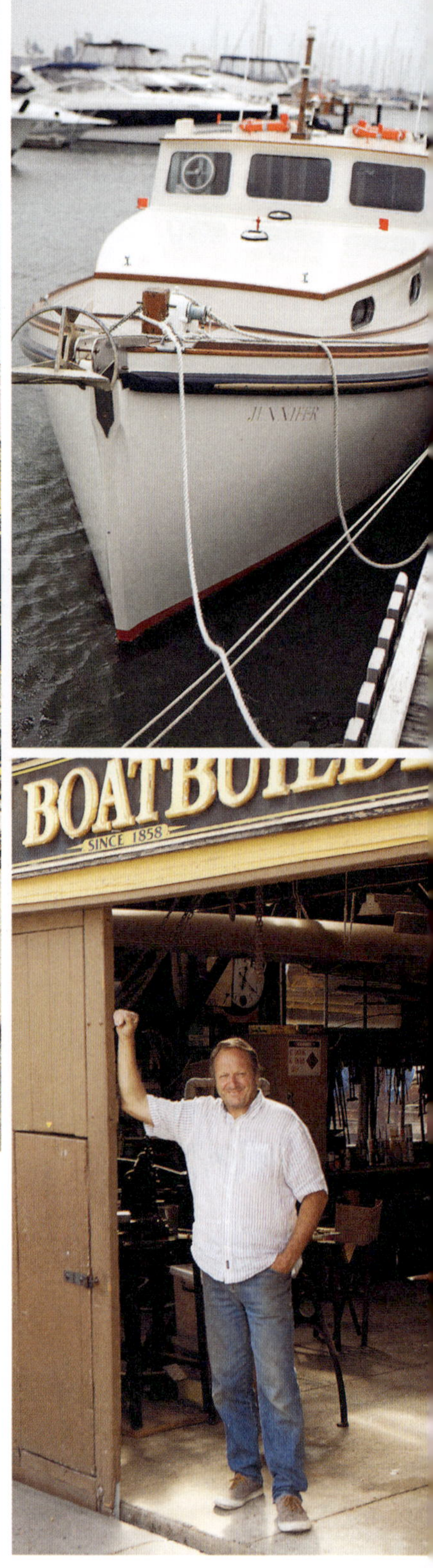

RIGHT Greg Blunt, fifth-generation boatbuilder.

OPPOSITE, TOP The slipway at the back is one of the few private slipways left in Australia.

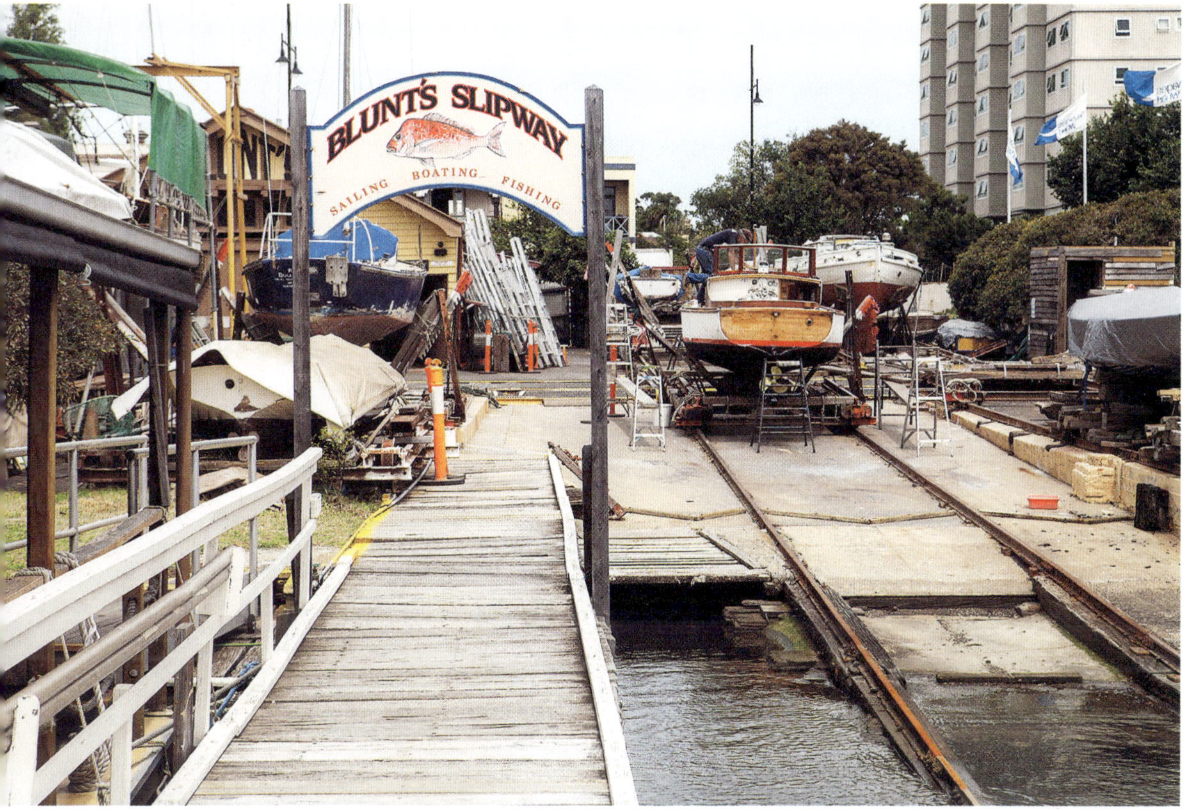

BLUNT'S SLIPWAY
SAILING BOATING FISHING
J244 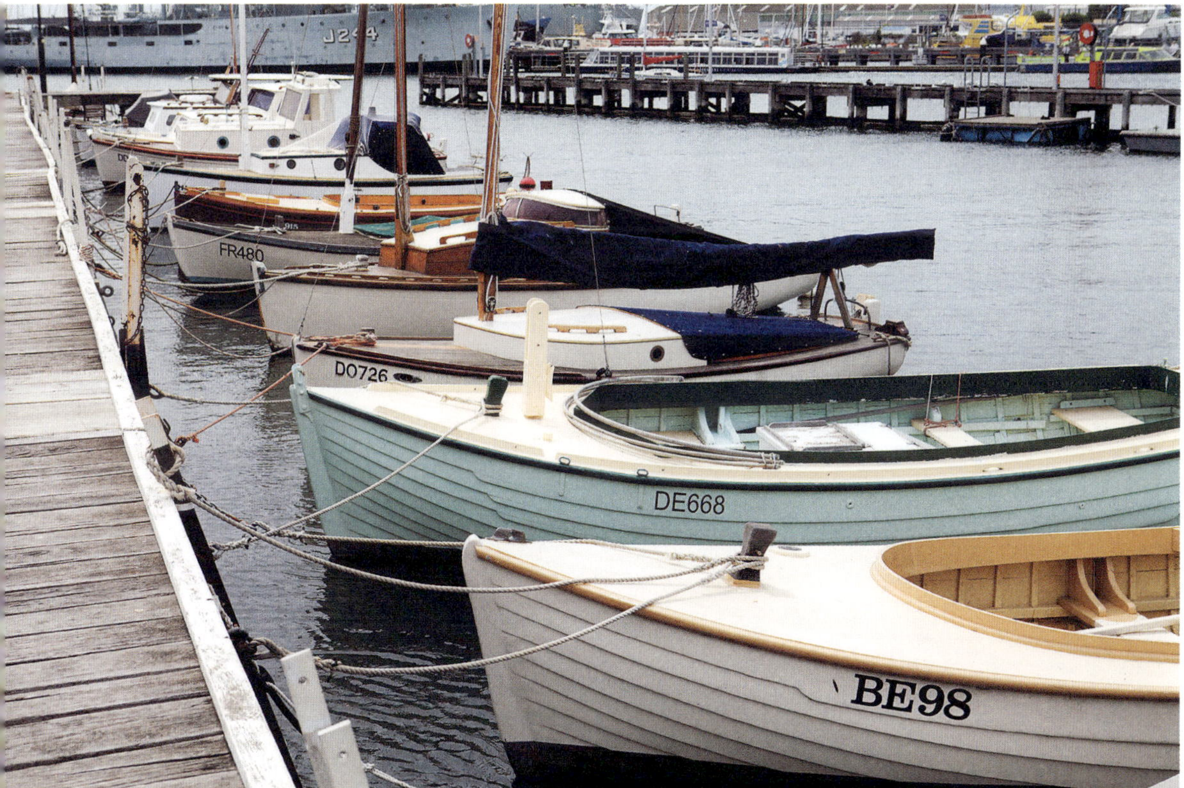
FR480
DO726
DE668
BE98

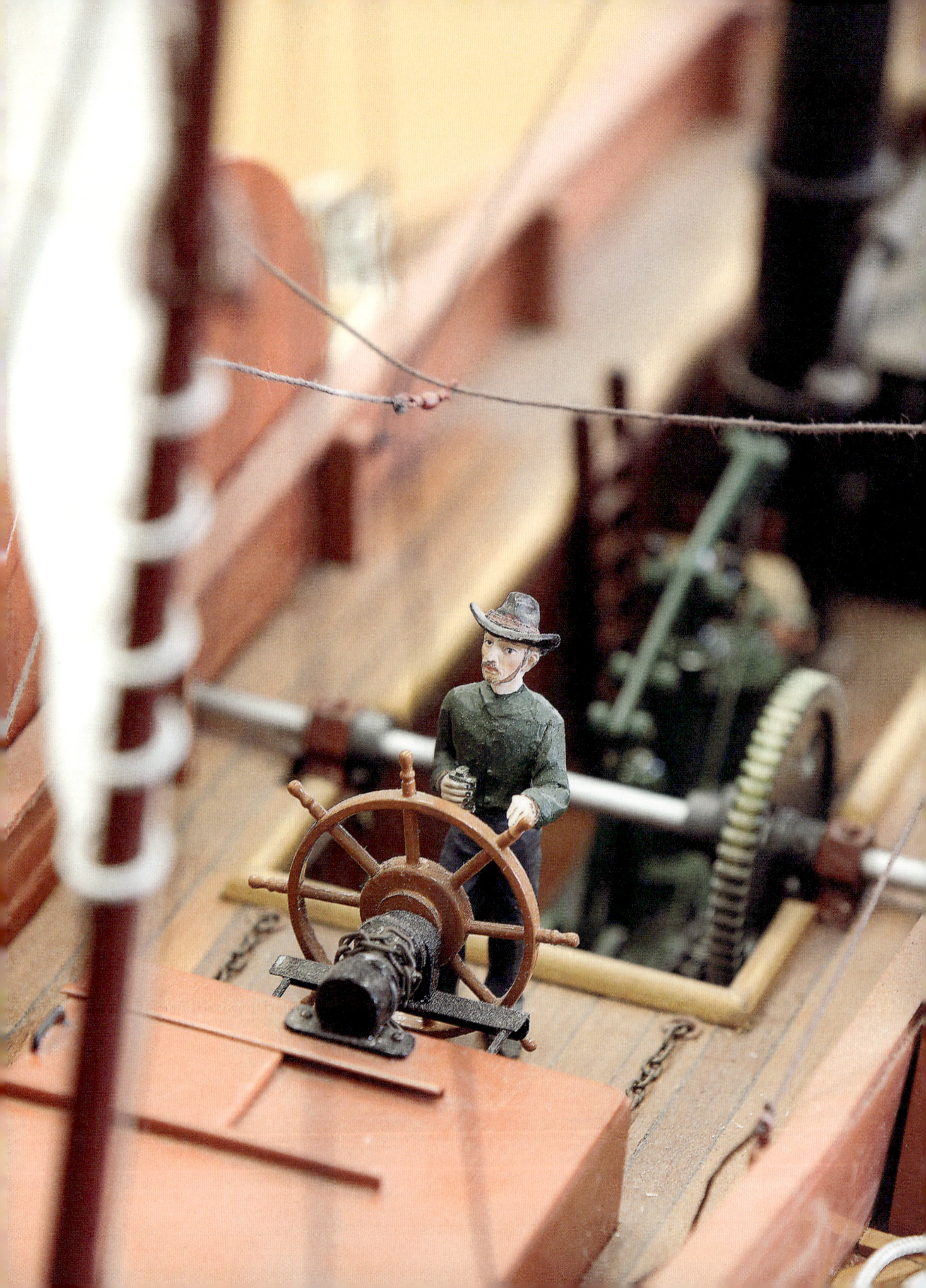

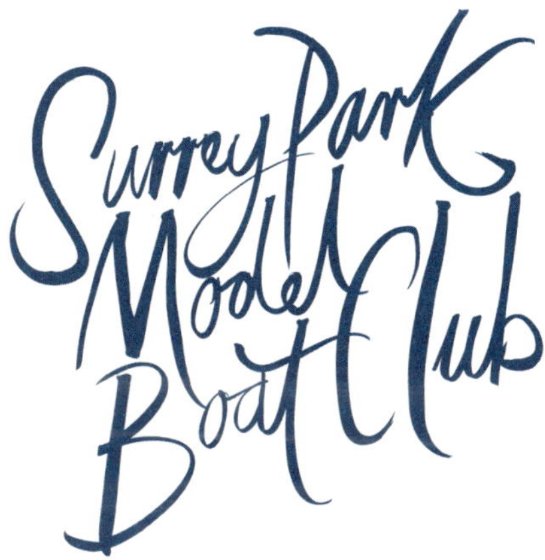

Formed twenty-seven years ago on Surrey Park Lake (also known as Surrey Dive) in Box Hill, Victoria, the Surrey Park Model Boat Club is the envy of many other model boat clubs, with a clubhouse on the lake and over 120 members.

Commodore Neil Spencer explains that it is a non-competitive club which caters for all forms of model-boating except internal combustion engines (no petrol engines), so you will find yachts, paddle steamers, steamships, tall ships, powerboats, fishing boats, naval boats, couta boats, Balmain bugs and just about any other type of boat you can think of.

The models are incredibly accurate, ranging in size from 15 centimetres to over 3 metres. Some people build models from kits and others build from scratch. Everyone has a great time and the club attracts a broad range of people: active and retired sailors, as well as people who just love building models. It's hard not to get caught up in the passion they all have for their boats. They fire up the barbecue and everyone sits down to a substantial lunch to discuss modelling and boats, boats, boats.

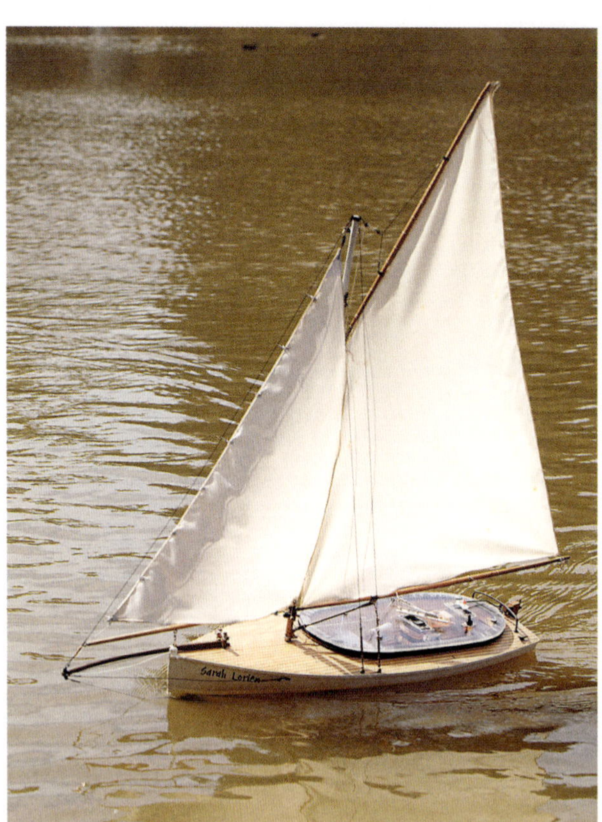

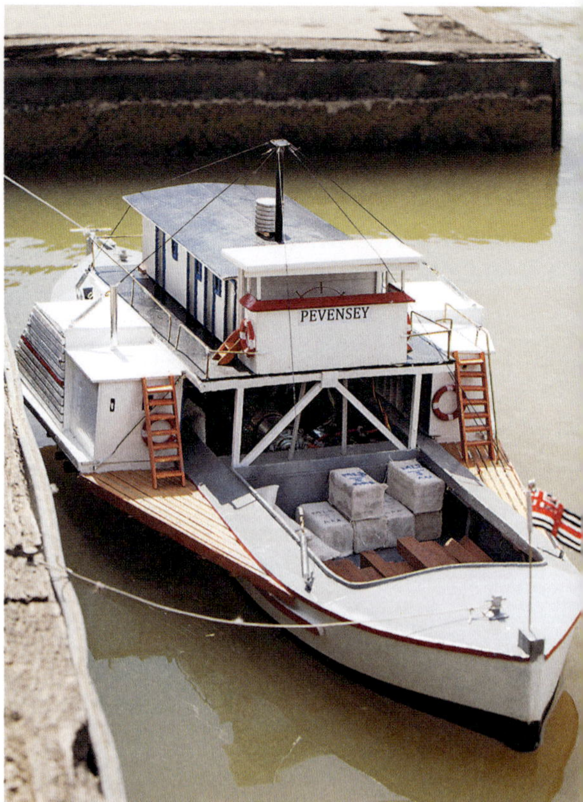

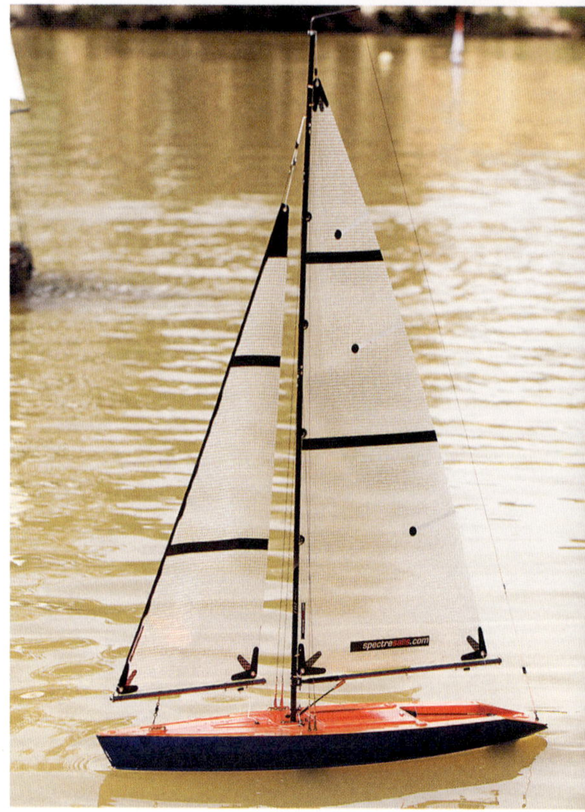

A selection of some of the many different types of boats the club members build and sail on the lake. There are model paddle steamers, yachts, couta boats, fishing boats and timber speedboats, just to name a few.

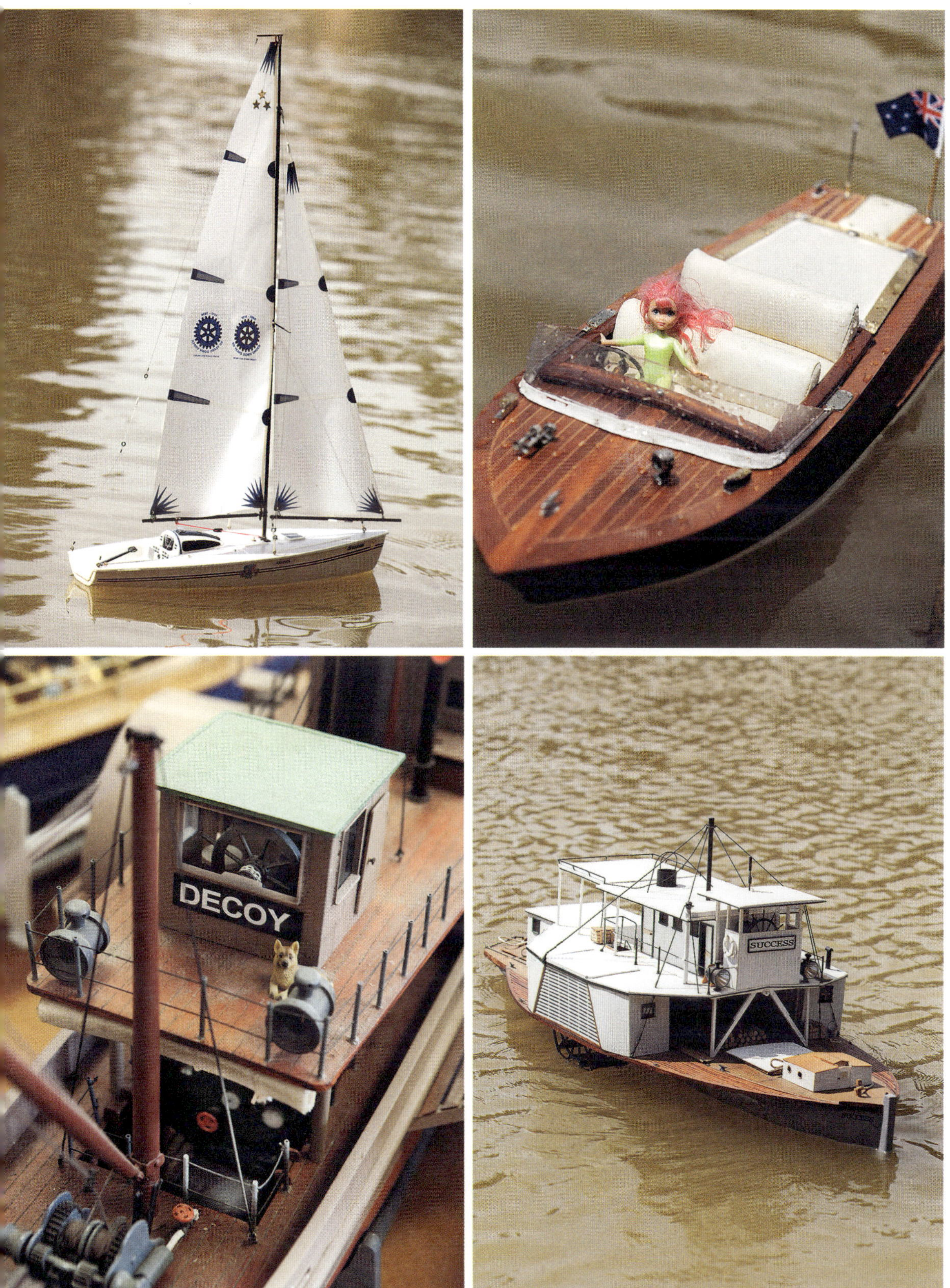
DECOY
SUCCESS

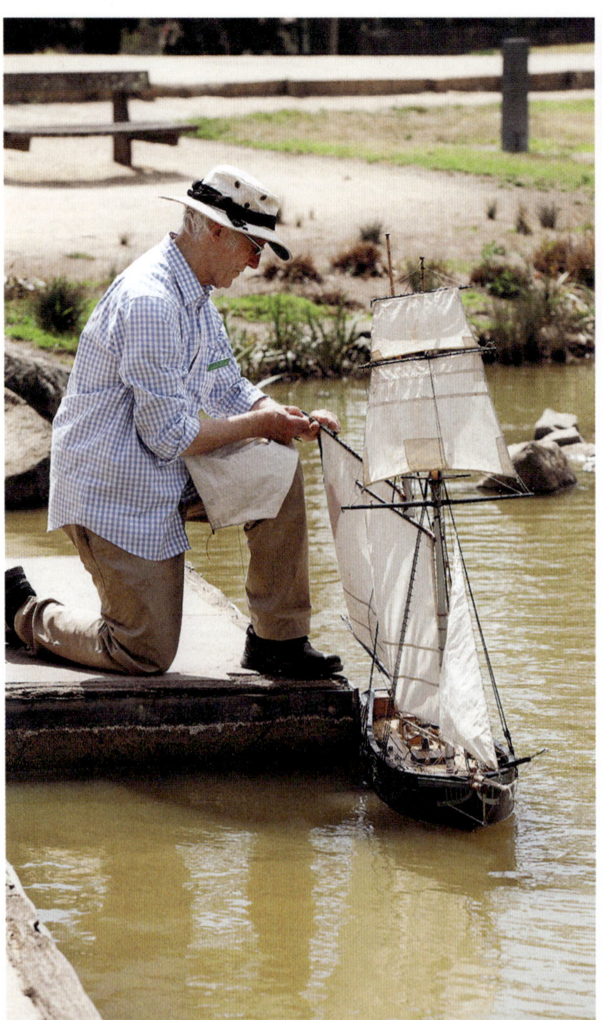

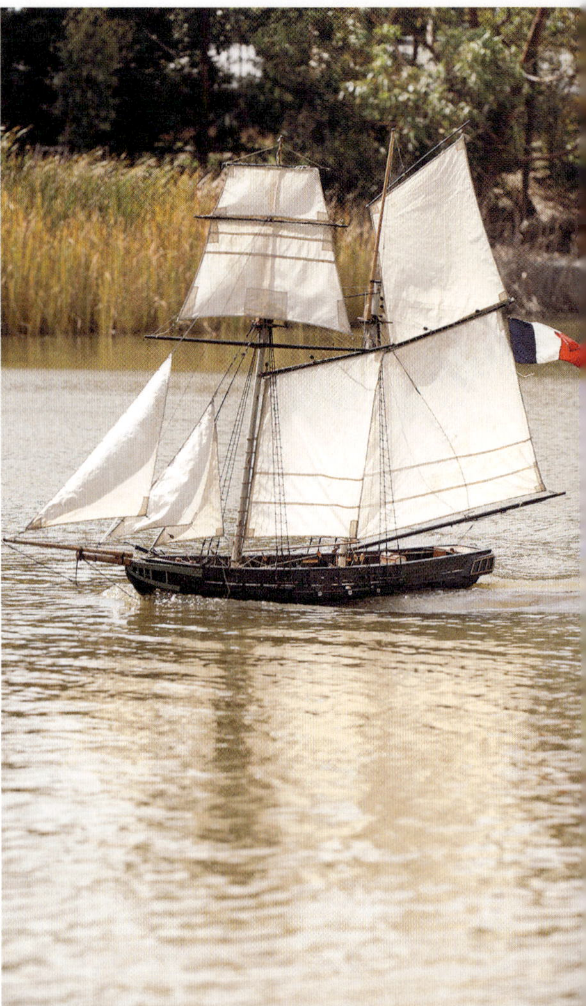

Claude Miller, a club member with *Toulonnaise*, a French, square-topsail schooner with copper-plated hull. She is faithful in every detail to the 1823 French Navy Schooner, *La Toulonnaise*, of which she is a replica, right down to her French flag.

OPPOSITE A contrast between the new and the old; modern model yachts made from hi-tech materials on the lake with Claude Miller's barque.

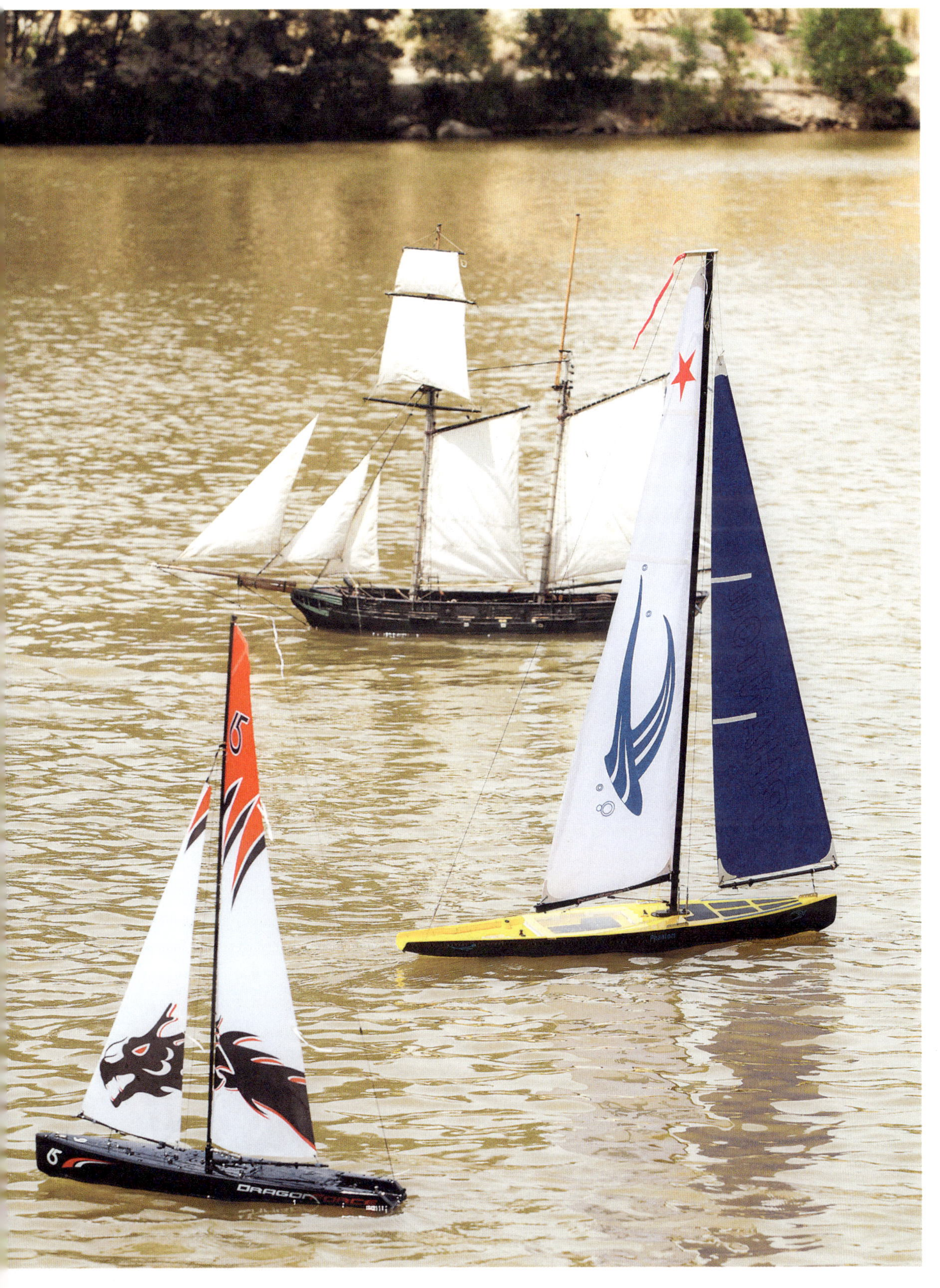
DRAGONFORCE

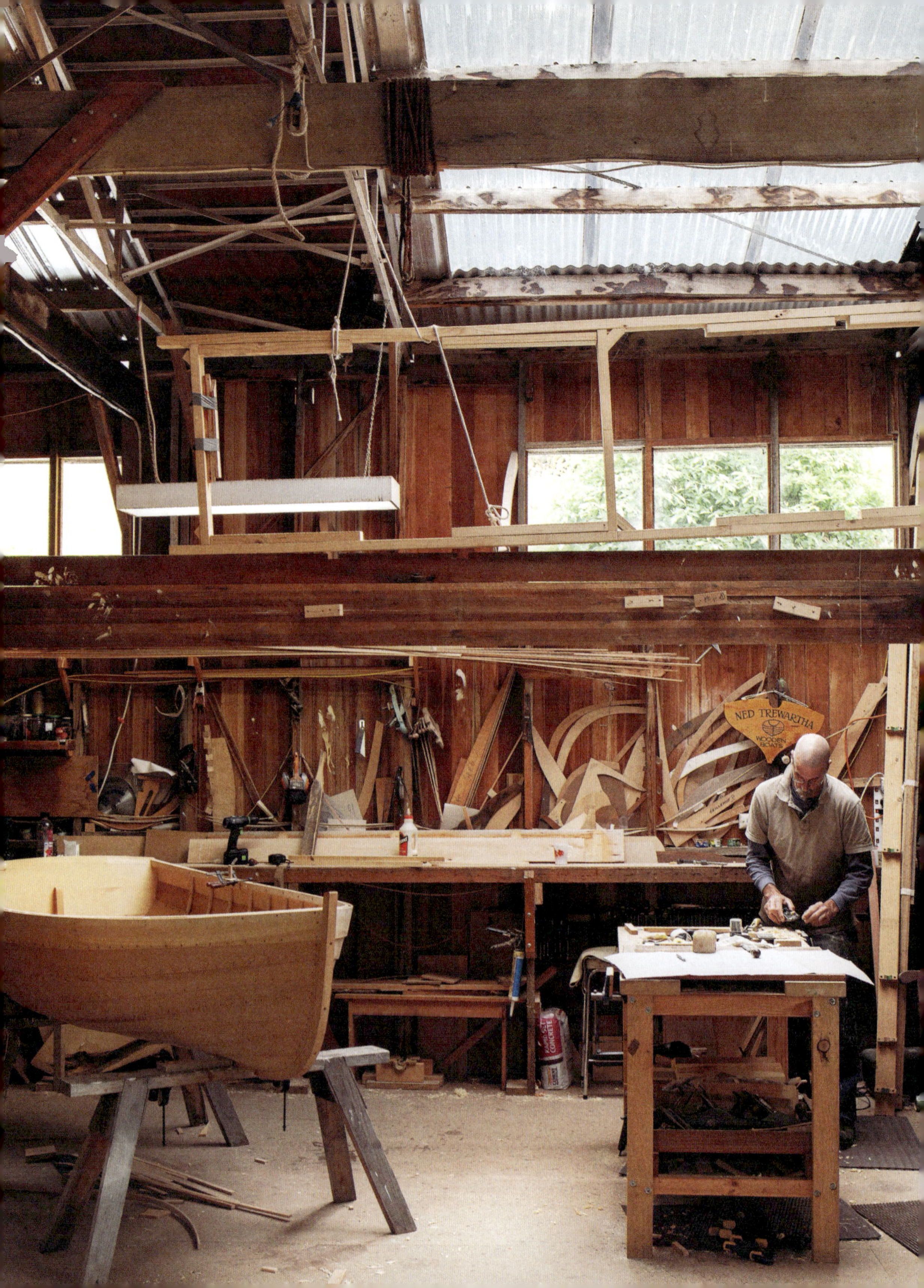
NED TREWARTHA
WOODEN BOATS

NED TREWARTHA

Ned Trewartha's boats have been described as having 'soul'; Ned's love of the materials he uses shines through in the quality and craftsmanship of his boats. Tasmania has some of the best boatbuilding timbers in the world: Huon pine, King Billy pine, Celery Top pine and myrtle. These timbers are beautiful to work with and last well in the water, and Ned puts them to great use in his boats. 'I feel incredibly privileged to work with such beautiful materials; timber is a finite resource but nothing gets wasted.'

Ned works from a shed in Gordon, Tasmania, crafting his beautiful boats. He has built a number of boats from plans by Iain Oughtred, the famous Scottish boat designer: they are classic boats with beautiful lines. Every detail is considered, down to the colour Ned paints his boats to how much timber is left exposed.

Ned has been building boats for about twenty years now. There is something about his boats that impels you to touch them – an impulse obviously shared by passers-by at the Australian Wooden Boat Festival in Hobart, whom I watched going up to Ned's boats to do just that.

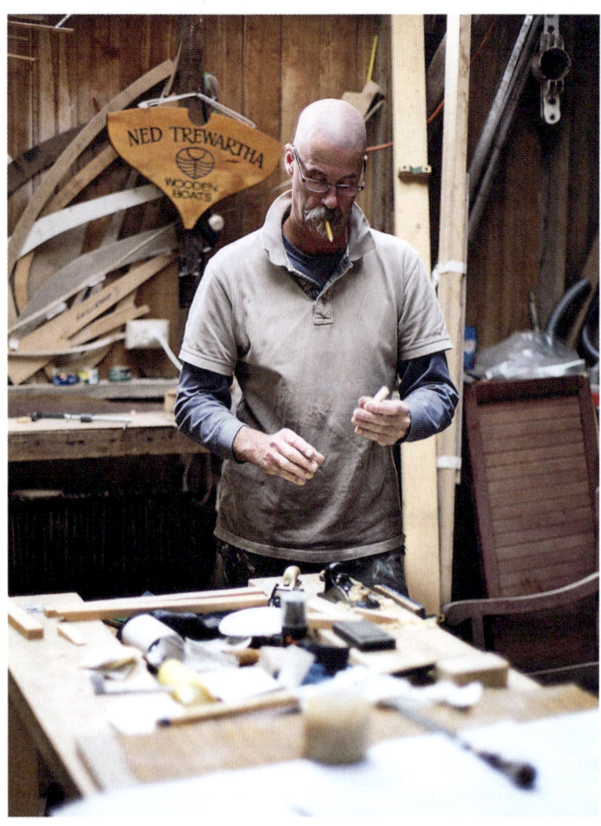

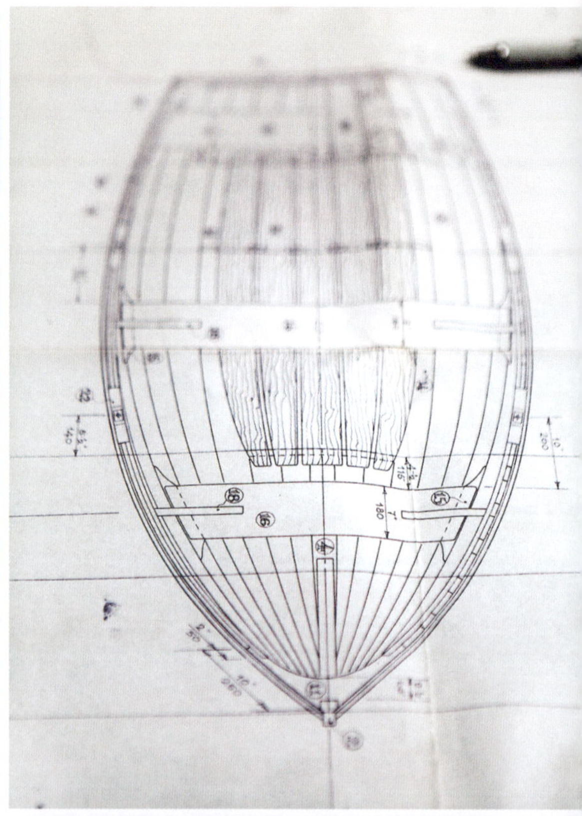

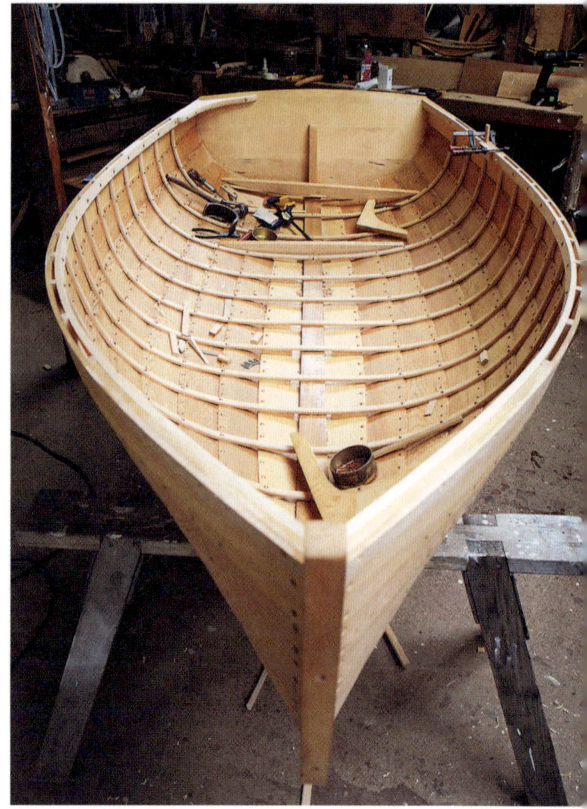

ABOVE, LEFT Ned hard at work in his shed.

ABOVE, RIGHT Ned often uses plans by acclaimed boat designer Iain Oughtred; you can see the detail that goes into one of his boats.

RIGHT Work in progress.

OPPOSITE, TOP Ned's shed, which has grown organically with the business. You can see a completed boat ready to go to its new owner.

OPPOSITE, BOTTOM RIGHT Patterns and templates for various boat parts in a corner of Ned's shed.

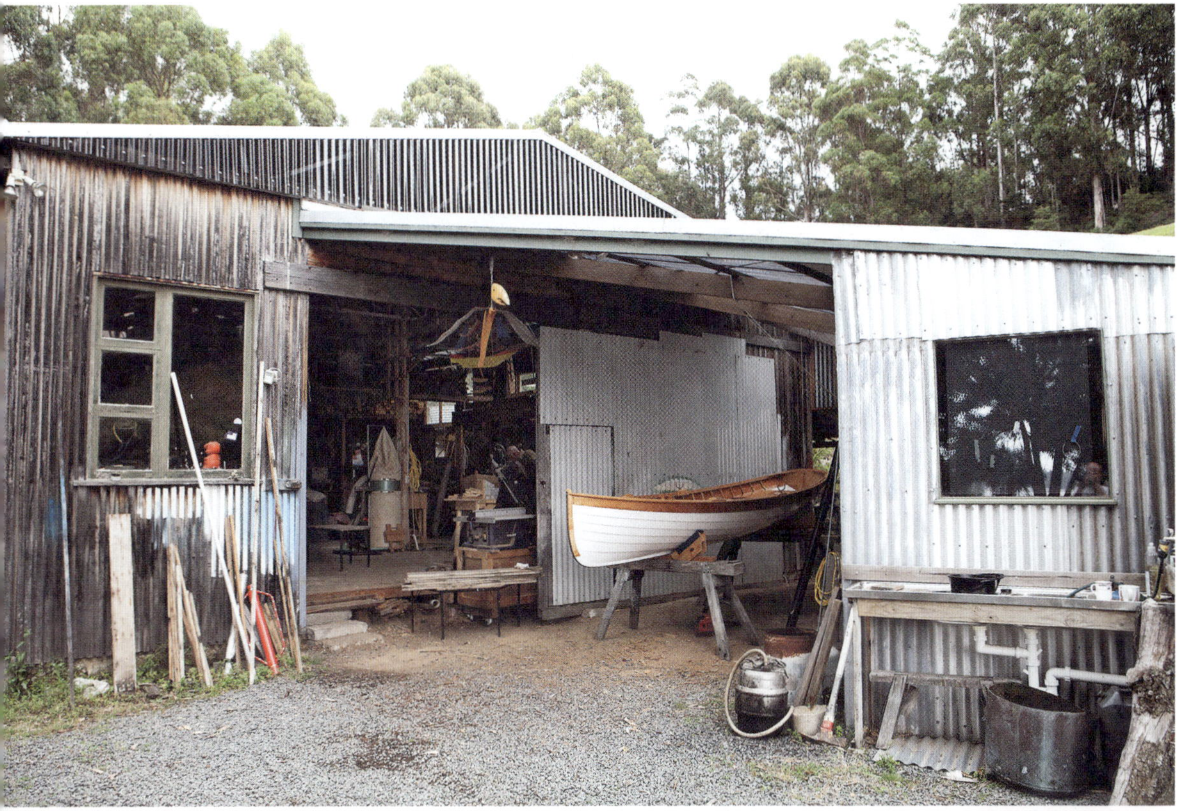

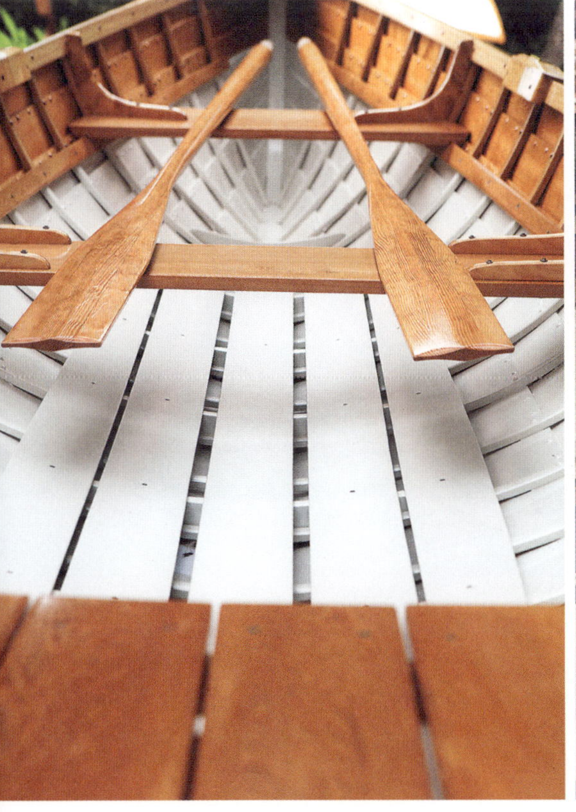

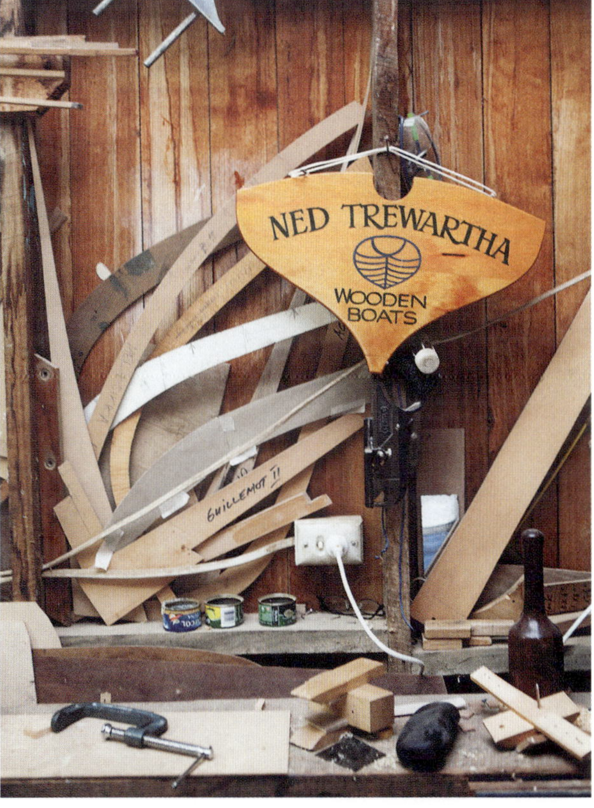
NED TREWARTHA
WOODEN BOATS
GUILLEMOT II

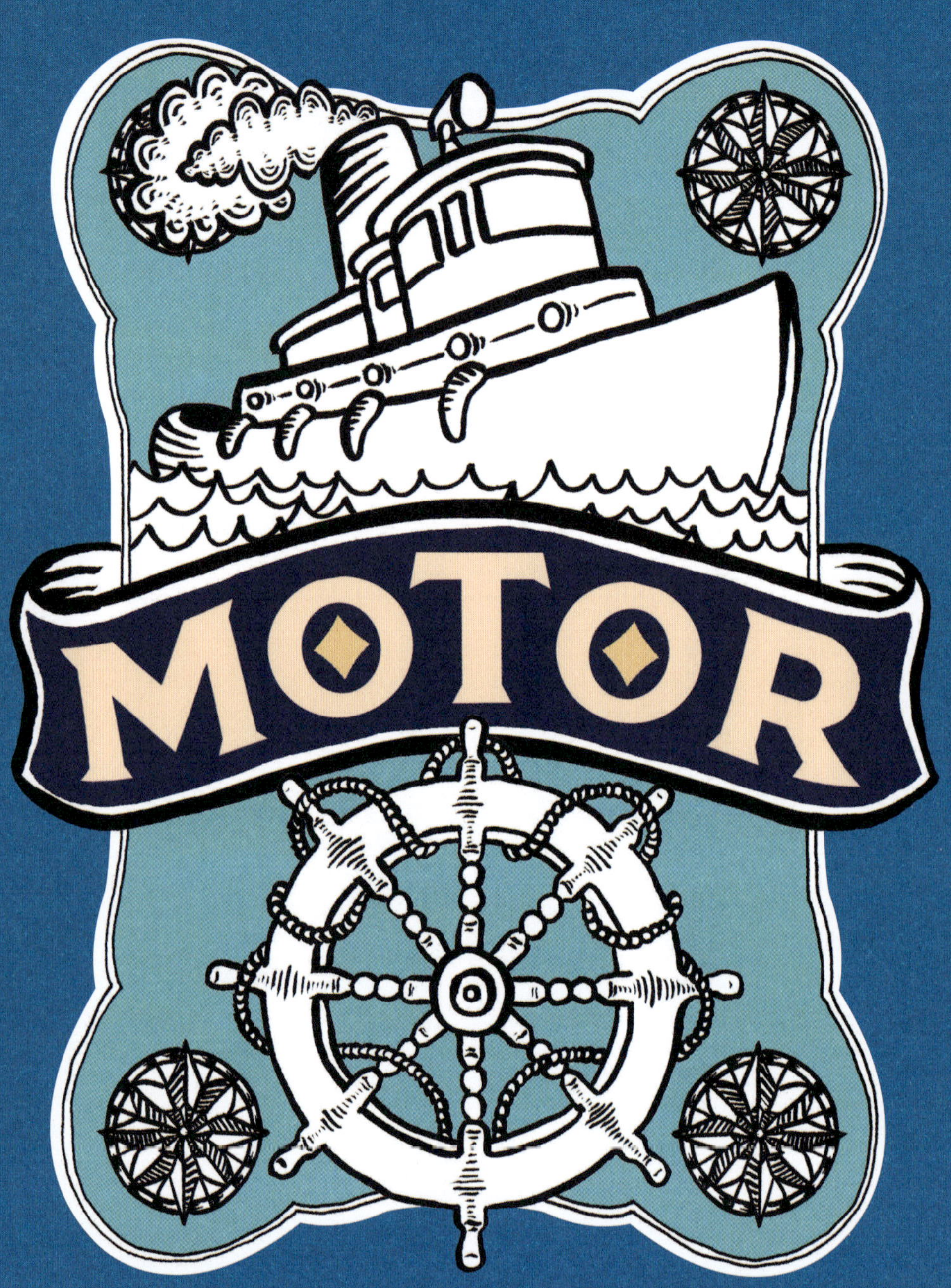
MOTOR

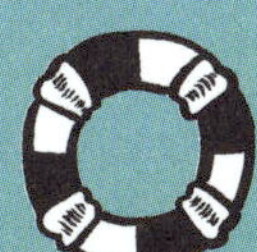

THE ENGINE STARTS AND WE ARE OFF. MODERN ENGINES HAVE TRANSFORMED THE BOAT. NO LONGER DO WE NEED TO WAIT FOR WIND, HAVE A CREW OF ROWERS OR BUILD UP ENOUGH STEAM TO MAKE A JOURNEY. FOR THOSE WHO FEEL THE NEED FOR SPEED IN THEIR LIFE THERE IS NOW THE SPEEDBOAT. OR PERHAPS YOU PREFER A FERRY RIDE ACROSS THE HARBOUR. THE ENGINE HAS TRANSFORMED THE WAY WE USE BOATS.

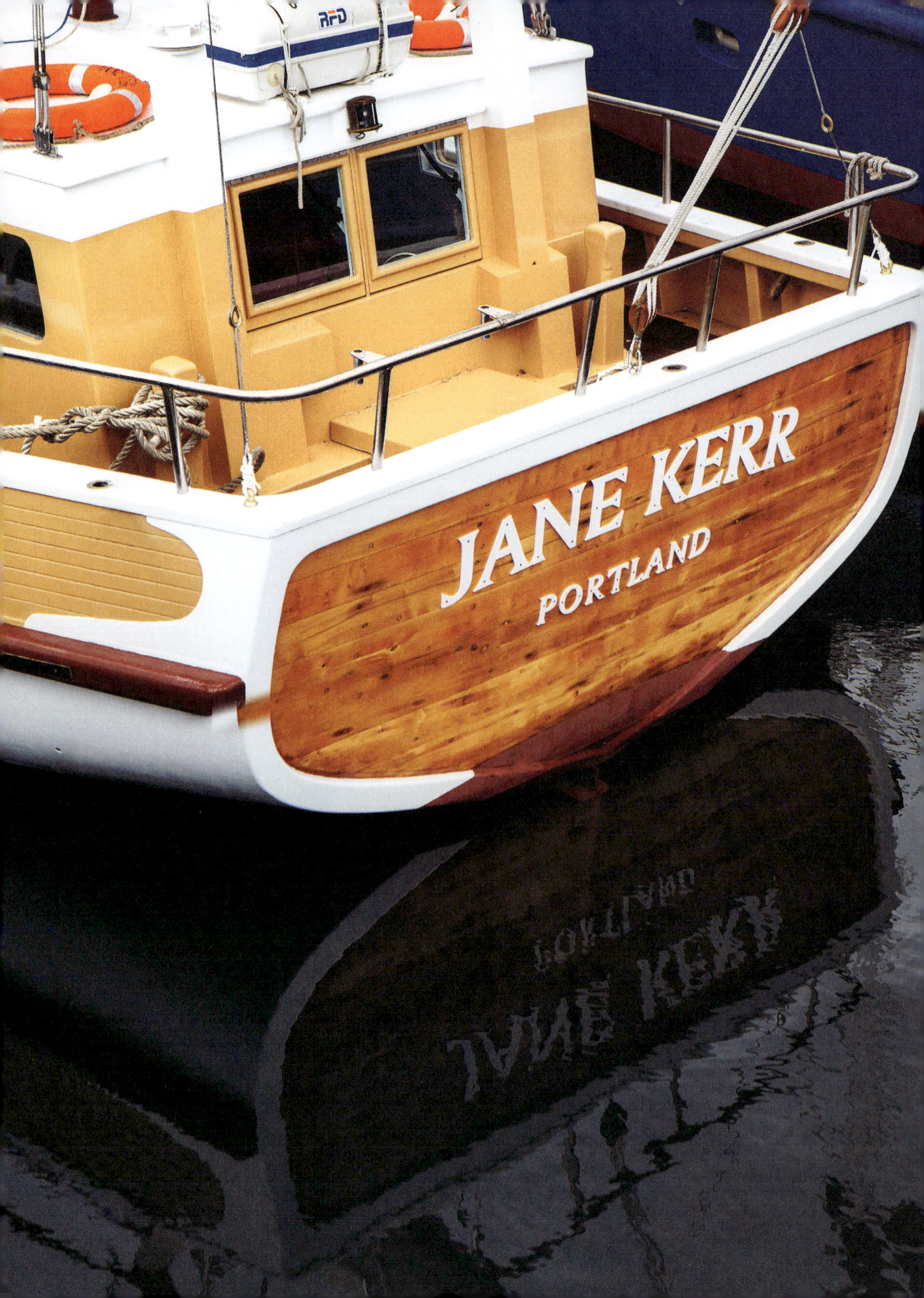
RFD
JANE KERR
PORTLAND

Jane Kerr

Jane Kerr, a purpose-built 50-foot Huon pine auxiliary ketch was commissioned by Garry Kerr and named after his daughter. Garry was a cray fisherman for over forty years on various boats out of Portland, Victoria, working as far afield as Bass Strait and the west coast of Tasmania. He is a boating legend who has owned quite a few boats over the years.

Jane Kerr was built by Port Fairy boatbuilder Gary Stewart from 2-inch-thick boards of Huon pine, and her framing and keel are made from West Australian karri. Launched in 1981, she was built to last as she had to be sturdy enough to tackle the rough seas of Bass Strait. She has a Gardner 6LXB engine, but is also ketch-rigged, with a jib, main and mizzen sails, so although she is here in the Motor chapter, she is technically a sailing fishing boat.

She was bought by Tim Phillips from the Wooden Boatshop, a specialist wooden boatbuilder in Sorrento, south of Melbourne, Victoria. He is especially passionate about working wooden boats, and also owns the beautiful *Storm Bay* on pages 26–33. Tim has given her a major overhaul and completely restored her to her original glory.

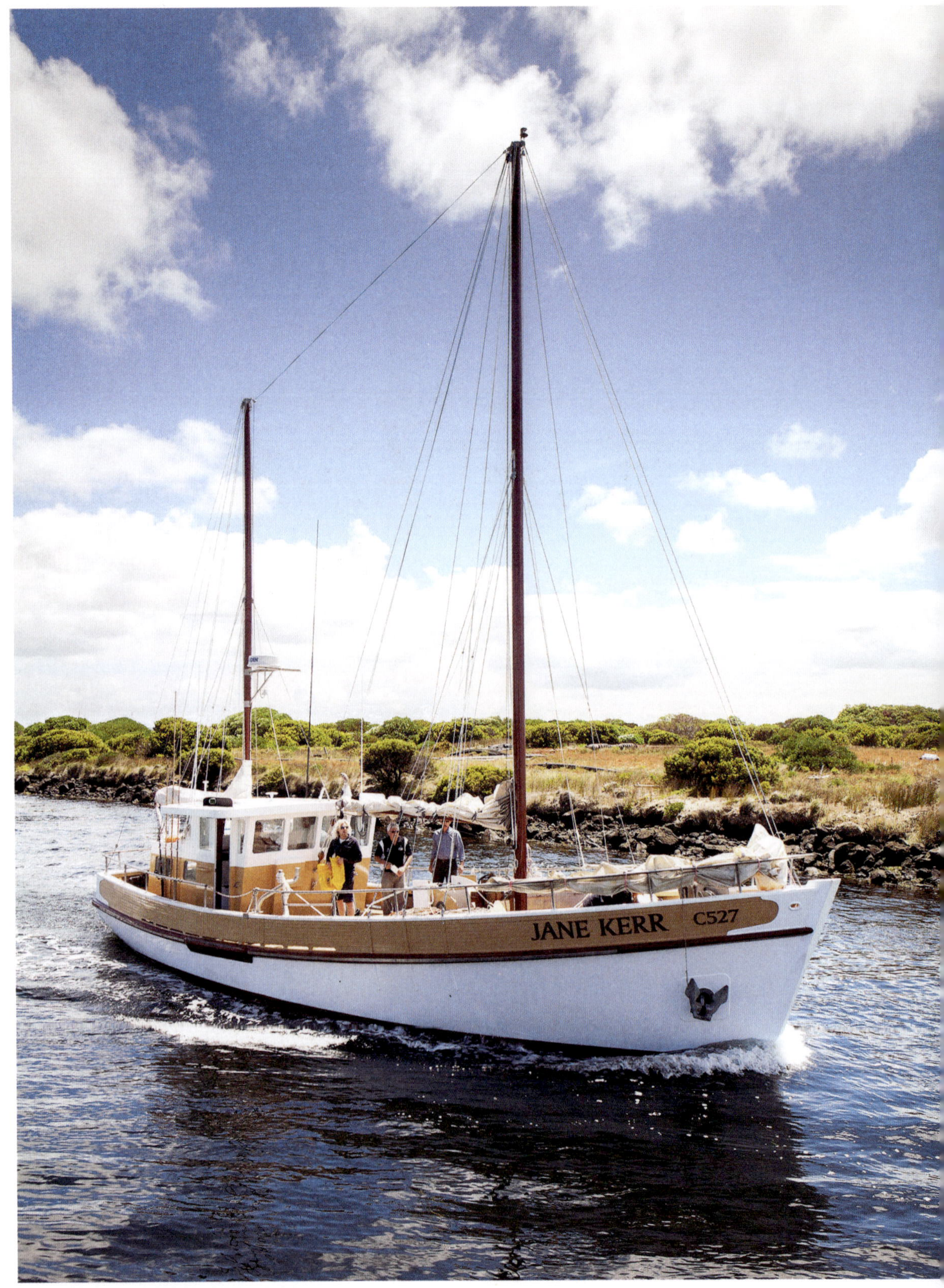

JANE KERR
C527

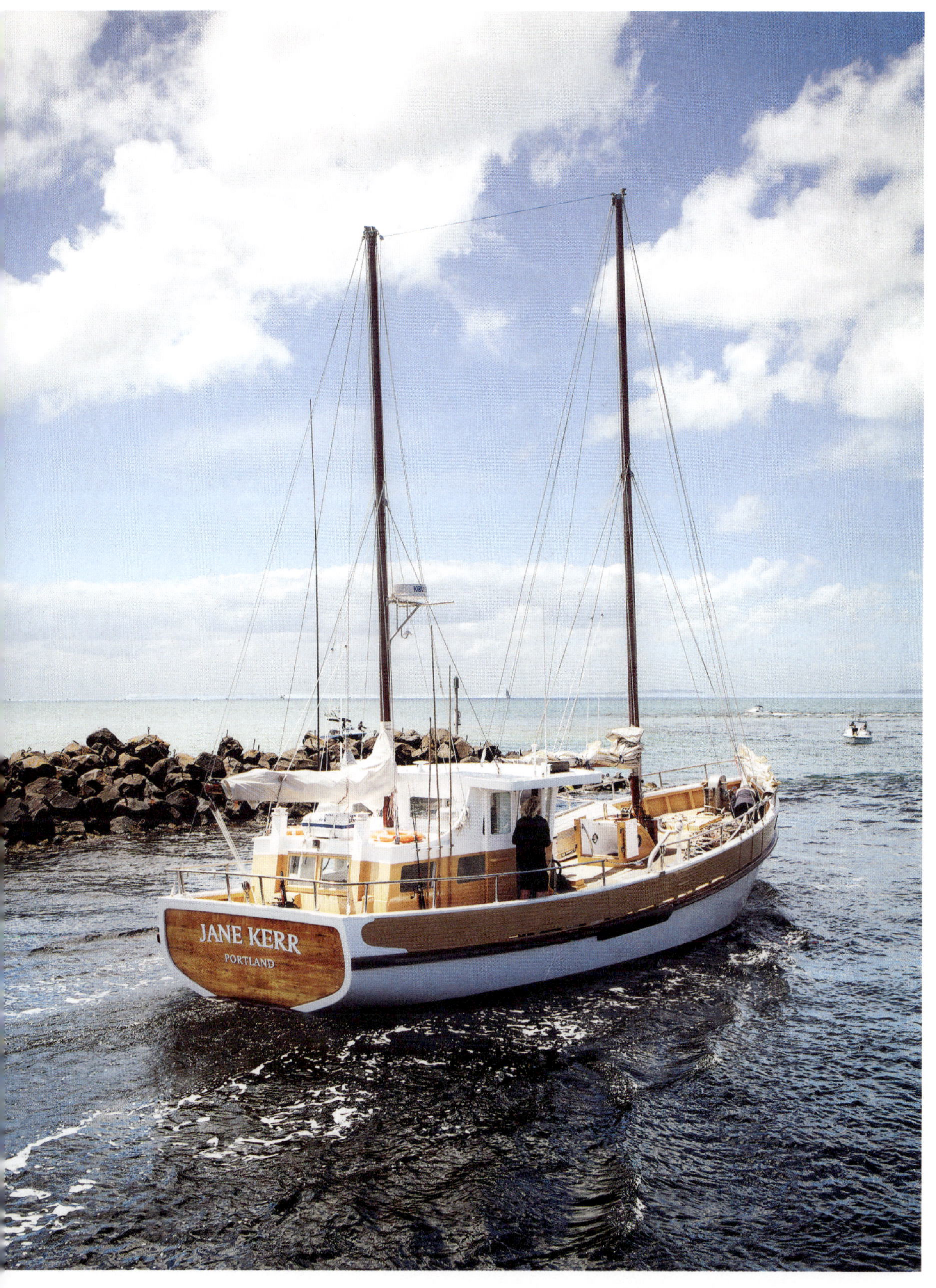
JANE KERR
PORTLAND

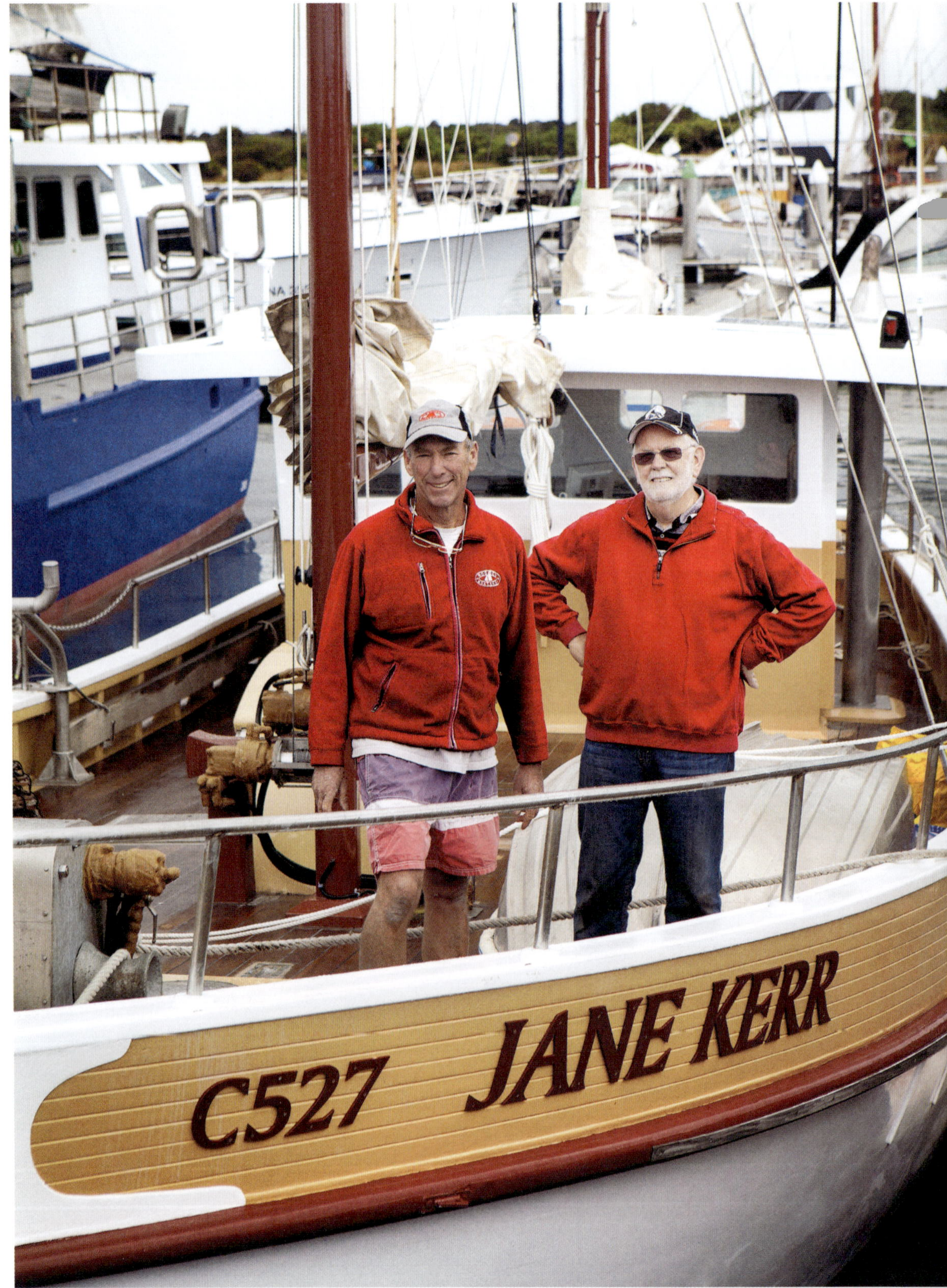
C527
JANE KERR

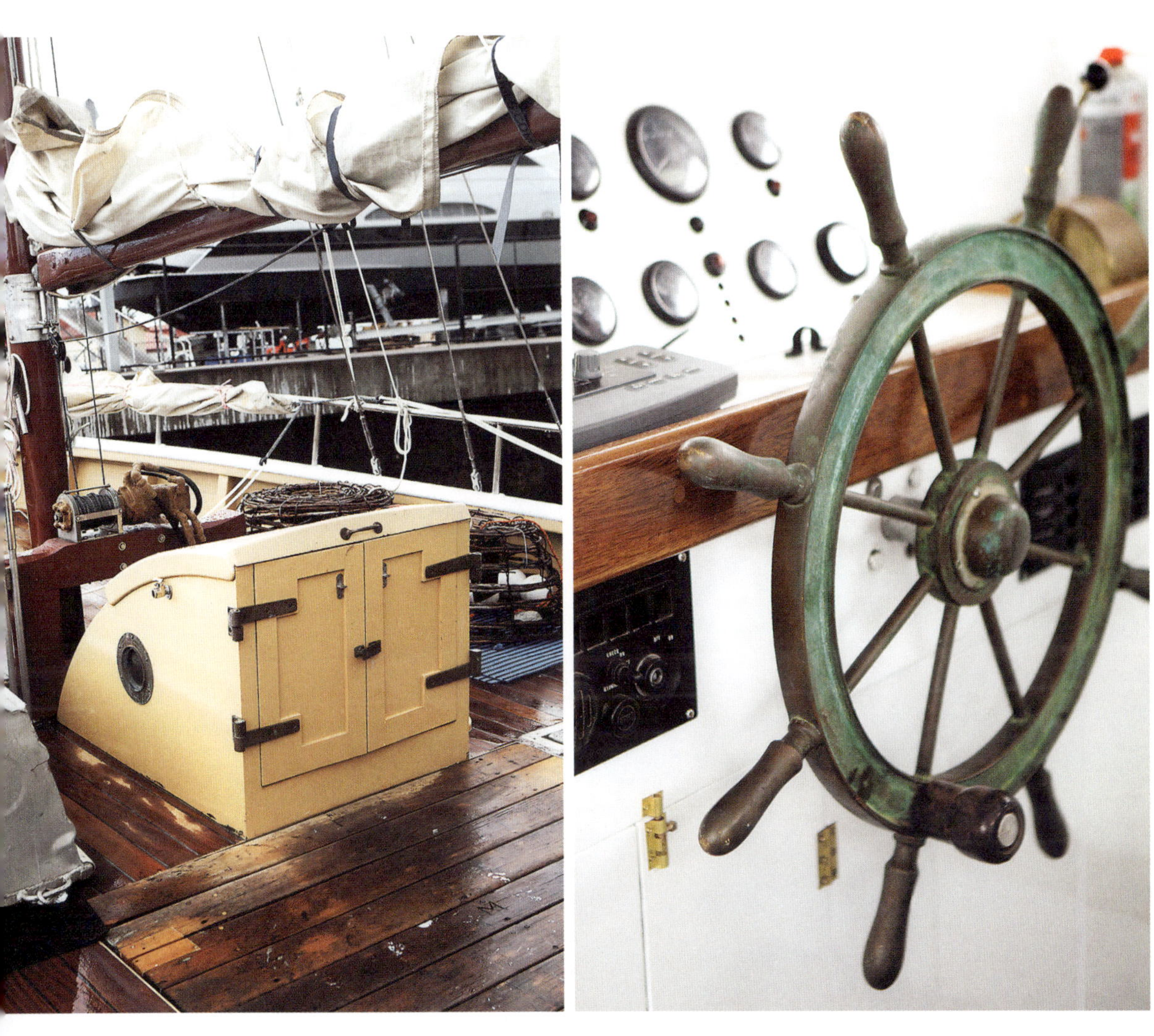

OPPOSITE Garry Kerr (at right), the original owner of *Jane Kerr*, with Tim Phillips, her current owner.

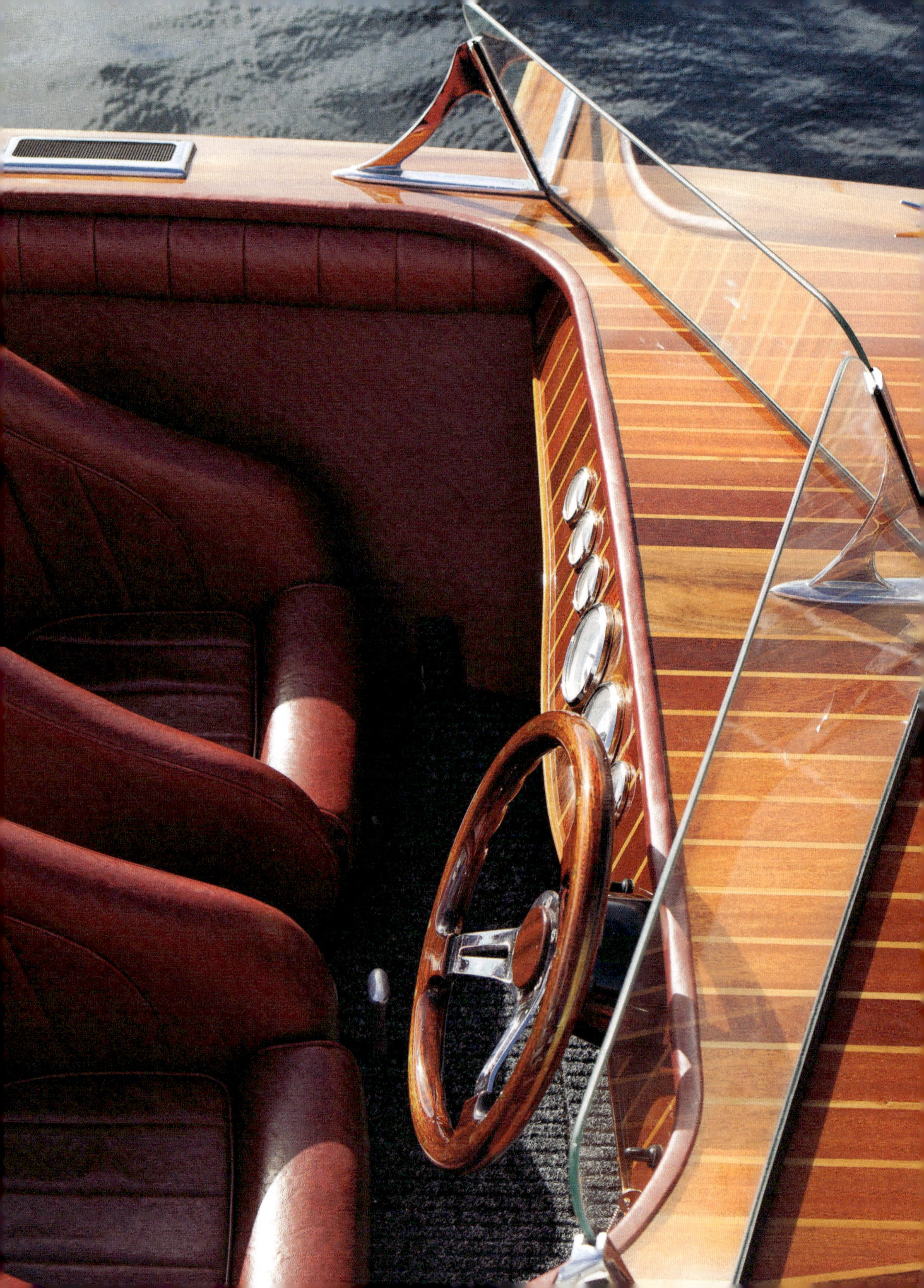

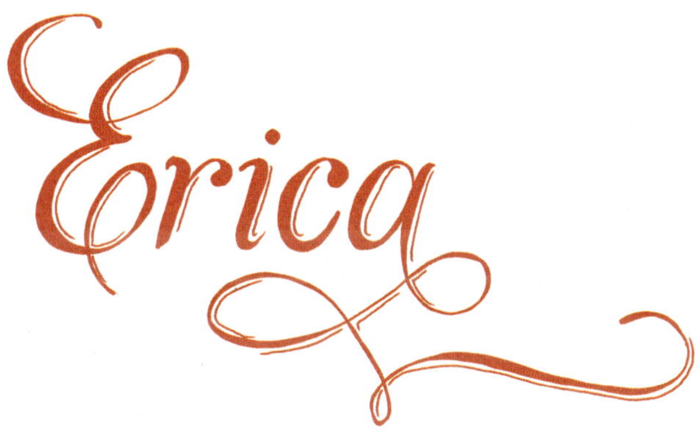

There is something deeply pleasing about the polished mahogany of a boat like *Erica*. She sits gleaming in the sun with her glassy finish and polished metal parts, a speed-lover's dream.

Craig Strike of Craig Strike Classic Runabouts in South Hobart spent thousands of hours building *Erica*, a mahogany, cold-molded powerboat, based on the designs of runabouts from the 1940s and 1950s. *Erica* is a Riviera, built to a design by Glen-L, who are based in the United States and have been supplying boat plans and kits for over sixty years. She is influenced by iconic American designs such as Chris Craft, Gar Wood, Hacker-Craft and Century.

Erica is 20 feet 4 inches long and powered by a 350 ci (cubic inch) Chevrolet engine. Since being photographed she has been sold to a happy customer and is now turning heads on the waterways around Melbourne.

Every detail of *Erica* is beautiful, from her leather seats and timber wheel to her gleaming dials and polished timber exterior.

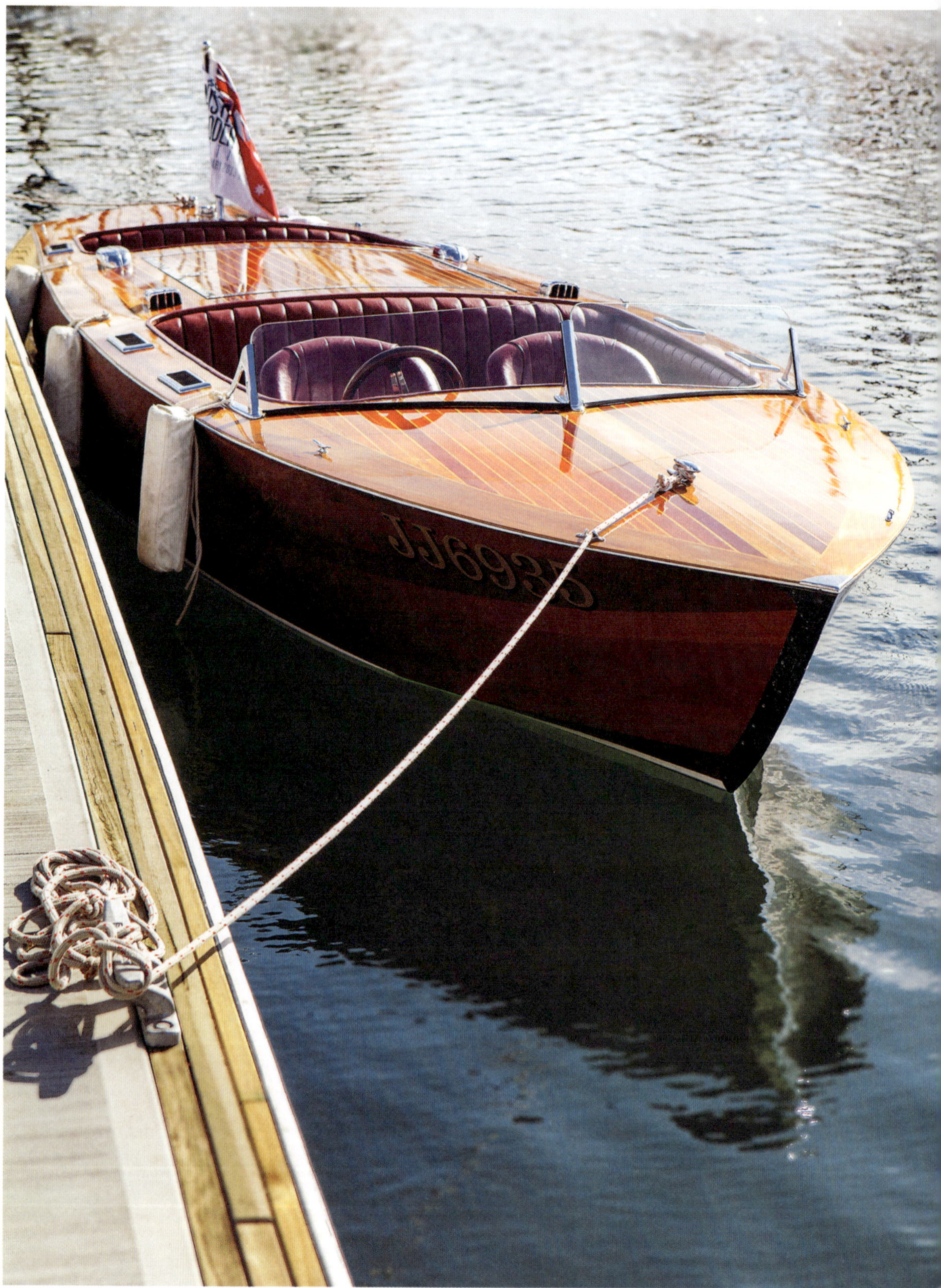
JJ6935

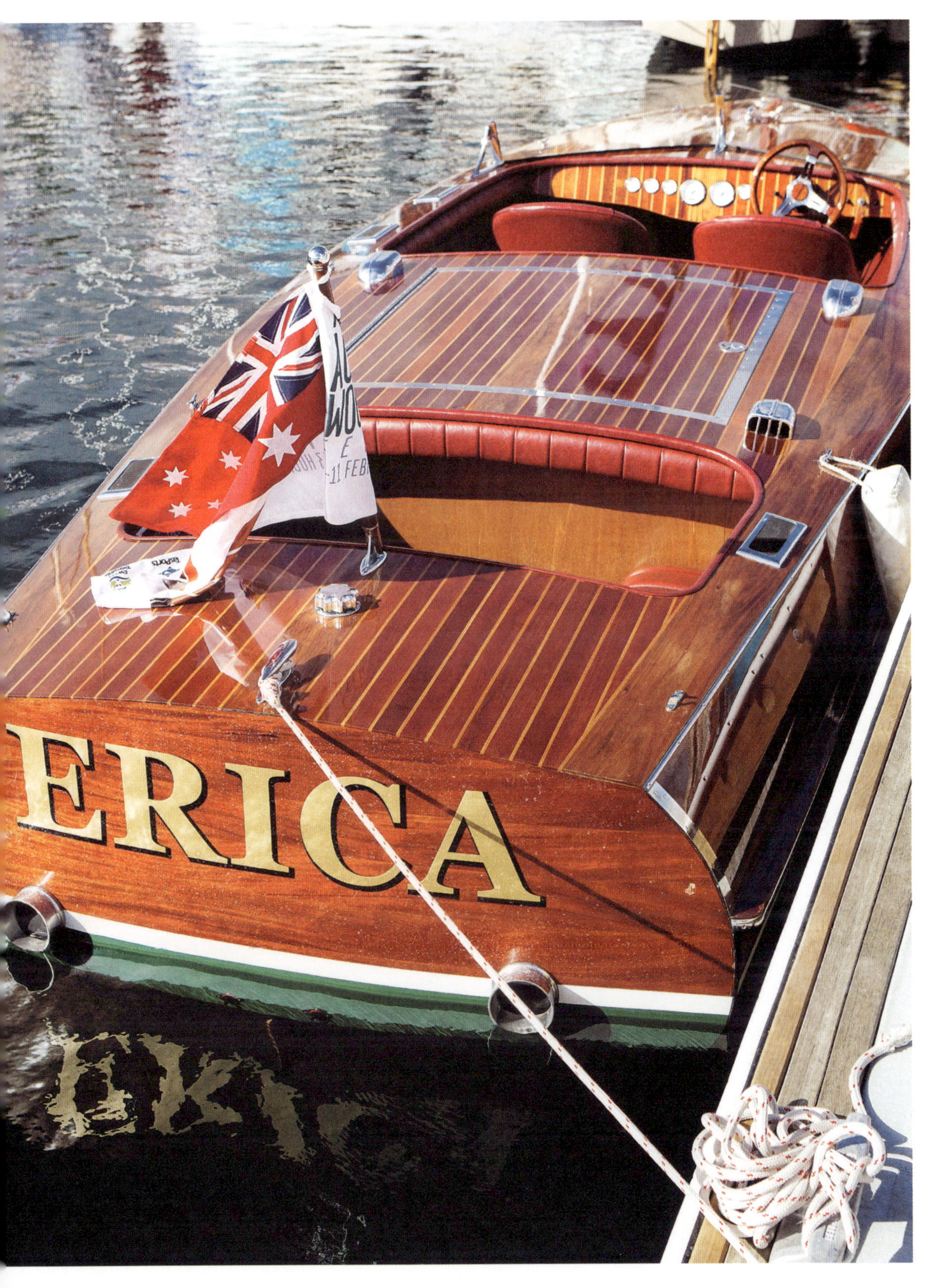
ERICA

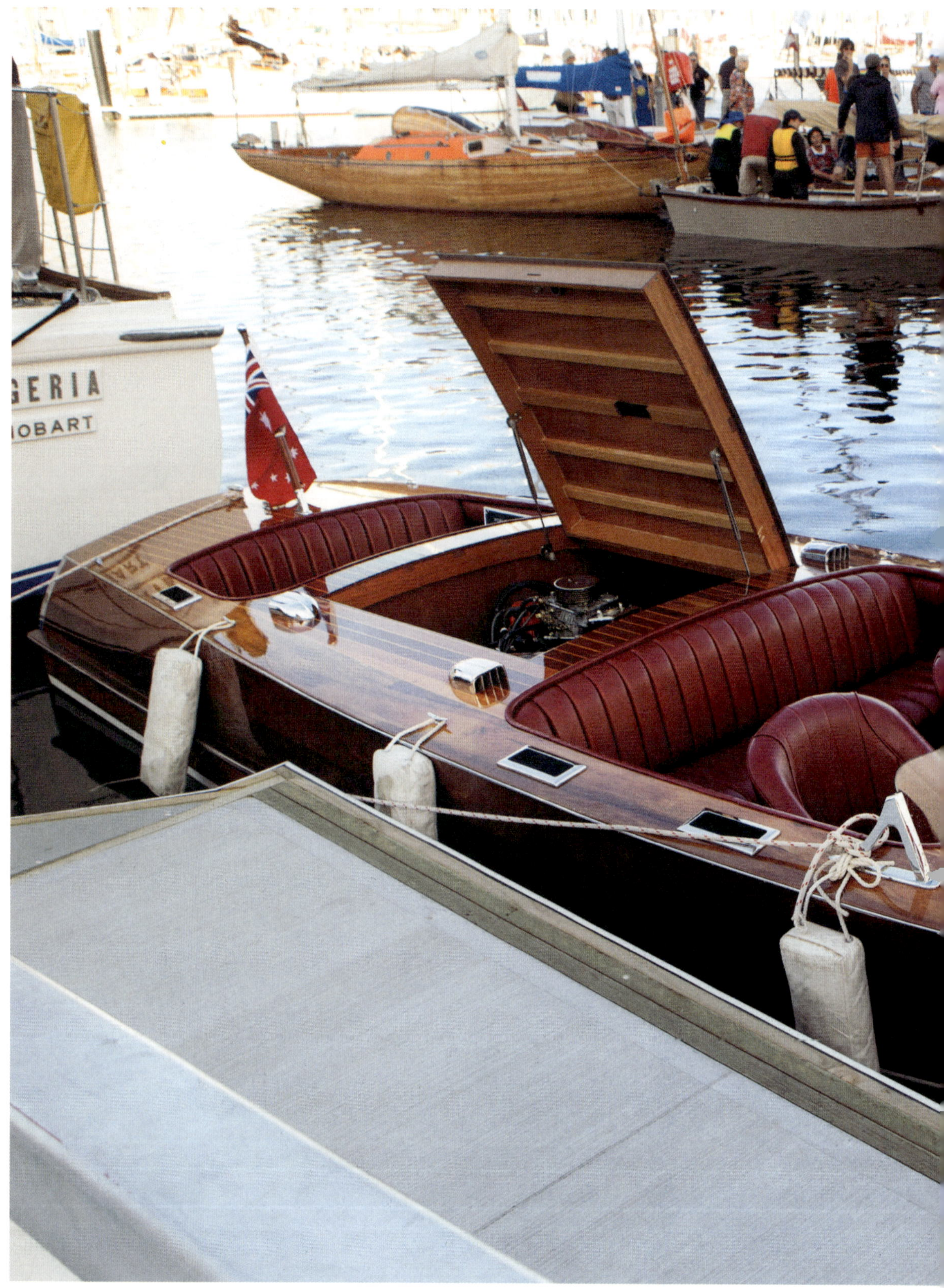
GERIA
HOBART

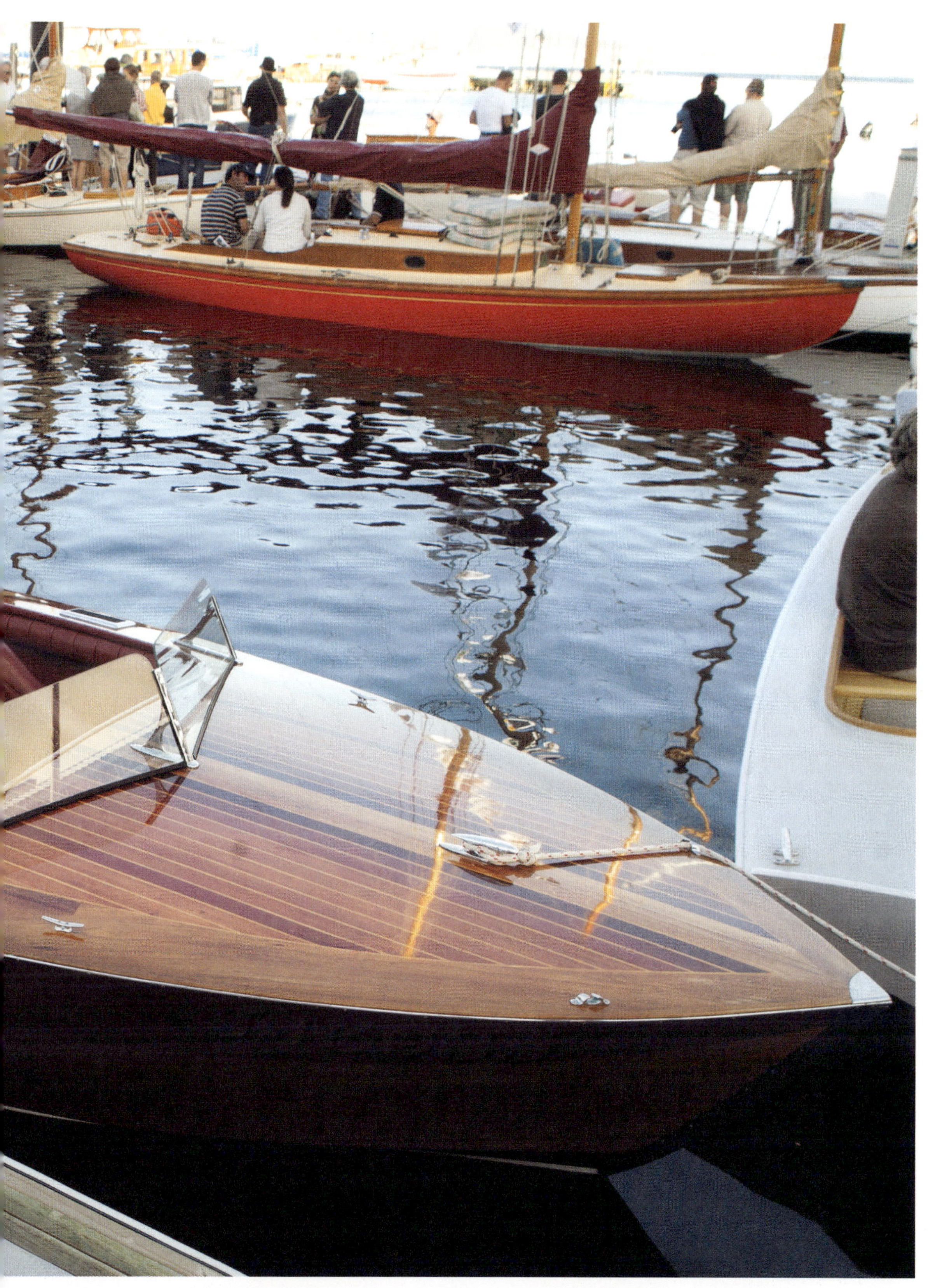

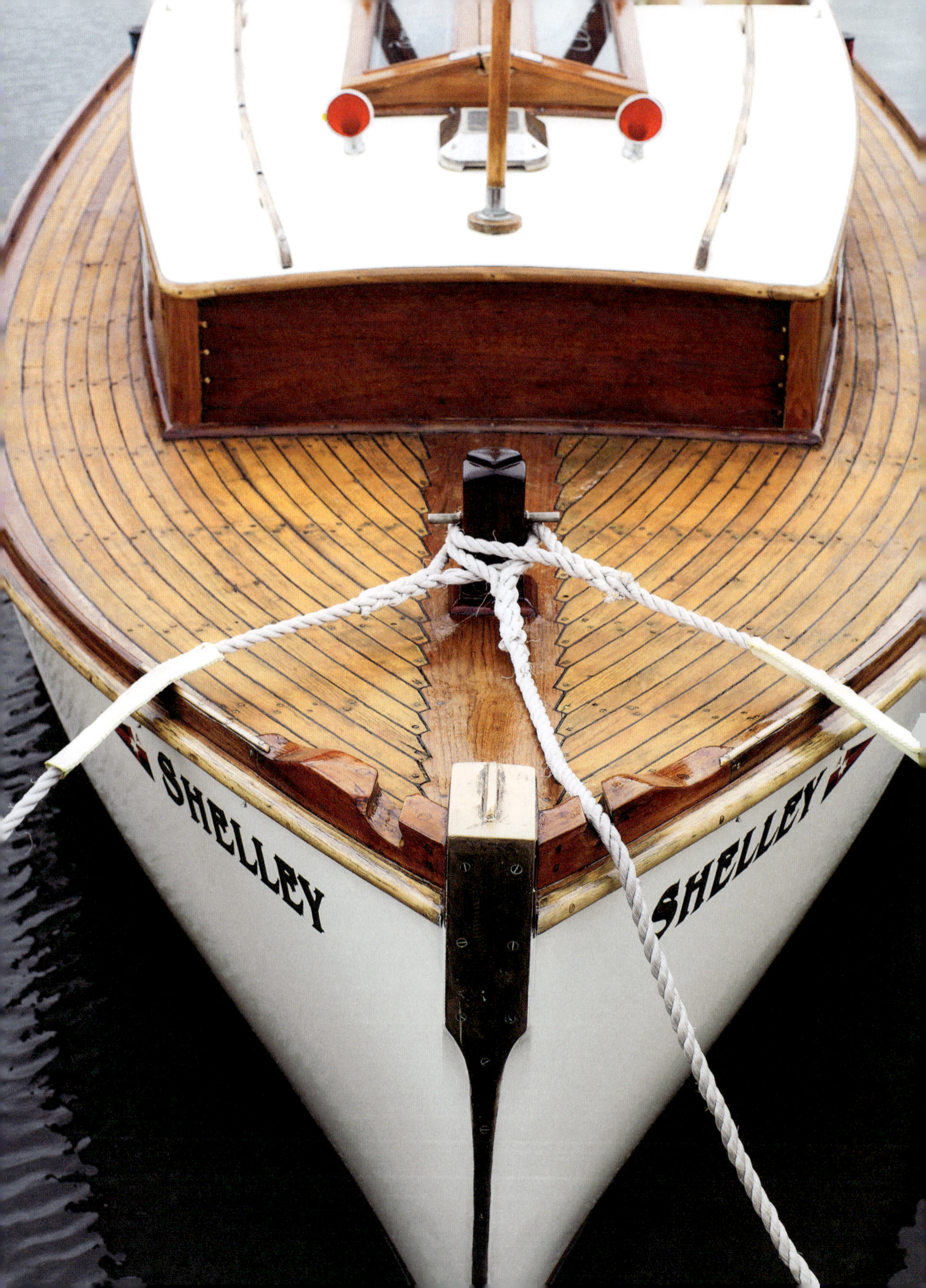
SHELLEY
SHELLEY

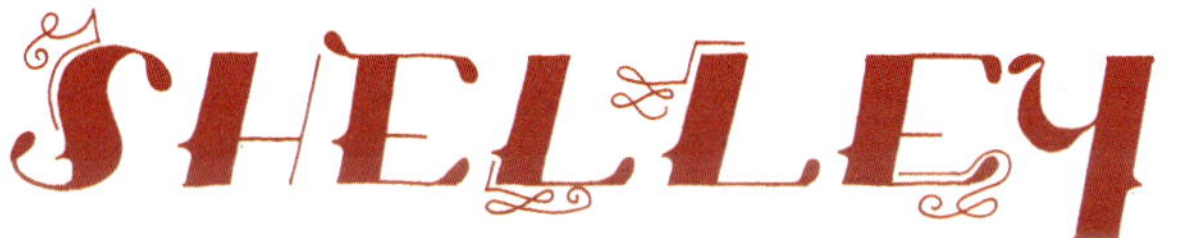

Shelley was built in 1968 by Robert Blunt, who named the boat after his daughter. She is 20 feet long, her beam is 7 feet 6 inches, and her draught is 2 feet, 6 inches. The Blunts also built Williamstown's first ever motorboat, *Ariel*.

This smart motorboat is now owned by Robert's son, Greg Blunt (see C. Blunt Boatbuilder, pages 88–97), who uses it as a runabout. 'She's beautiful, isn't she?' says Greg, with a wink. You can often see him whizzing around Williamstown, Victoria, in *Shelley*.

Shelley has a 22-horsepower Petter diesel engine and is made of Huon pine and mahogany. When not in use, she spends her life moored at the Blunts' jetty, not far from where she was built.

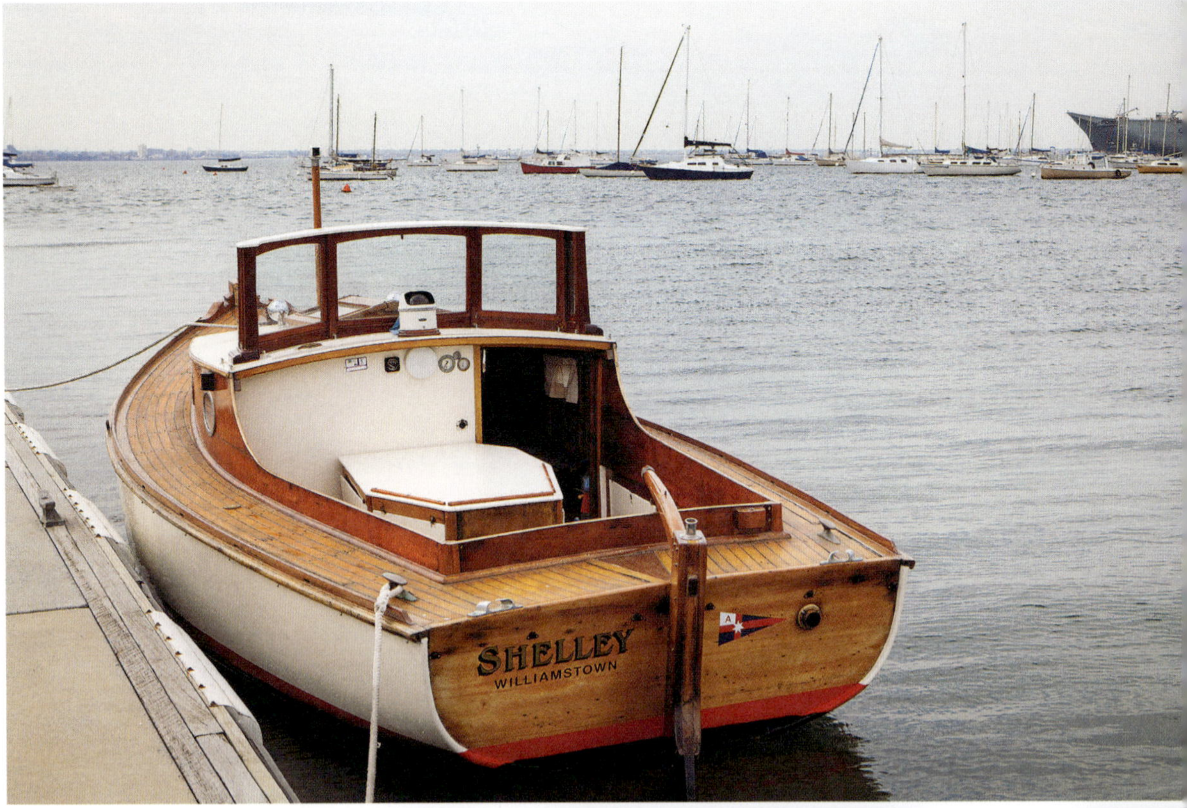
SHELLEY
WILLIAMSTOWN

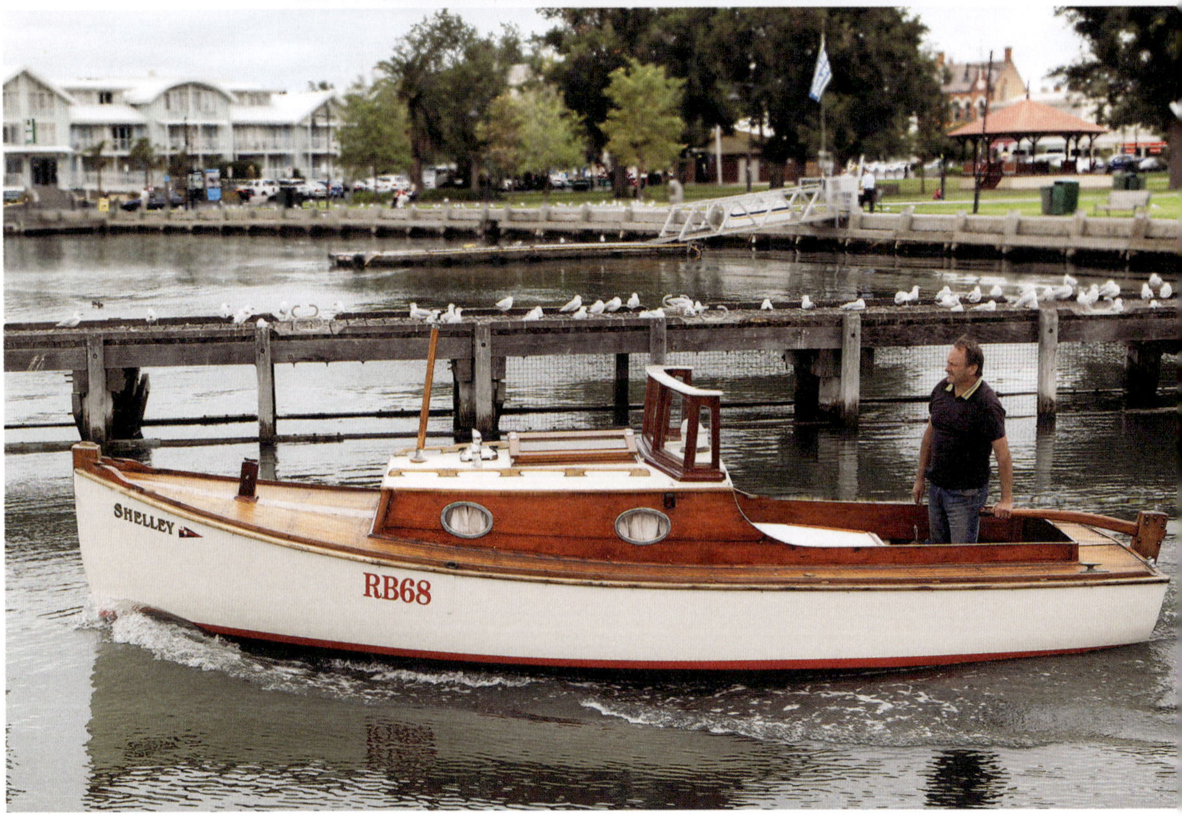
SHELLEY
RB68

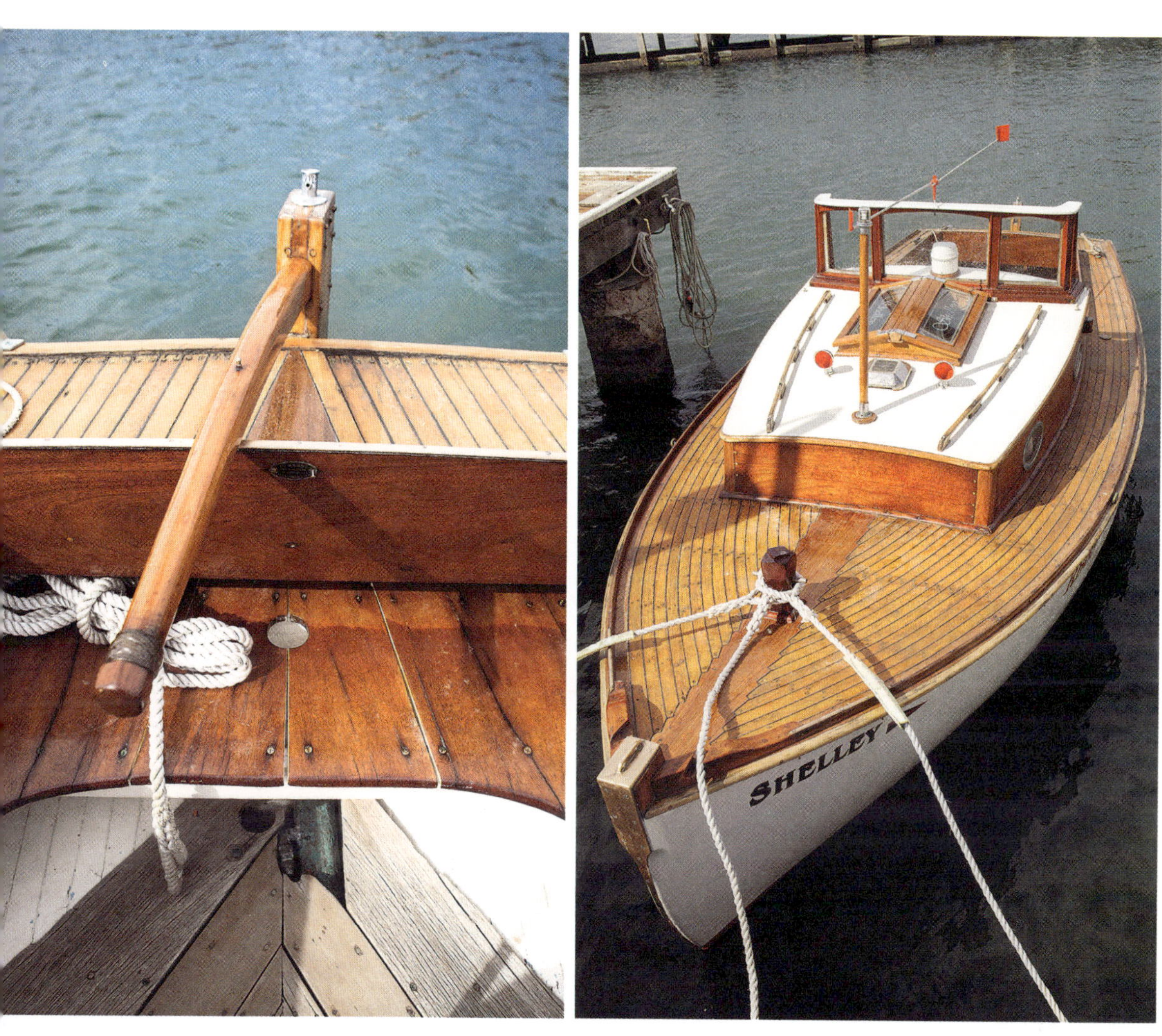

Built from Huon pine and mahogany, *Shelley* is a real beauty. She has tiller-steering and a 22-horsepower Petter diesel engine. Greg has just had her name repainted in gold leaf, as befits such a beautiful vintage craft.

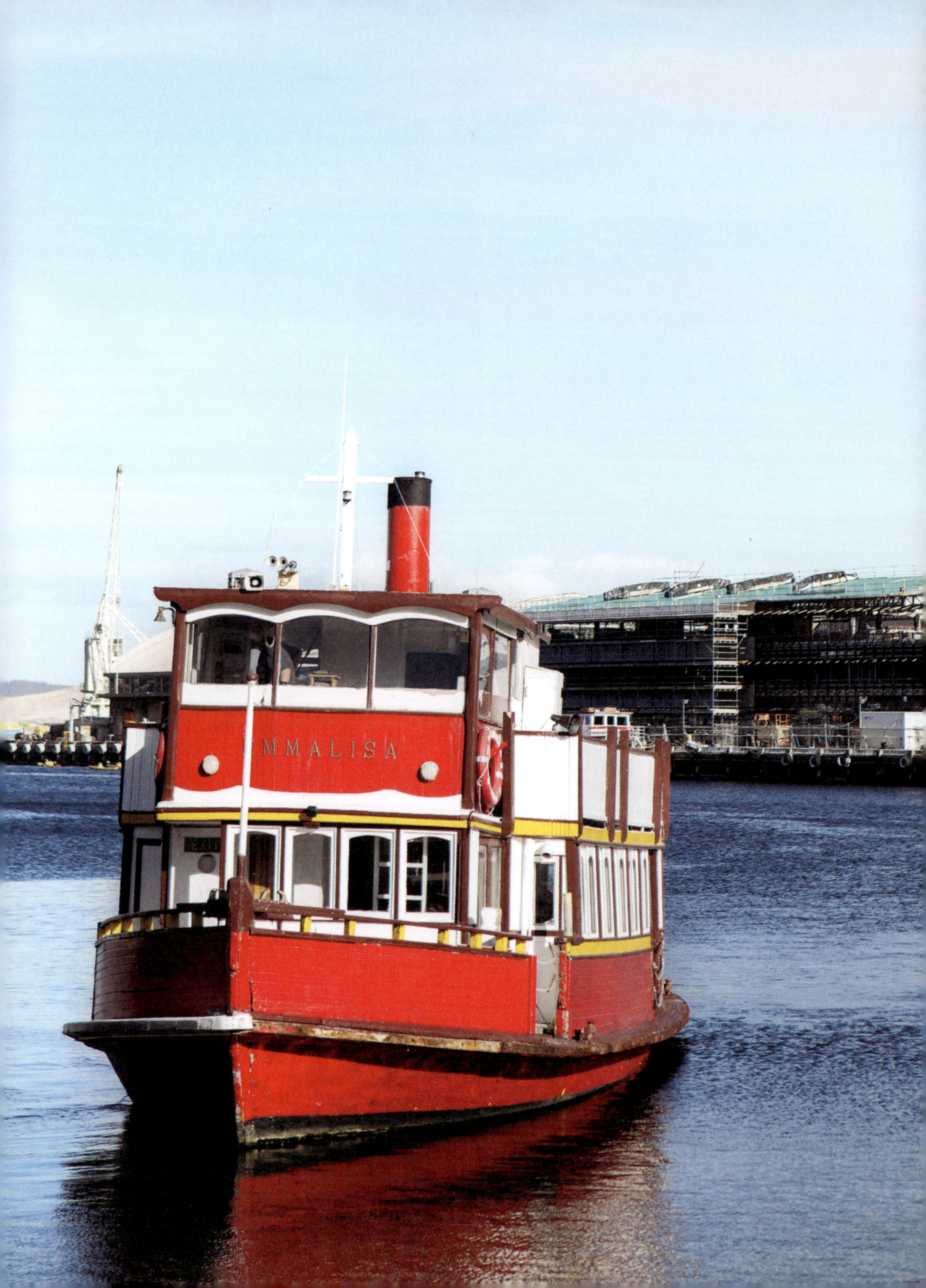
EMMALISA

M.V. Emmalisa

M.V. Emmalisa may look like a charming old ferry, but she started out life being commissioned by the Royal Australian Air Force in 1942, at the height of World War II, for the purpose of carrying bombs out to Catalina flying boats on Lake Macquarie for bombing raids.

After the war she spent time on the Hawkesbury River, before being converted in 1952 to a ferry to operate in Sydney Harbour, where she worked for many years before arriving in Hobart in 1981. She now does charter cruises around the Derwent and has become part of the landscape in the historic Port of Hobart.

She is 50.9 feet long, her beam is 16 feet, and her draught is 5 feet. She weighs 33 tons, and travels at a speed of 8 knots, and she is very popular with both adults and children.

M.V Emmalisa is moored in the middle of the Port of Hobart and has become part of the visual landscape. Her cheery red paint and shrill whistle mean you can't help but notice her.

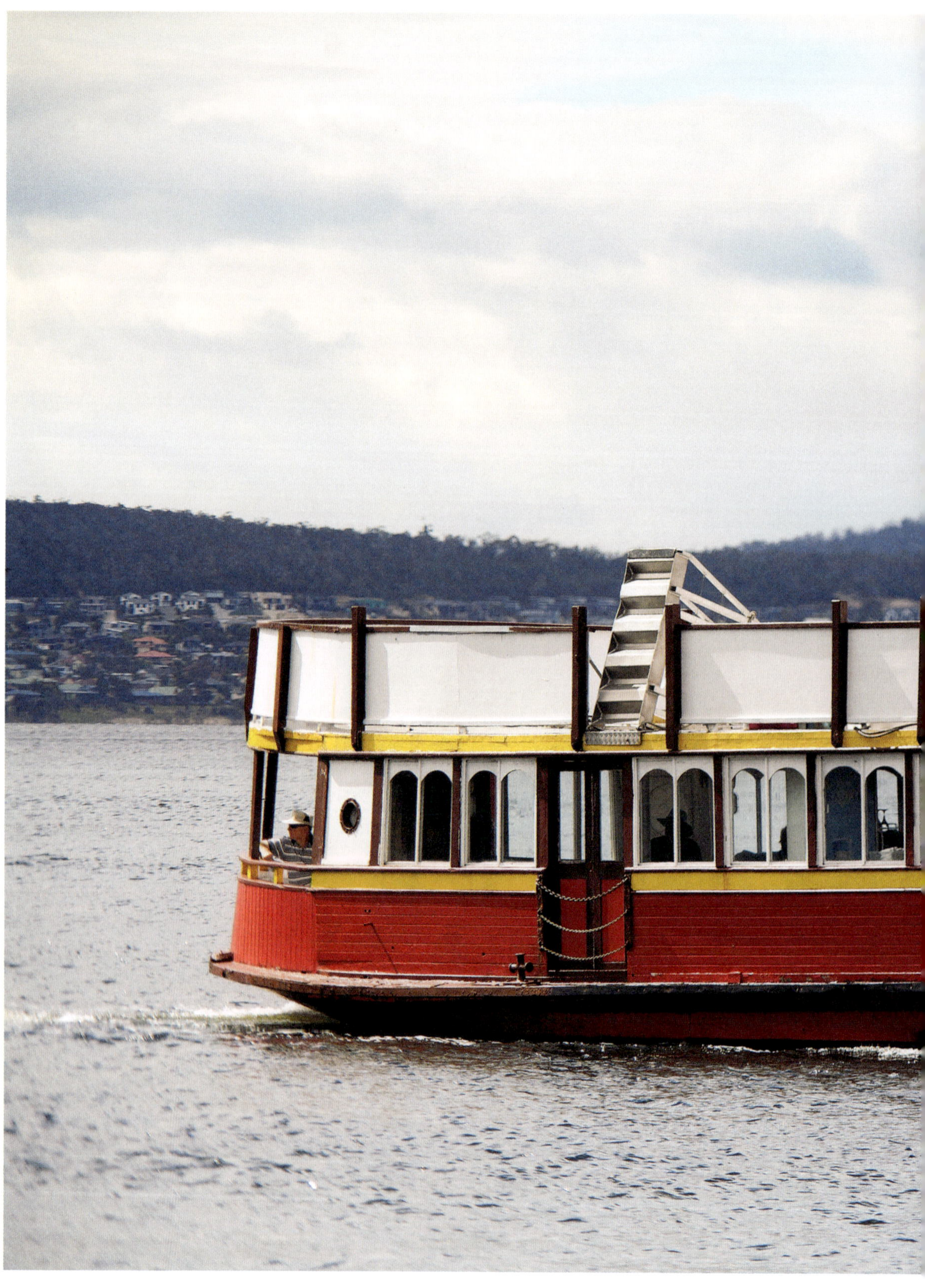

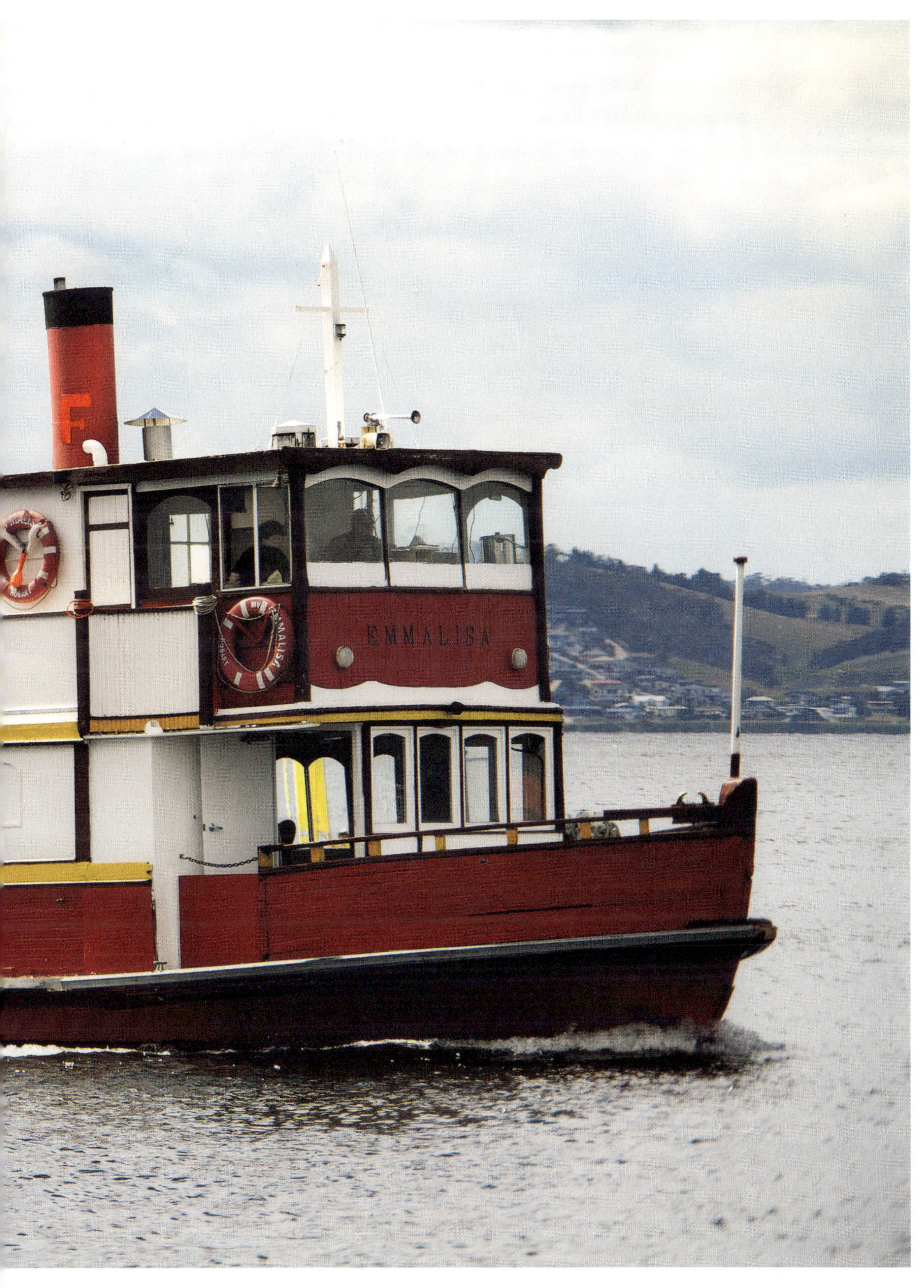
EMMALISA

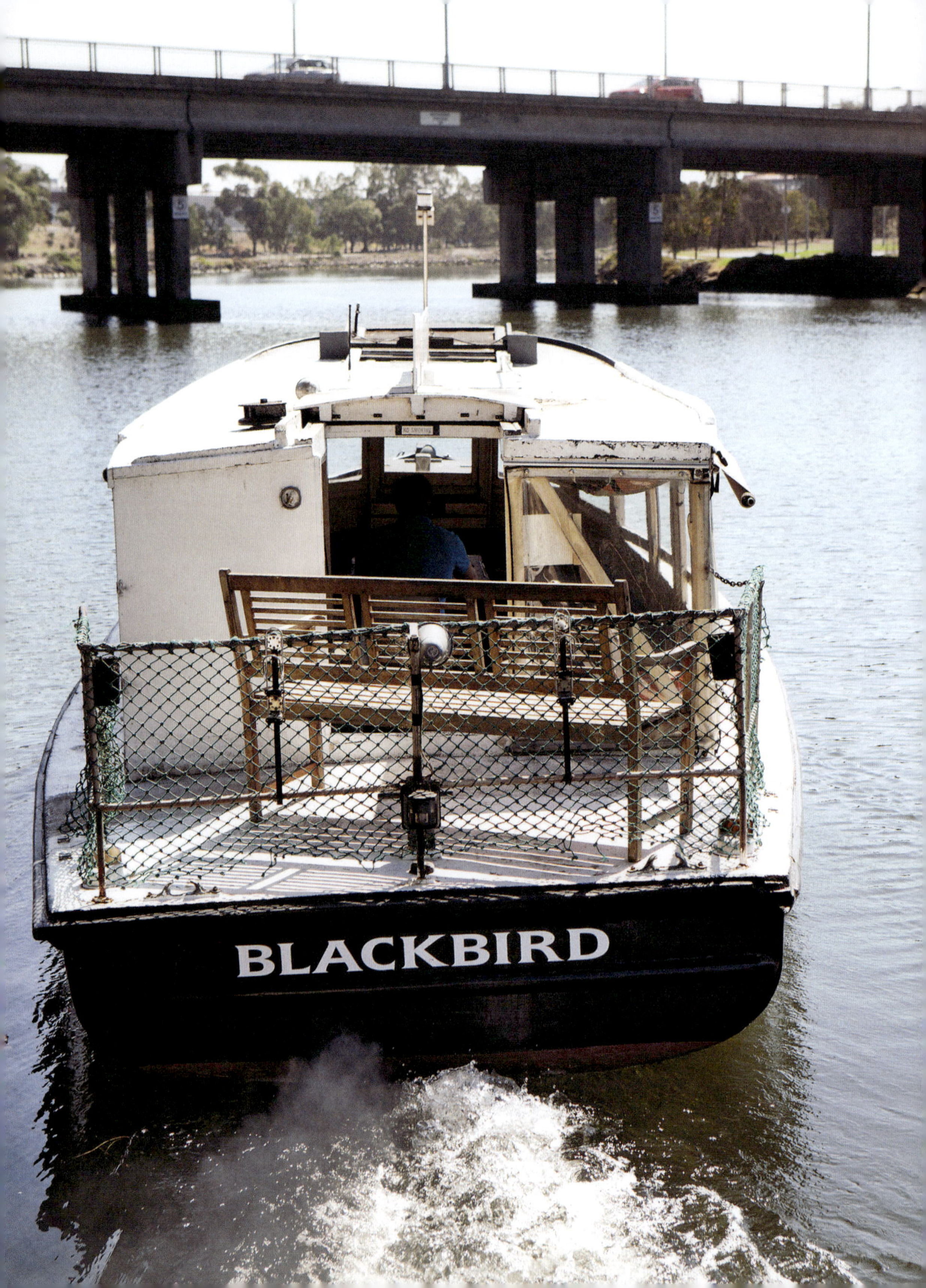
BLACKBIRD

BLACKBIRD

From their office in a 1950s shed on the Maribyrnong River, Peter Sommerville and his son Warwick operate *Blackbird,* a traditional ferry from Lakes Entrance in eastern Victoria. *Blackbird* was built in 1926 for the Peel family, along with sister ships *Bluebird* and *Bellbird* – both of which are still cruising.

Peter bought *Blackbird* in 1979 and has been operating Blackbird Cruises ever since; he won the only Great Yarra Riverboat Race in her and has a rather large trophy to show for it. She has a kauri hull, is 36 feet in length and has a four-cylinder diesel engine.

Peter is a walking history of Melbourne; he tells me that the opposite bank of the river used to be a shipyard employing some 700 men. Today it's just part of the container terminal.

A cruise on *Blackbird* is a very pleasant way to spend a couple of hours, and with Peter as a guide and captain you will learn about some of the early history of Melbourne at the same time.

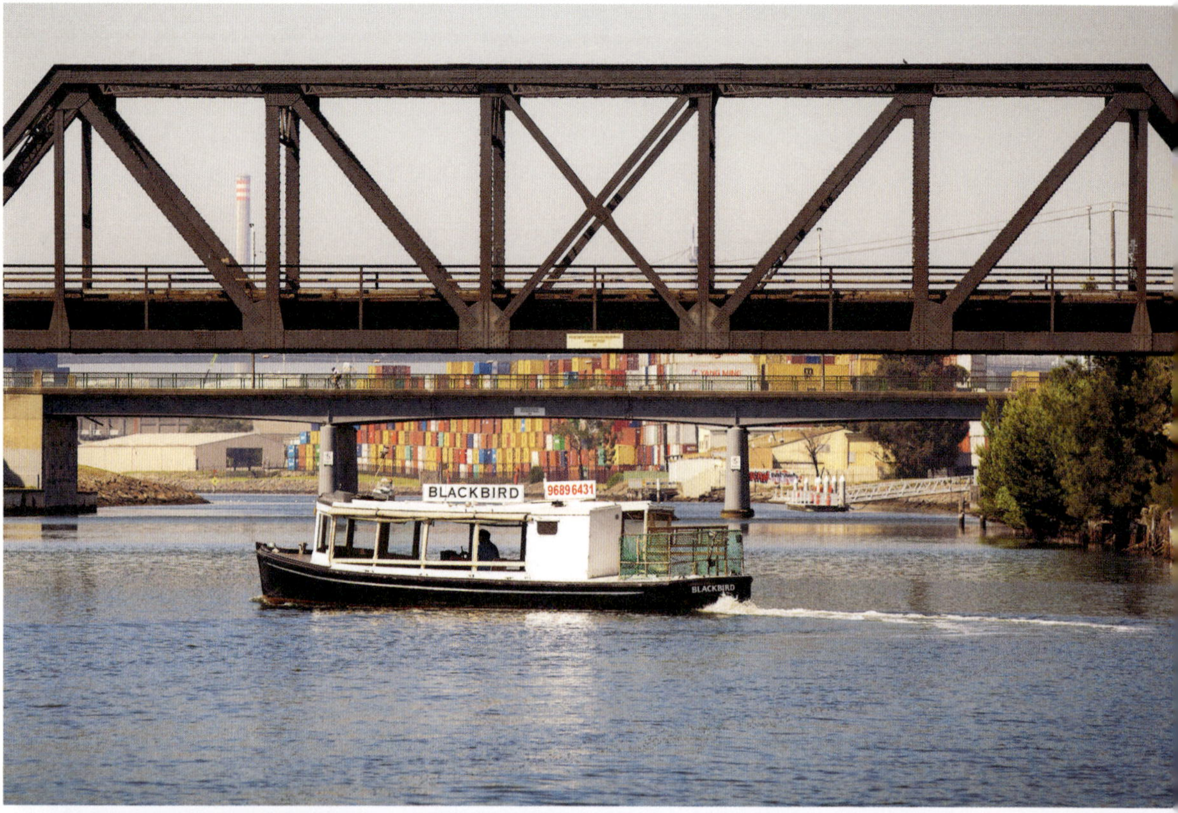
BLACKBIRD
9689 6431
BLACKBIRD

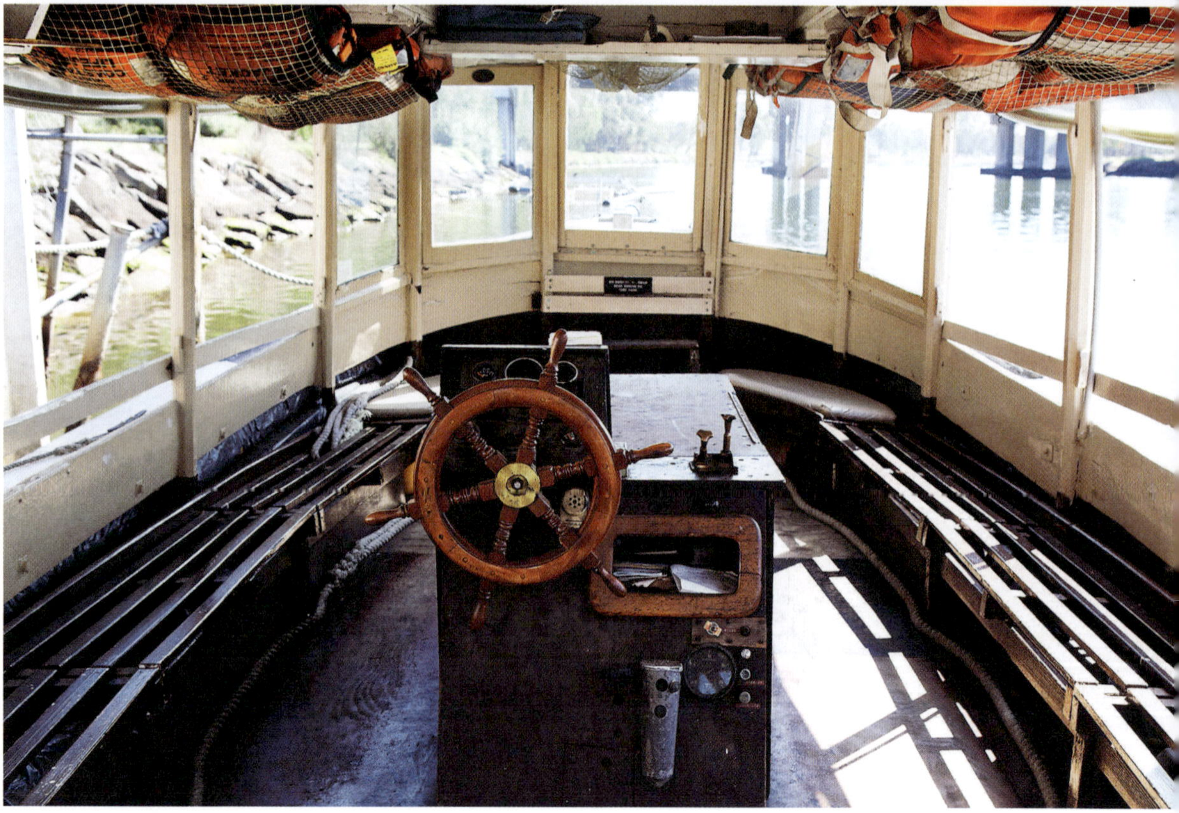

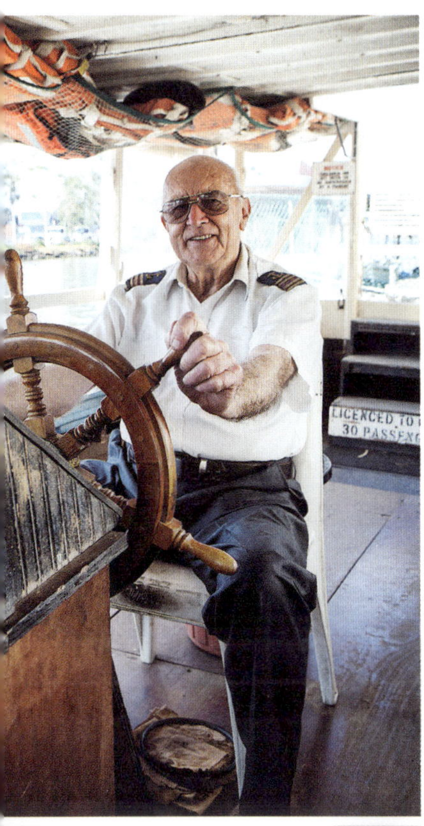

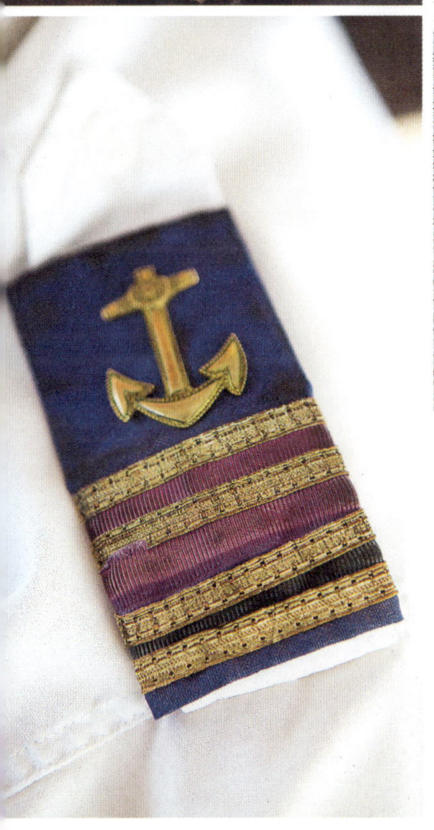

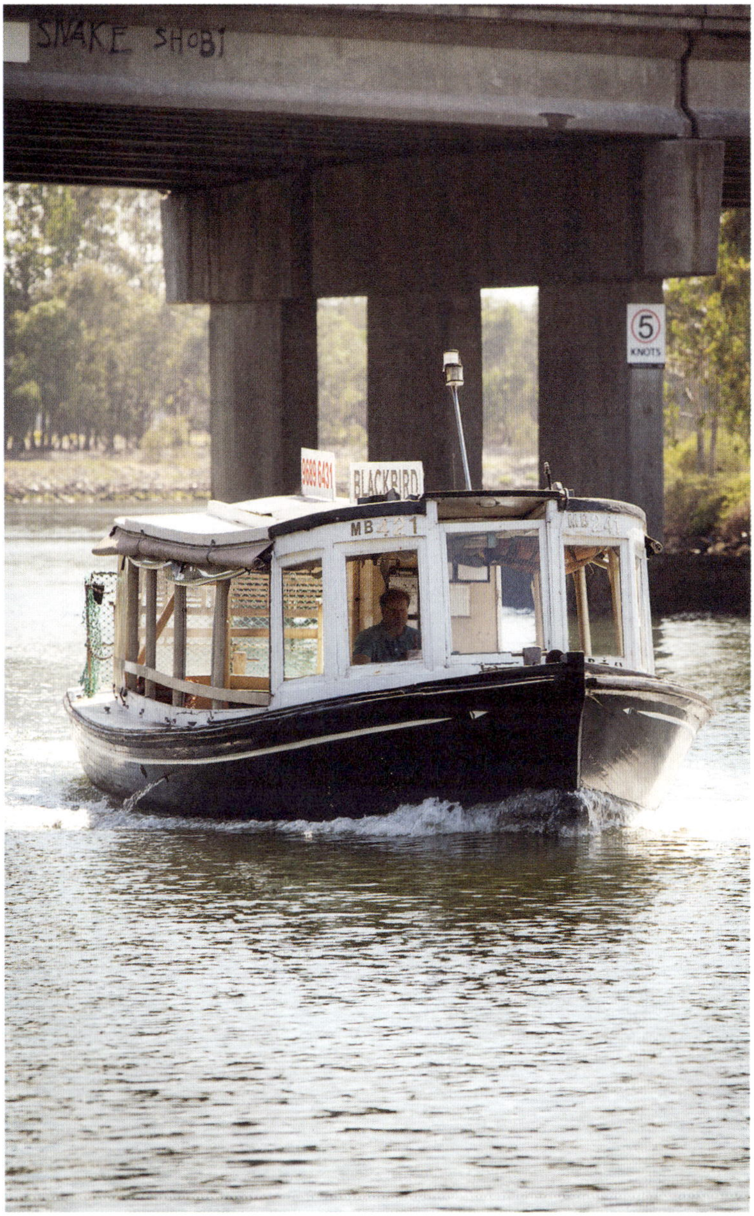

Blackbird operates on the Maribyrnong, the forgotten river of Melbourne, showing her passengers a hidden side to the city. Nothing could be more relaxing than a leisurely cruise down the river aboard this vintage ferry.

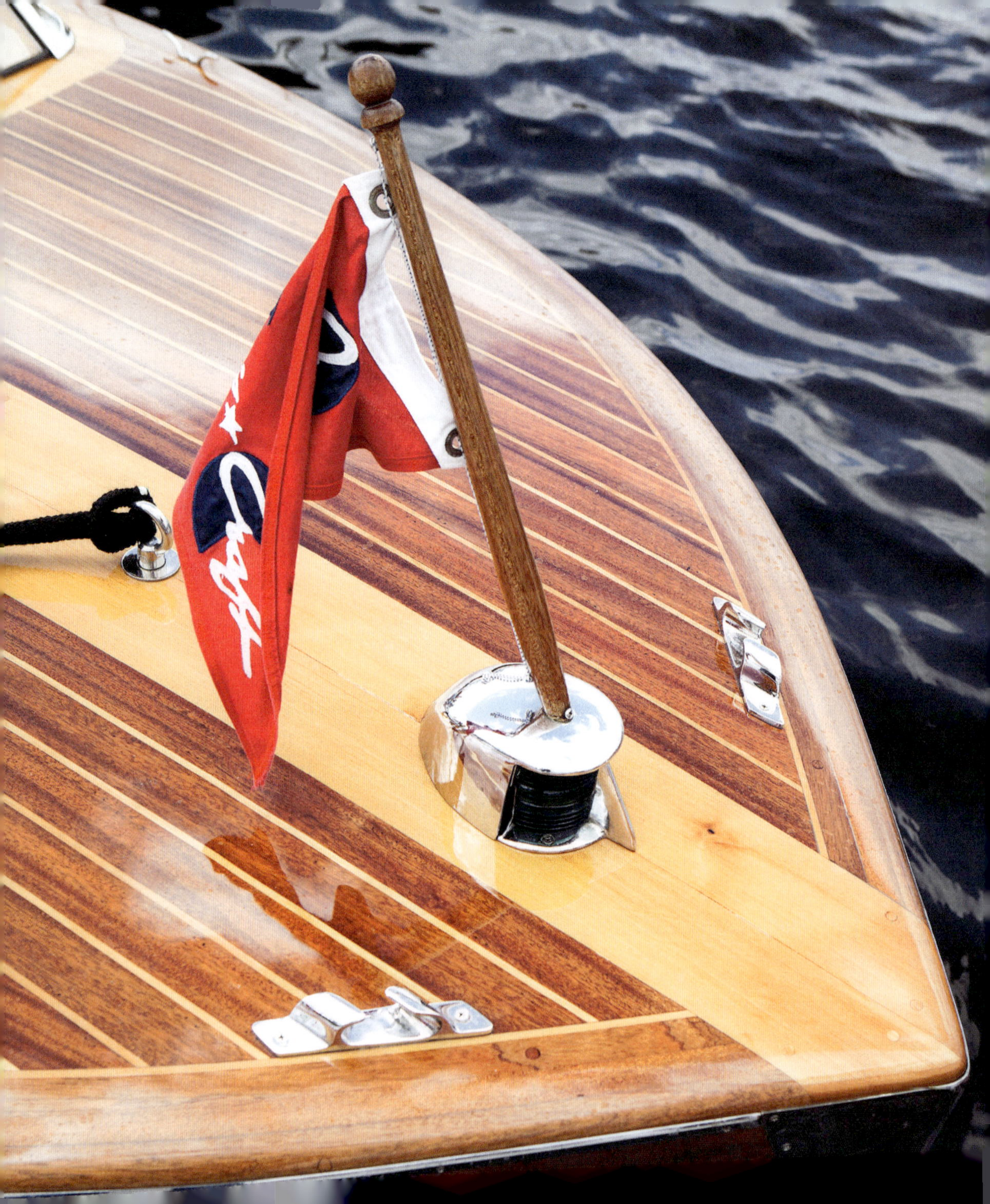

Fleetwood

There is something really pleasing about the mirror-finish varnish and the detailing on a beautiful Chris Craft speedboat; it's the type of boat you expect to see a Hollywood star travelling in, and indeed Frank Sinatra, Elvis Presley and JFK all owned boats made by this prestigious American company. The Chris Craft is considered by many to be the quintessential American 1950s runabout.

Fleetwood, a classic 18-foot replica of an 1950 Chris Craft Riviera, was built by Gordon Scrim in Tasmania. Riviera was Chris Craft's most popular design. It took Gordon three years to build *Fleetwood*, with her beautiful detail and finish, using a balsa core with ply and glass and finishing her with Philippine mahogany topsides and deck.

It is obvious how much care Gordon lavishes on his pride and joy; from her crisp, red upholstery to her wooden wheel and the red Chris Craft logo flag that flutters on her bow, she's a real star.

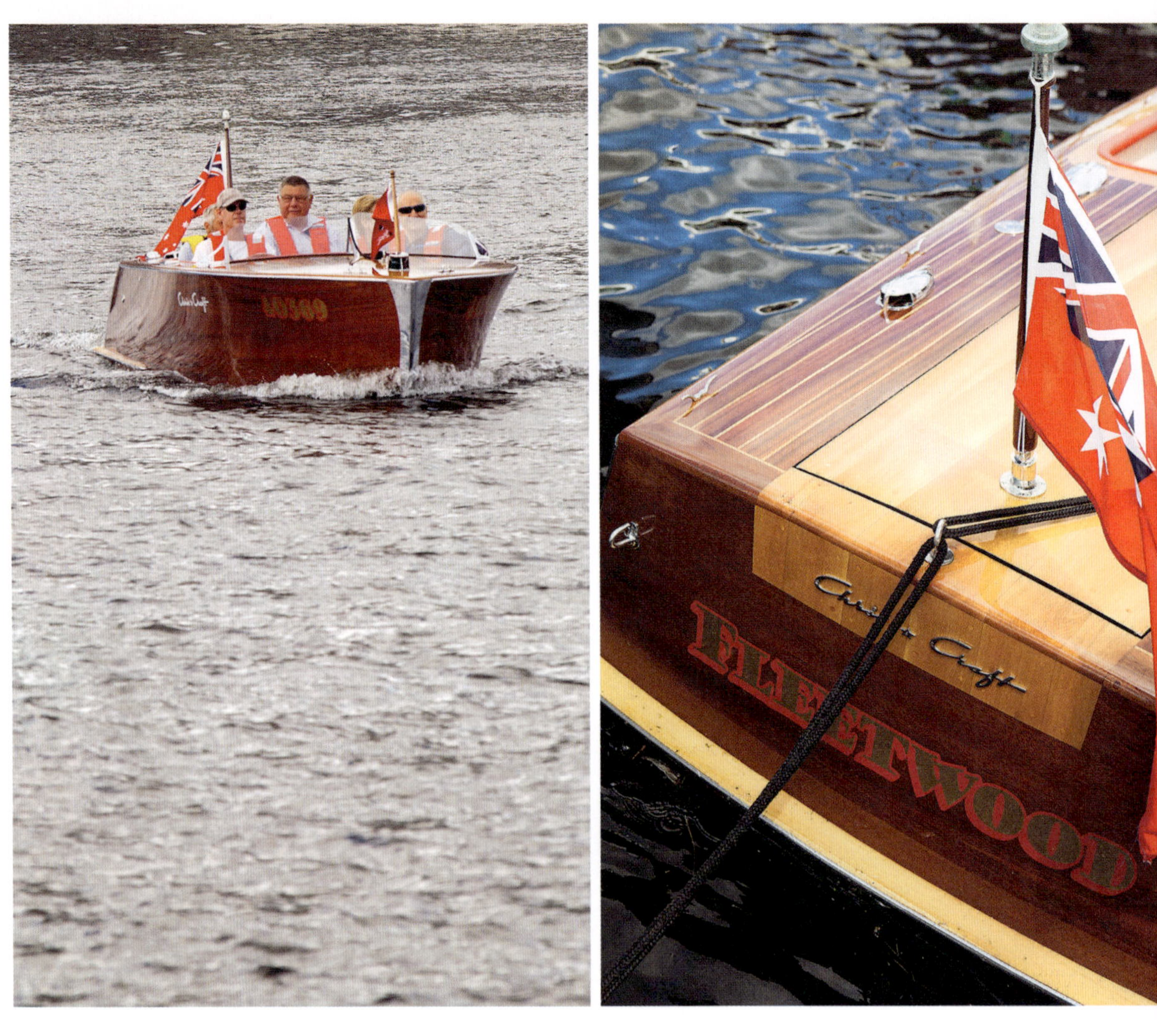

Fleetwood is all polished timber, chrome and glamour; it is no wonder that Chris Craft boats have been used by celebrities over the years. Every detail of *Fleetwood* is beautifully finished; she is Gordon Scrim's pride and joy.

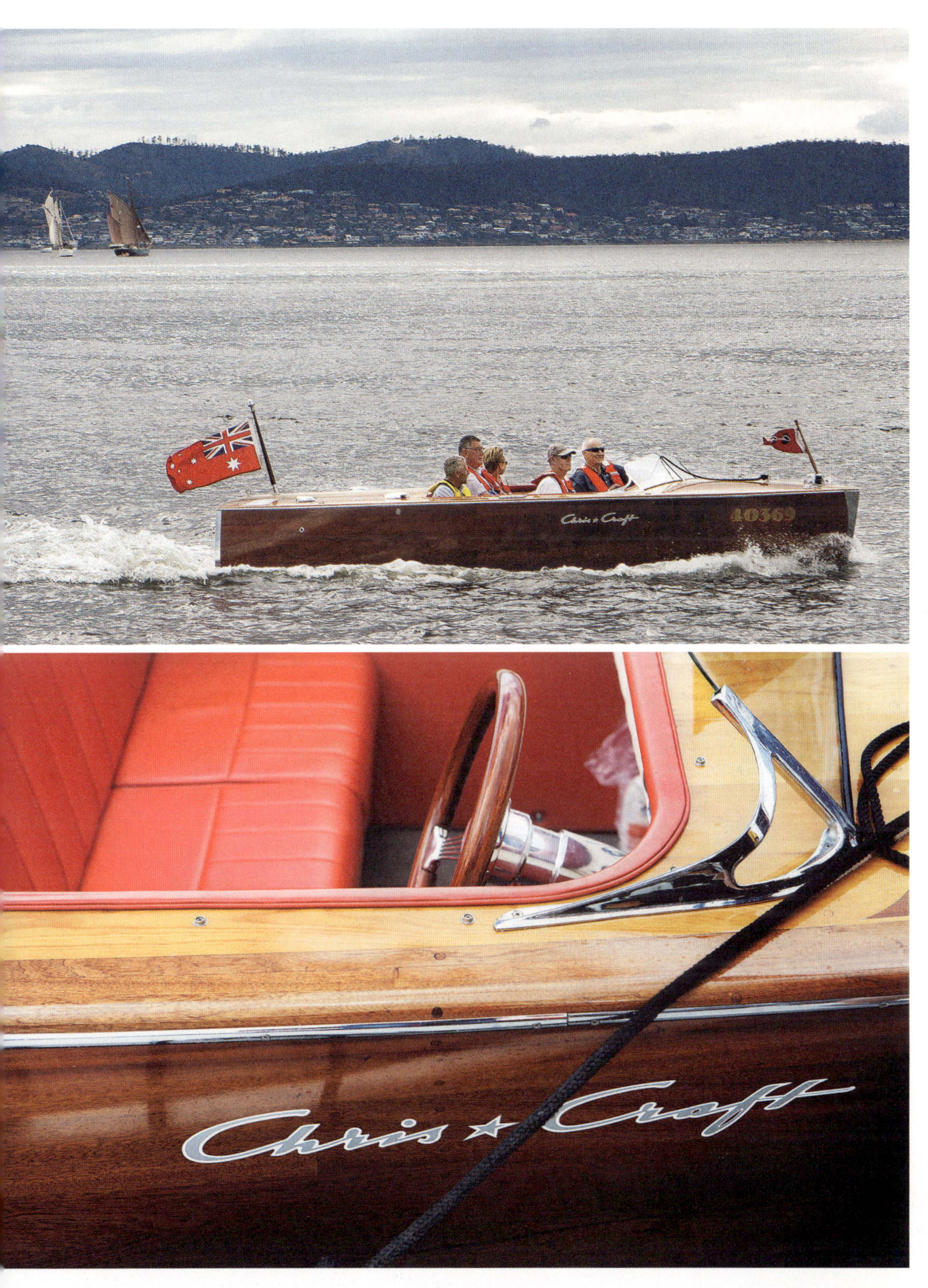
Chris ★ Craft
40369
Chris ★ Craft

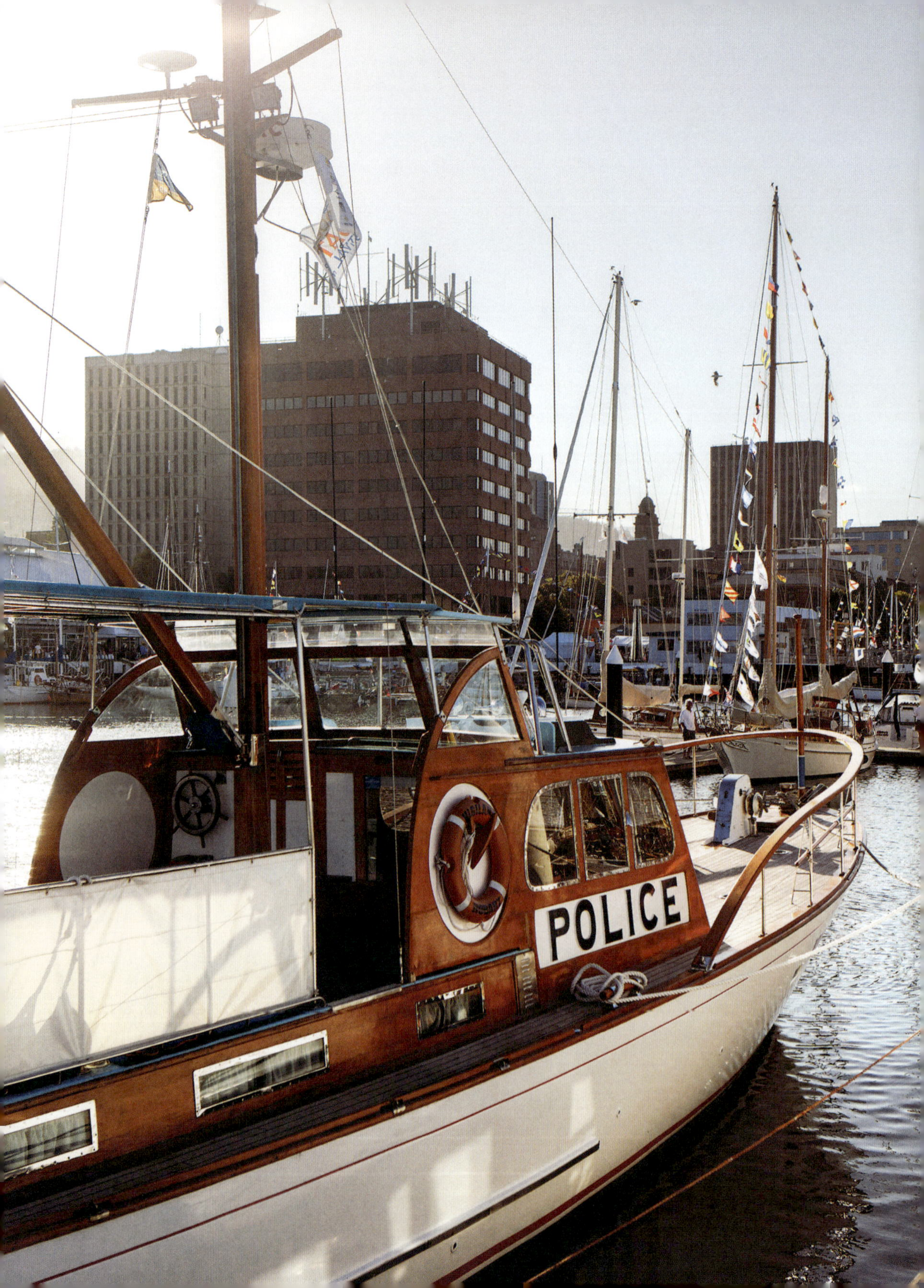
POLICE

VIGILANT

Vigilant, probably the only wooden police boat operating in the Southern Hemisphere, was purpose-built for the Tasmanian Police by Ray Kemp. Commissioned in 1971, the Huon pine carvel-planked launch has twin 185-horsepower Cummins diesel engines. She is 52 feet 10 inches long, her beam is 15 feet and her draught is 6 feet. She weighs 26 tons and her top speed is 12.5 knots. She sleeps six people.

Vigilant is used as an offshore patrol vessel for search-and-rescue operations, fishery patrols and community events. She has also performed a vital role in rescue operations for such disasters as the sinking of *Blythe Star* in 1973 and the collapse of the Tasman Bridge in 1975.

Tasmania is the only state where the police are responsible for enforcing fisheries regulations. *Vigilant* has played a major part in this, spending sixty to seventy days at sea each year in this role. Skipper Rob Round tells me that positions working on any of the three Tasmanian police vessels are highly sought-after.

Vigilant has seen over forty-four years of active service and, no doubt, has many left in her.

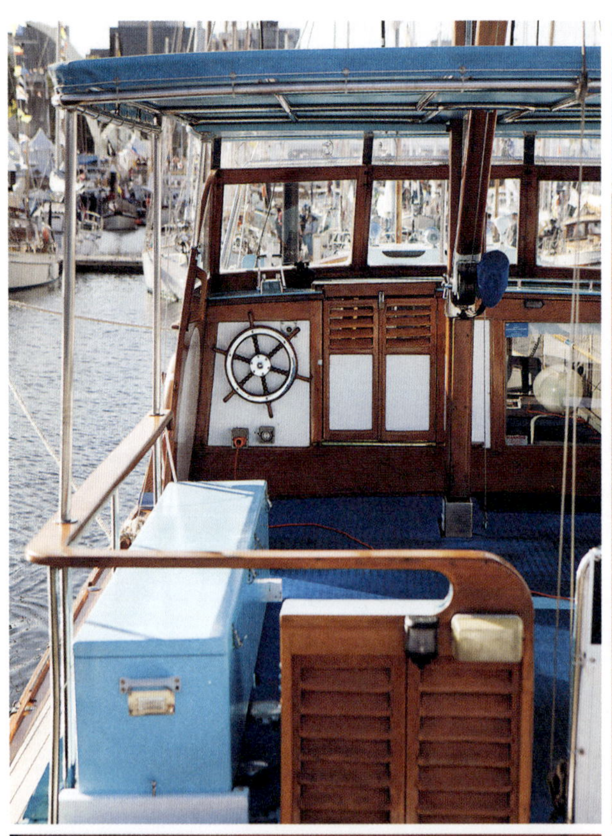

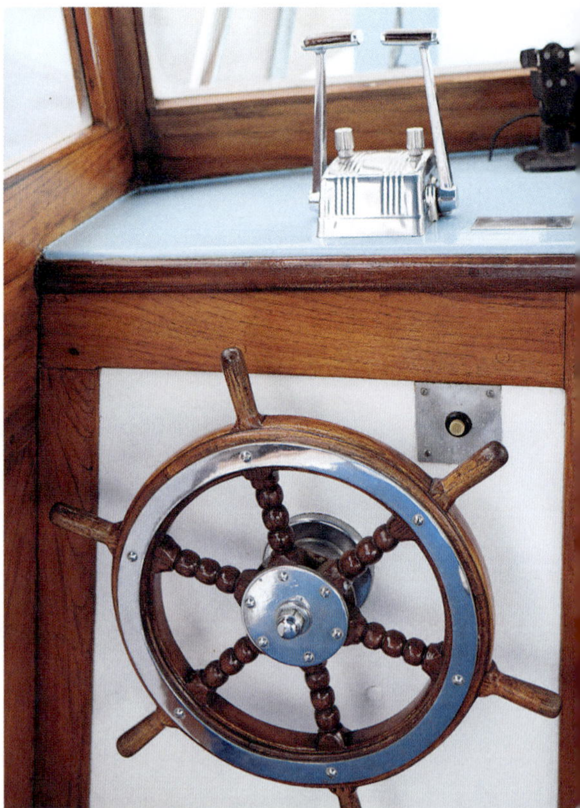

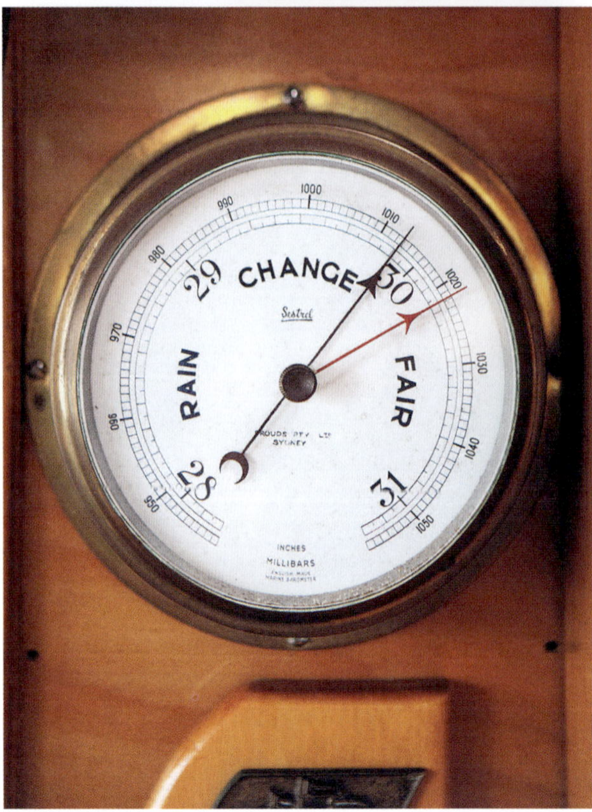

CHANGE
RAIN
FAIR
29
30
28
31
INCHES
MILLIBARS

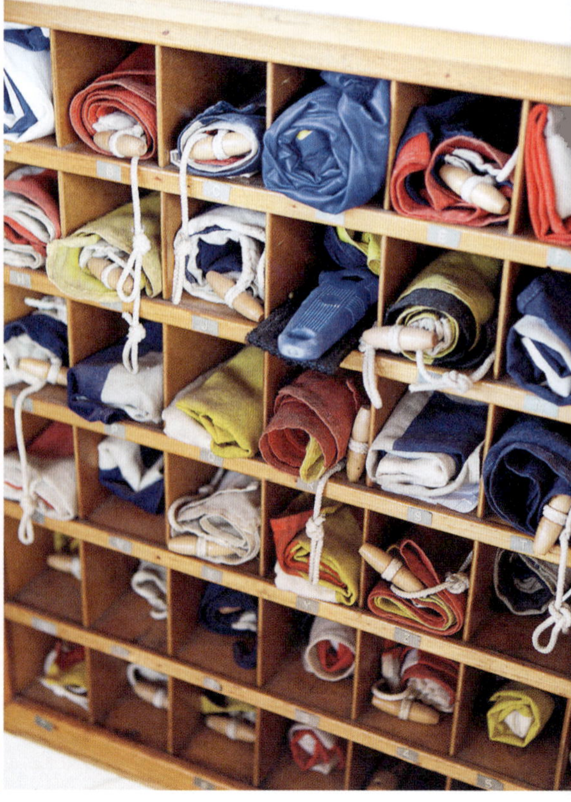

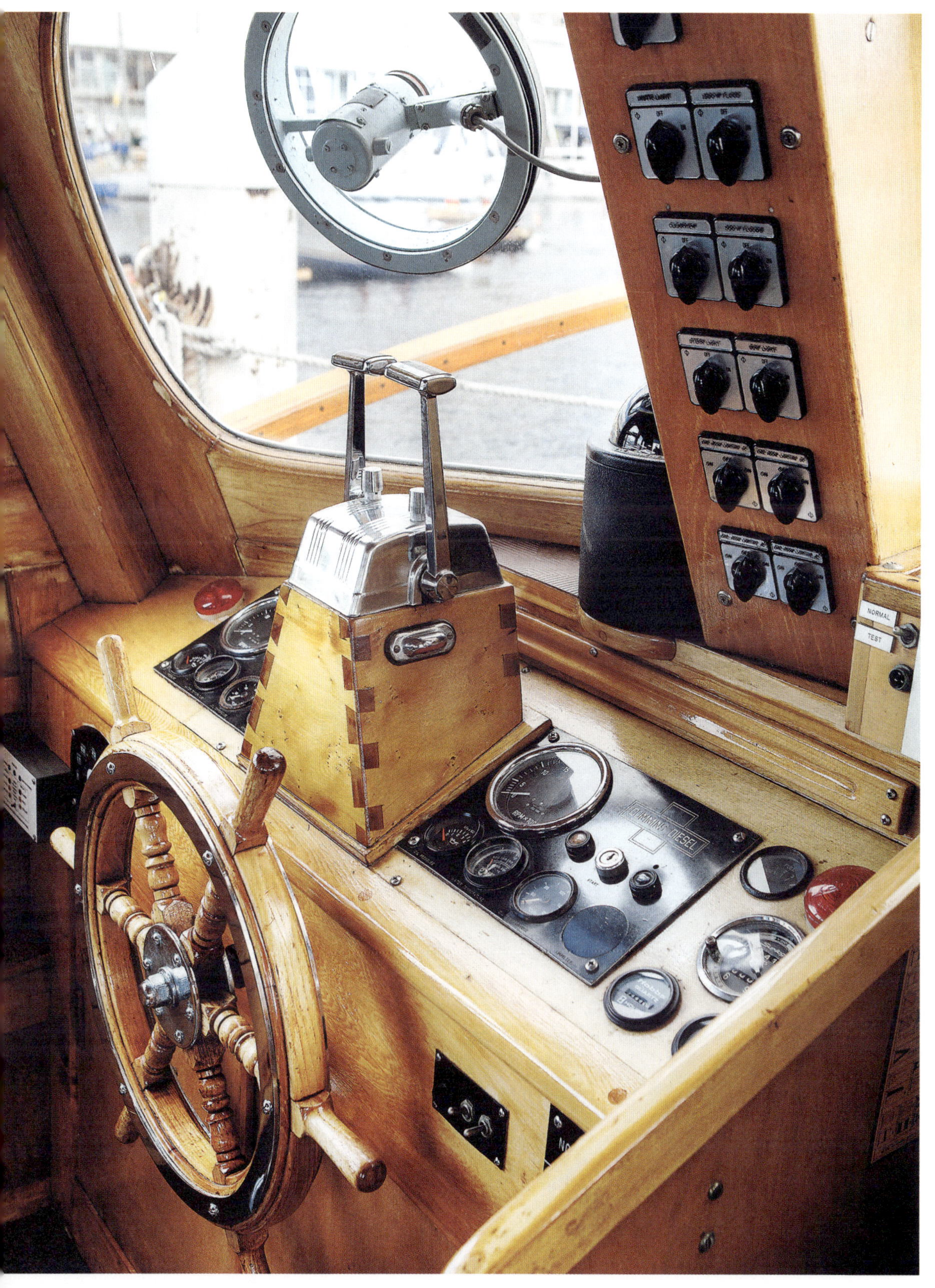
NORMAL
TEST
CUMMINS DIESEL

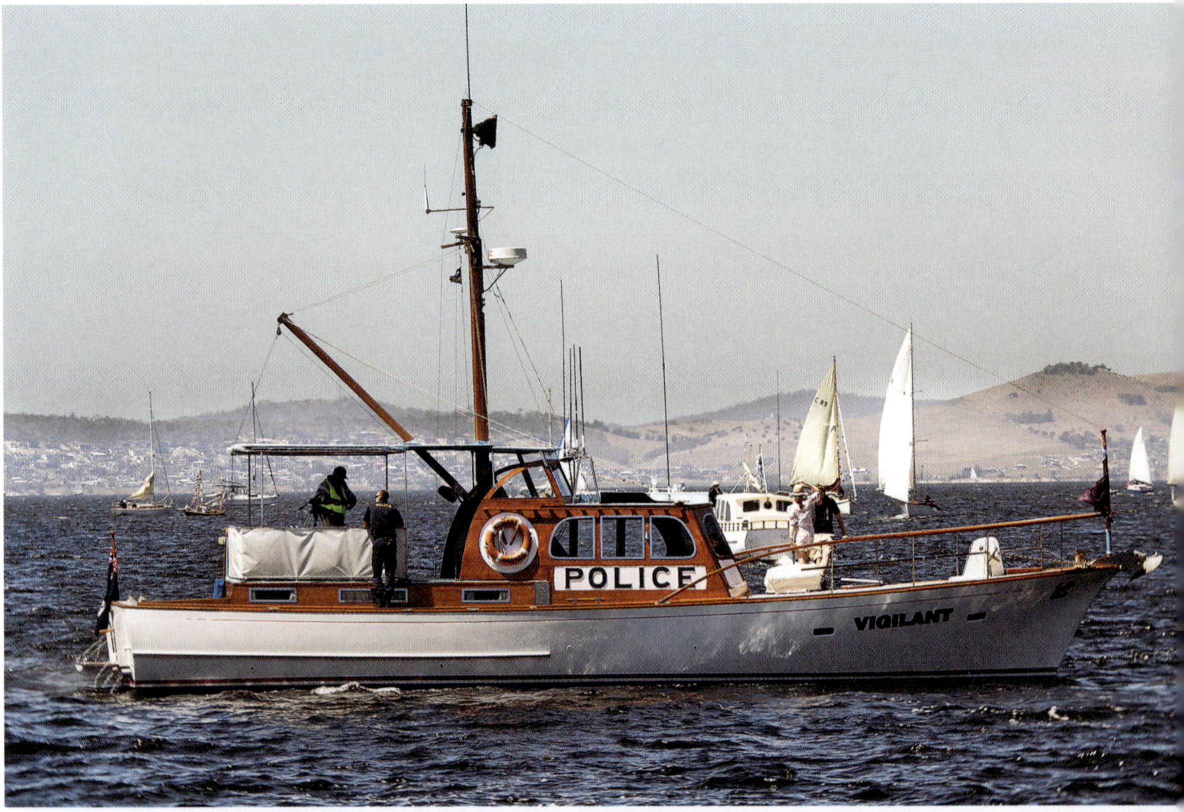

POLICE
VIGILANT
POLICE

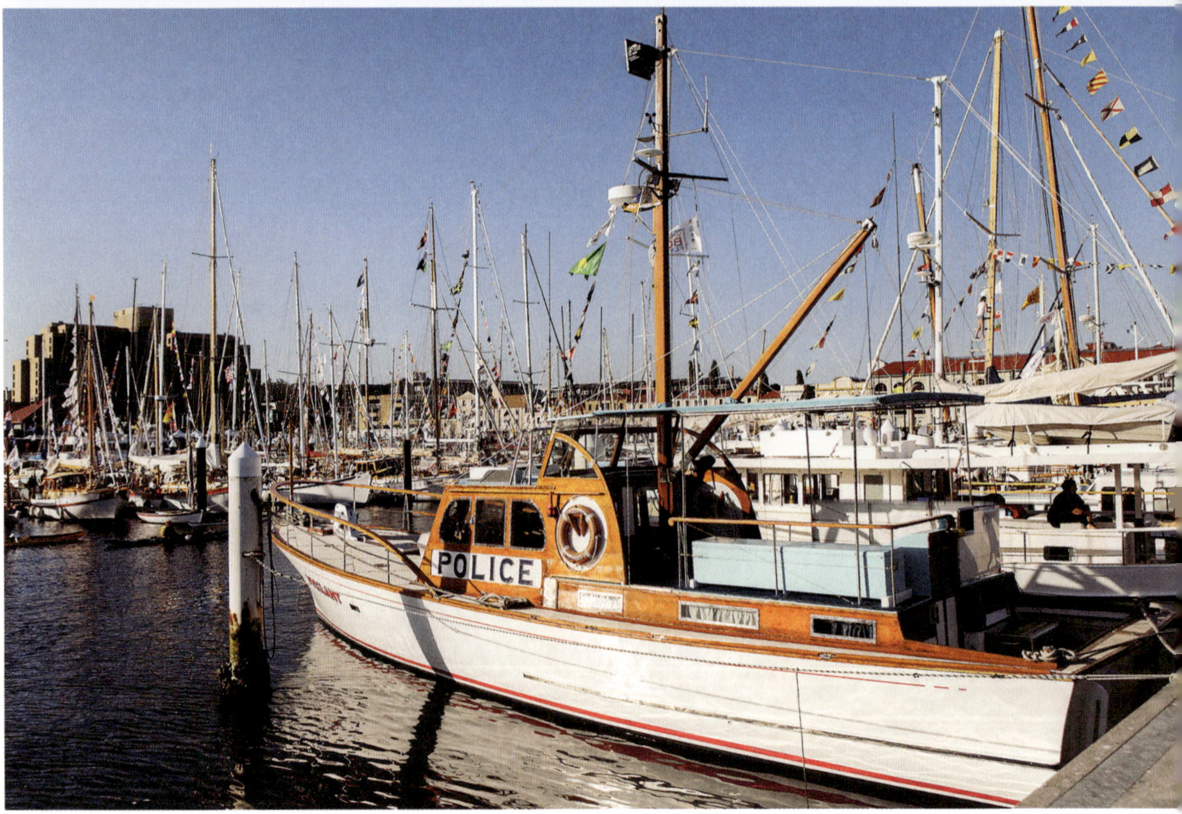

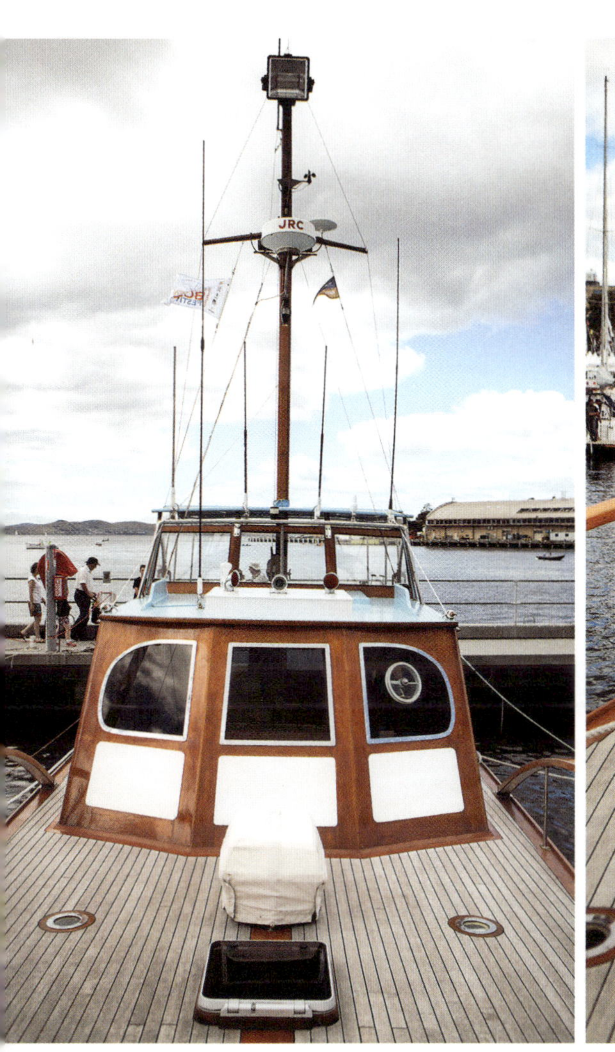

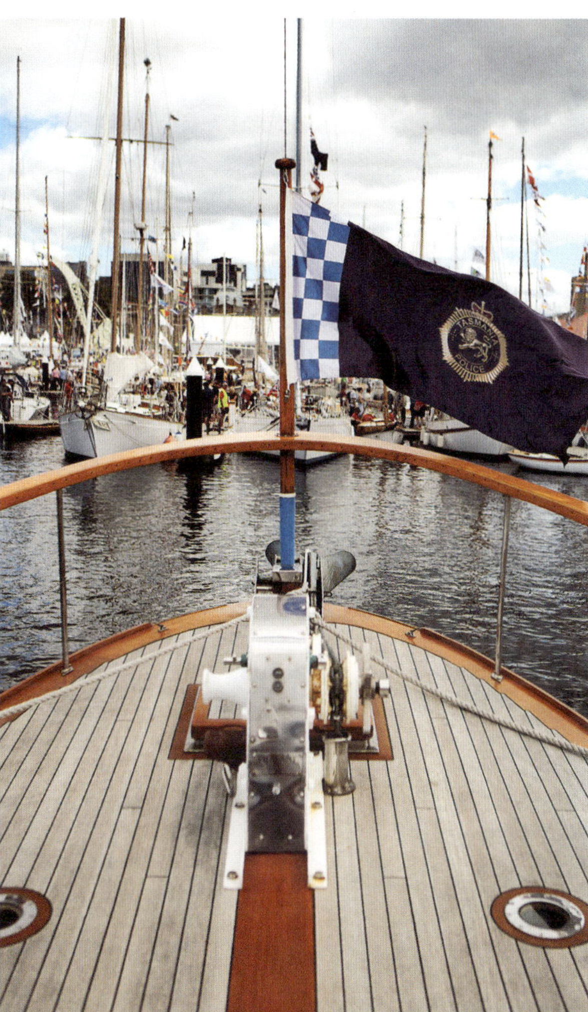

Vigilant, locally designed and built, contains everything the Tasmanian Police require for their boating operations and patrol work; she is virtually a floating police station. As she is a working boat, every inch of her is dedicated to protecting Tasmania's people and her coastline.

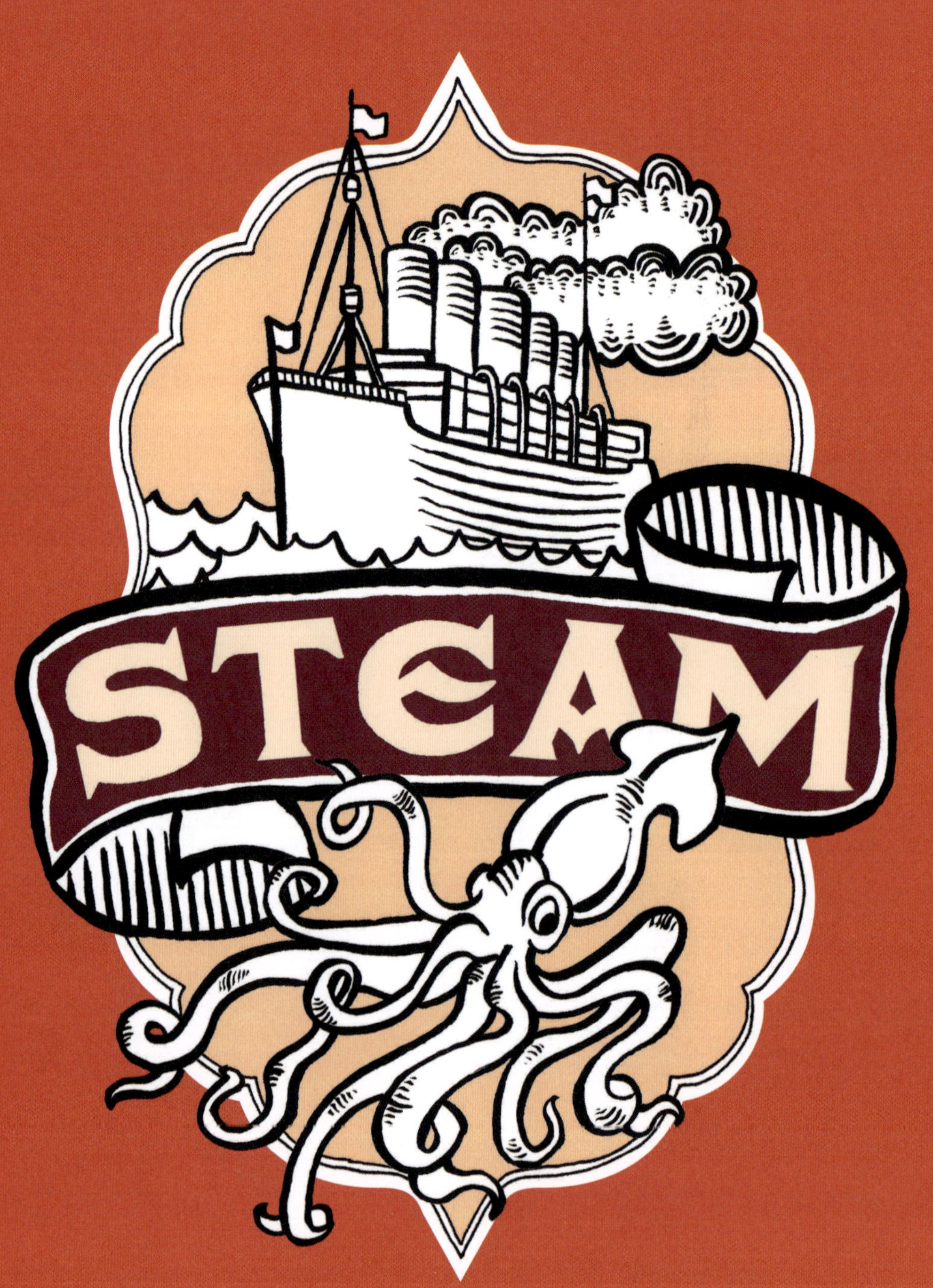
STEAM

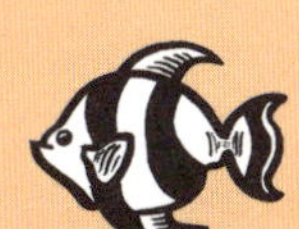

STEP ON BOARD A STEAMBOAT AND YOU ARE STEPPING BACK IN TIME, WITH THE POLISHED BRASS, THE SMELL OF THE OILED ENGINE, THE HISS OF STEAM, THE SPINNING WHEELS AND PISTONS AND THE SHRILL SOUND OF THE STEAM WHISTLE. THE FIRST STEAMBOAT WAS PATENTED BY JONATHAN HULLS BACK IN 1737, BUT ALTHOUGH THE AGE OF STEAM MAY HAVE PASSED, STEAMBOATS STILL HAVE A HUGE FOLLOWING AMONGST BOAT ENTHUSIASTS.

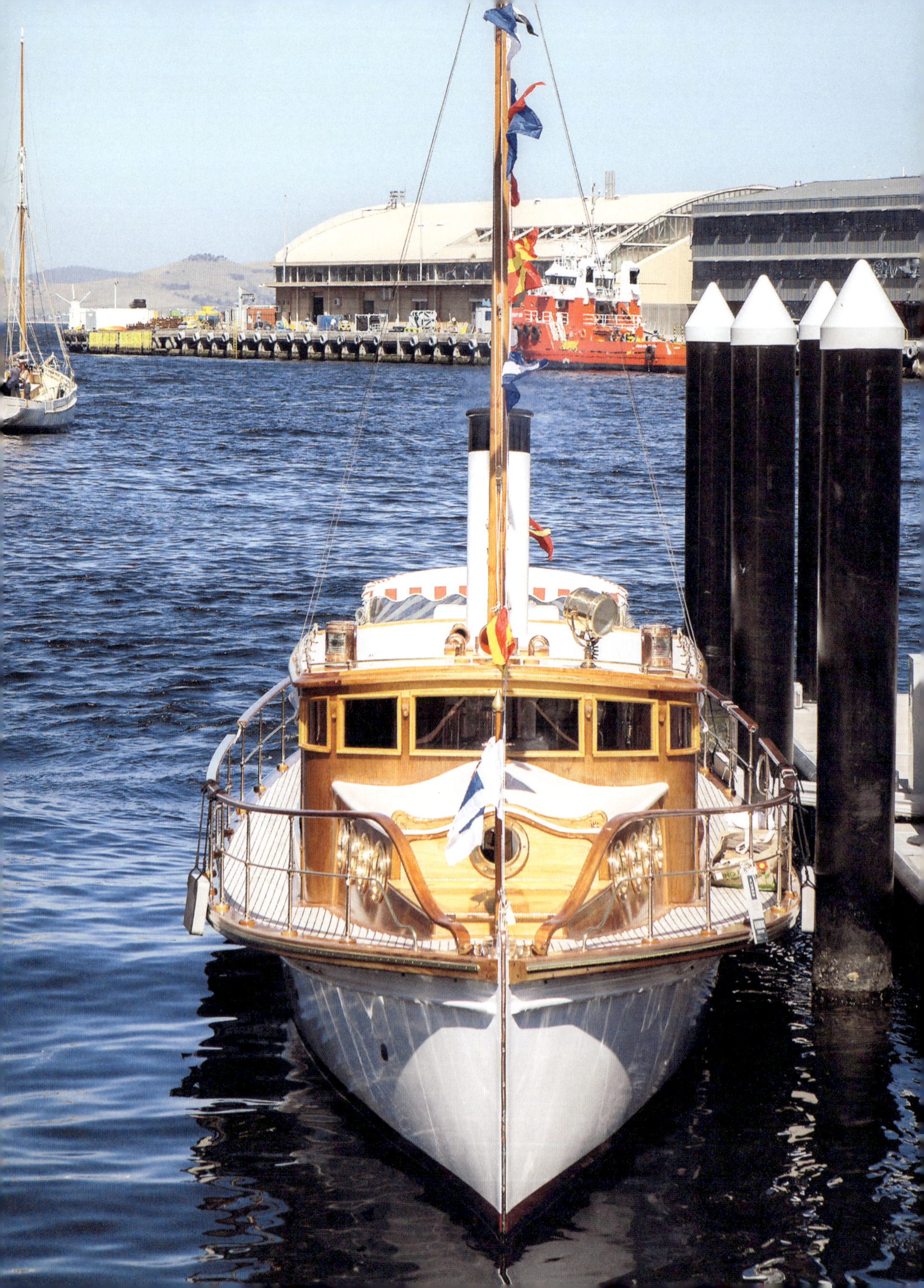

S. Y. Preana

Built in Hobart in 1896 for businessman and M.P. the Rt Hon William Gibson, *S.Y. Preana* ferried Gibson across the Derwent River from his home to his flour mill in Hobart. After he died she fell into disrepair and was converted into a fishing boat. Her steam engine was removed.

When Jim Butterworth found her in 1992 she was hauled up on the mud of Prince of Wales Bay – a real wreck. Jim set up the Preana Trust, and that, unfortunately, was to be the beginning of sixteen years of problems. One of these was Jim's inability to find a Simpson Strickland triple steam engine to replicate the original one, but he did eventually locate a 40-horsepower US Navy type E compound engine that was the right size. The engine is truly a work of well-oiled, steel and bronze art; the century-old compound steam engine works away, quietly propelling the elegant boat across the Derwent.

S.Y. Preana was relaunched in 2005 and is available for cruises and dinner parties. She is 55 feet long, her beam is 13 feet, her draught is 4 feet 6 inches and she weighs 13 tons.

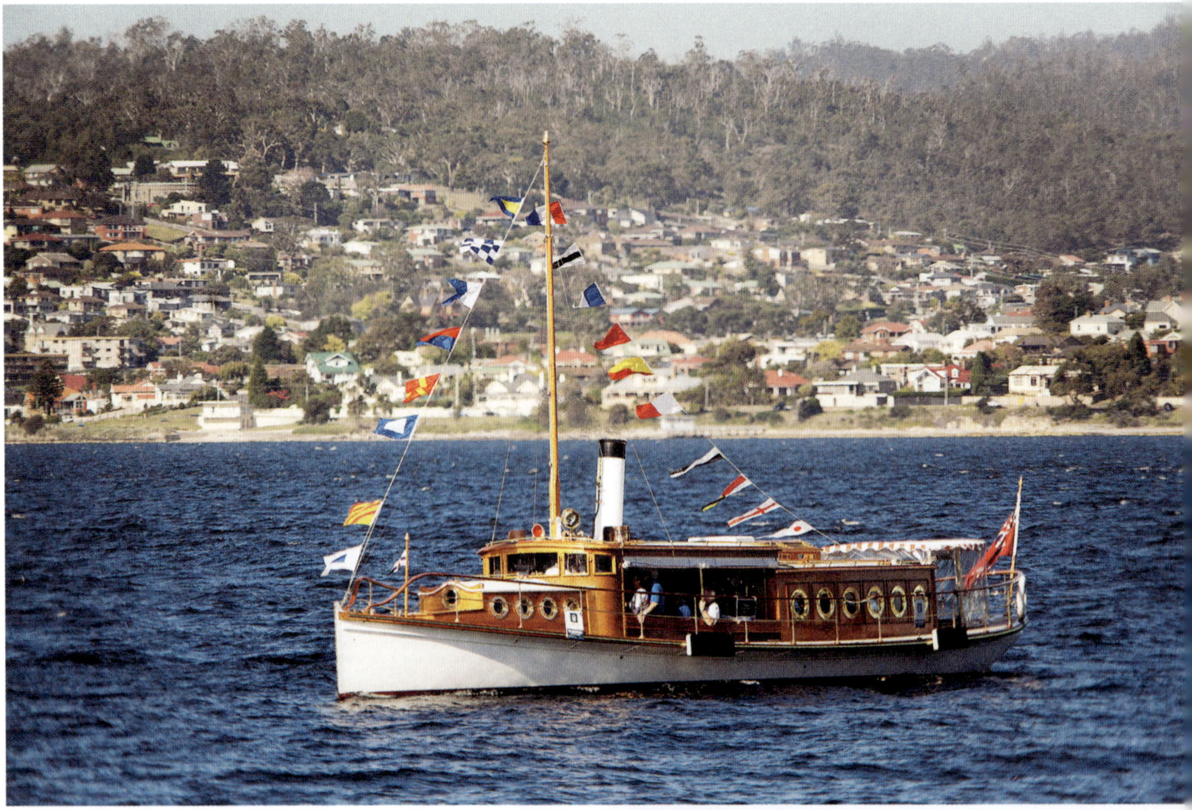

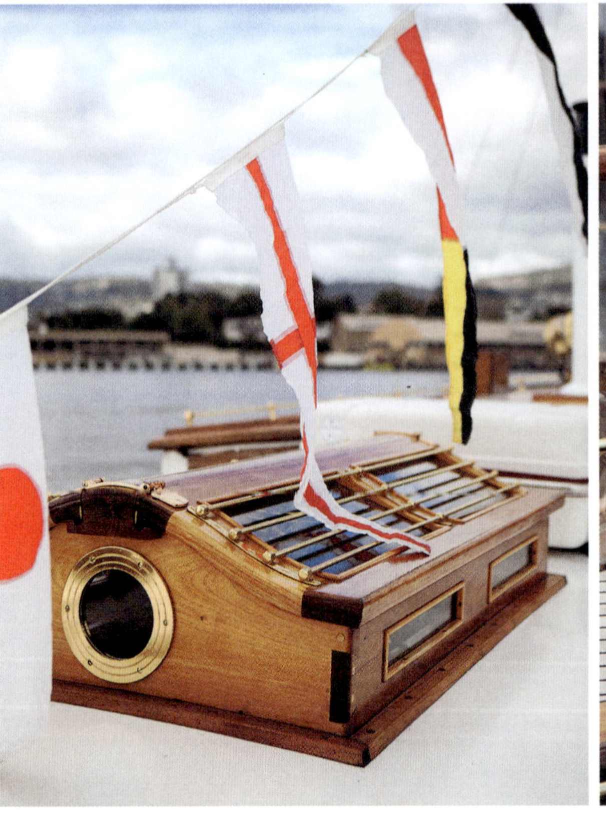

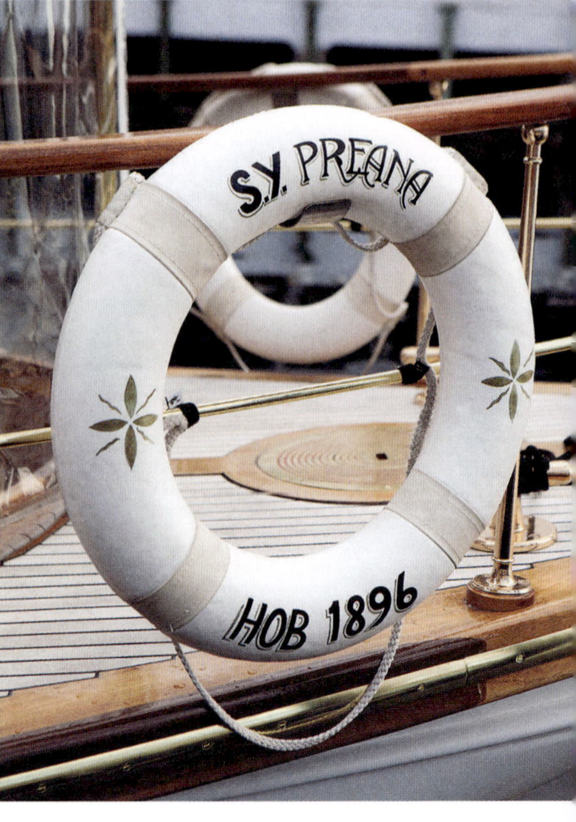
S.Y. PREANA
HOB 1896

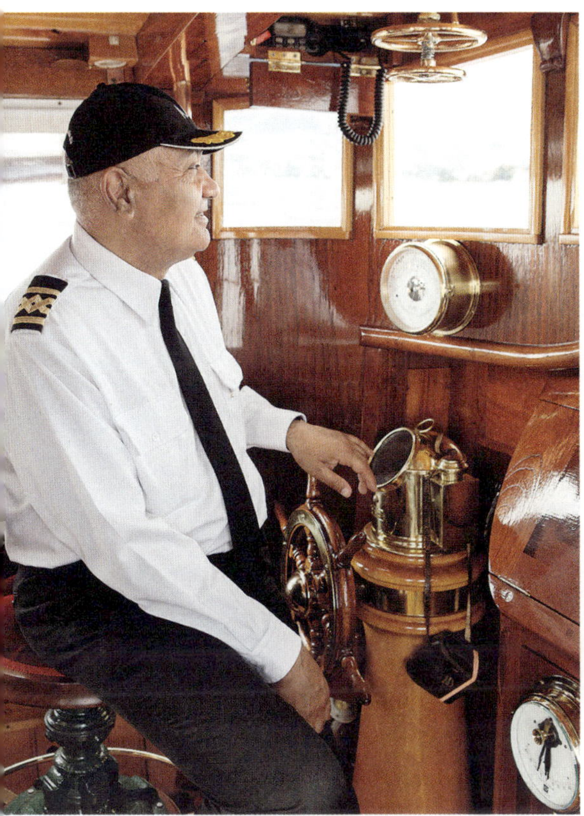

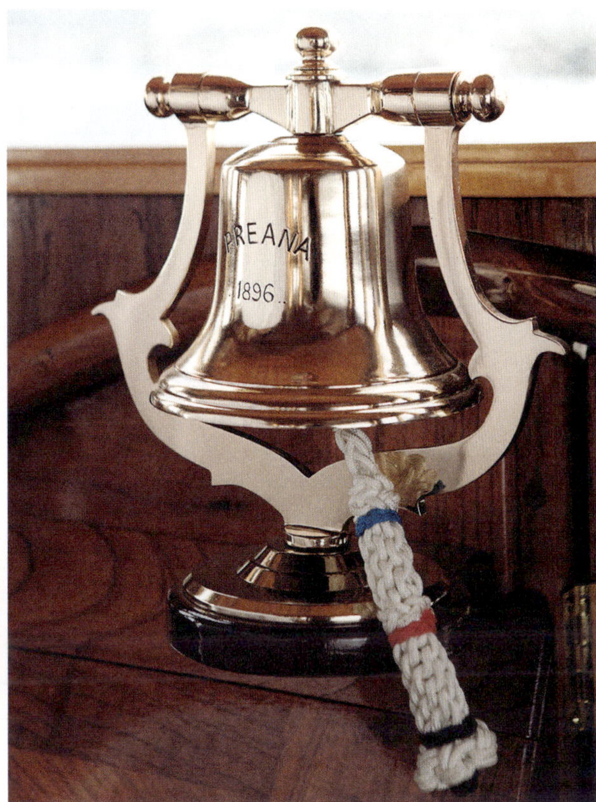

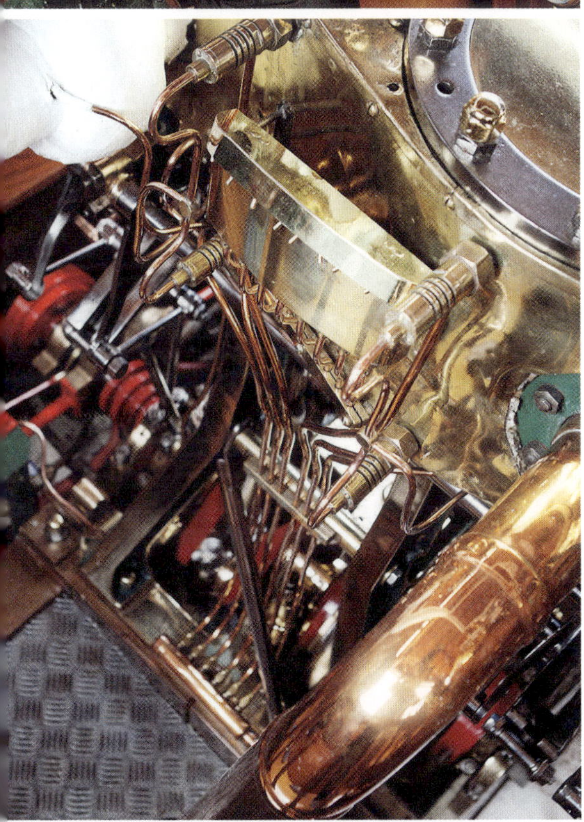

All of the original details have been reinstated; *S.Y. Preana* is now a symphony of polished brass and beautiful timber as she sails the Derwent once again, proud captain at the helm.

S.Y. Preana has today been restored to her former glory.

FOLLOWING PAGES Her interior is most elegant, with burgundy velvet buttoned lounges and smartly polished brass and red cedar fittings.

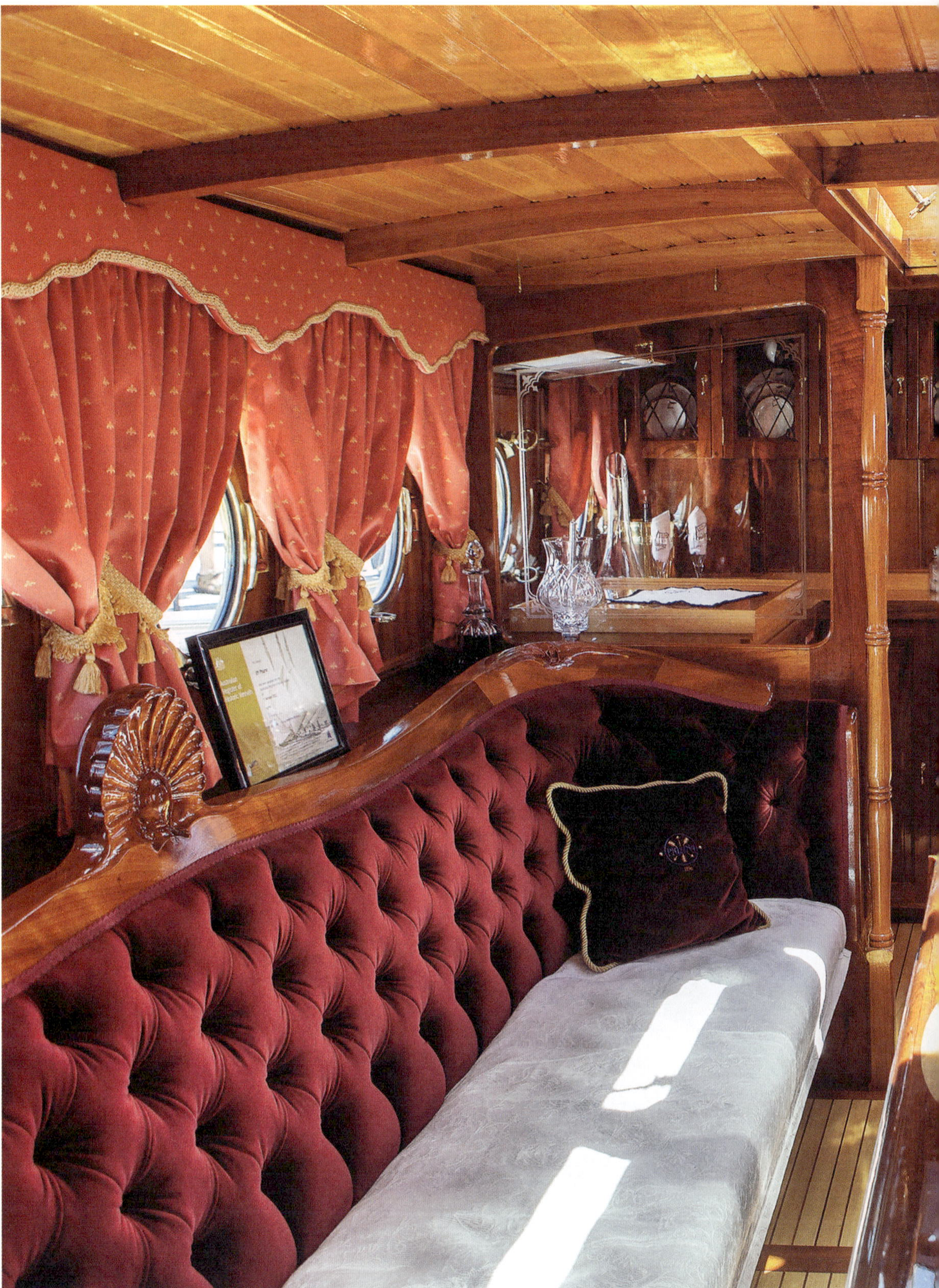

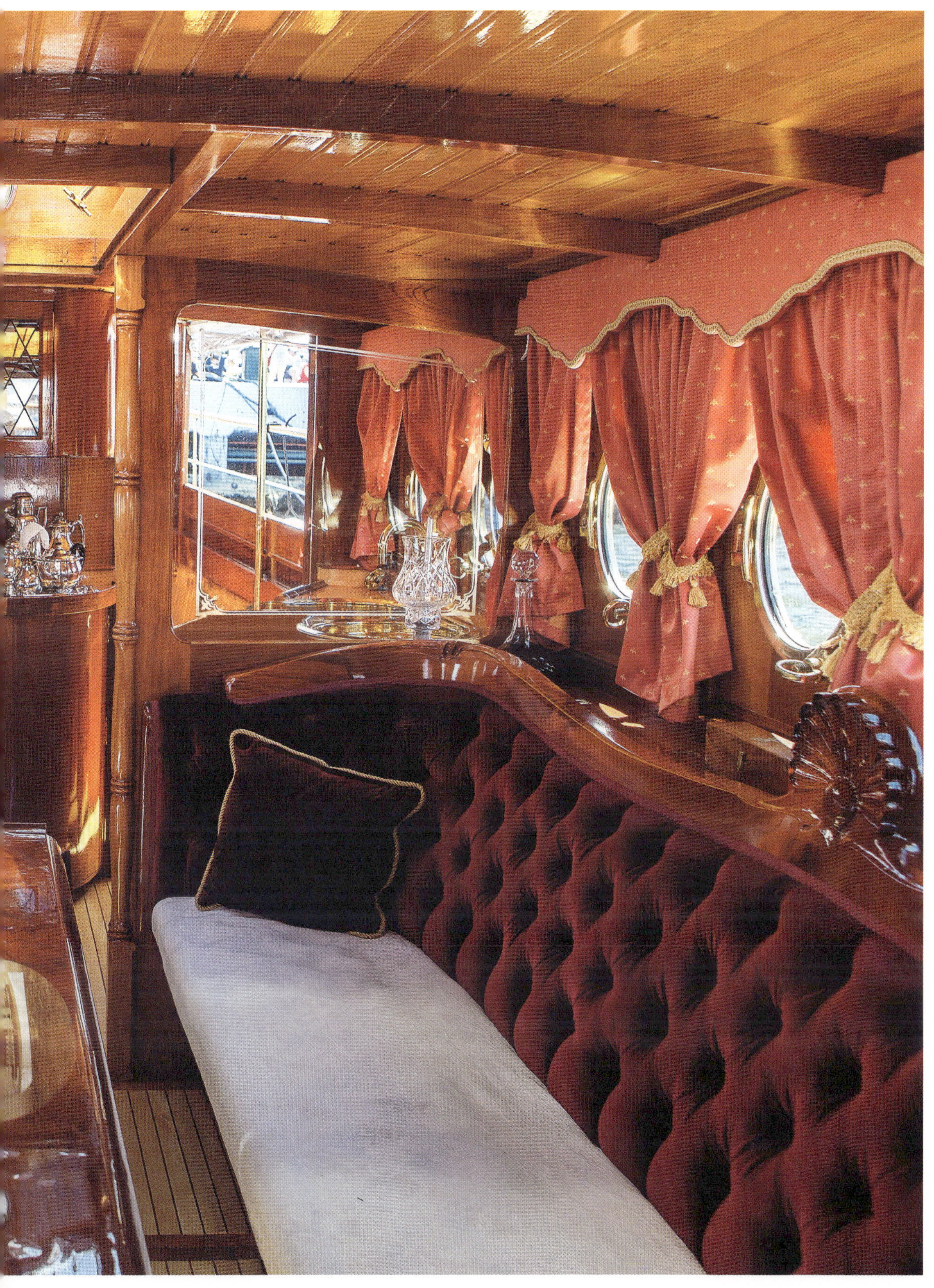

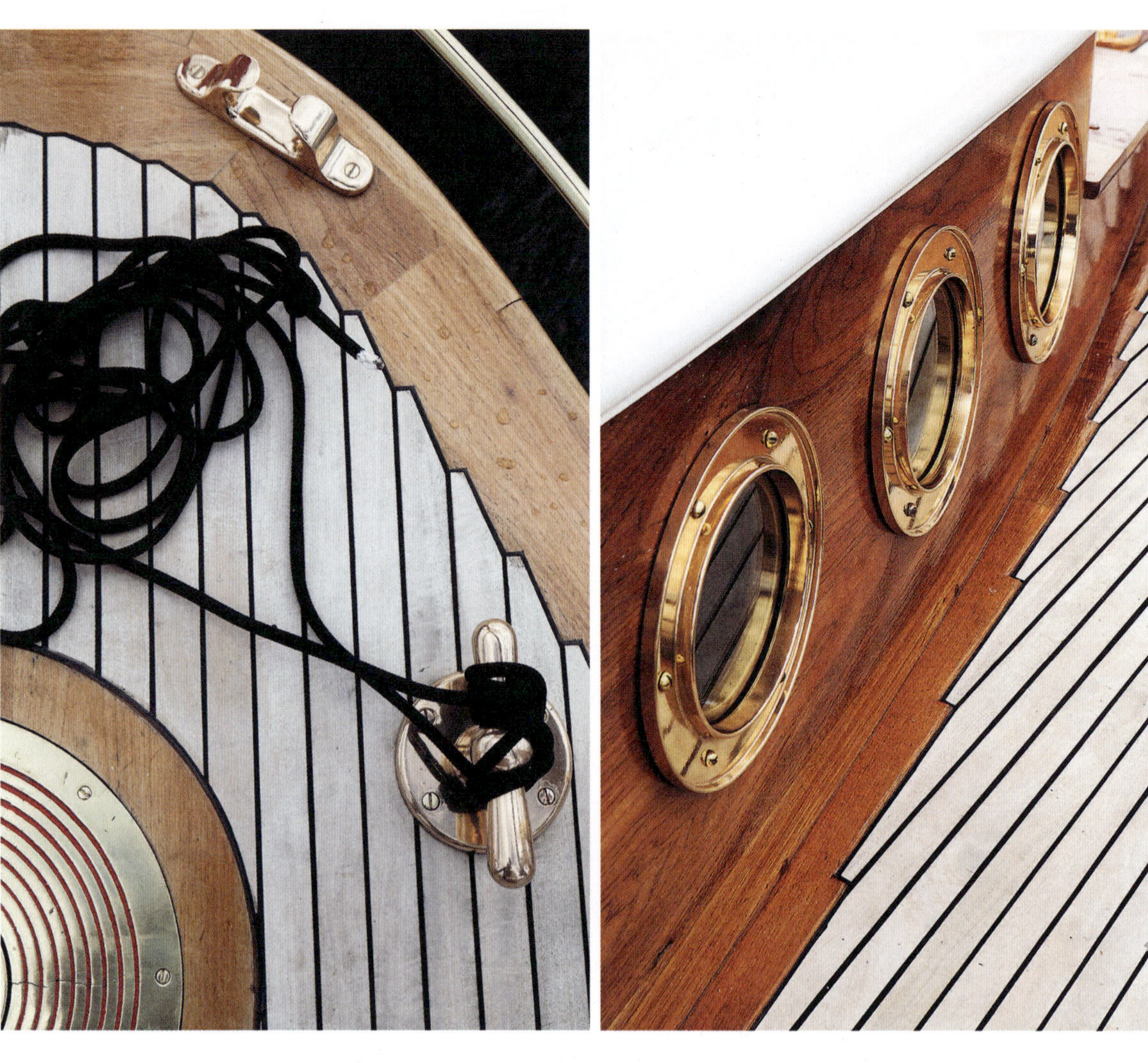

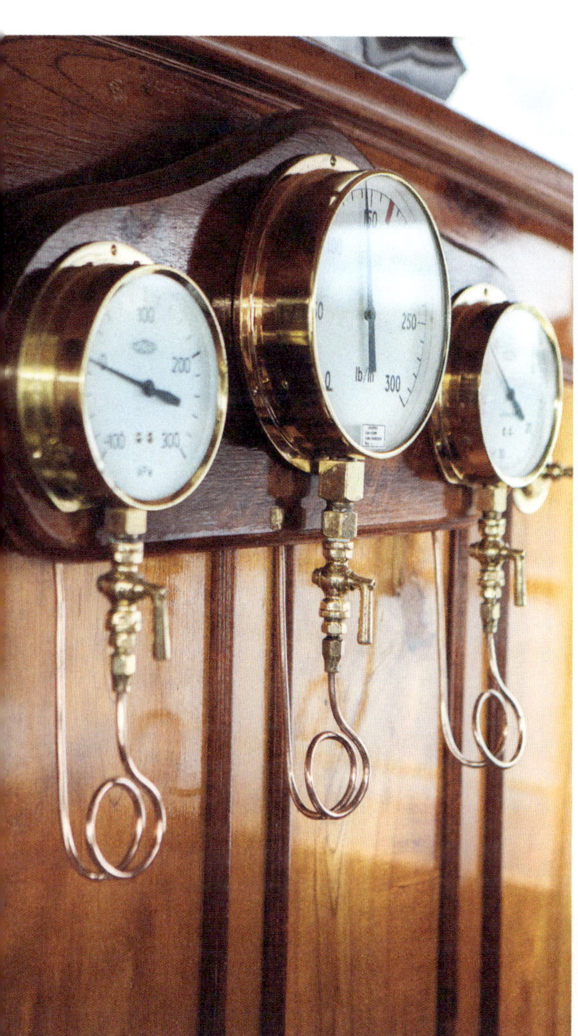

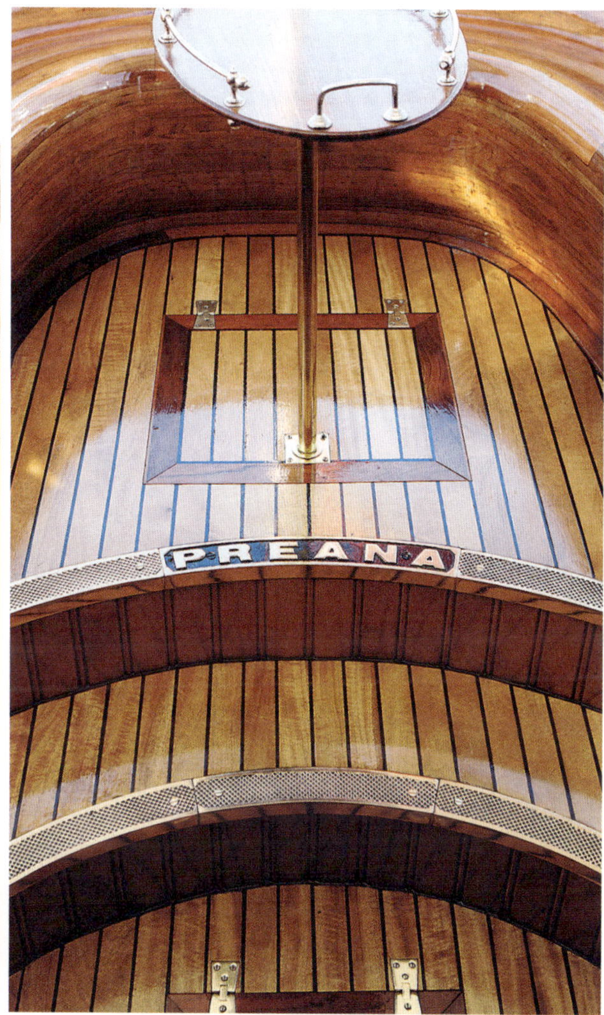

A trip on *S.Y. Preana* is like a huge step back in time, with her polished brass and timber interior and lavish fitout.

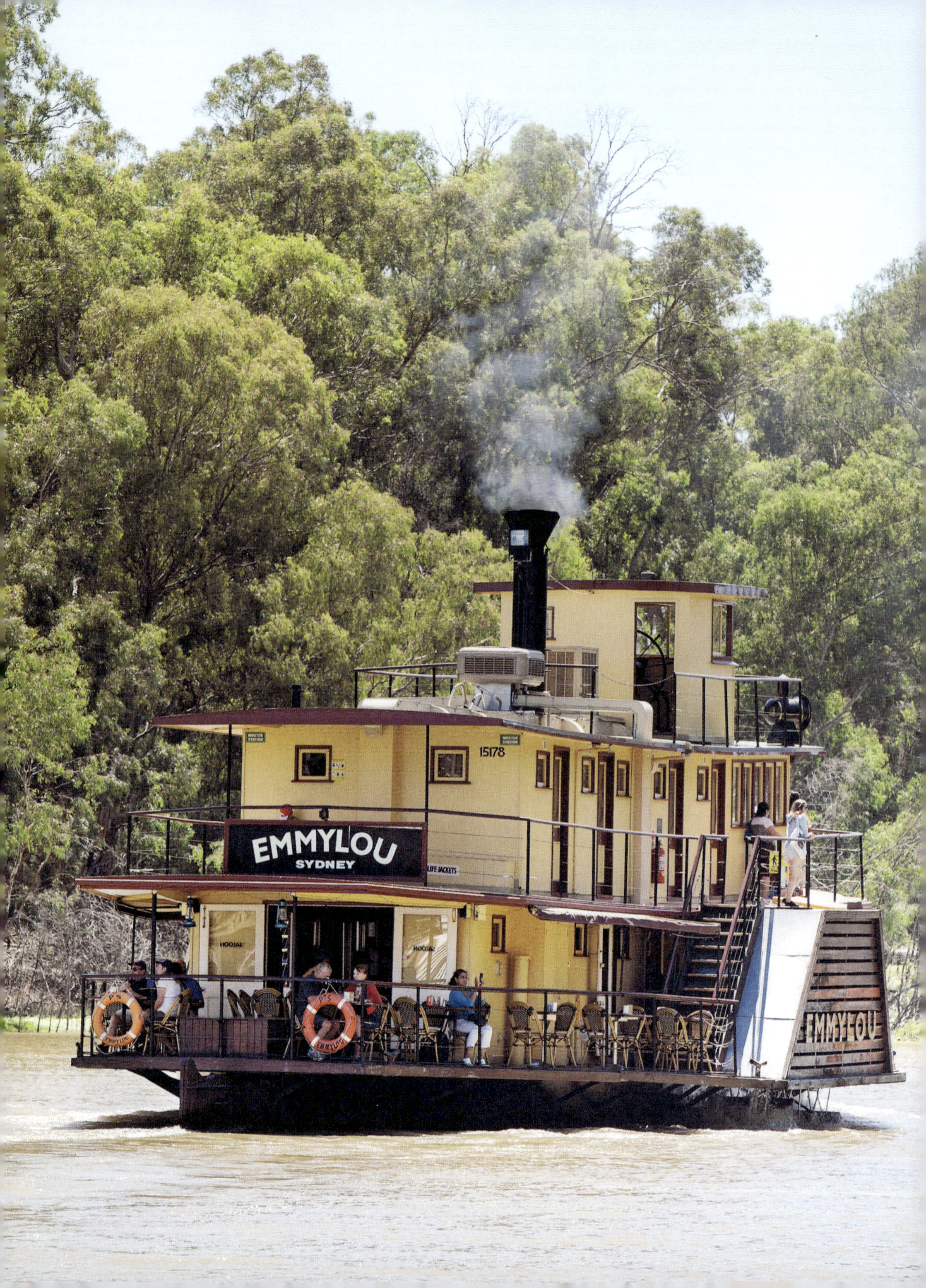
EMMYLOU
SYDNEY
15178
LIFE JACKETS
EMMYLOU

P. S. Emmylou

There is something about the smell of the river on a hot day, combined with the smell of towering River red gums, the steam and oil, and the deafening sound of the steam whistle as *P.S. Emmylou* leaves dock. The port of Echuca, on the border of New South Wales and Victoria, is home to *P.S. Emmylou*, a steel-hulled, timber-decked paddle steamer driven by a restored 1906 steam engine. She was built locally between 1980 and 1982 in the style of a nineteenth-century riverboat, and she fits in well with the other original paddle boats on the river. She is 90 feet long and her beam is 30 feet.

Captain Darren Mann steers the boat down the Murray River on this hot, lazy summer's day. The decks are full of passengers; excited children rush around as the engineer oils the engine and stokes up the firebox with red-gum logs. Lots of people are having morning tea aboard as we slowly make our way down the river, to the gentle sound of the paddles hitting the water and propelling the boat along.

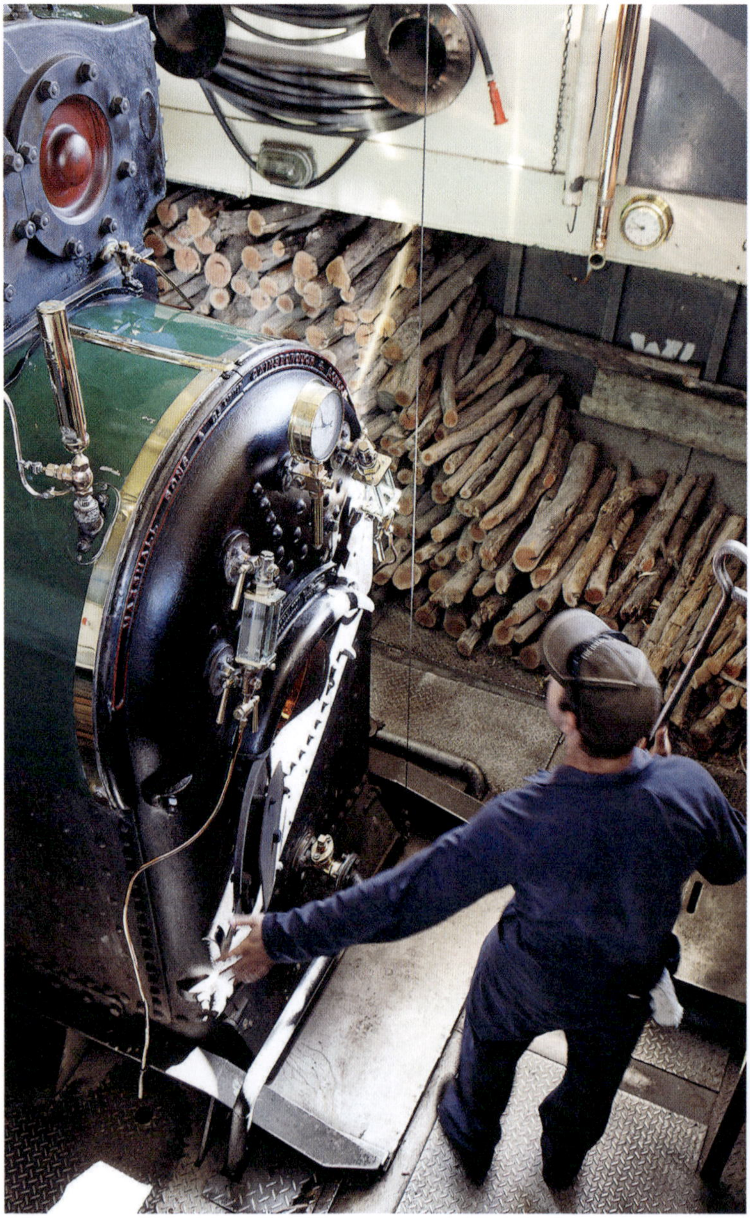

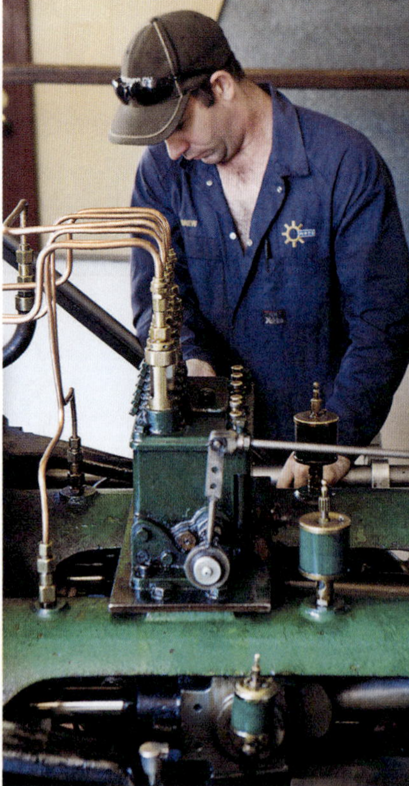

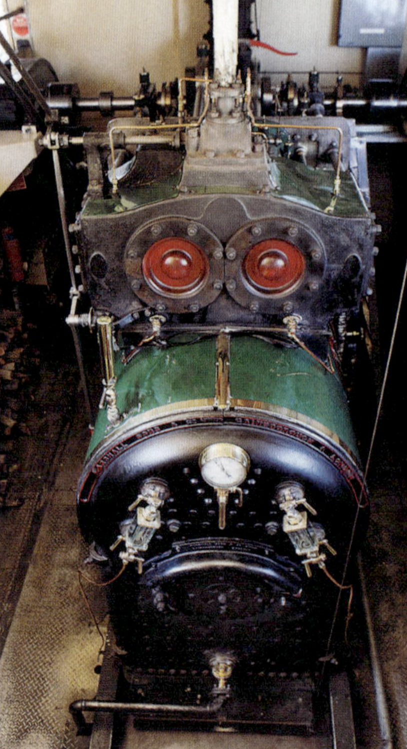

The engineer keeps the restored 1906 steam engine, the heart of *P.S. Emmylou*, in mint condition. Every inch of the engine is polished and kept shipshape, and she is powered by local timber.

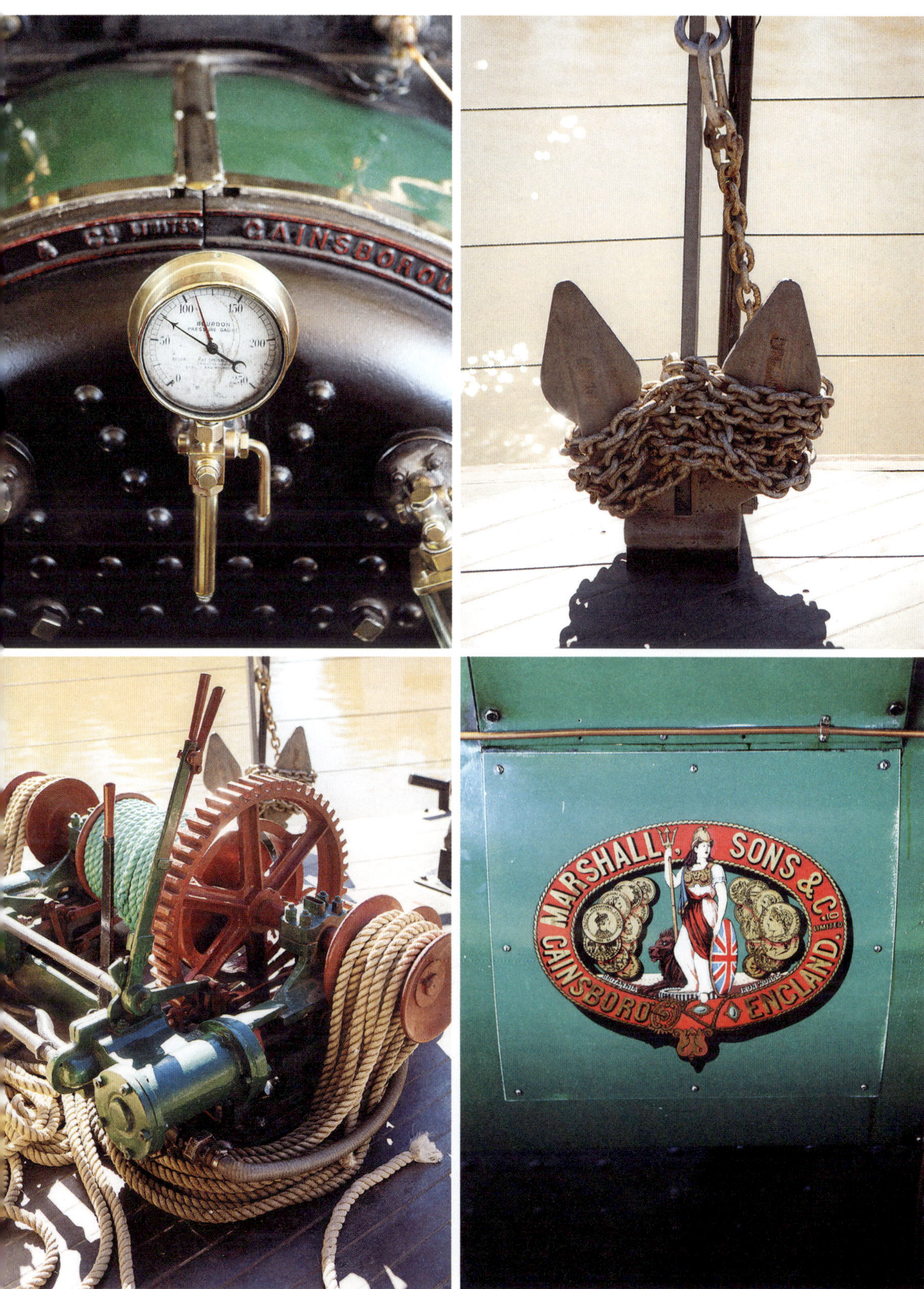
BOURDON PRESSURE GAUGE
MARSHALL, SONS & Co
LIMITED
GAINSBORO ENGLAND

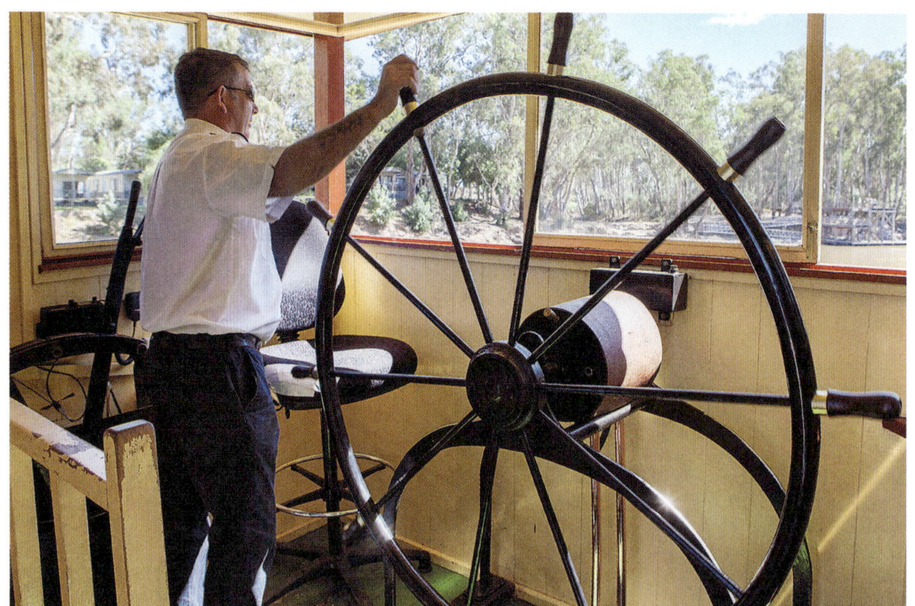

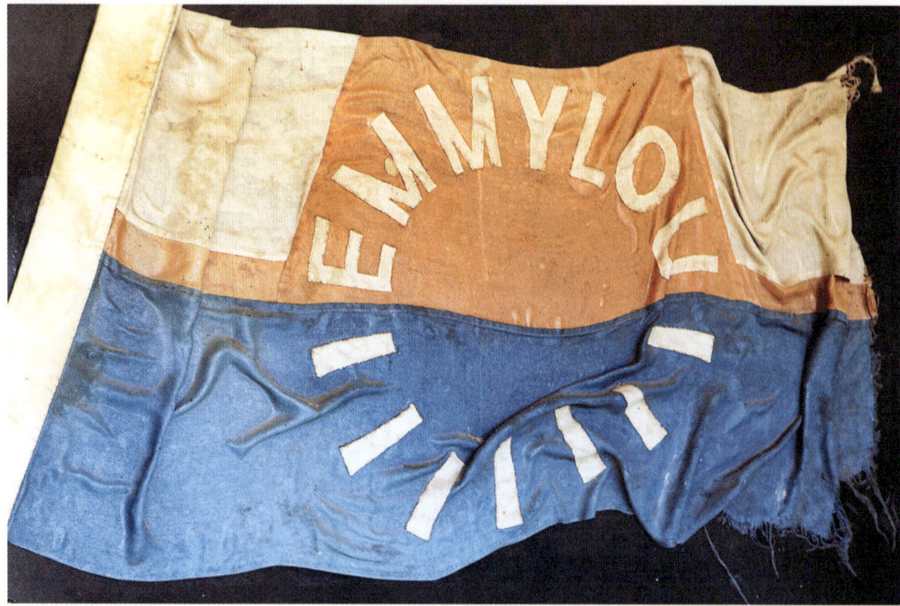

The captain, Darren Mann, steers *P.S. Emmylou* from his cabin at the top of the paddle steamer.

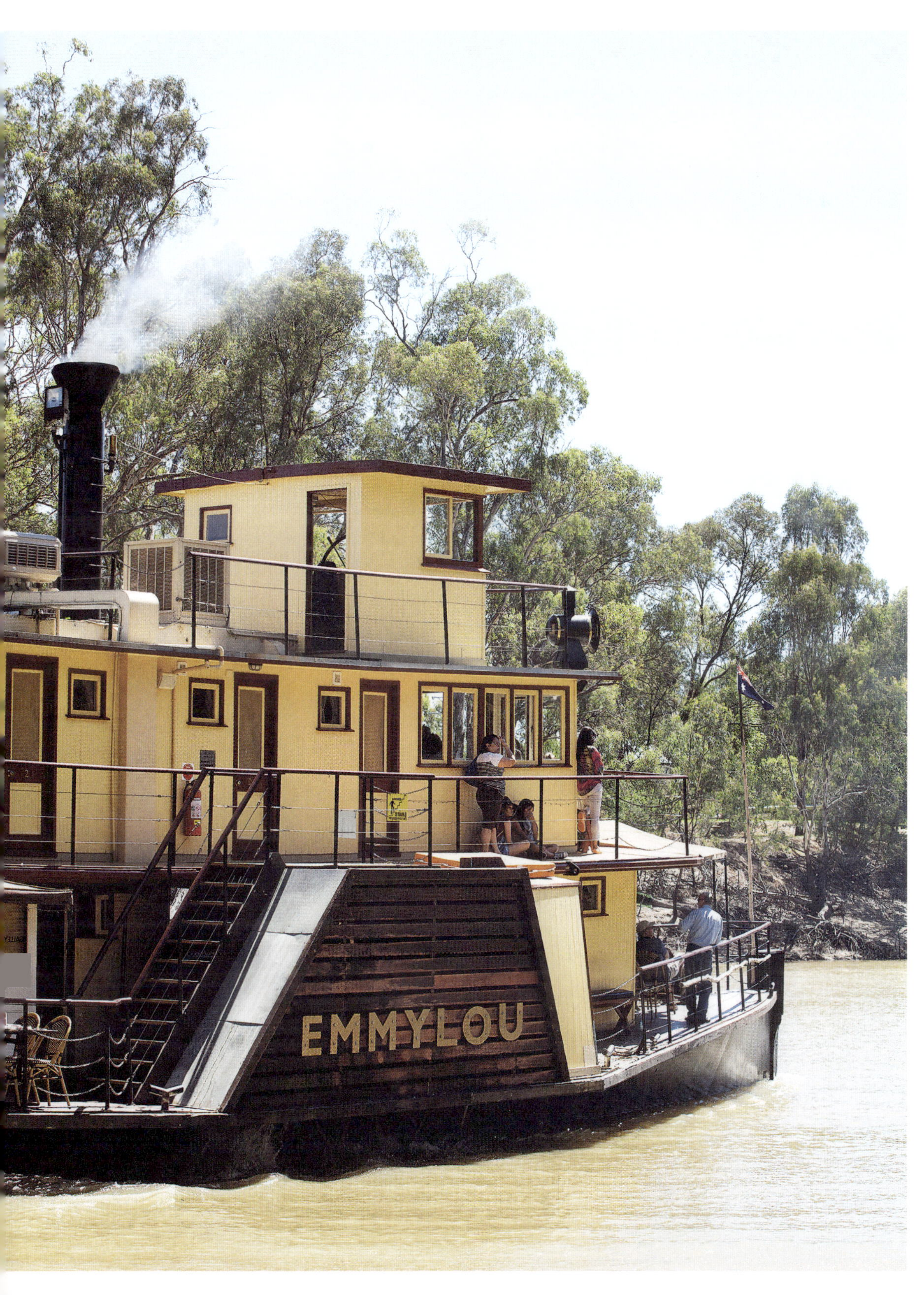
EMMYLOU

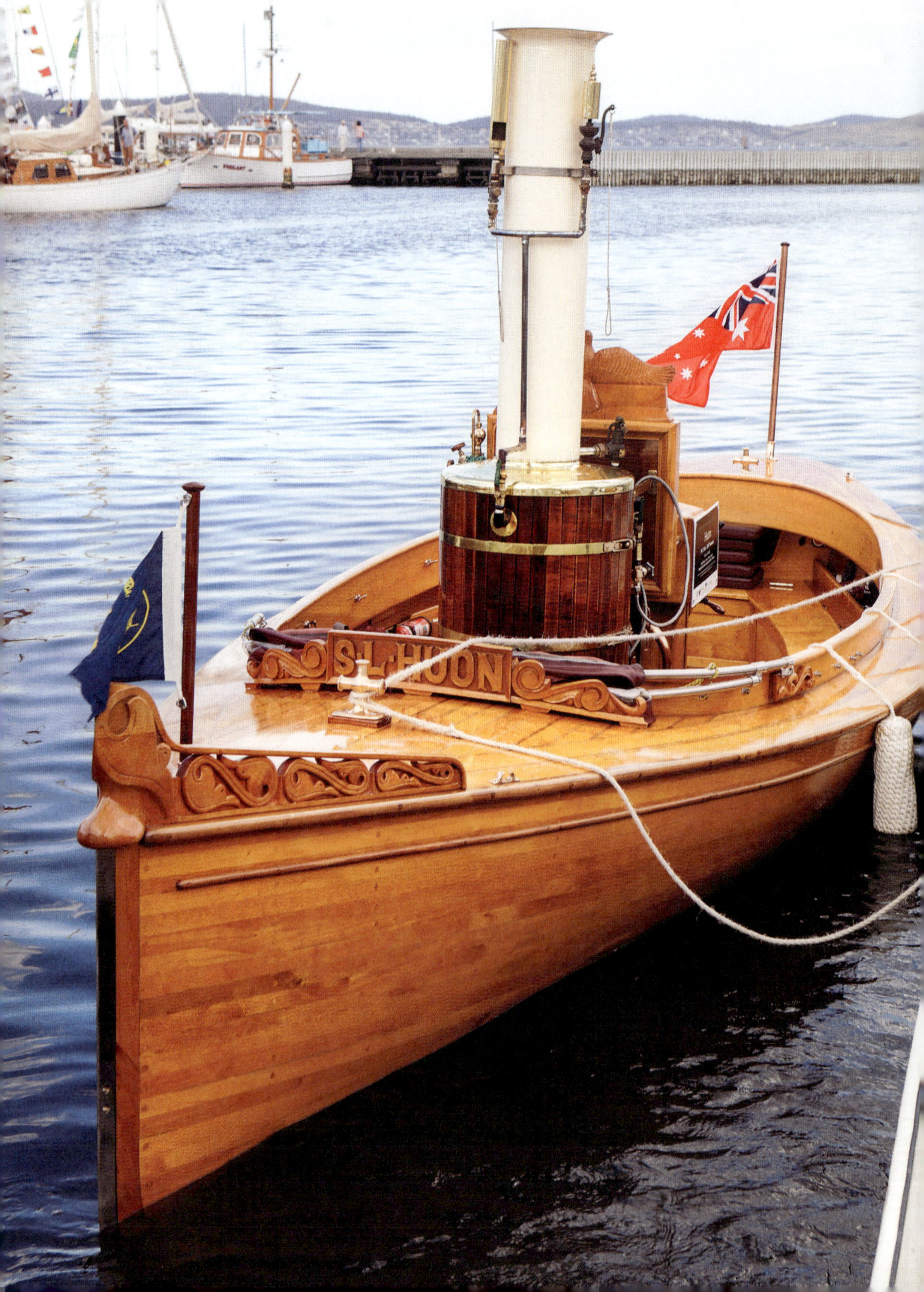
S.L. HUON

S.L. Huon

Bruce Jessup is the proud owner of *S.L. Huon*. She is a replica of an 1875 carvel steam launch used on inland waterways in the United States, all smartly polished brass with lots of detail in the timberwork. A carved bird with a fish in its claws perches above the brass steam gauges, while two steam whistles sit atop the funnel.

Built in Launceston, Tasmania, she was launched in 2006. She is made from Huon pine over Celery Top pine, fitted out with birds-eye Huon pine and Fiddle-back blackwood and propelled by a bronze propeller. She is 24 feet long.

The boiler, designed by Strath Steam of Goolwa in South Australia, is powered by brown coal. The engine is a York Compound, engineered by Charles Singleton of Westbury, Tasmania.

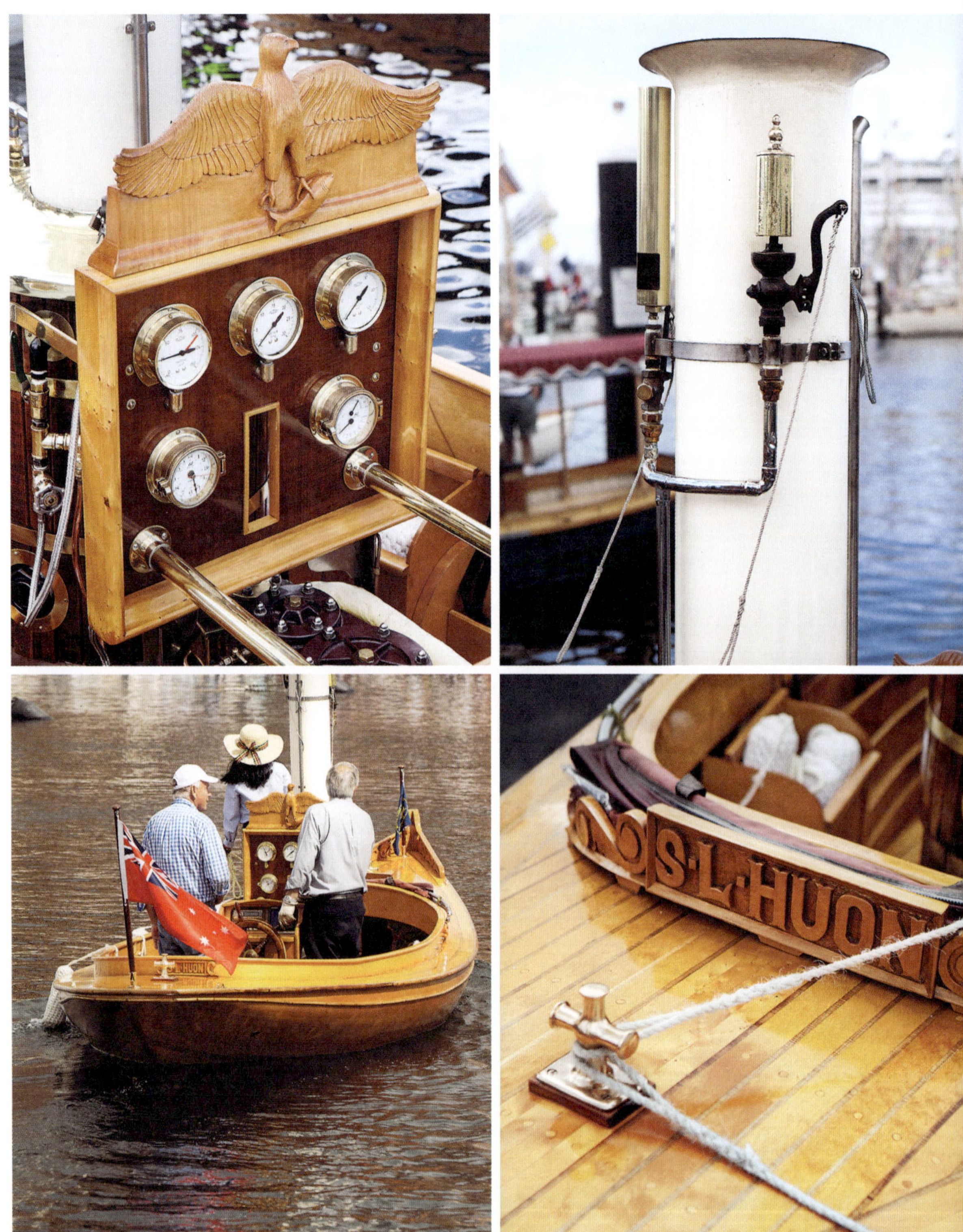
S·L·HUON

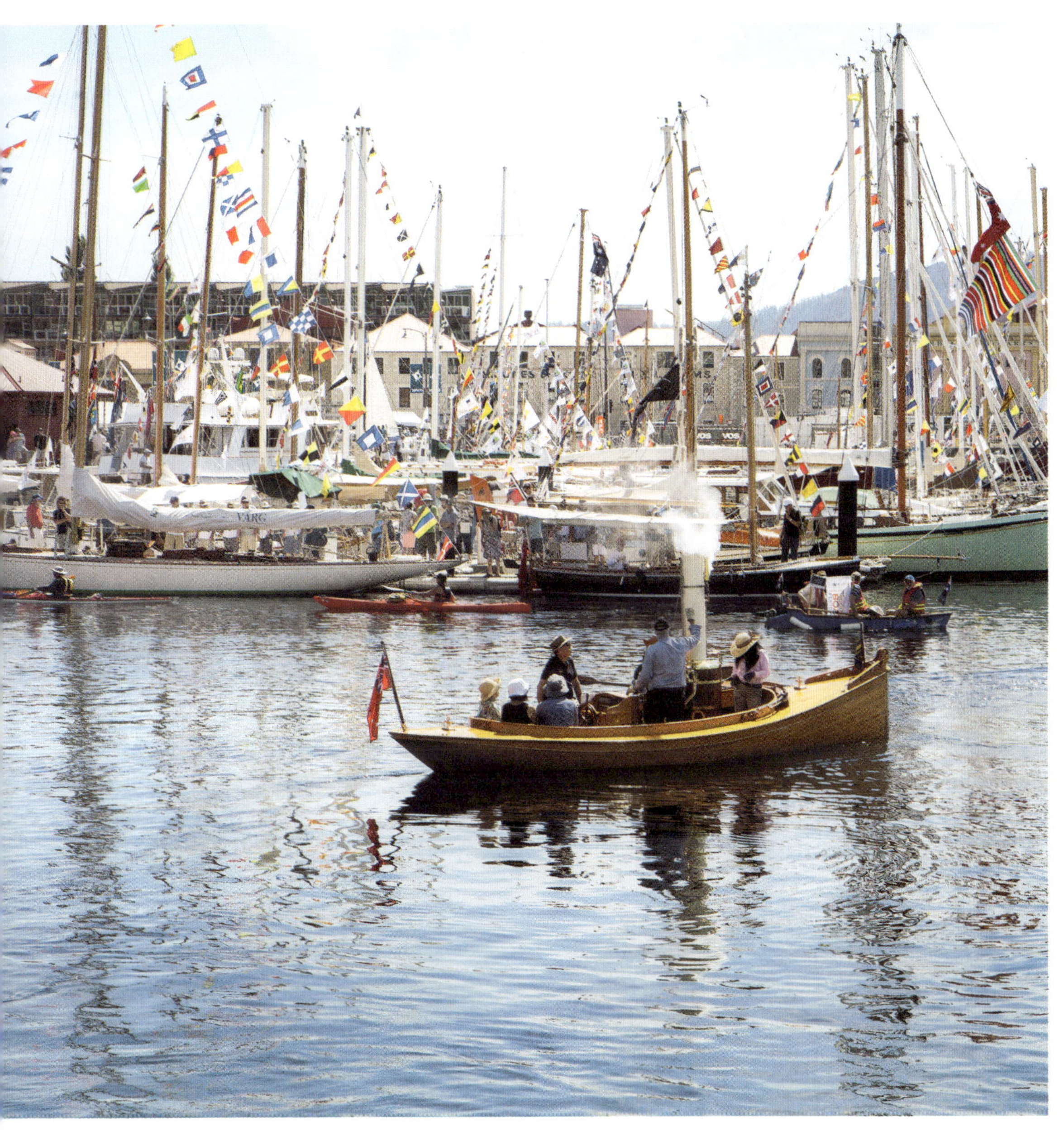

OPPOSITE, TOP LEFT Polished brass steam gauges gleam in the sunlight, with a carved wooden bird sitting above them, a freshly caught fish in his talons.

ABOVE What could be more enjoyable than a jaunt on a steam-powered boat?

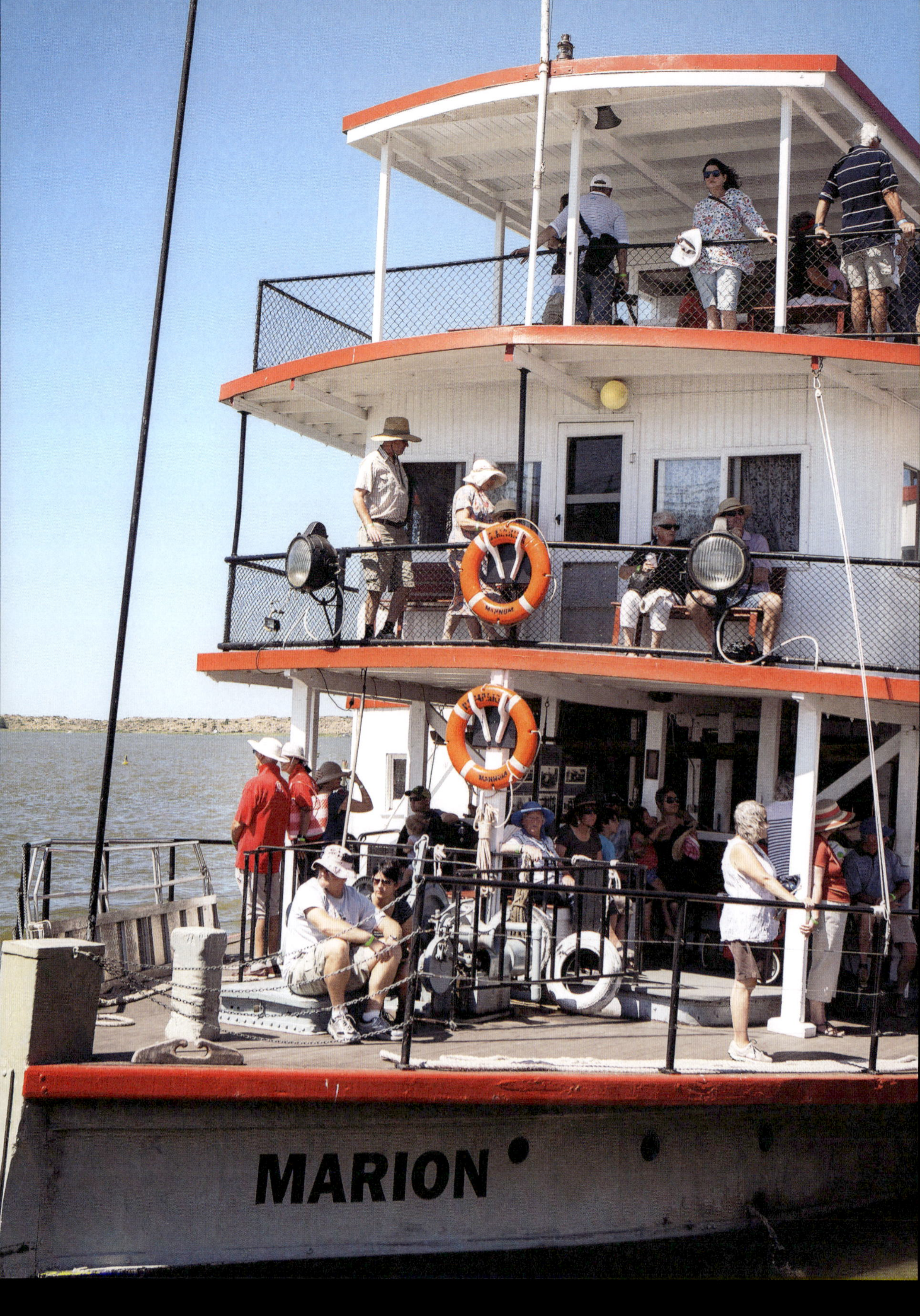
MARION

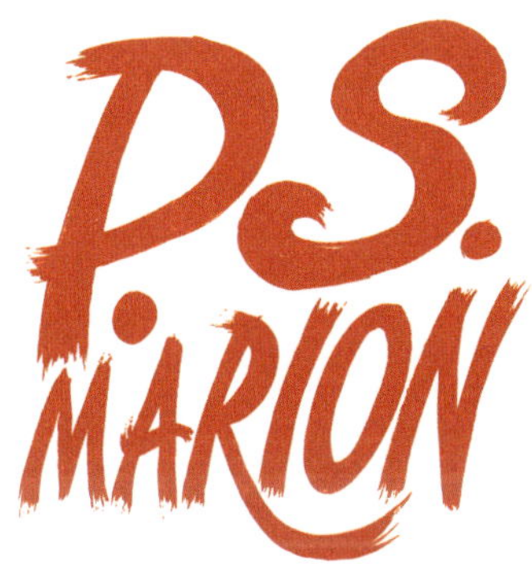

Prominent Adelaide businessman and M.P. Mr George Swan Fowler commissioned *P.S. Marion* in 1896 from Milang shipbuilder A.H. Landseer. Unfortunately Mr Fowler died soon after building had begun, so his trustees decided to complete the hull and sell her as a barge. She floated in 1897.

In 1900, William Bowring bought her. He built a superstructure on her, and imported a Marshall & Sons of Gainsborough engine. She is still powered by that engine. Over the years her function changed, from shipping cargo to passengers.

As a passenger steamer, *P.S. Marion* went on regular summer cruises until 1963, when she was bought by the National Trust, which maintained her for over thirty years as part of the static Mannum Dock Museum.

In 1989, it was decided to restore *P.S. Marion* to full operation. After a long and thorough restoration she was recommissioned in 1994. Based at Mannum on the Murray River in South Australia, she is now open every day for passenger trips.

P.S. Marion is recognised as one of the flagships of river transport and operates as a living museum.

FOLLOWING PAGES
A pleasant way to view the boats at the Australian Wooden Boat Festival in Hobart (see pages 174–185).

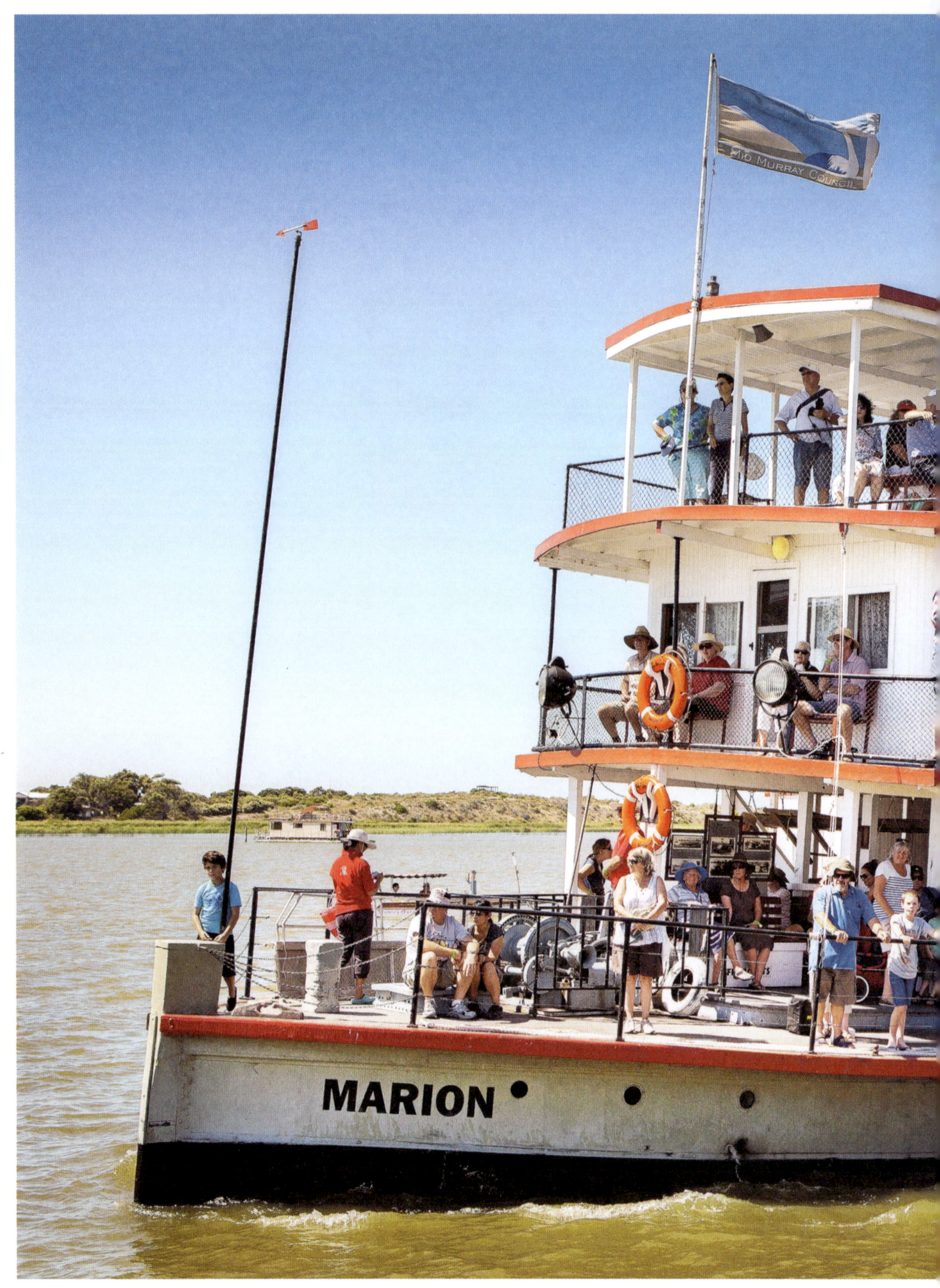
MID MURRAY COUNCIL
MARION

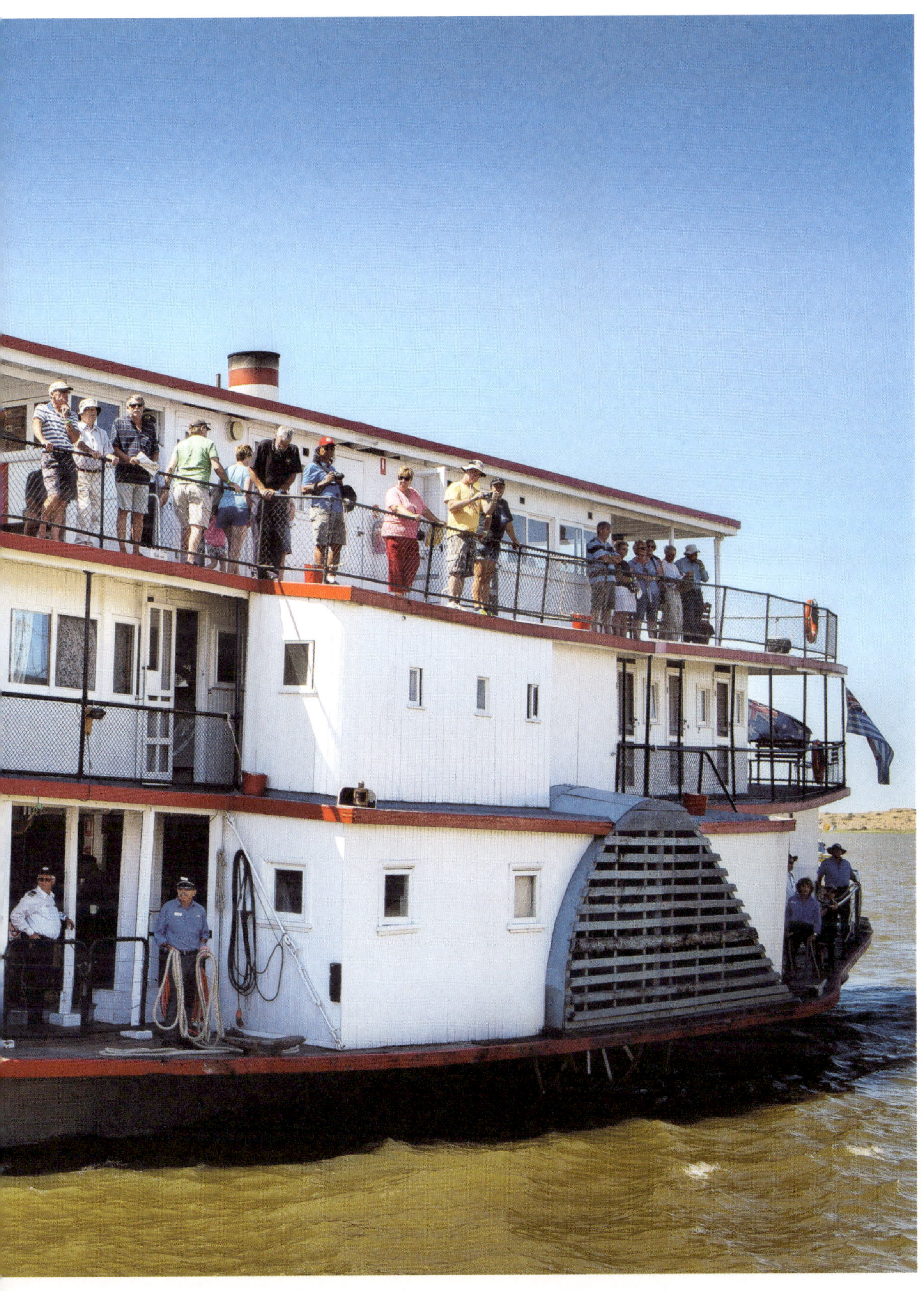

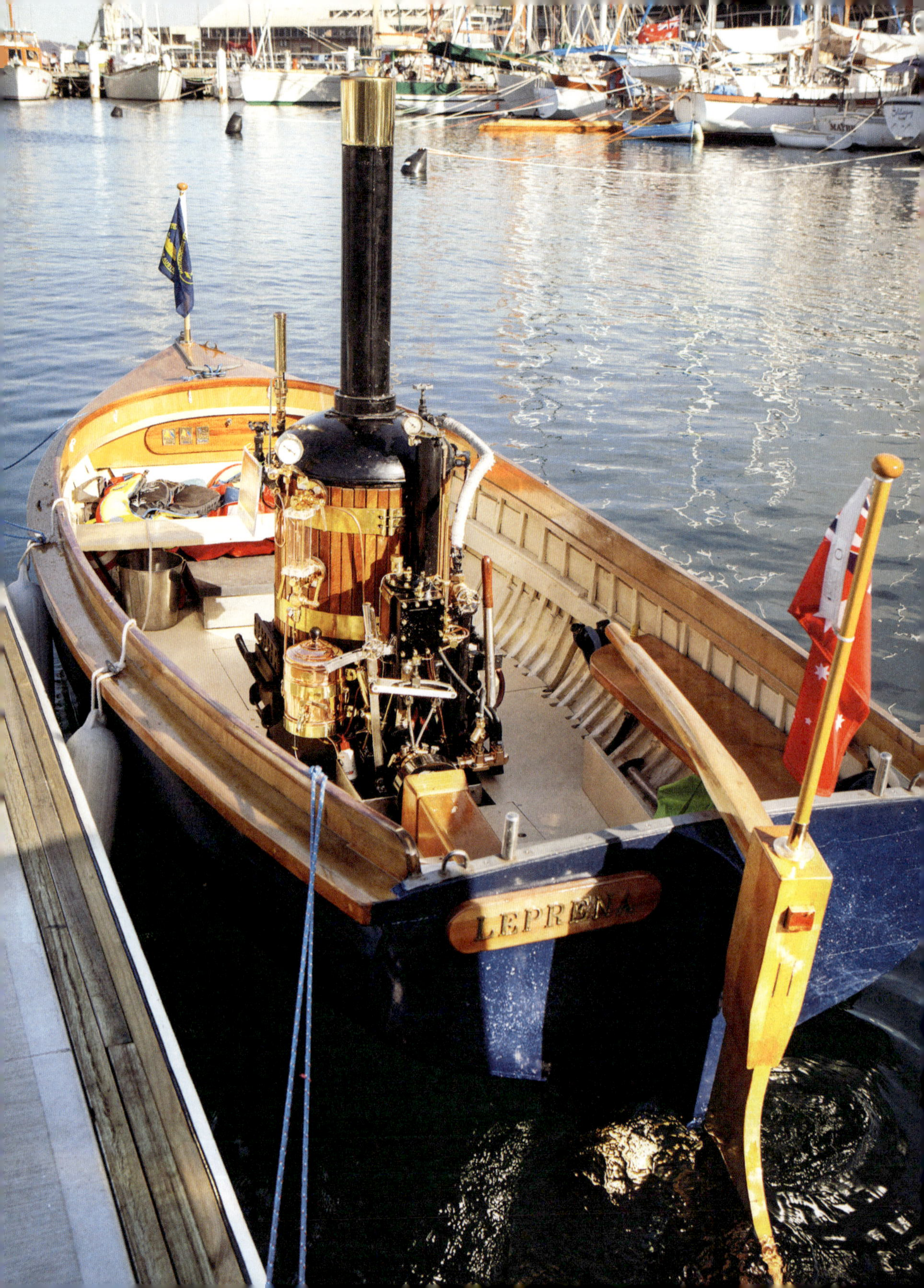
LEPRENA

S.L. LEPRENA

This boat started life as a six-oared jolly boat aboard the larger *S.L. Leprena,* a 110-foot schooner built to take timber from Recherche Bay to Hobart. She was built by Purdon and Featherstone in 1922 and is clinker-built in King Billy pine. She is 16 feet long. In 1925, the original schooner was wrecked just north of Eddystone Point, on a rock later named Leprena Rock. The jolly boat was then fitted with a petrol engine and used for many years for fishing at Recherche Bay, near the southern tip of Tasmania.

S.L. Leprena jolly boat was restored in 1998 by Bart Hutchings, who also built and fitted the Cleveland Dolphin steam engine and C&M Wear wood-fired fire tube boiler. Andrew Perkins bought *S.L. Leprena* in 2012 and restored her, converting her so that she ran on bio-mass or wood pellets. She is now truly a steam launch of the twenty-first century, as wood pellets are 100 per cent renewable, a non-fossil fuel and a sustainable energy source.

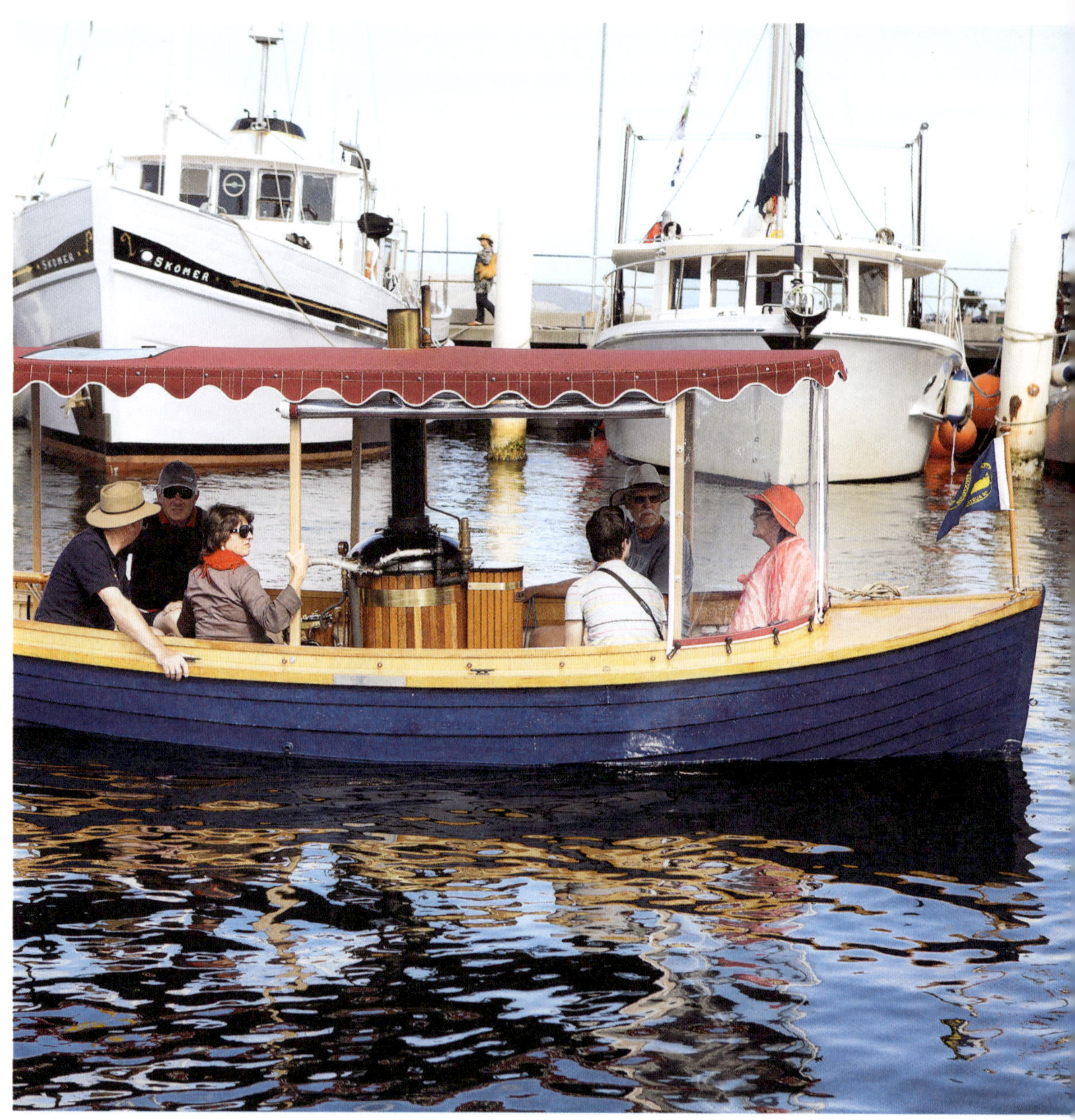

ABOVE From jolly boat to steam launch, *S.L. Leprena* has had an interesting and varied life.

OPPOSITE, LEFT *S.L. Leprena's* boiler and engine are always neatly polished; in fact, everything about her is as neat as a pin.

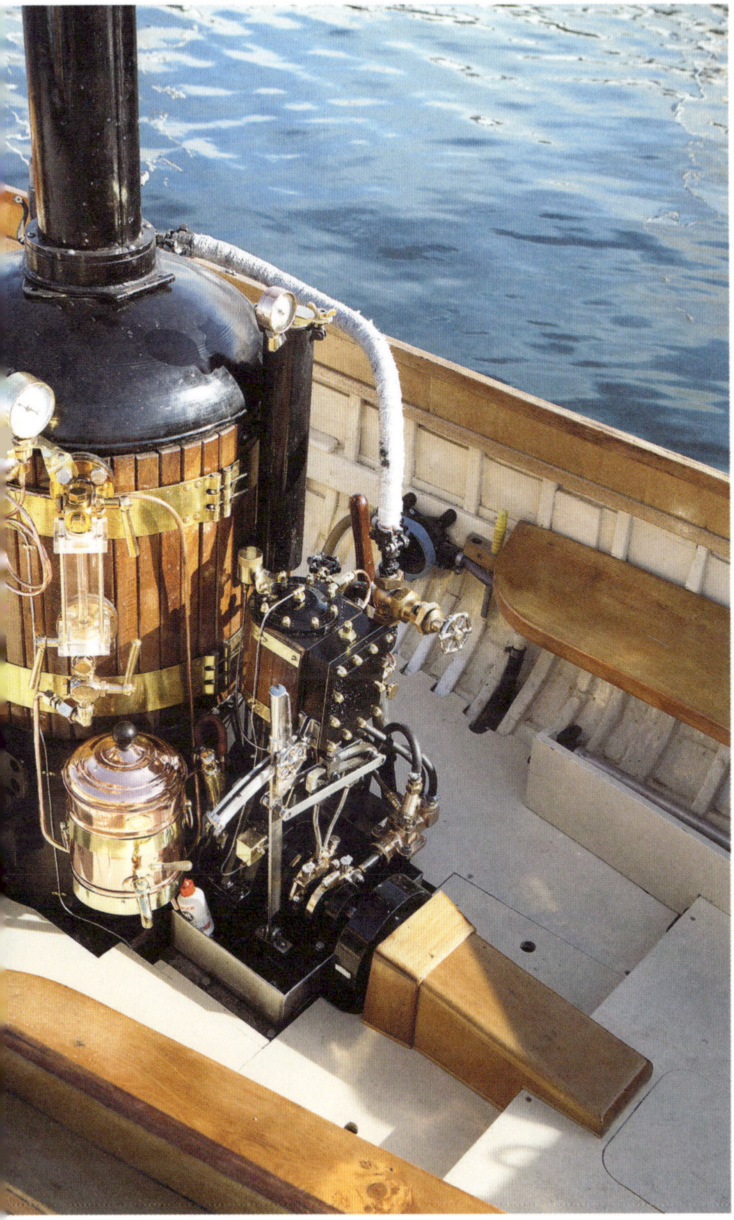

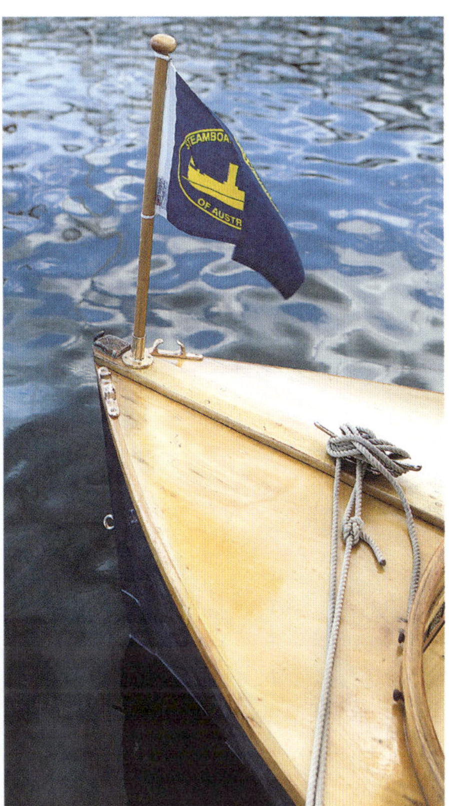

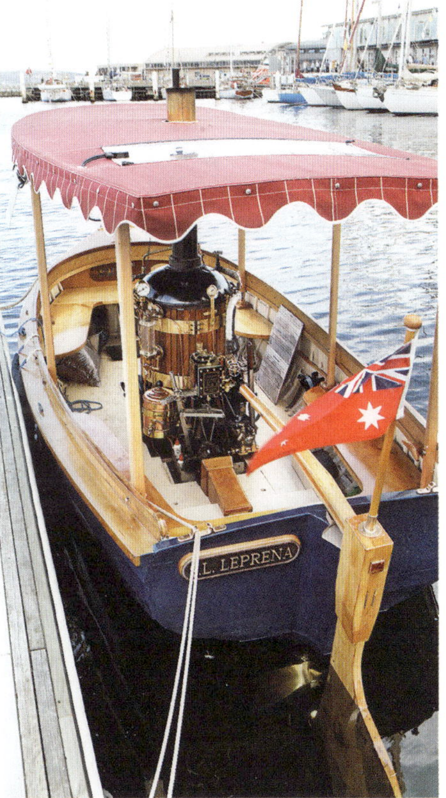
L. LEPRENA

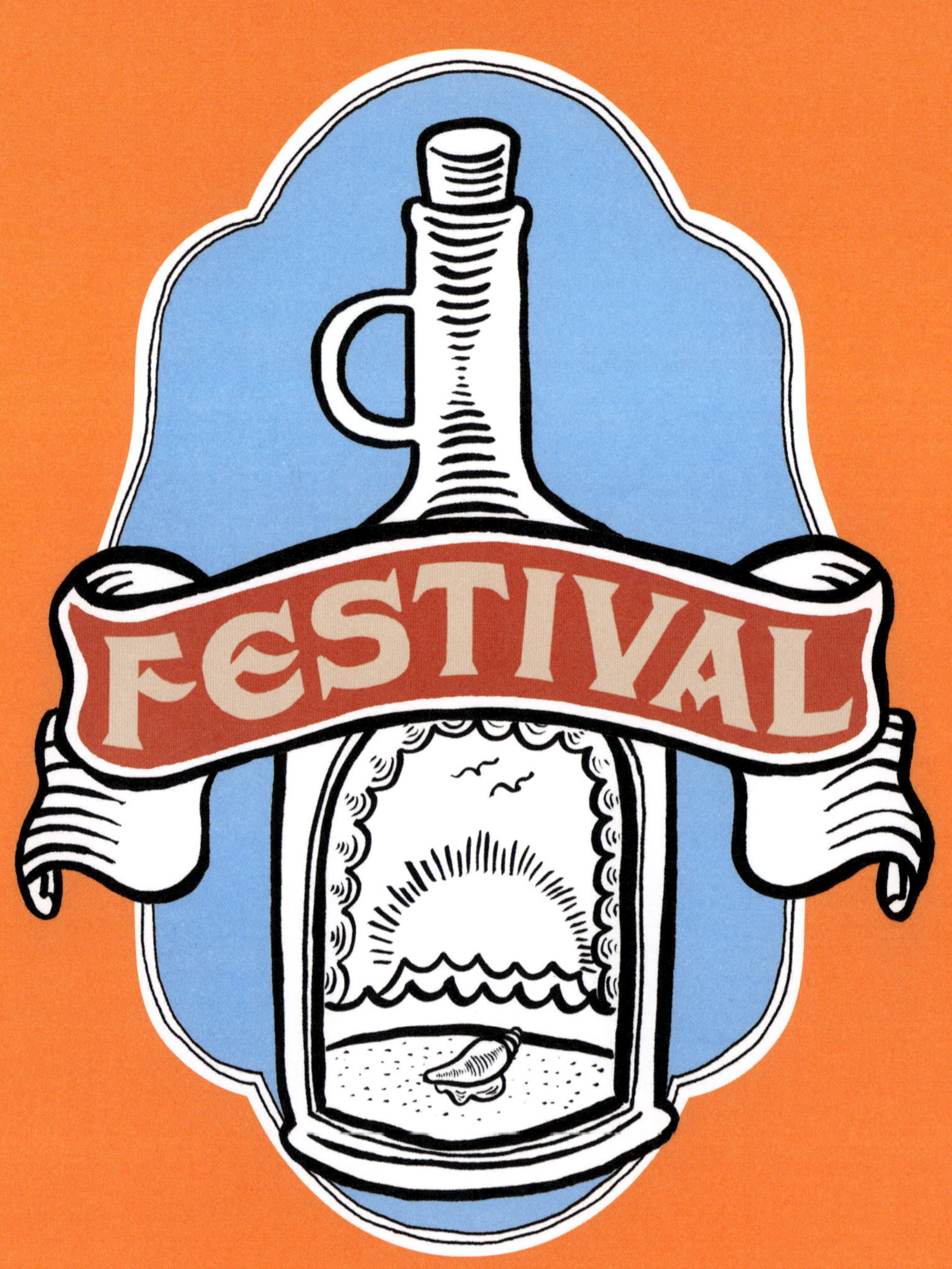
FESTIVAL

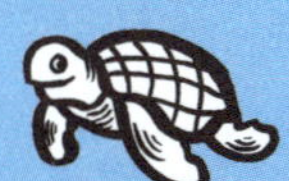

AUSTRALIA HAS PLENTY OF BOAT FESTIVALS. A FESTIVAL IS THE BEST WAY TO SEE LOTS OF GREAT BOATS IN ONE LOCATION. IT IS ALSO JUST THE PLACE TO FIND THE BOAT OF YOUR DREAMS, MEET A BOATBUILDER WHO CAN BUILD IT FOR YOU, OR BUY SOME PLANS TO BUILD IT YOURSELF. OR YOU CAN JUST LOOK AND DREAM.

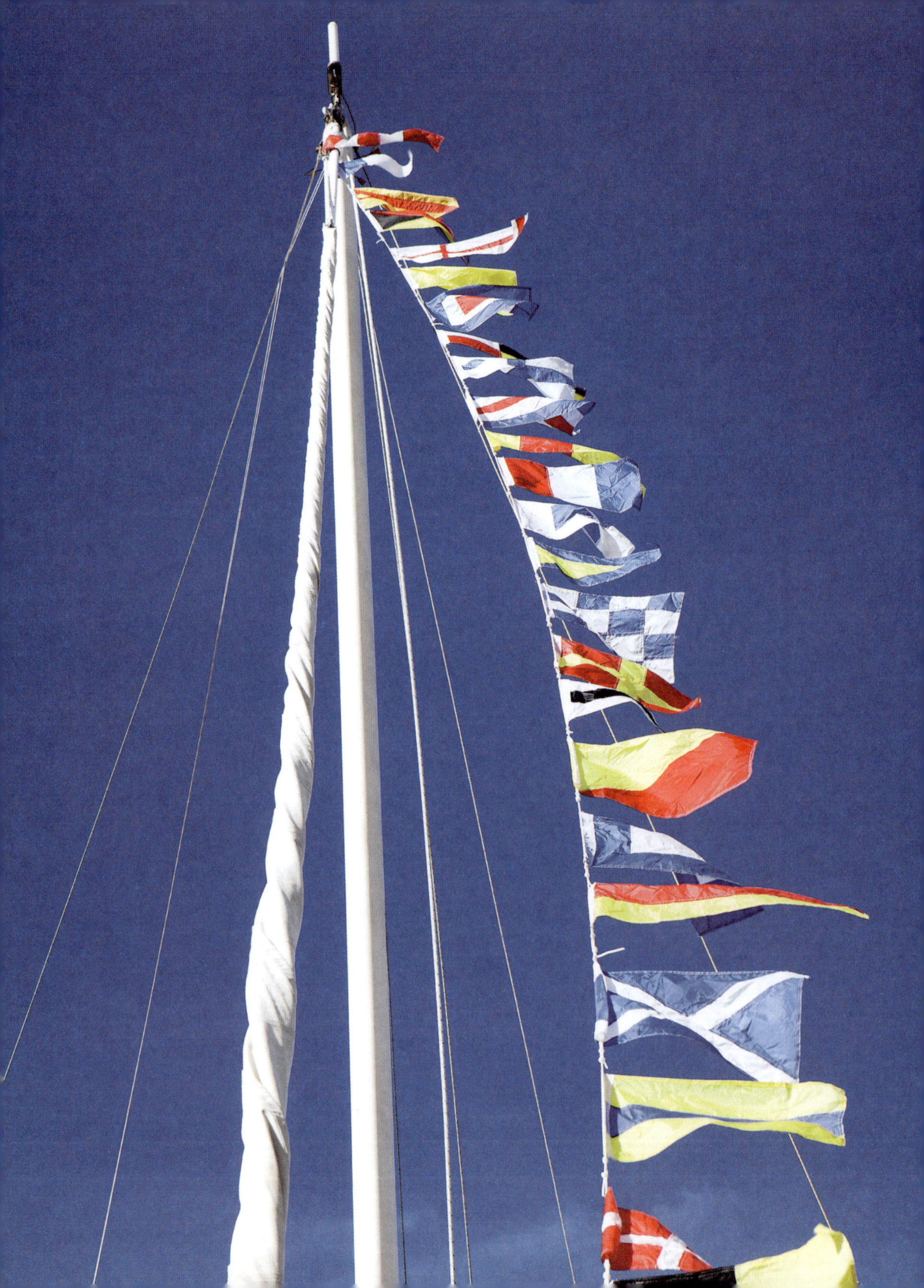

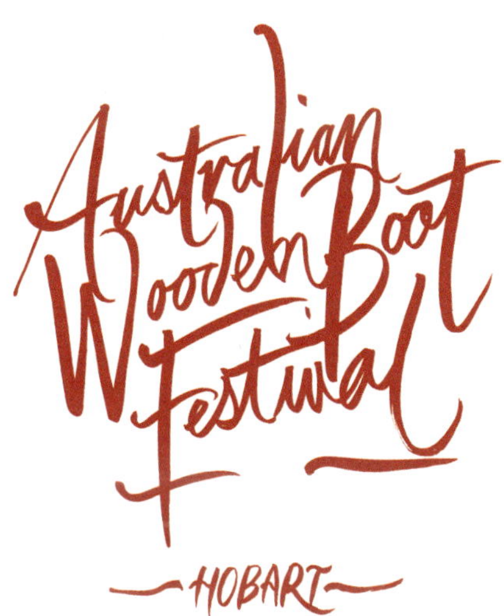

Started in 1994, this is without a doubt the best boat festival I have ever been to. The people of Hobart, where it is held, really know how to turn on a festival – theirs is the biggest wooden boat festival in the Southern Hemisphere. The historic Hobart waterfront comes alive with hundreds of boats of all descriptions.

You will find all manner of wooden boats here, from tiny models to classic tall ships and everything in between. You can also meet boat owners, boatbuilders and boat restorers, cruise on magnificent tall ships and steam launches, buy a boat from some of the boatbuilders who set up displays or go to presentations about boating history or boat maintenance.

The whole harbour area is buzzing with people and stalls selling Tasmanian gourmet produce. Traditional boatbuilding skills are on show in demonstrations, and the opening 'Parade of Sail' is an amazing display of boats of every description.

The festival is held over four days in February of each odd-numbered year and it takes at least three days to see everything and take it all in.

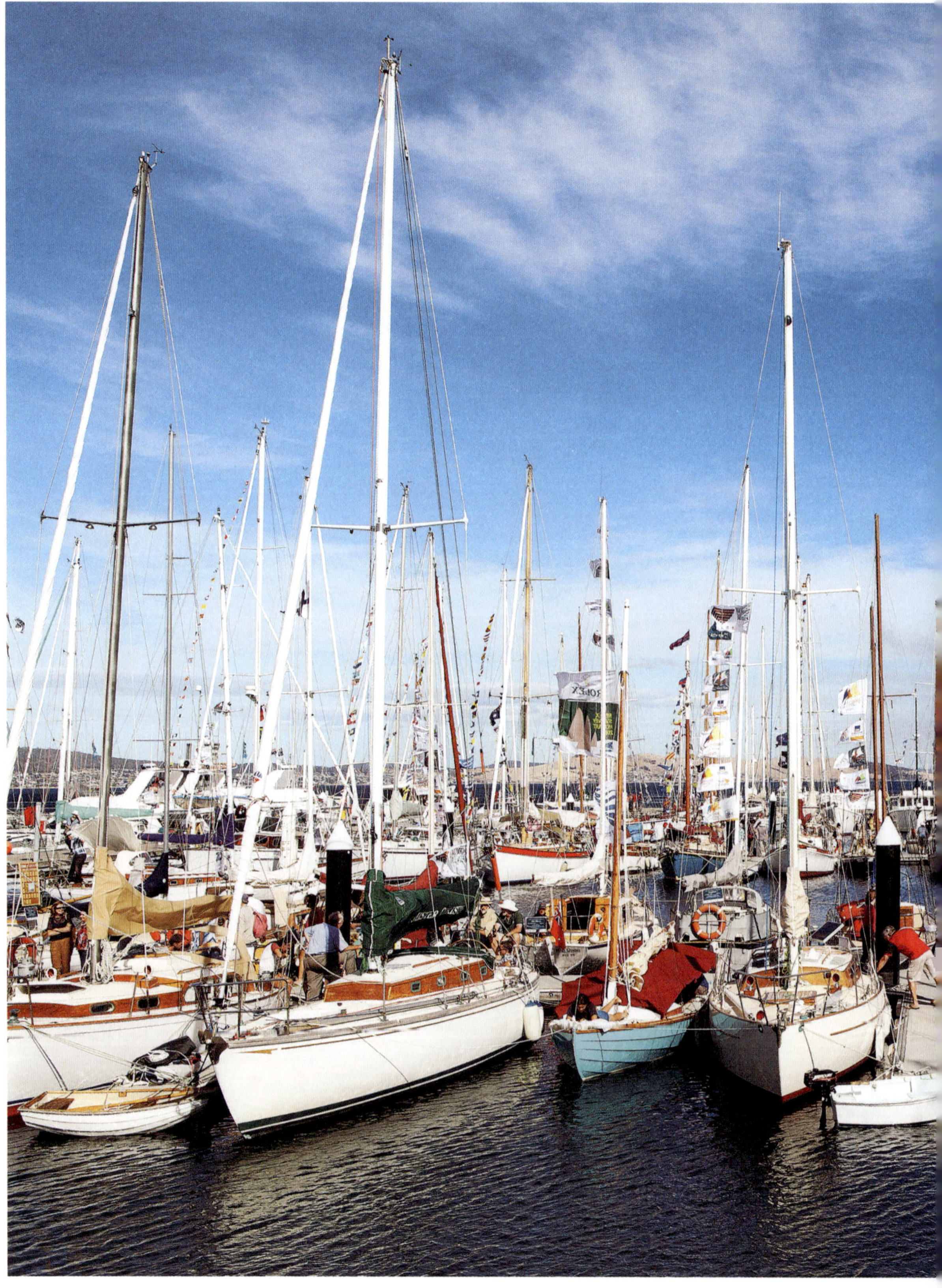

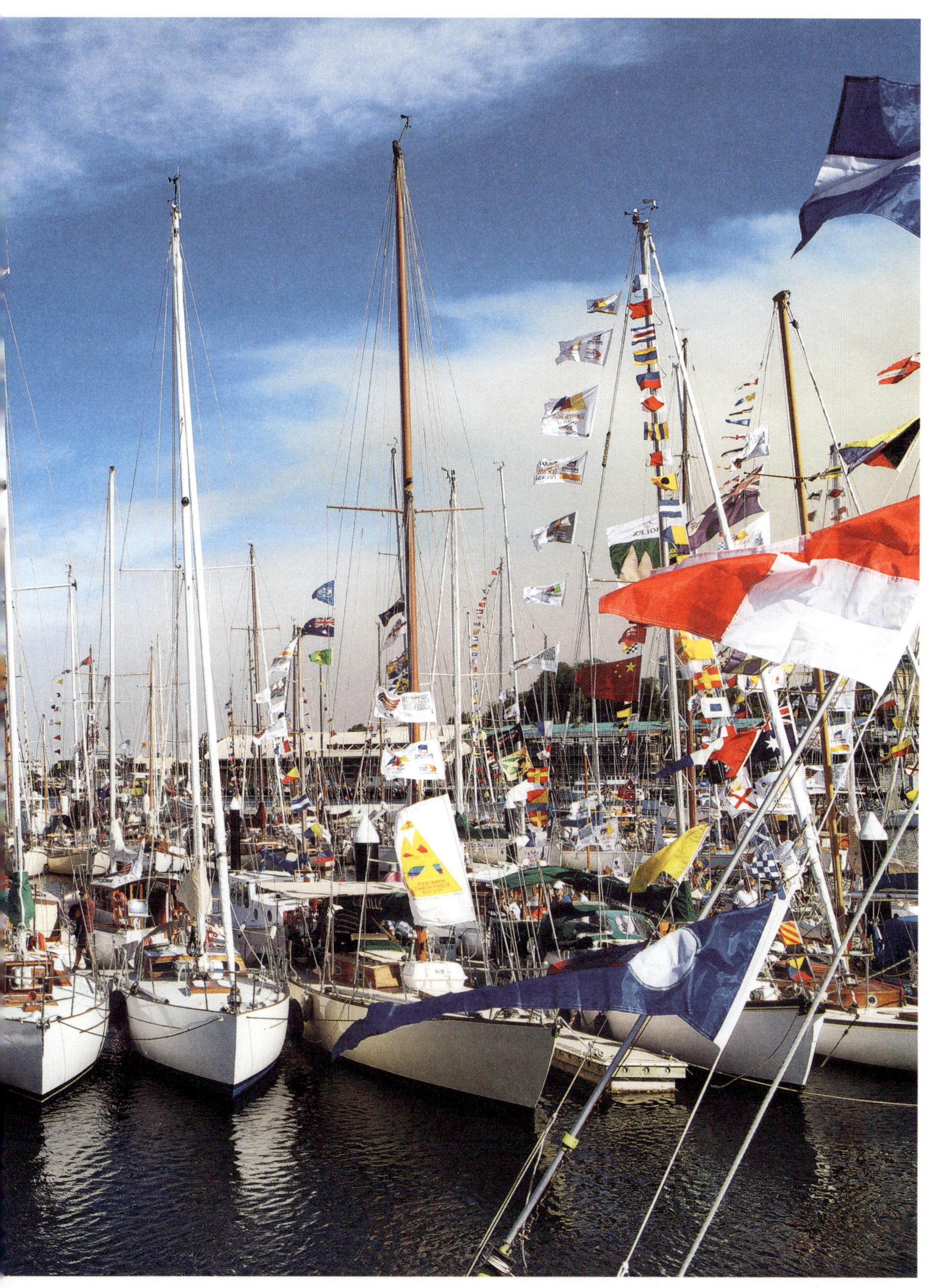

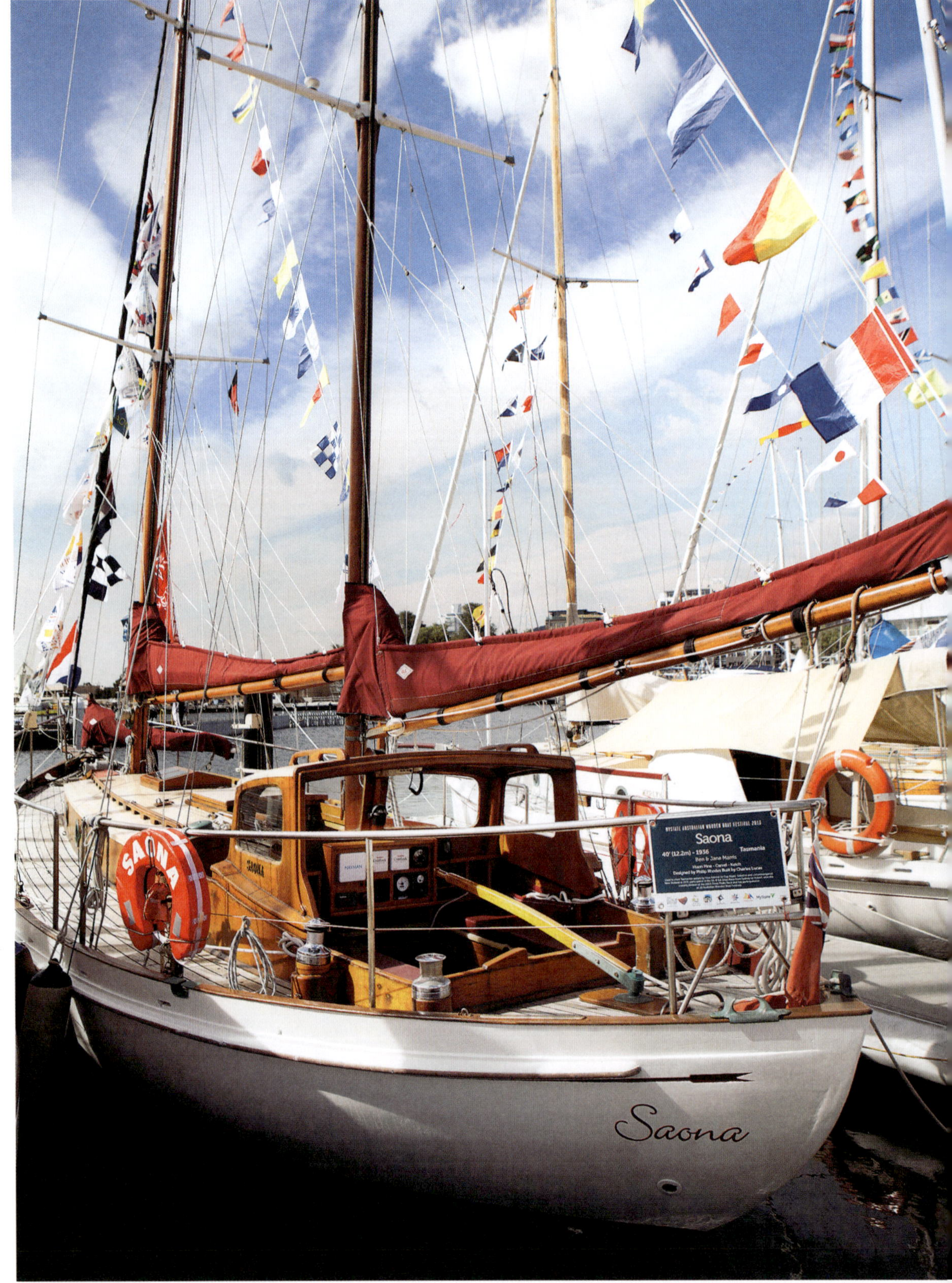
SAONA
Saona
Tasmania
40' (12.2m) - 1936
Ben & Jane Marris
Huon Pine - Carvel - Ketch
Designed by Philip Rhodes Built by Charles Lucas
MyState
Saona

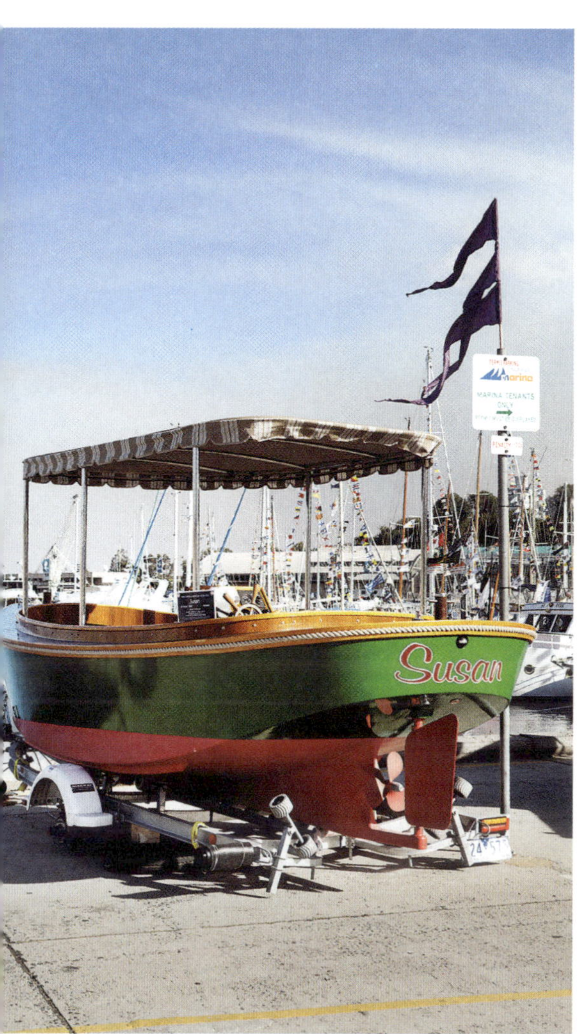

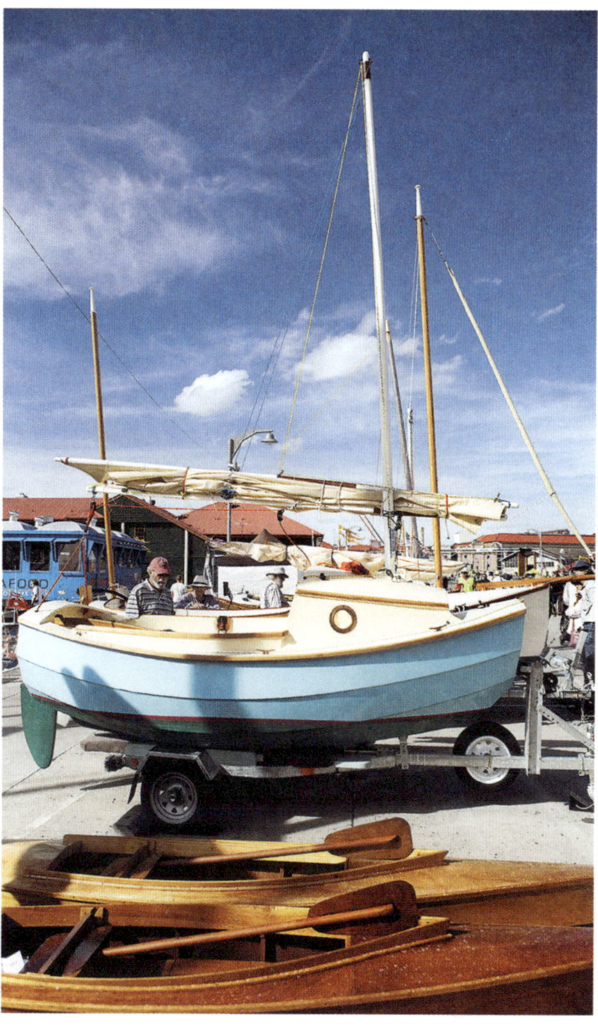

There are wooden boats of every size and shape at the festival. Whether your passion is for model boats, fishing boats, yachts or tall ships, there is something for everyone.

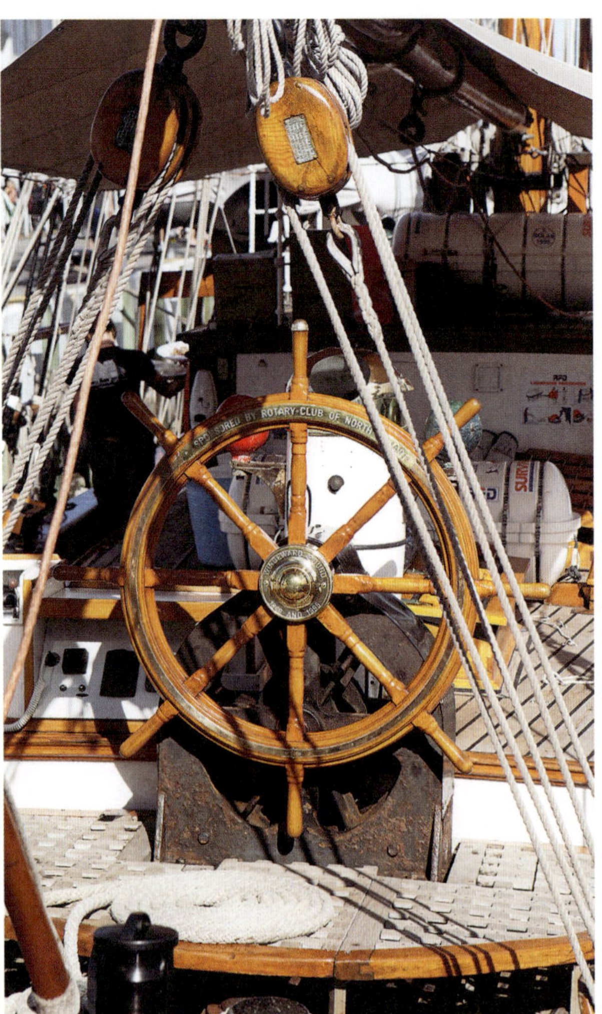

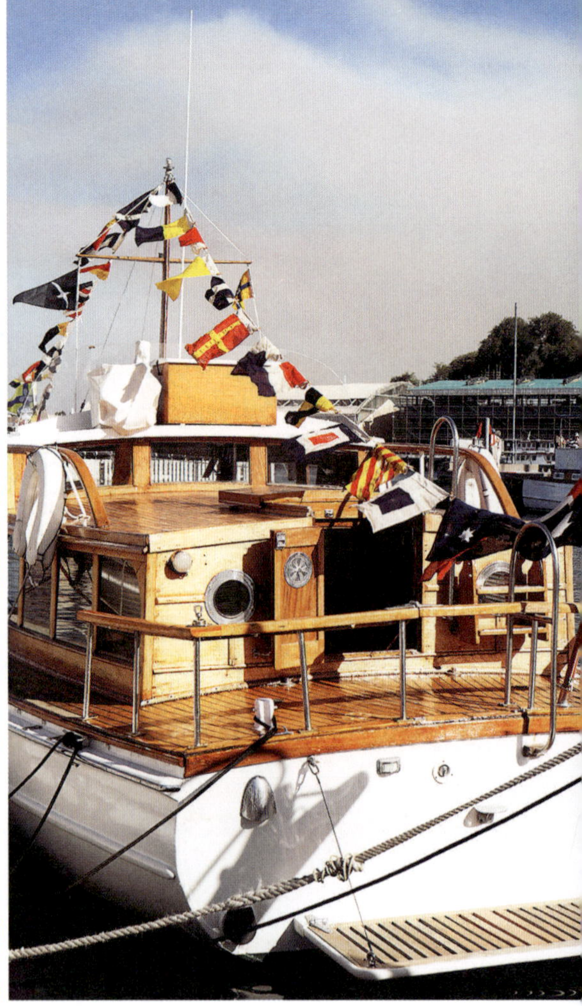

The whole Port of Hobart comes alive during the festival. The boat owners get into the action too, with everyone flying flags and joining in the fun.

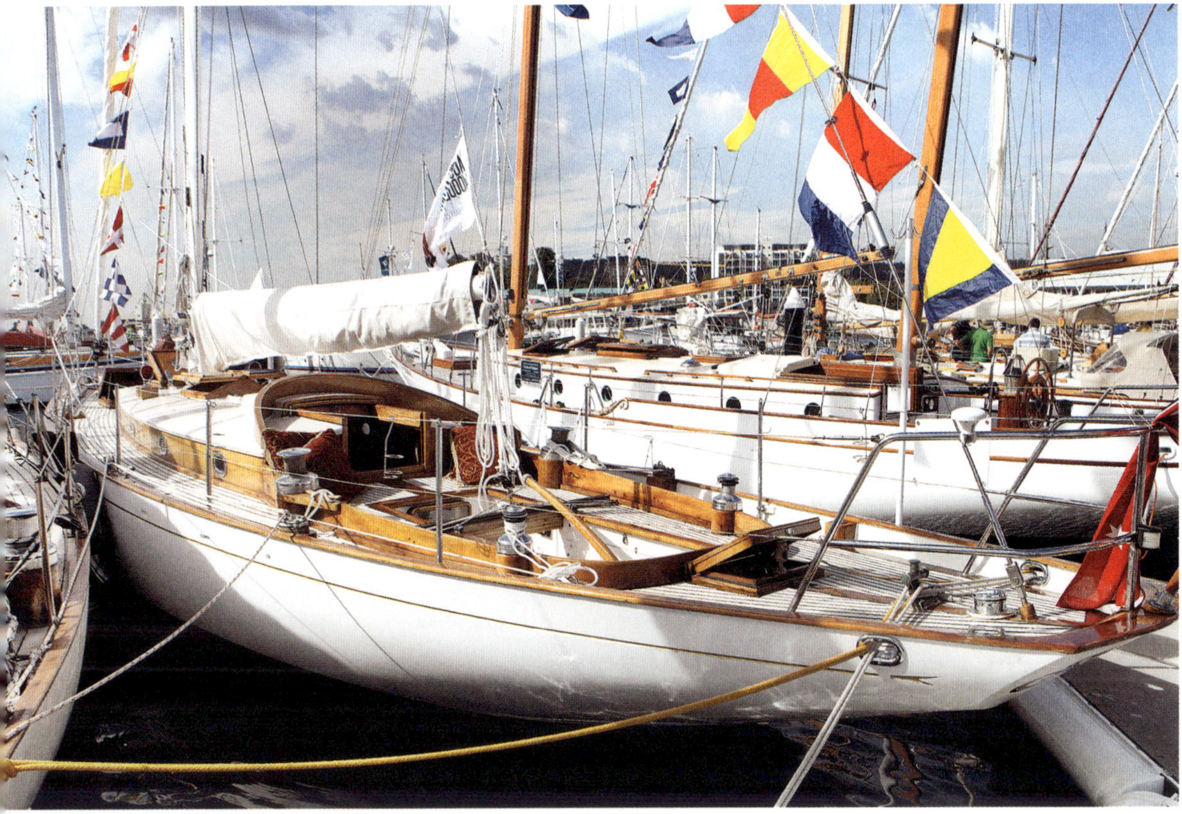

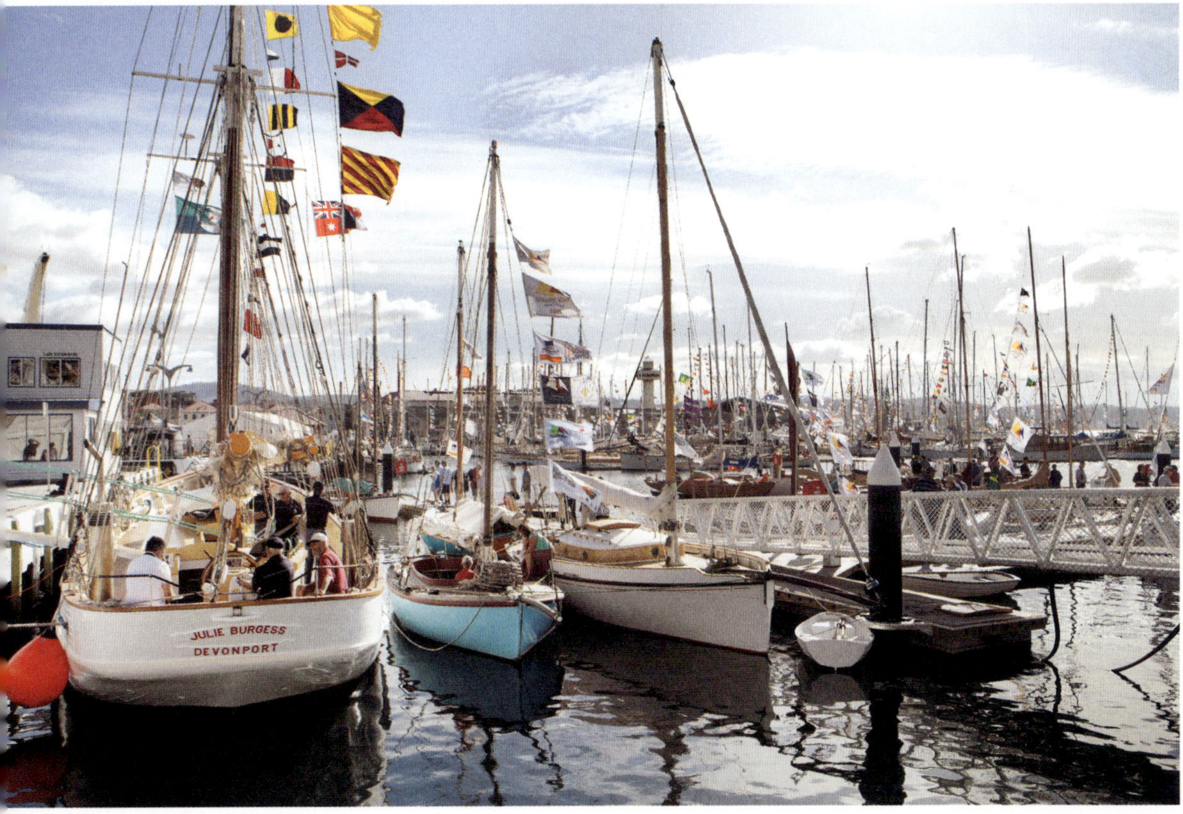

JULIE BURGESS
DEVONPORT

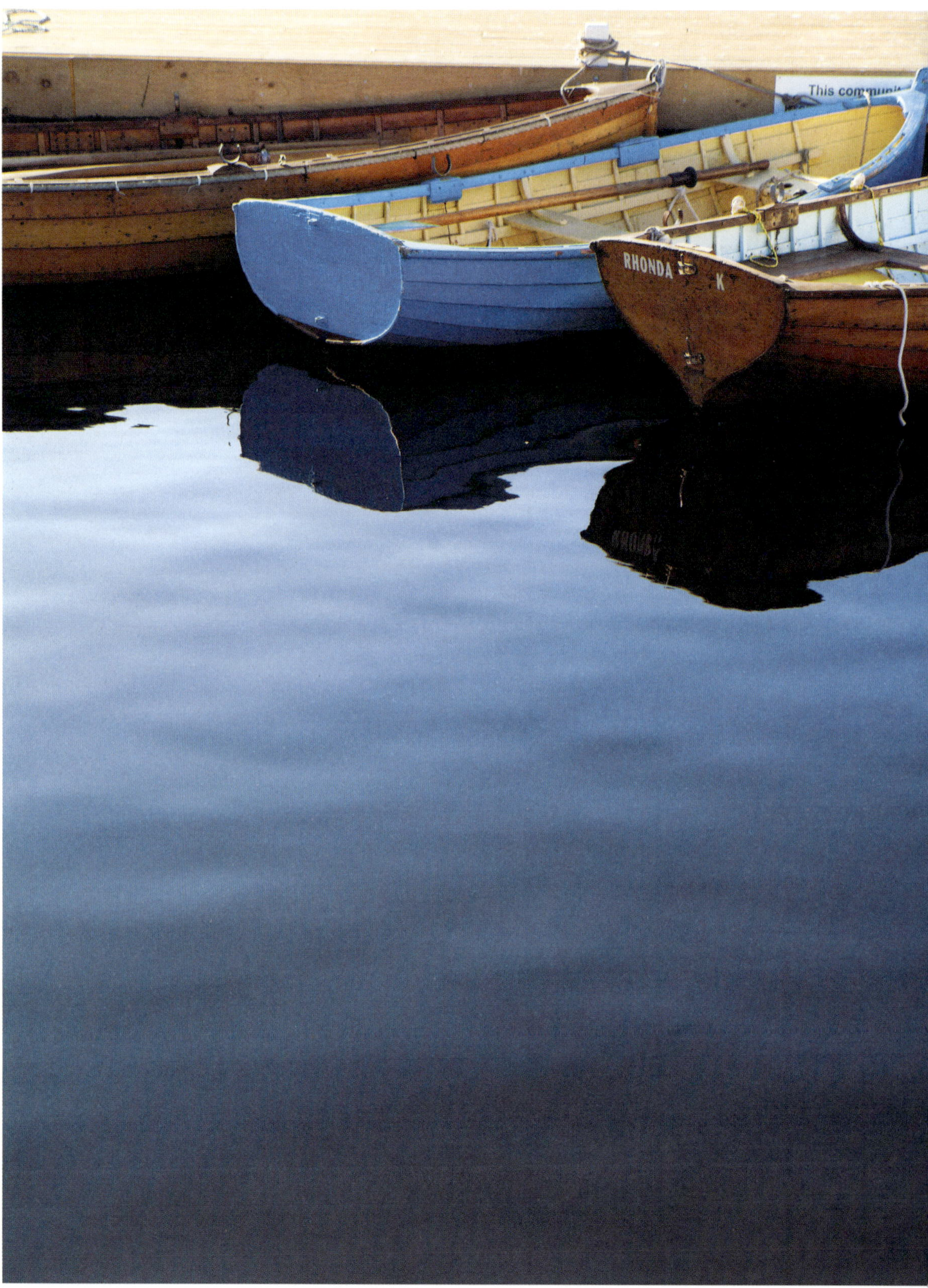
RHONDA
K

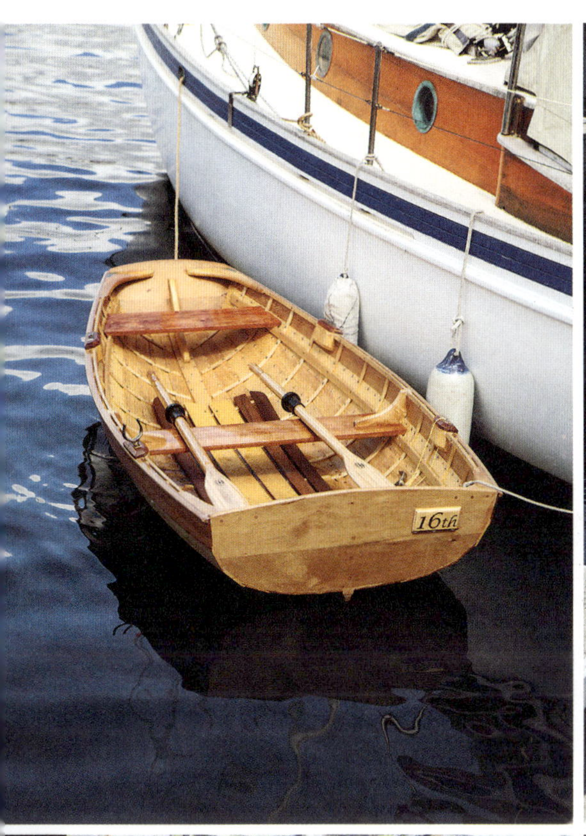
16th

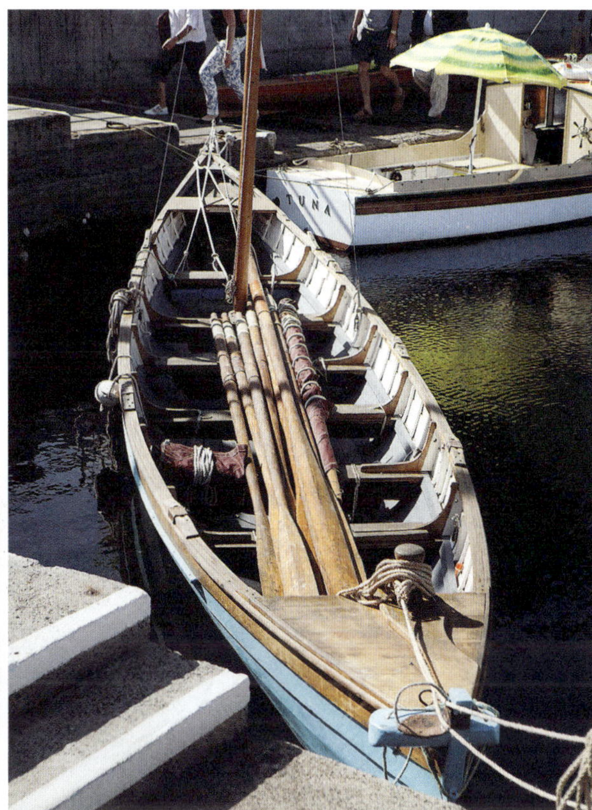

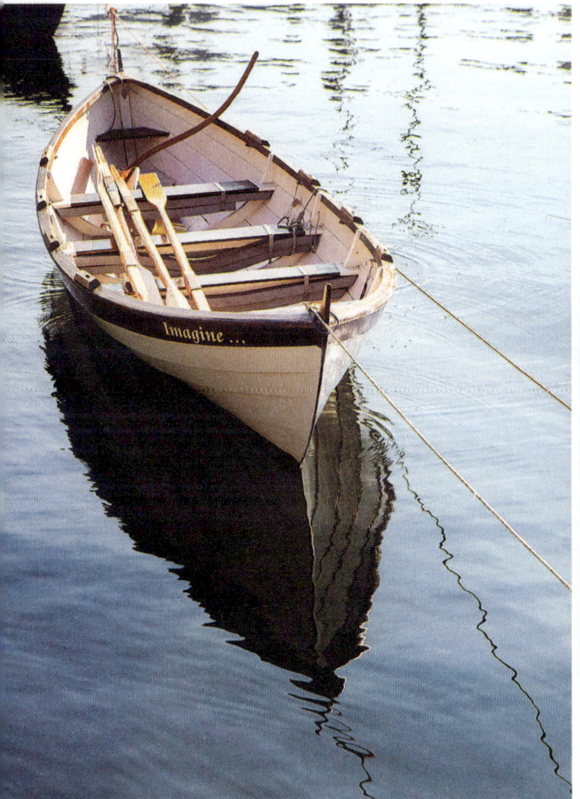
Imagine ...

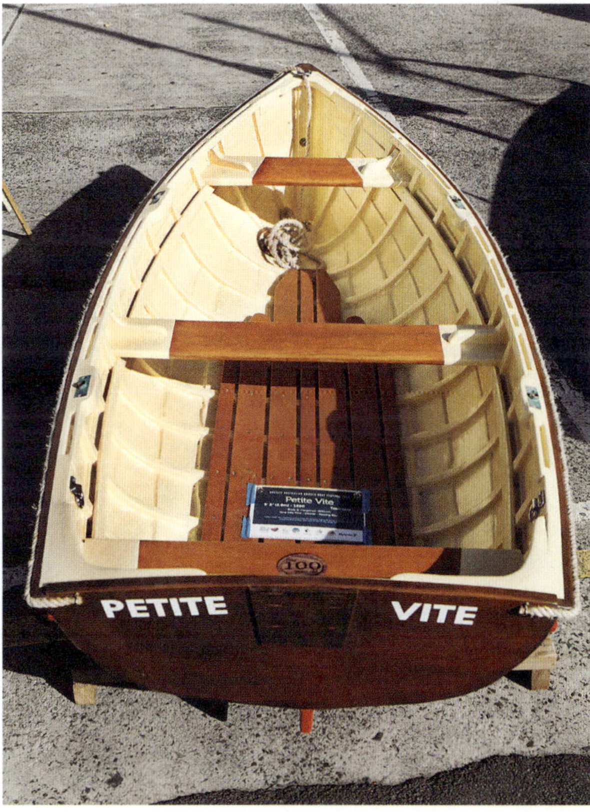
Petite Vite
100
PETITE VITE

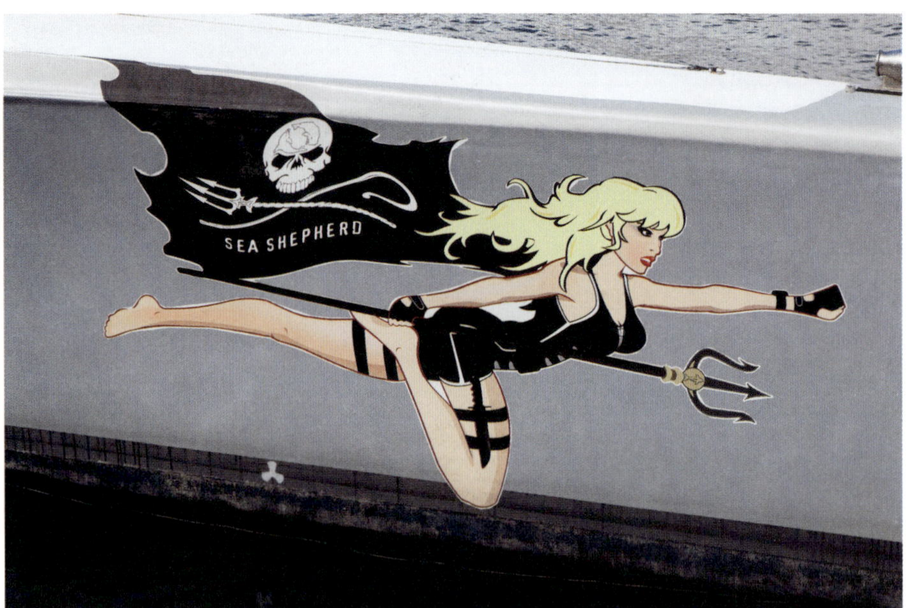

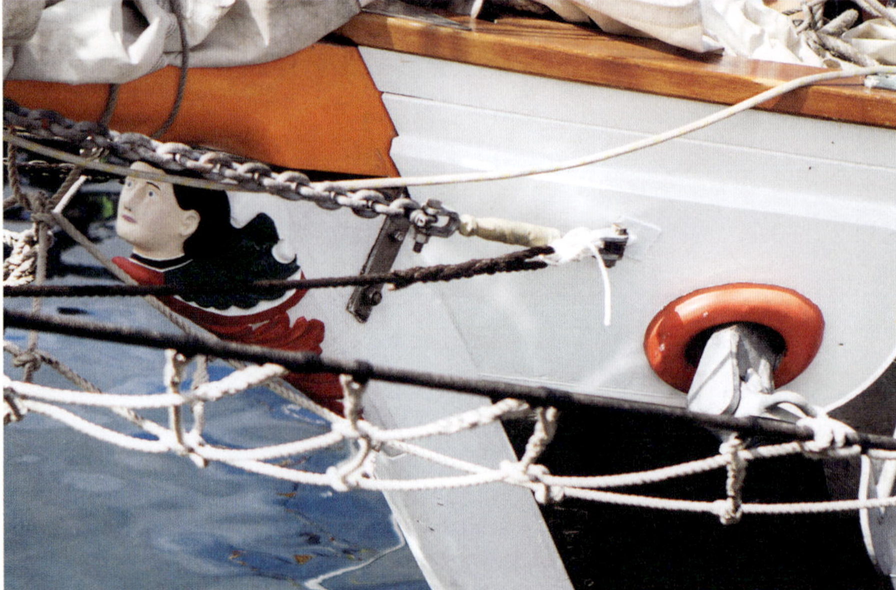

ABOVE Boats from the *Sea Shepherd* fleet are used to protect and defend the marine environment. They always have distinctive logos.

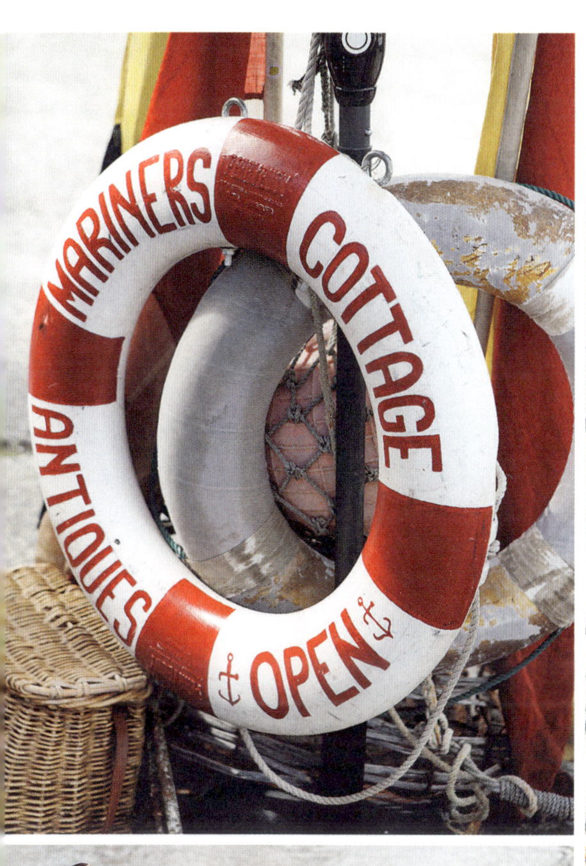
MARINERS
COTTAGE
ANTIQUES
OPEN

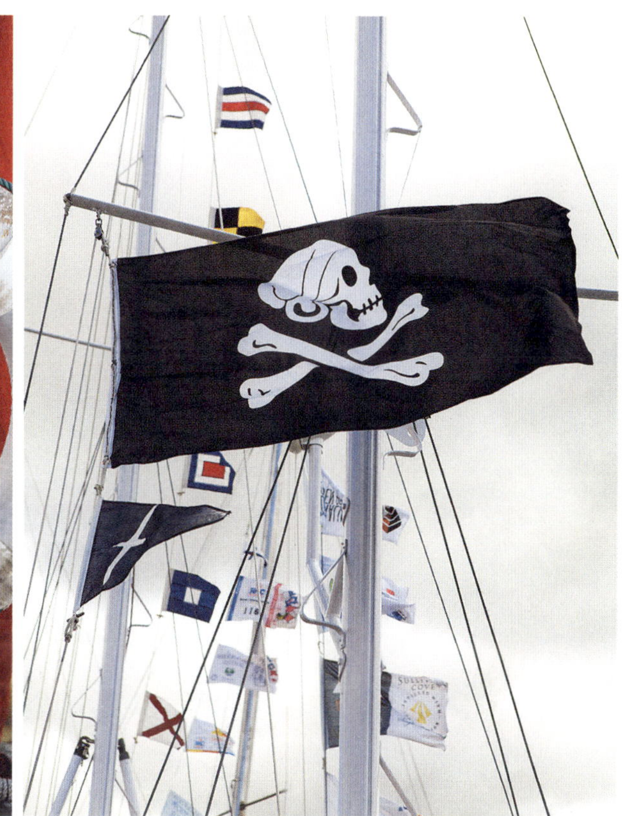

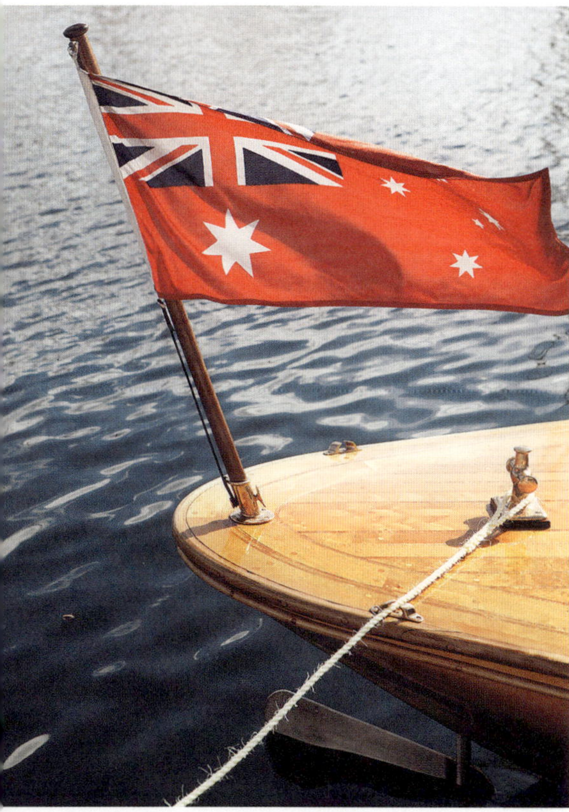

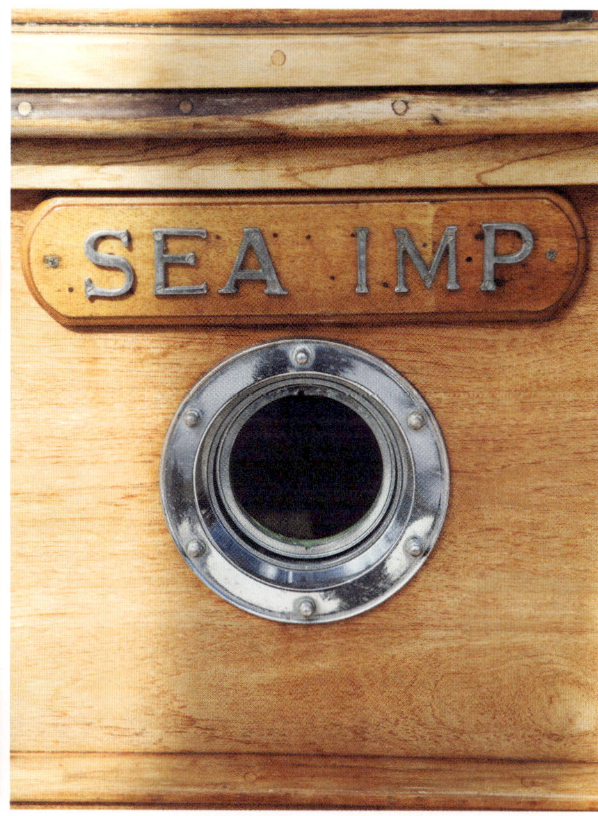
SEA IMP

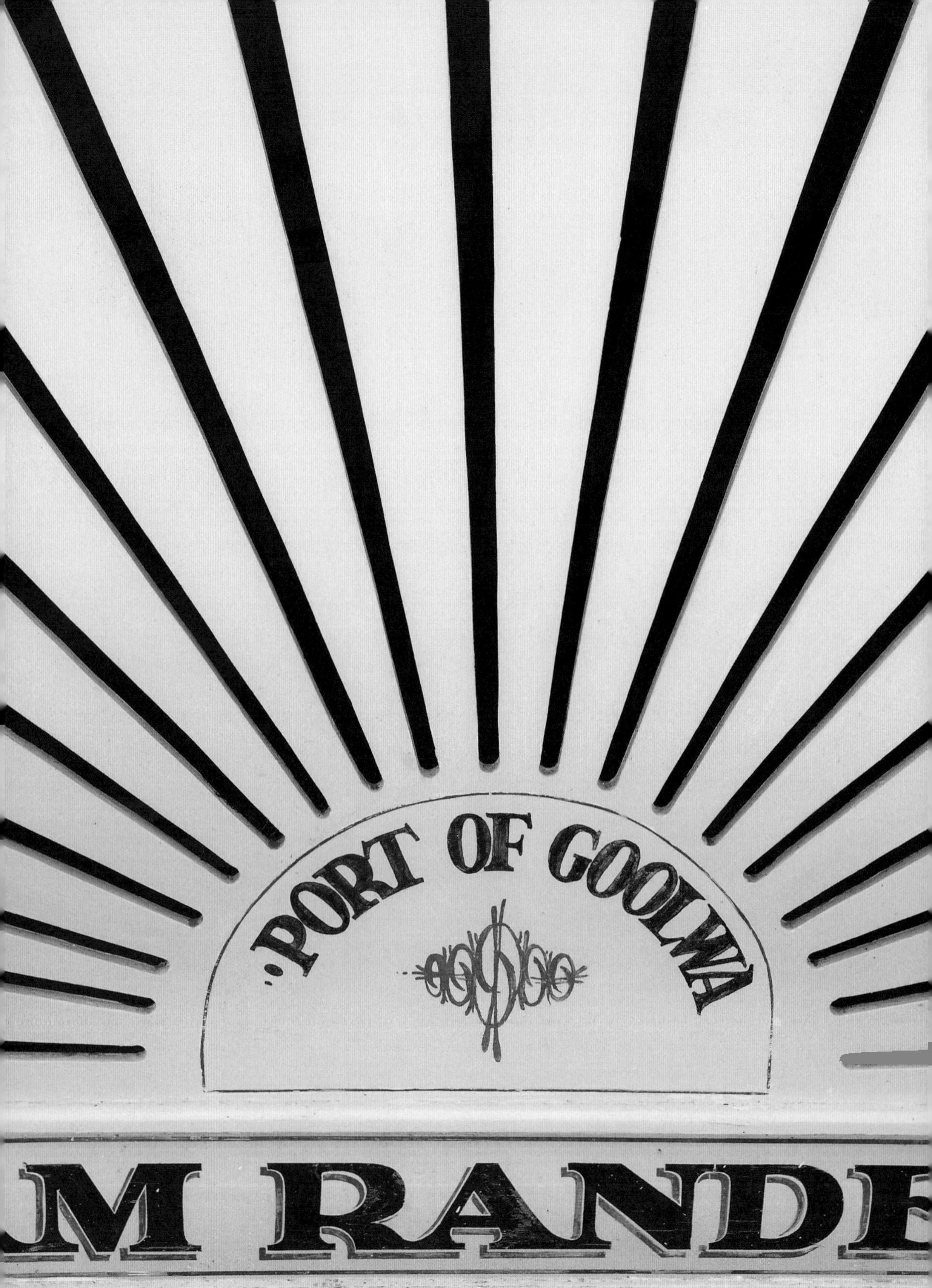
PORT OF GOOLWA
M RANDE

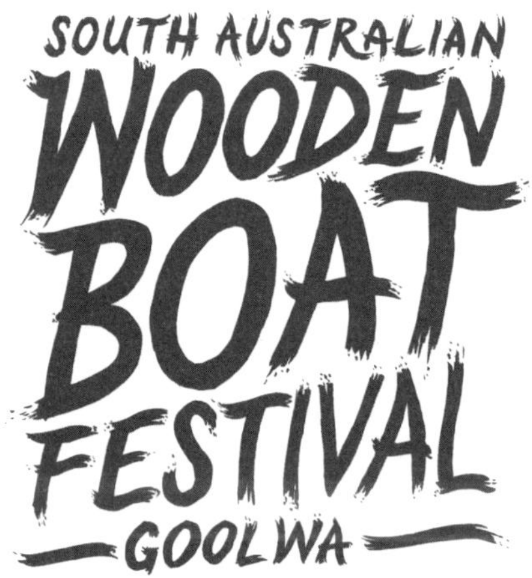

Goolwa is 83 kilometres south of Adelaide, at the southern end of the Fleurieu Peninsula. It is a State Heritage-listed area, and the last town on the Murray before the river meets the sea. Its port is famous as a trading point along the Murray.

The South Australian Wooden Boat Festival is held every two years over two days in February at the Goolwa Wharf Precinct, next to the Hindmarsh Island Bridge. It's great fun, with river boats and historical boats to see, plenty of events and demonstrations to visit, and lots of boat owners to talk to. Not to mention the boats: paddle boats and steam launches, putt-putts, and cruisers – take your pick.

There's also plenty of entertainment on land, with children's activities, maritime displays and music, as well as regional food and wine. You can soak up the atmosphere and go for a ride on a historic paddle steamer, or just wander around the docks and look at the boats.

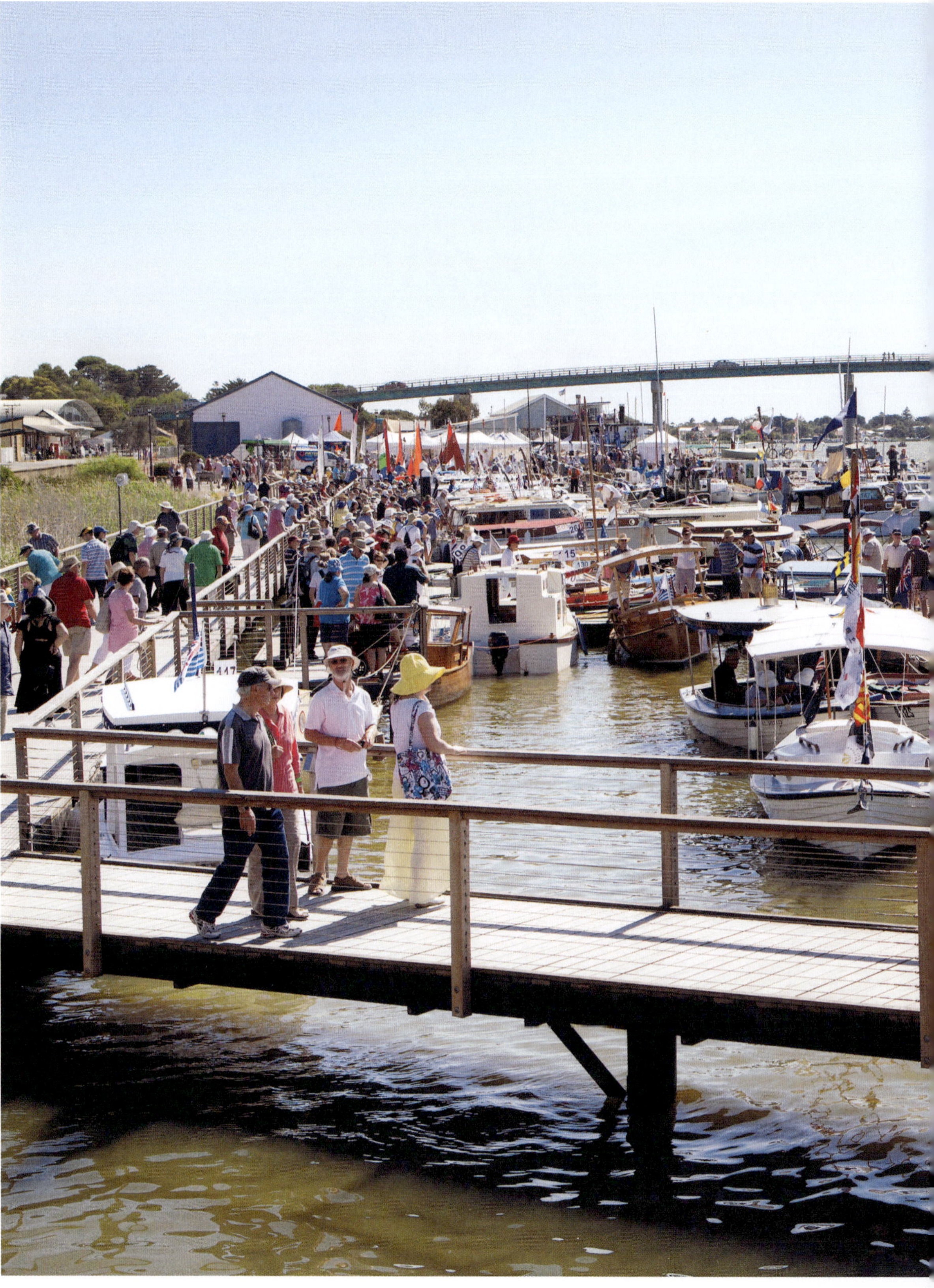

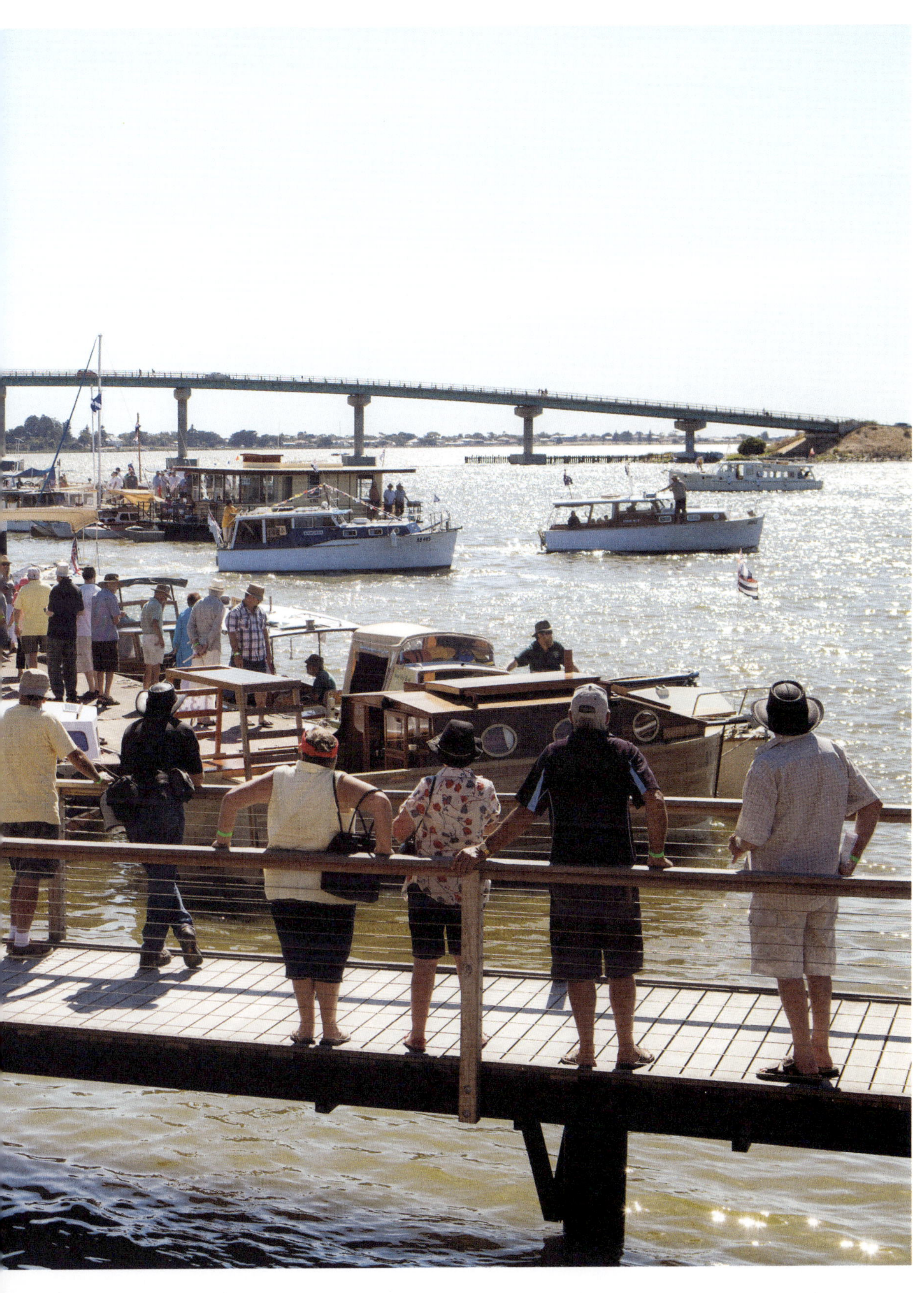

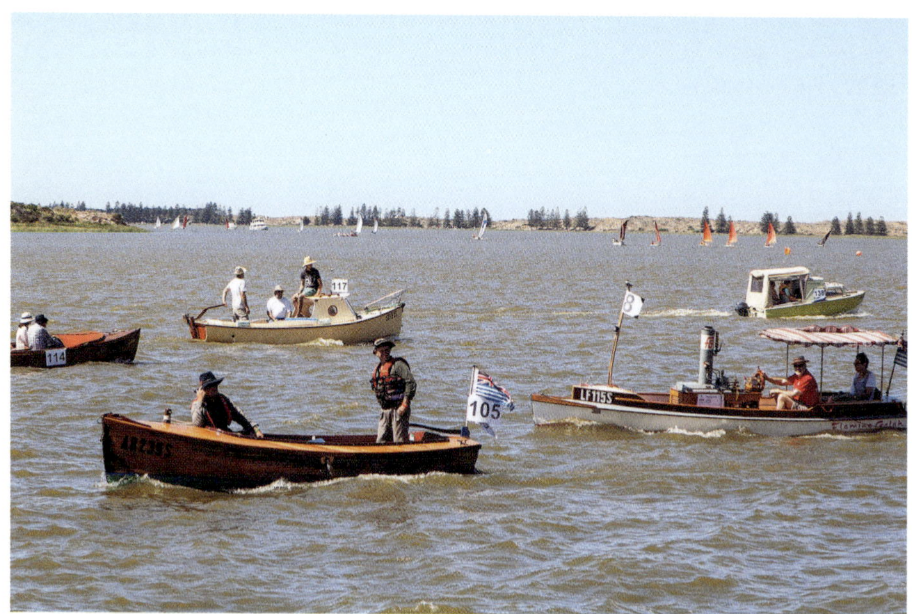

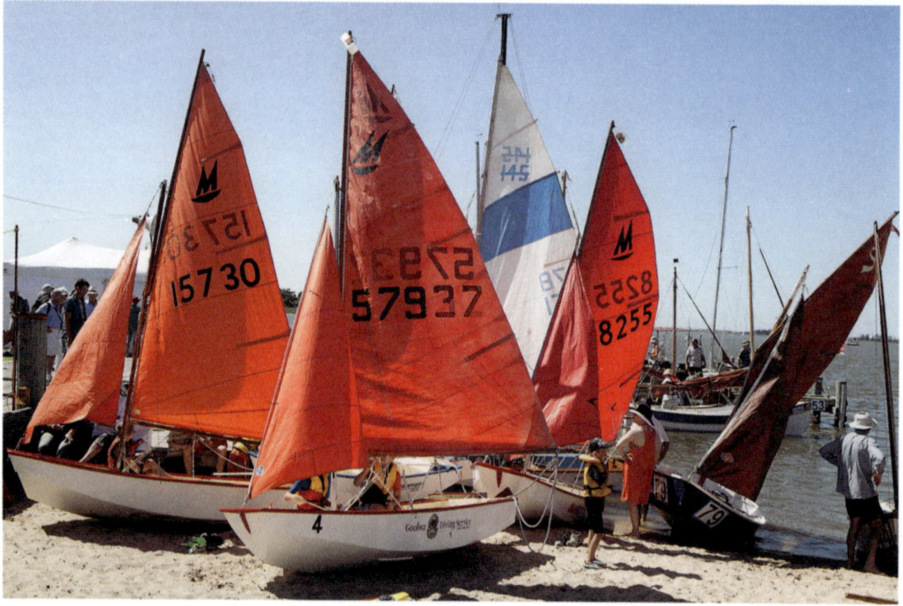

River-boating at its best at the South Australian Wooden Boat Festival in Goolwa, with its amazing array of vessels: boats to sail on, boats to ride on, paddle steamers, yachts and dinghies.

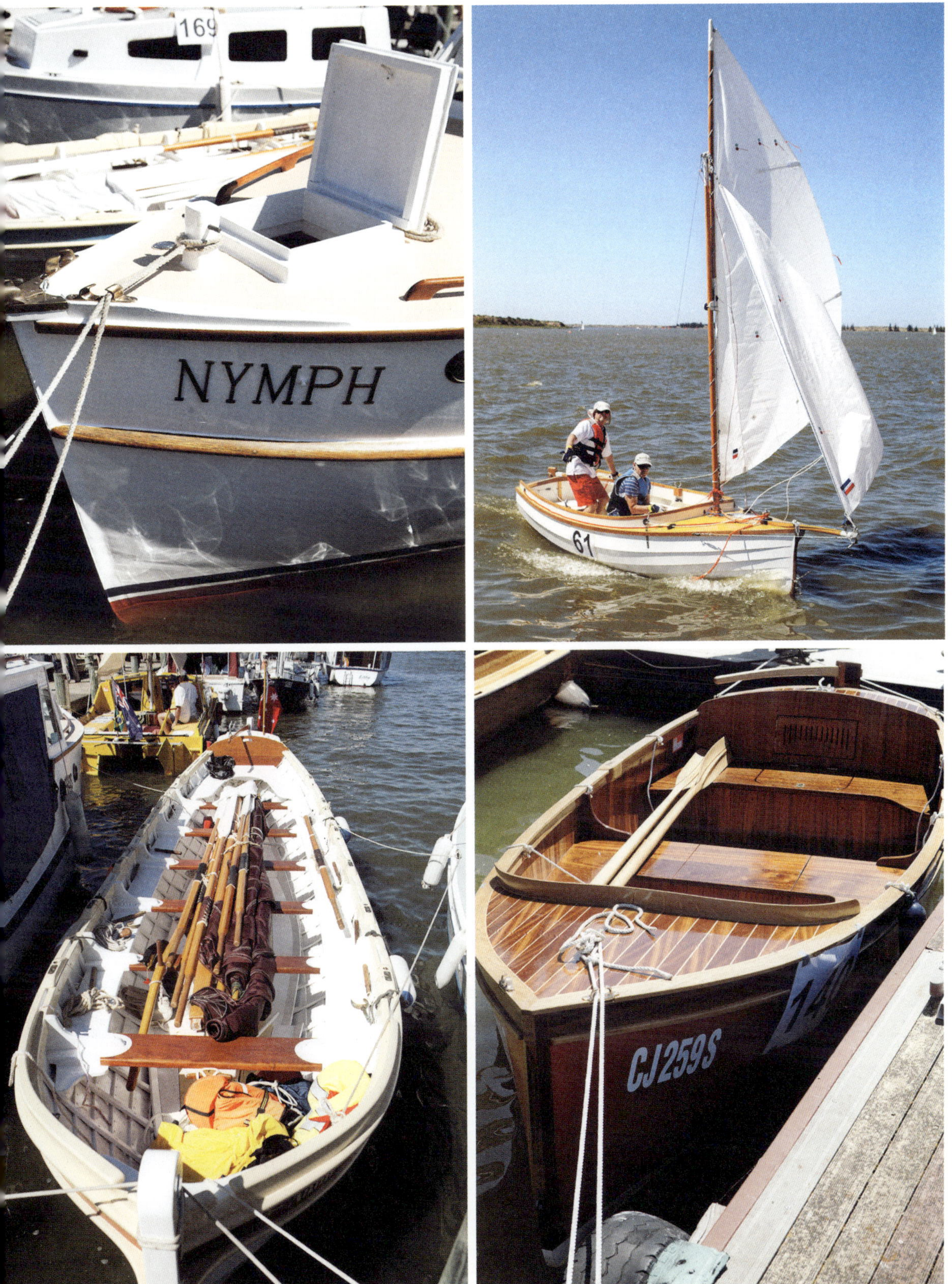
169
NYMPH
61
CJ259S

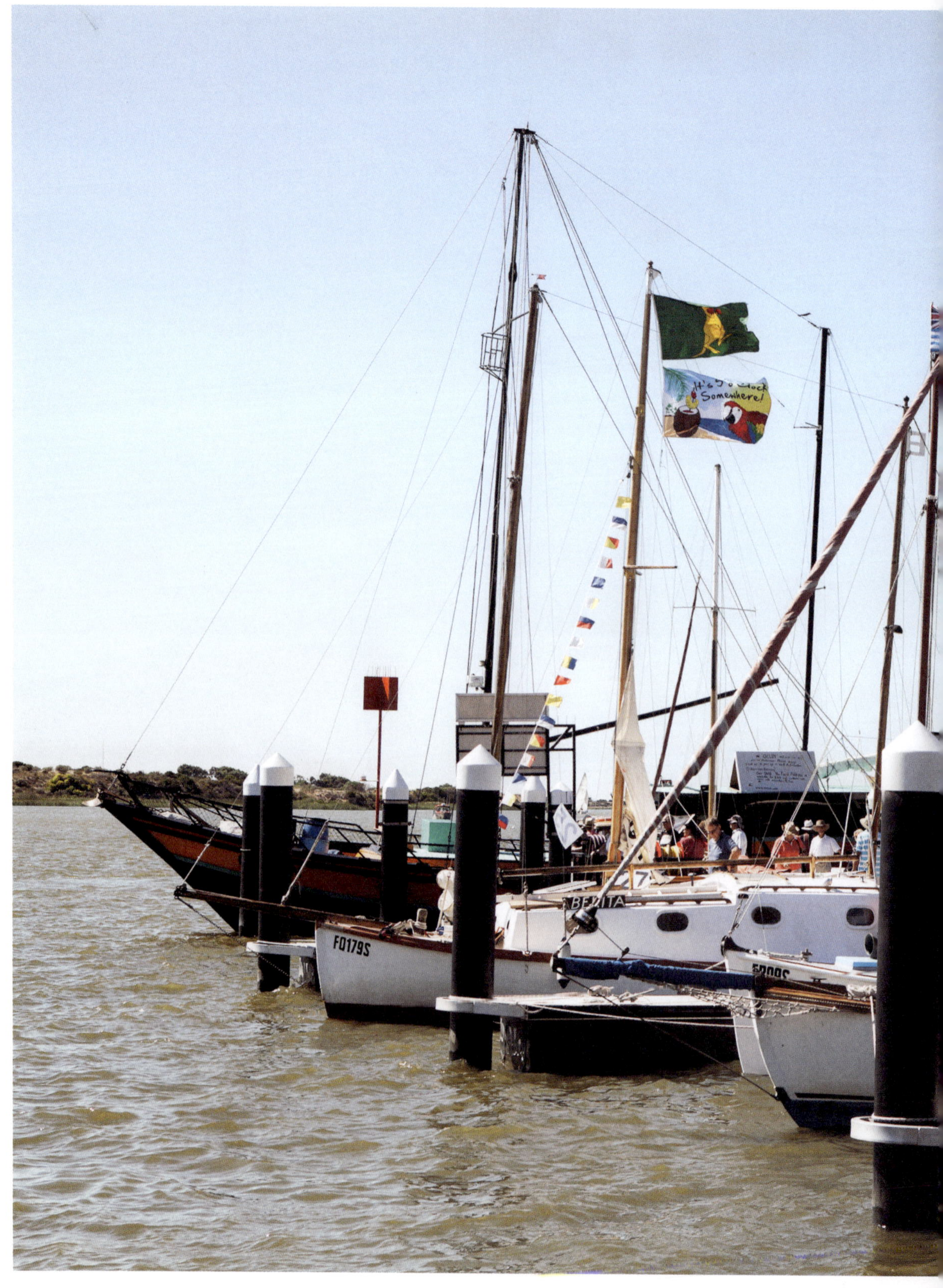
Somewhere!

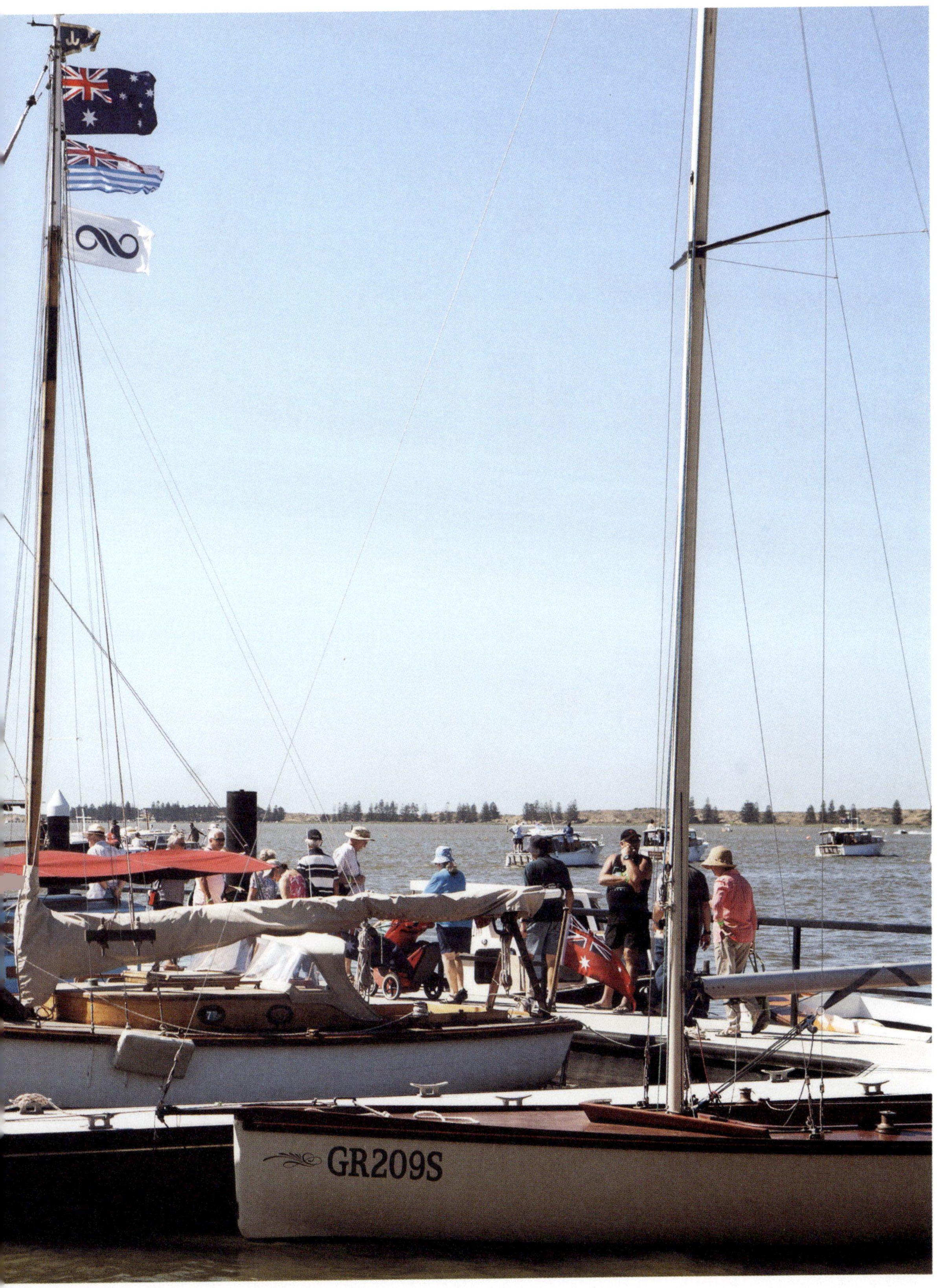
GR209S

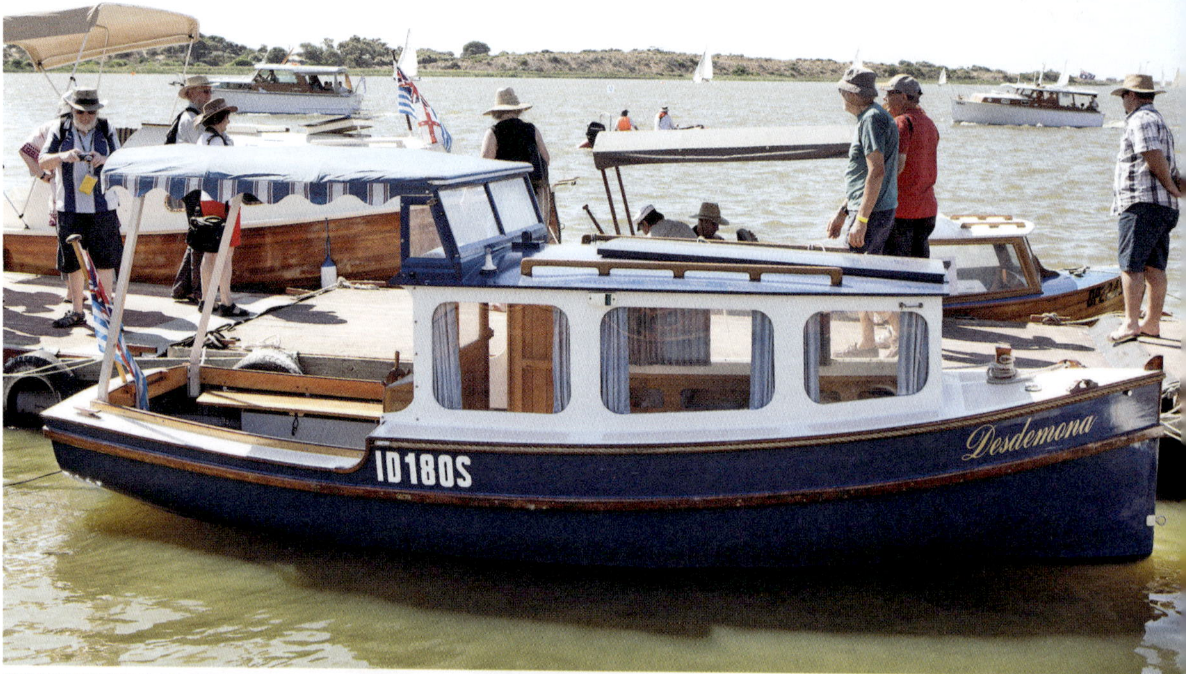

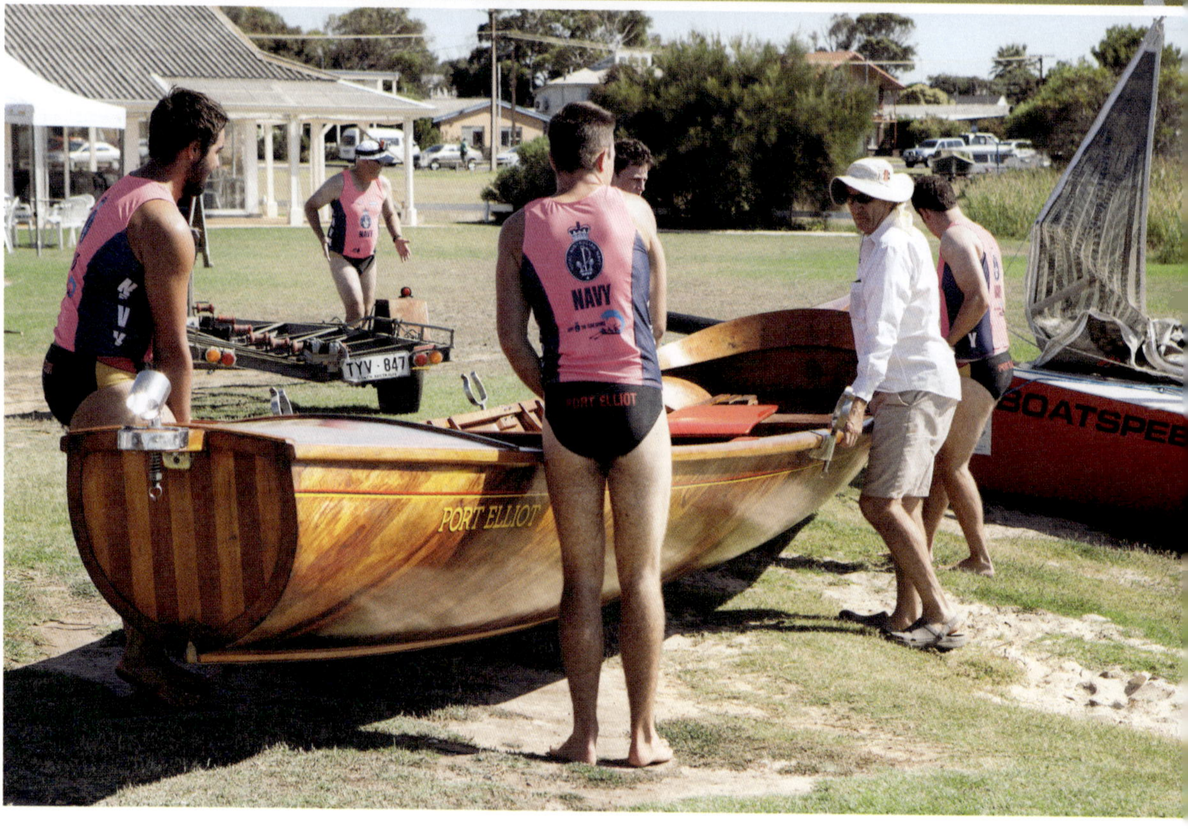

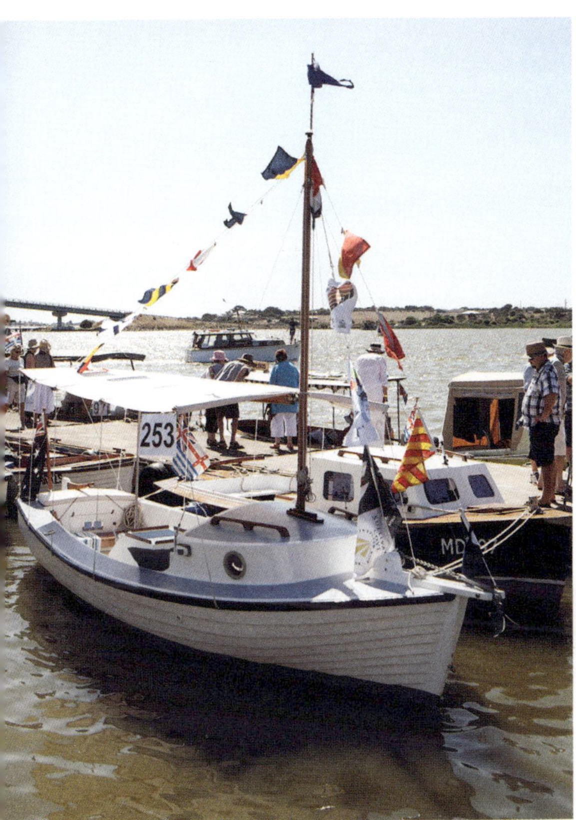

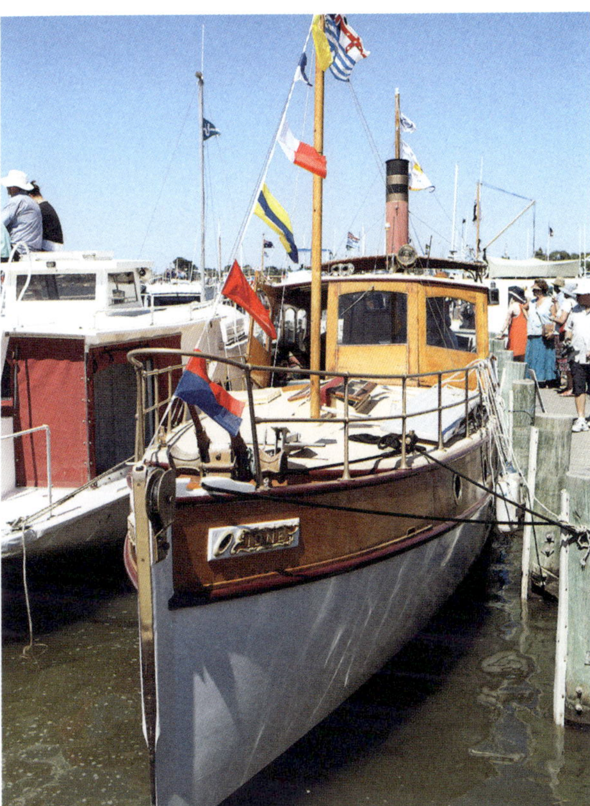

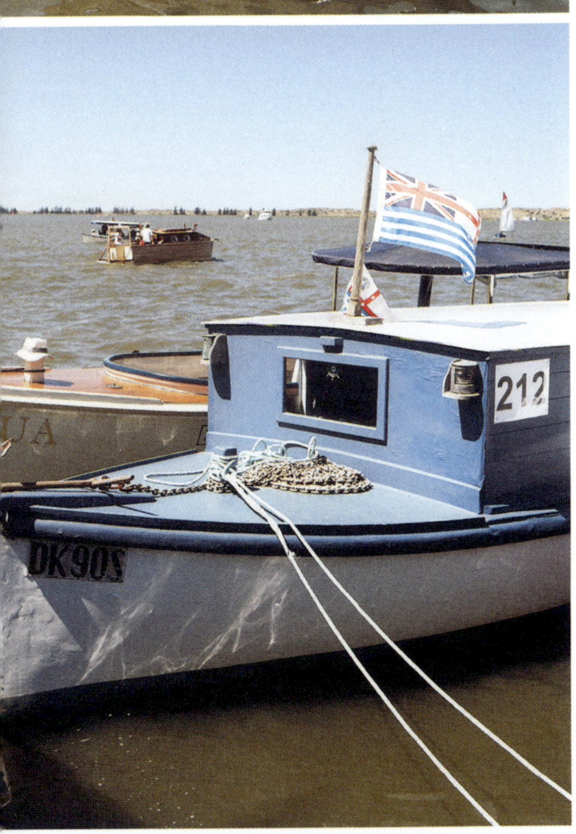

It is a great set-up for everyone involved, with all the boat owners only too happy to chat about their boats and invite you onboard.

OPPOSITE, BELOW Navy rowers prepare for the Grand Parade or sail-past.

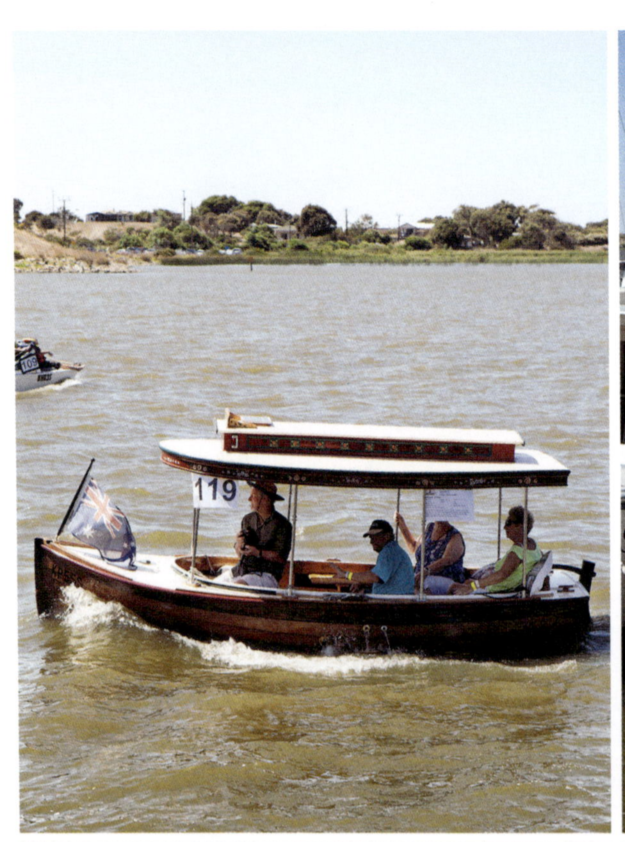
119

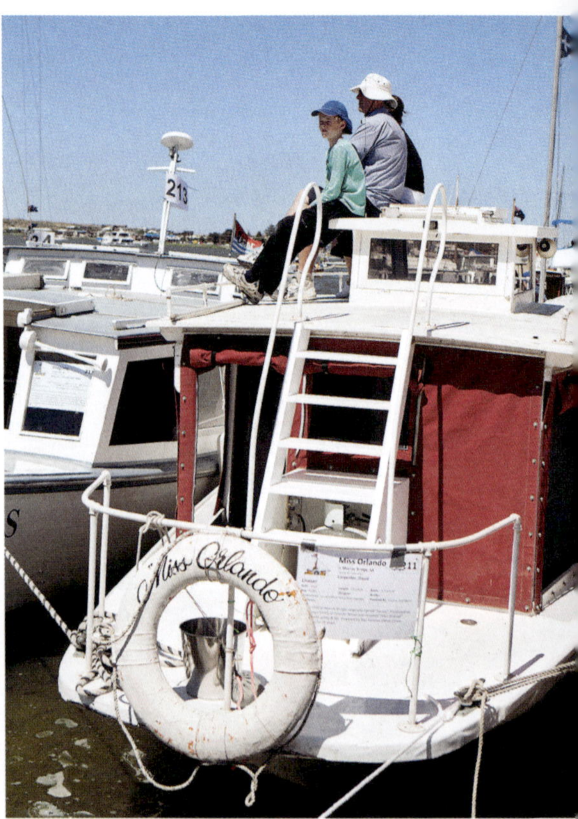
213
Miss Orlando

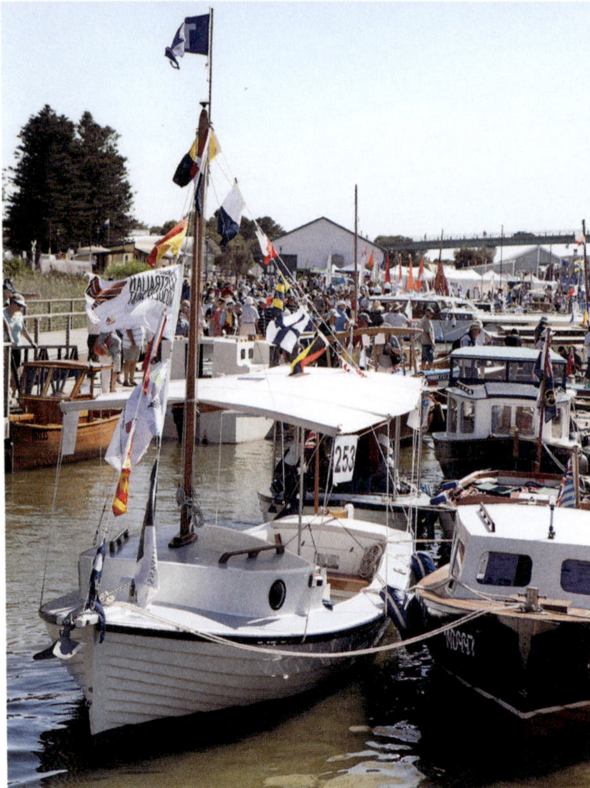
253

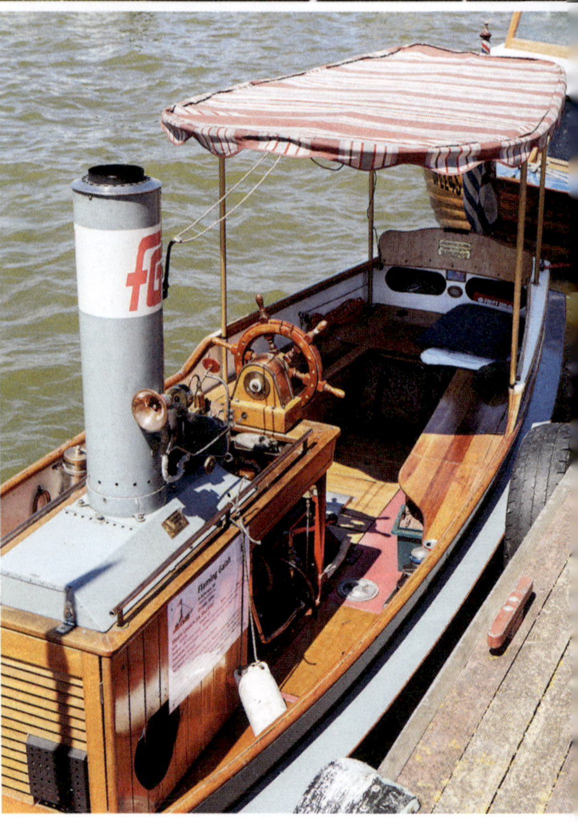

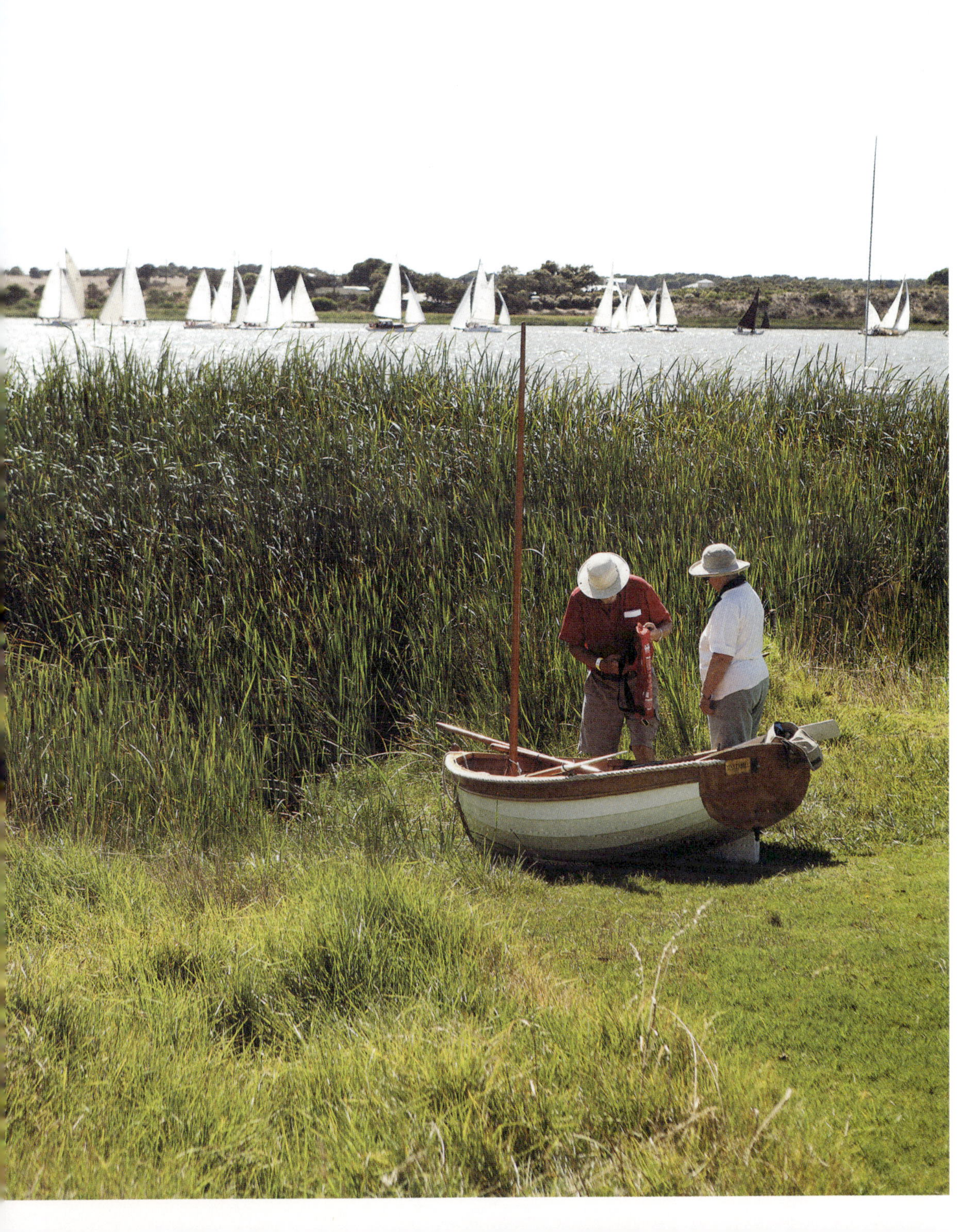

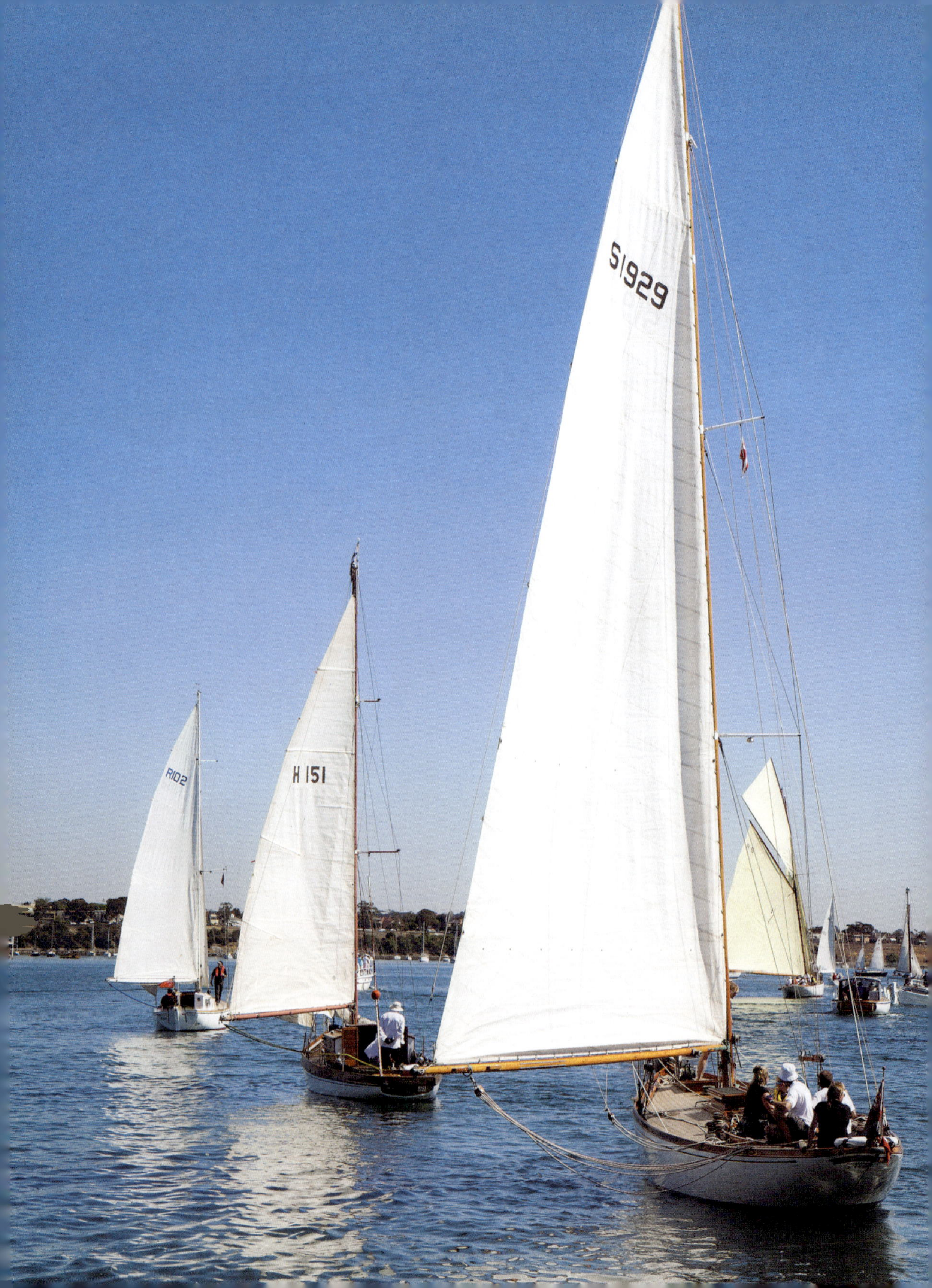
S1929
H 151
R102

GEELONG WOODEN BOAT FESTIVAL

The picturesque Geelong foreshore just south of Melbourne is home to the Geelong Wooden Boat Festival. Australia has a wealth of wooden boat festivals and Geelong's, although not huge, is lots of fun. There are many local boats on show and plenty of boat owners and boat people to talk to. The highlight of the day is the grand parade of boats, when the boats do a sail-past and you get to see them all under sail, steam or motor. *Enterprize* is there too, so you can book a sail on Melbourne's very own tall ship.

There is a great variety of historic and new boats, with lots of couta boats, boating events and boatbuilding displays, as well as plenty of water-based and shore-based activities. As well as the grand parade, there are a number of races, including the Corio Bay Couta Boat Cup and the Corio Bay Classic Wooden Yacht Cup. It is well worth a trip to Geelong to see the Festival.

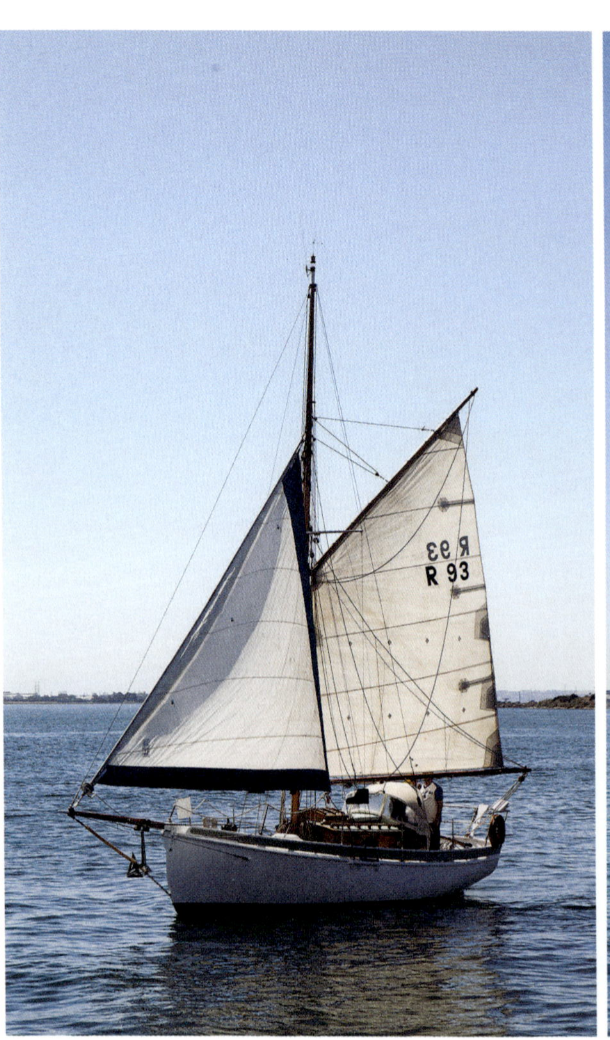
R 93
R 93

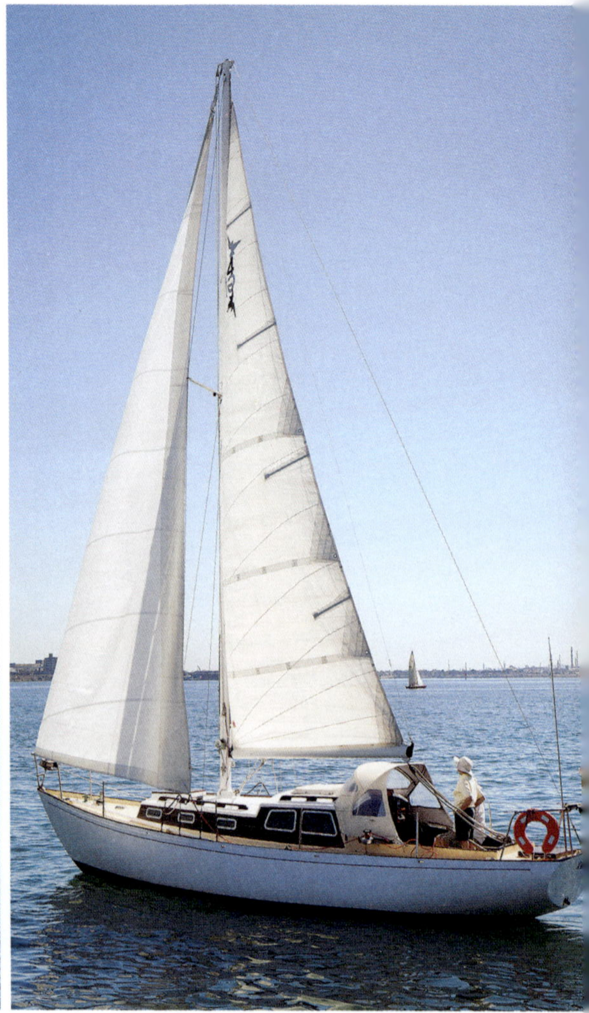

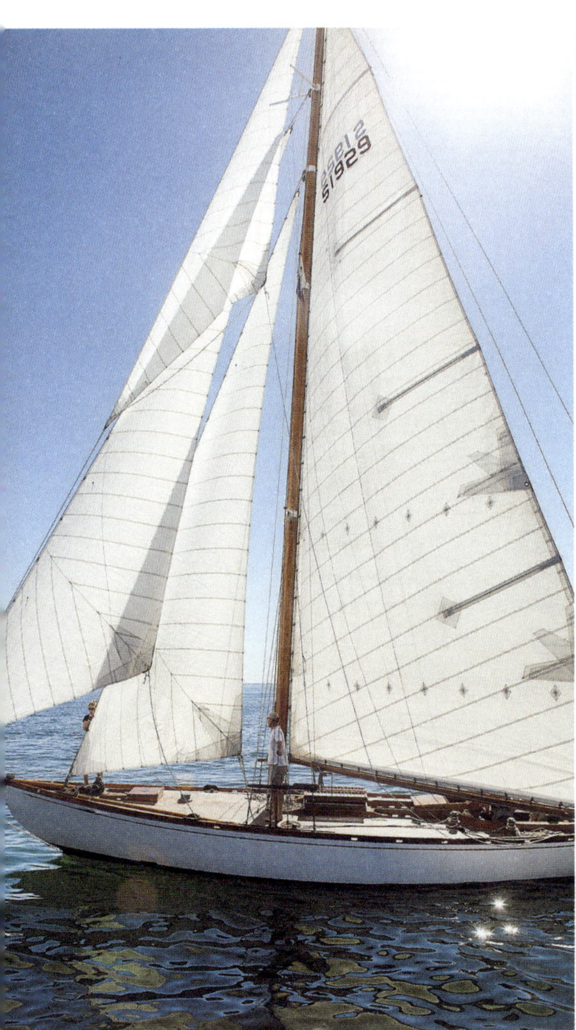

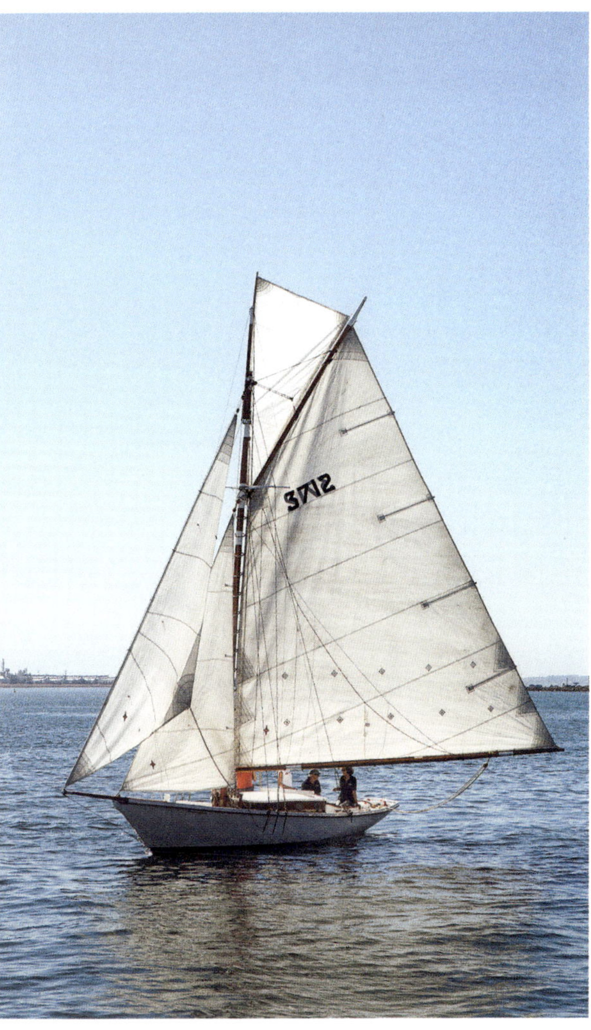

The sail-past is the highlight of the festival; it is amazing to see all the boats under sail, steam, or engine power.

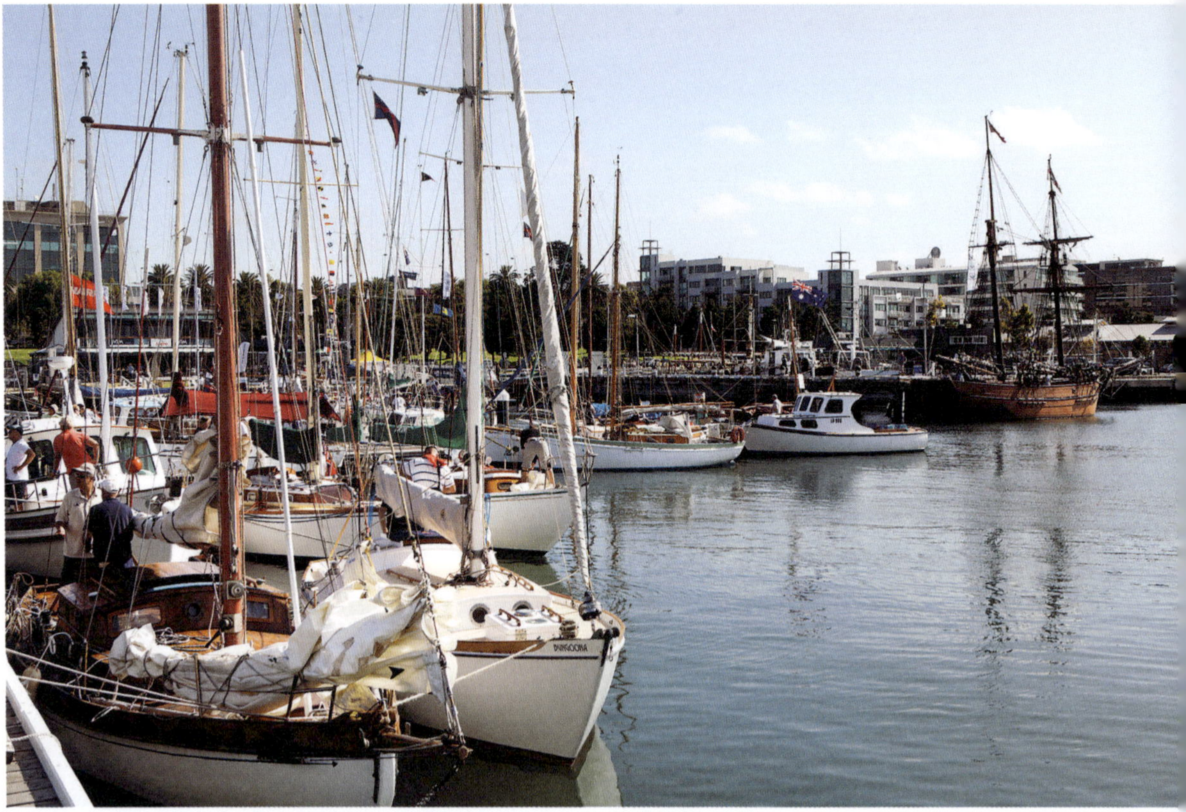

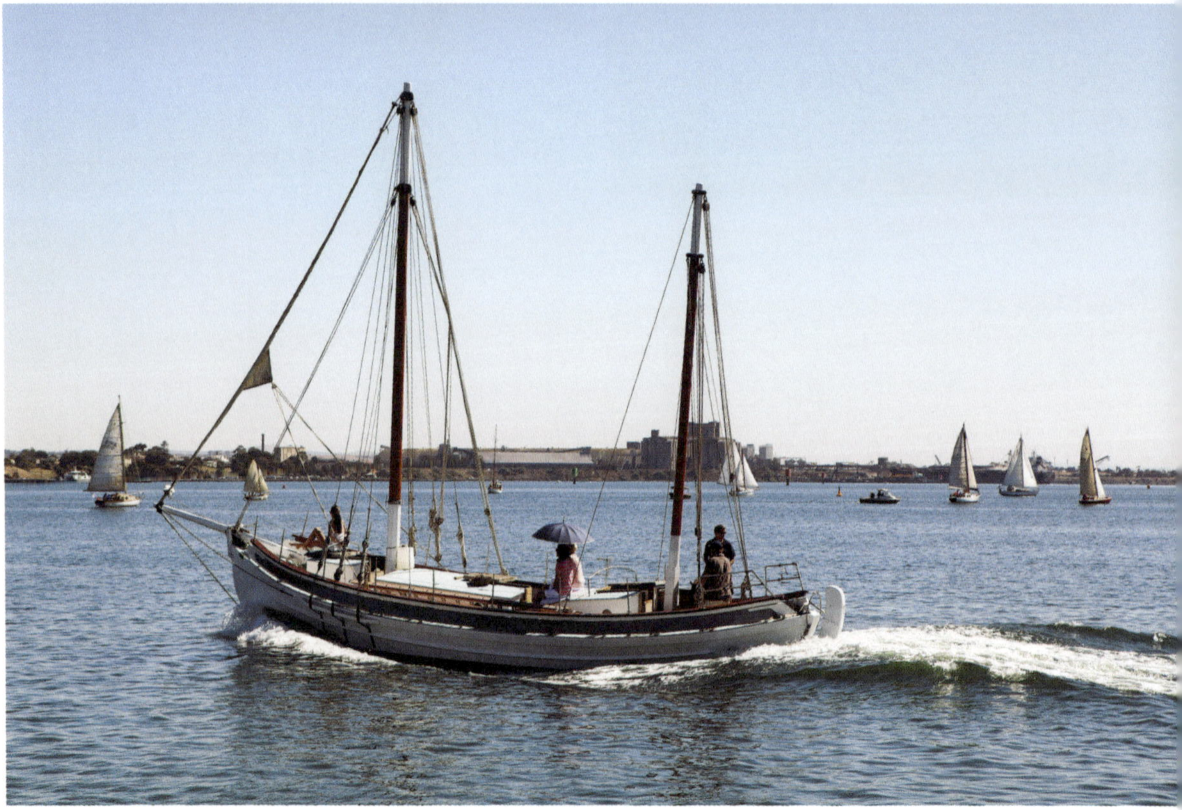

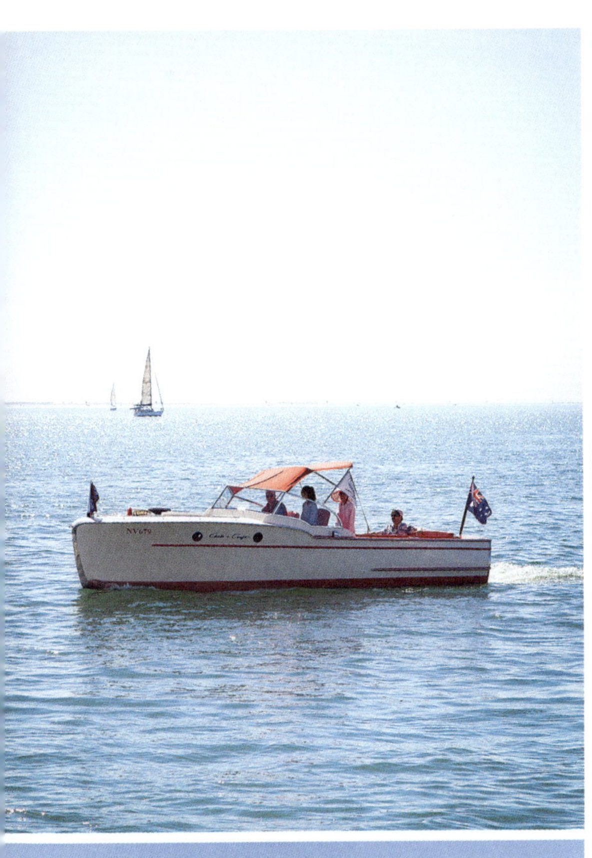

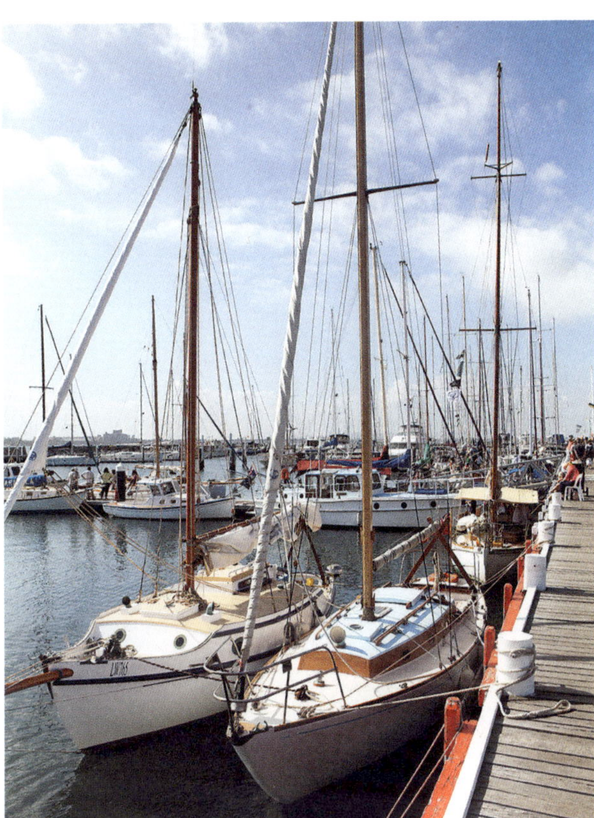

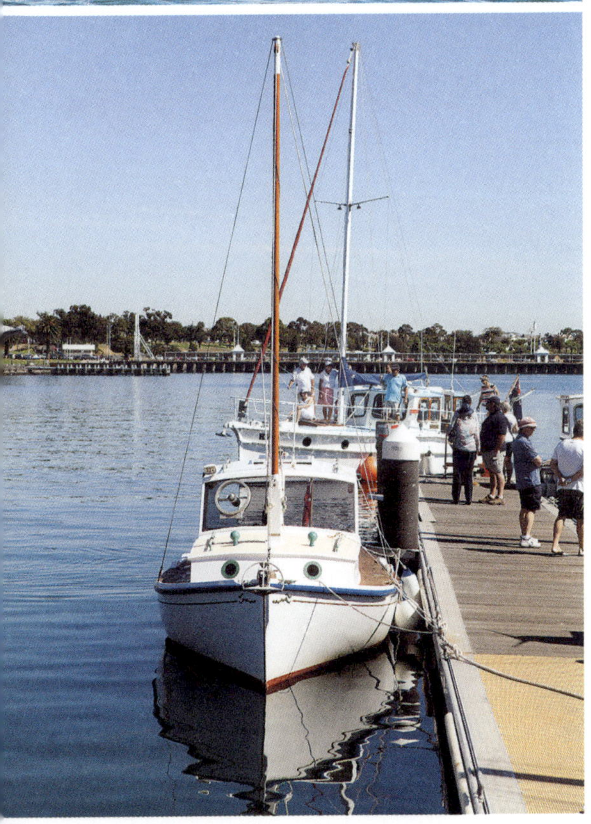

Geelong really comes alive during the festival; it is a side of the city a lot of people don't get to see.

GLOSSARY

Balmain bugs: model racing yachts, which had their heyday from the 1870s to the 1950s.

Barque: a boat with at least three masts, all of them square-rigged except for the aftermost mast, which is fore-and-aft rigged.

Beam or breadth: the measurement of the width of a boat at its widest point.

Bobstay: a rope, chain or rod used to exert downward tension on the bowsprit and keep the boat steady.

Bow: the front end of the boat.

Bowsprit: a pole extending from the prow of a sailing boat or ship.

Centreboard: a retractable keel for a sailing boat.

Carvel: a method of building the hull of a boat so that the edges of the planks are fastened edge-to-edge, producing a smooth finish. This method produces a stronger hull than the clinker method.

Clinker: a method of building the hull of a boat so that the wooden planks overlap along their edges, producing a ridged finish. Clinker-built boats are lighter and faster than carvel-built boats.

Cold-molding: a boatbuilding method that involves laminating layers of wood veneers to each other at right angles (sometimes called 'double diagonal'). It produces boats that are light but strong.

Commission: to put a boat into active service, with a captain and a crew.

Couta boat: originally fishing boats, couta boats date back to the 1870s and are associated with historic fishing ports in Victoria such as Queenscliff, Port Fairy and Portland. They are now sailed by boating enthusiasts who have either restored old ones, or built new ones from scratch.

Decommission: to remove a boat from active service.

Draught: the vertical length of a boat from the waterline to the bottom of the keel. It is the minimum depth the boat can safely navigate.

Fire tube boiler: a type of boiler in which the by-products of combustion, or flue gas, travel through tubes surrounded by hot water (the reverse occurs in a water tube boiler). These boilers are easy to install and operate, and were commonly used in steam locomotive engines.

Gaff rig: a sailing rig with a fore-and-aft sail supported by a spar (pole) called a gaff. Due to the rigging, the sails are four-cornered, a style common on old-fashioned boats.

Halyards: the lines that pull the sails up the mast.

Hull: the body of a boat – the part that floats on the water.

Jolly boat: one of a ship's small boats, used in the eighteenth and nineteenth centuries to carry people to and from shore.

Keel: the backbone of a boat, running lengthways along the hull from the stem to the stern. The shape of the keel governs how the boat sails and how it turns. The 'full keel' or 'ballast keel' is a downward extension of the keel that helps a boat keep its balance and prevents it going sideways.

Ketch: a sailing boat with two masts.

Shipwright: someone who builds or repairs ships.

Slipway: a ramp down to the water used to move ships in and out of the water.

Skiff: a small, light boat for rowing or sailing, usually used by one person.

Sloop: a single-masted, fore-and-aft-rigged sailing vessel.

Smack: a nineteenth-century term for a fishing boat.

Spar: a general term for any mast, yard, boom or bowsprit on a boat.

Stem: the front section of a boat – the most forward part of the bow. Sometimes it is carved or decorated.

Stern: the back of a boat.

Strip-building: a common boatbuilding method used by home builders. A form of carvel planking, it involves attaching thin, flexible strips of wood to the spine of the boat.

Waterline: the line on the hull where the water meets the air when the boat is in the water.

Whale boats: long, narrow boats that are pointed at both ends. They were formerly used for whaling, but are now used as rowboats.

Yawl: A two-masted fore-and-aft-rigged sailing vessel, with a larger mainmast and smaller second mast, or a ship's small boat crewed by four or six rowers (also known as a jolly boat).

ACKNOWLEDGEMENTS

A big thank you to my wonderful publisher, Julie Gibbs. We have worked together for over twenty years and had many adventures together.

To the wonderful Evi O: your design is amazing. Thank you so much.

And Nicole Abadee, a joy to work with: thank you for your patience and hard work making my words look good.

A BIG thank you to all of the boat owners for allowing me to include all your wonderful boats.

Many thanks to Greg Blunt of C.Blunt Boatbuilder for coffee, advice and contacts.

A big thank you to Joy Phillips and Phillip Myer for an amazing day spent on *Holger Danske*.

And a big thank you to Sir James Hardy and David Hardy for a perfect Sydney day on *Nerida*.

Heartfelt thanks to Ian Creber, for all of your help in finding the best Sydney boats.

Thank you also to:

Australian Wooden Boat Festival (Hobart)
www.australianwoodenboatfestival.com.au

Blackbird
www.blackbirdcruises.com.au

C. Blunt Boatbuilder
www.bluntboats.com.au

David Emery
www.davidemery-furnituremaker.com.au

David Hunt Model Boats
Tel: (03) 6243 5544

Derwent Skiffs
www.rowandsail.com.au

Enterprize
www.enterprize.org.au

Garry Kerr
For books and Dvds
email garry.k@westvic.com.au

Geelong Wooden Boat Festival,
Royal Geelong Yacht Club
(03) 5229 3705

James Craig
www.shf.org.au

M.V. Emmalisa
www.hobarthistoriccruises.com.au

P.S. Emmylou
www.emmylou.com.au

P.S. Marion
www.psmarion.com

Patterson Lakes Radio Model Yacht Club
www.plrmyc.com

Portland Whale boat
www.facebook.com/portlandwhaleboat

S.L. Leprena
Andrew Perkins
(03) 6272 8344

S.Y. Preana
www.preana.org

South Australian Wooden Boat Festival
www.woodenboatfestival.com.au

Storm Bay
Wooden Boatshop
www.woodenboatshop.com.au

Surrey Park Model Boat Club
www.spmbc.org.au

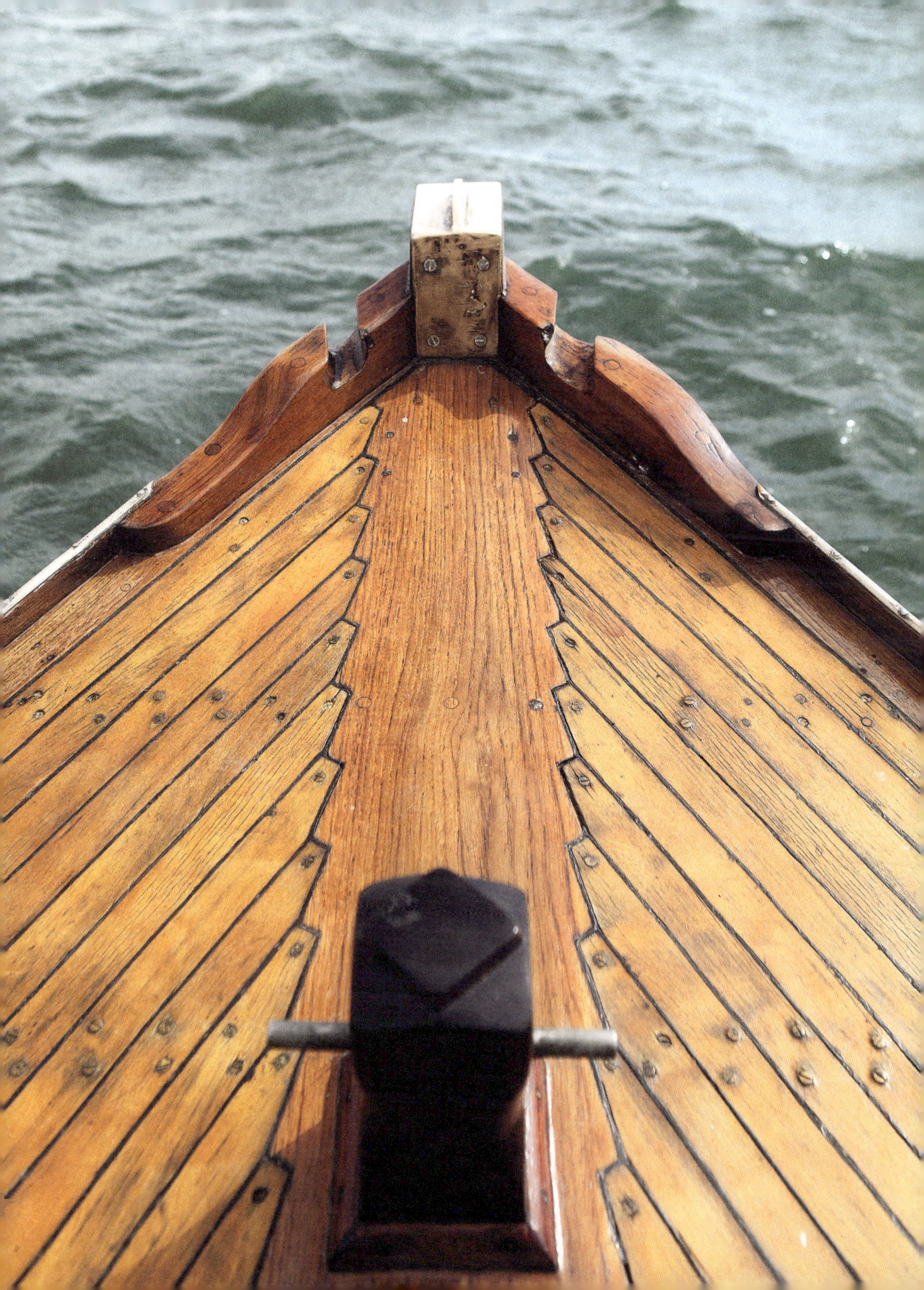

LANTERN

UK | USA | Canada | Ireland | Australia
India | New Zealand | South Africa | China

Penguin Books is part of the Penguin Random House group of companies whose addresses can be found at global.penguinrandomhouse.com.

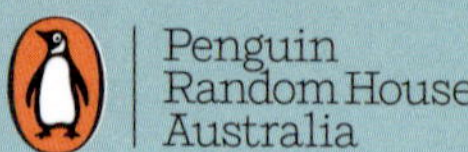

First published by Penguin Group (Australia), 2015

1 3 5 7 9 10 8 6 4 2

Cover and text design by Evi O. © Penguin Group (Australia)
Cover photograph by Simon Griffiths
Typeset in Cochin by Post Pre-press Group, Brisbane, Queensland
Colour separation by Splitting Image Colour Studio, Clayton, Victoria
Printed and bound in China by 1010 Printing International Ltd

National Library of Australia Cataloguing-in-Publication entry

Griffiths, Simon (Simon John), author, photographer.
Boat / Simon Griffiths.
9781921383403 (hardback)
Boats and boating--Pictorial works.
Boatbuilding--Pictorial works.

778.993872

penguin.com.au/lantern

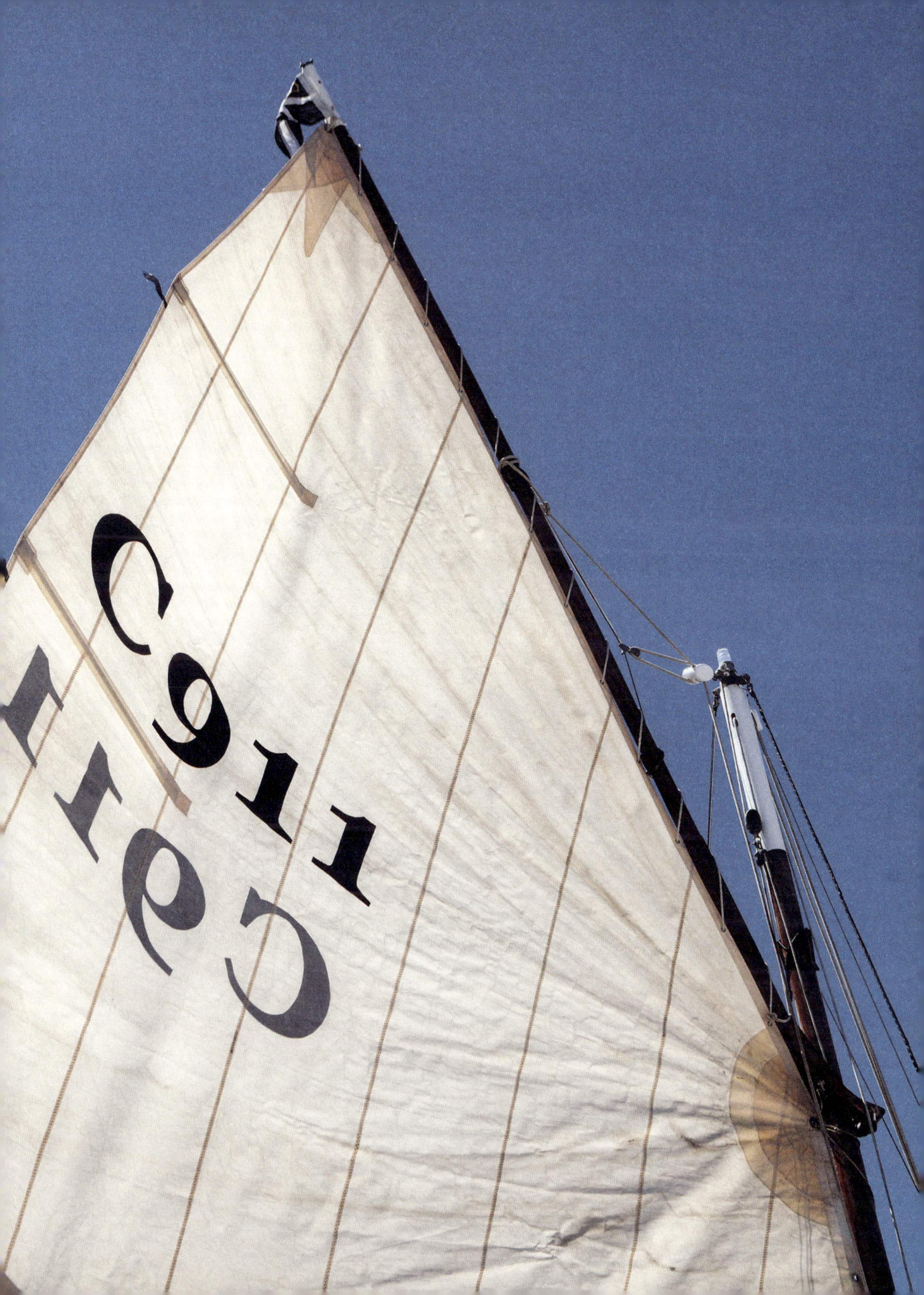
C911

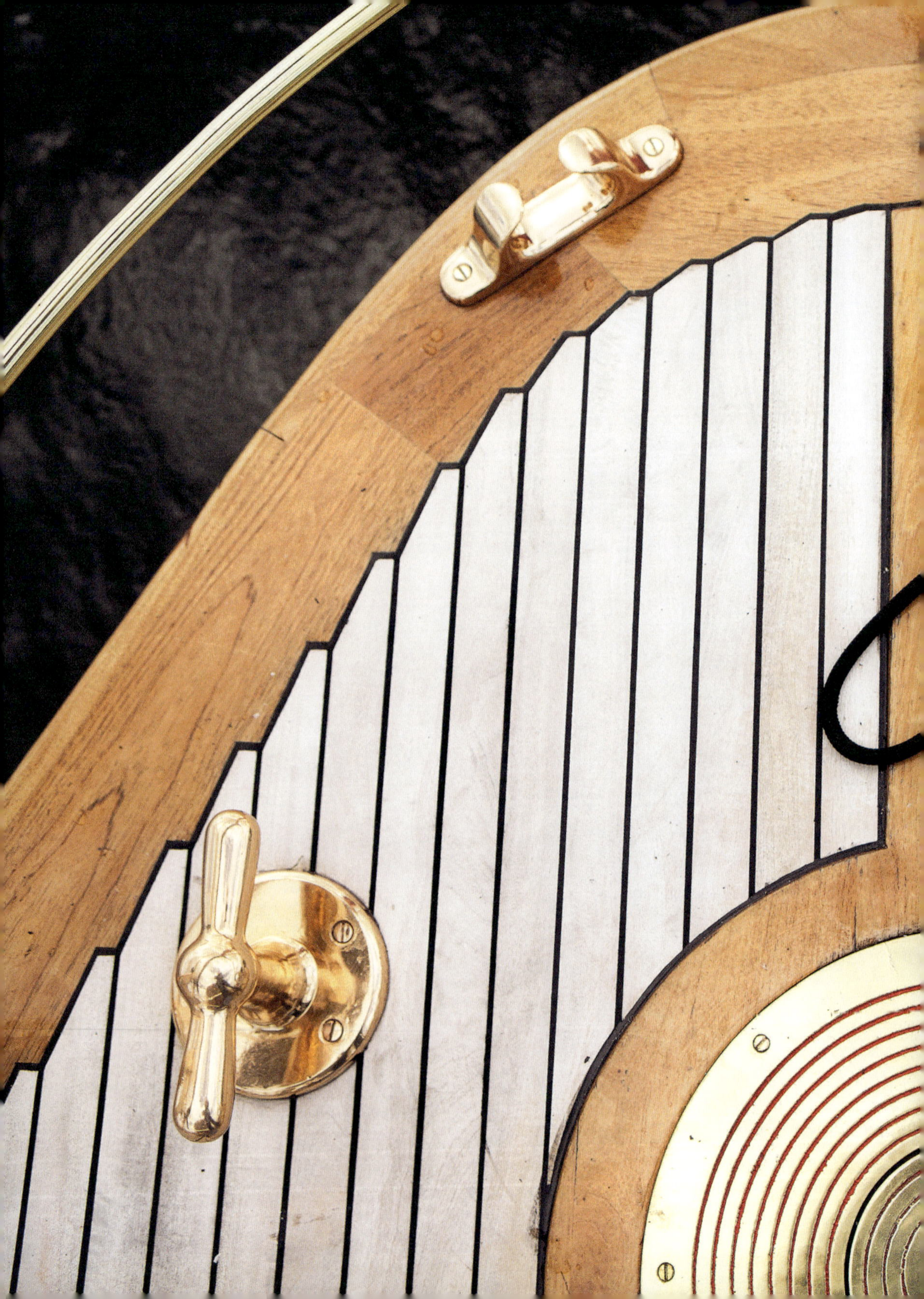